Fly-Fishing
Northern
California Waters

Roadside, Backcountry, and Wilderness Destinations

Lily Tso Wong, Ph.D.

Frank
Amato
PORTLAND

Fly-Fishing
Northern
California Waters

Roadside, Backcountry, and Wilderness Destinations

Lily Tso Wong, Ph.D.

Frank Amato
PORTLAND

About the Author

Lily Tso Wong, Ph.D., is a native of California. For over two decades, she ventured into countless challenging and rewarding watersheds in Northern California and the High Sierras. A fly-fishing instructor at the American River College and Sacramento City College, Lily is the recipient of the California Fly Fishers Unlimited 1991 Distinguished Member Award. The award stems from her many years of outstanding leadership serving as President, President-Elect, Vice President, Newsletter Editor, and Outings Chairperson. She is the seventh member to receive the honorable award from over 200 memberships since the club's inception in 1962. Lily participated as guest speaker at the Federation of Fly Fishers' International Conclave in Oregon, numerous Northern California Fly Fishing clubs, and other organizations. Her fly-fishing skills touch on where, when, and how to fly-fish for salmon, trout, and steelhead in California waters. Besides taking pleasure fishing her favorite waters, she has led large groups of fly-fishers to many trout and steelhead waters.

Dr. Wong's articles have appeared in several issues of fly-fishing. One of her primary interests in fly-fishing is to investigate fish habitat and how each species of fish adapts to changing conditions in nature's ecological surroundings. This led to spectacular fishing adventures in primary and lesser-known waters throughout California. In addition, Lily adds new touches of creativeness to her fly tying skills by creating her own favorite fly patterns with confidence. Lily credits the fly patterns she designs to her artistic background.

Dedication

To Joey,
for sharing many adventurous hours fly-fishing numerous exciting waters with me, and
understanding my devoting countless hours unlocking the mysteries of my journeys.
To Kevin Wong and Justine Wong,
my companions in many wondrous wilderness treks and fly-fishing destinations.
To Loretta and Corinne Wong,
for sacrificing many weekends to be with me on fishing and camping trips.
To Thomas Bruice, Jenna Sierra Wong-Fortunato, Jiavanna Wong-Fortunato, our future fly-fishers.
To Frank Amato,
for having supreme faith in me to take on this enormous book project.

Acknowledgments

In order to cover all aspects of fly-fishing, additional research data was needed. It is an extraordinary privilege to have cooperation and support from many individuals who provided data and information for inclusion in my book. The information was an invaluable tool for the compilation of a fly-fishing reference and guidebook covering the Golden State, California.

My sincere thanks to the California Department of Fish and Game fish biologists Paul Chappell, Almo Cordone, John Deinstadt, Glen Delisle, Eric Gerstung, David Lentz, Dennis Maria, and Darrell Wong; Fisheries Management's Ken Hashagen, Jr., Mas Yamashita, and Ray Banthin for generously supplying data concerning fisheries in various parts of the state. The generous miscellaneous information Fish and Wildlife Assistant Anthony Ries and DFG Production Coordinator Joan Prince supplied me are deeply appreciated.

Many thanks go to several individuals who provided pertinent data and information on this project. State Water Resources Control Board Analyst Suzanne Lewin; U.S. Forest Service Fish Biologists Sara Lee Chubb, Georgina Sato, and Jerry Ward; U.S. Bureau of Land Management Wildlife Biologist Nancy Williams; Desert Fishes Council Fishery Biologist Edwin (Phil) Pister; and J. S. Wong, Assistant Engineer, State Department of Water Resources, for providing watershed data.

A special thanks and appreciation to my publisher Frank Amato for his understanding and patience in the completion of my book. I am also indebted to my spirit guides for their encouragement and guidance through the path of dreams many years ago.

Softbound ISBN: 1-57188-255-3
Softbound UPC: 0-66066-00444-4

Frank Amato Publications, Inc.
P.O. Box 82112, Portland, Oregon 97282
(503) 653-8108 • www.amatobooks.com
Printed in Hong Kong

1 3 5 7 9 10 8 6 4 2

Contents

Preface

Centuries ago, anglers from various parts of the world attempted to fish by winding feathers onto a hook to imitate insects and catch fish. From that period on, fly-fishing expanded in many modes and directions.

This outdoor activity has become one of the fastest-growing recreational pastimes. Many anglers explore watersheds to fulfill their appetite for solitude. Thus, the number of travelers venturing into the backcountry and wilderness areas has increased tremendously. With this in mind, it is my desire to fill a need by creating an in-depth fly-fishing reference and guidebook on California waters; providing a diversity of angling information for recreational enthusiasts.

This book serves a dual purpose: as both a reference and a guidebook. It was designed to provide fly-fishing information on a wide range of adventurous waters, covering premier lakes and streams for roadside, backcountry, and wilderness destinations.

My quest for challenging and rewarding fly-fishing waters was endless. It is fascinating to observe how each watershed has a distinct personality of its own. Each lake and stream possesses its own unique features and landscapes.

While enjoying this aspect of fly-fishing, I experience an inner peace while surrounded by mountain ranges, rolling forested landscapes, and hearing the distant sounds of roaring streams. Besides being my dearest outdoor companions, streams, lakes, and ponds have provided me with the golden opportunity to catch and release various species of trout, keeping me spellbound forever.

I have explored many of Northern California's coastal and inland waters for more than two decades as an avid angler, hiker, backpacker, and skier. I spent many cherished years conducting widespread fieldwork gathering information for this book. In addition, I researched and collected useful data to go along with my field experience. This creative project has been a labor of love.

California's exquisite wilderness holds many special memories for me. This book shares the information that you will need in order to explore the heart of our Golden State.

Weed patches provide excellent trout habitat.

Introduction

Premium waters and superb angling prevail in the coastal and inland waters of California. Through the years, I have kept a journal with resources on fly-fishing destinations, effective fly patterns, and other significant data on all of the waters I have visited in the Golden State. The inspiration for this book came as I was reminiscing while looking through photos of my fly-fishing expeditions. I asked myself, why not share this information with other fly-fishers? The excitement led me to design a somewhat different approach to illustrating the wide range of adventures I've had while fly-fishing. This publication covers waters from the Nevada state line to the Pacific Ocean, sharing the richness and diversity of the lakes and streams in the northern Coast Ranges, Klamath Mountains, southern Cascade Range, Modoc Plateau, and Great Basin provinces.

My focus is on the Smith, Eel, other North and Central Coast, Klamath system, Pit, McCloud, Sacramento, its tributaries, and other major and lesser-known waters. Each region has its own historical, geological, geographical, and topographical features. All waters within our national forests, wilderness areas, national parks, state parks, and other recreation areas exhibit a diversity of these features.

The headwaters of most major river systems start at the alpine levels. Their flows traverse down the valley to their final destination, the sea. Rainbow, golden, redband, brown, cutthroat, and brook trout inhabit the waters of Northern California. (In addition, Northern California's coastal rivers and tributaries in Sonoma, Mendocino, Humboldt, Del Norte, Siskiyou, and Trinity counties harbor some of the most challenging western anadromous fisheries.) Graced with towering redwoods, primeval forests, and swift wild rivers, anglers will find an astonishing paradise awaits them.

Although I've had numerous roadside, backcountry, and wilderness fly-fishing adventures, they are too numerous to include in one book. However, other destinations in the Northern and Southern Sierra Nevada Province waters are covered in my two forthcoming volumes. The goal will be to provide enough information to give you an idea of what each body of water, in various geographic sections, has to offer. This will give you the opportunity to explore them at your leisure.

An endless search for knowledge is a trait many fly-fishers share. Learning opportunities abound from one source of information to another. Based on responses from students in my fly-fishing classes and participants in my workshops and seminars, I designed this book to benefit beginning fly-fishers, as well as fly-fishers with more skill.

To help you plan adventures to selected waters, I've included basic information on map and compass resources, California's public lands, backcountry, and wilderness areas. I have also incorporated other important resources, such as origins of names, fish stocking programs, watershed accessibility, and recreational opportunities. Emphasis is placed on the characteristics, distribution, and environment of trout and sea-run game fish. Other information includes: individual descriptions identifying various species of fish, habitat, their food resources, and suggested fly patterns. In addition, I briefly cover fishing strategies, reading water, and water types—moving and still waters—as they are important skills to know for optimum fishing.

However, due to many factors, such as severe winters, winterkills, drought, or other environmental factors, habitat rearrangement can alter the course of streams, streambeds, lake bottoms, and vegetation. In some instances, these changes can drastically affect the fish, as well as the food sources of previously productive waters.

Most destinations require a short drive directly to the water for shore fishing, wading, float tubing, boating, or for other various types of watercraft. For the more ambitious and energetic angler seeking a challenge, there's information for leisurely day hikes, adventurous backpacking treks, and horse pack trips to remote backcountry and wilderness watersheds.

I have compiled fish distribution data for trout and anadromous fish inhabiting most lakes and streams in 16 Northern California counties. The data includes all lakes and streams by county, drainage, lake elevation, and species of fish. It also identifies the most current U.S. Geological Survey (USGS) 7.5 Minute Series Topographic Quadrangle maps for each body of water. (Topographic Quadrangle maps are available for purchase through many recreational supply and equipment outlets. Also, you may purchase them through the Western Mapping Center, U.S. Geological Survey, 345 Middlefield Road, Menlo Park, CA 94025.)

The primary objective of the Fish Distribution is to show additional waters other than those mentioned in the text. It can help the angler explore a wide spectrum of lakes and streams throughout Northern California. In addition, I have included a directory listing fly-fishing and environmental organizations, as well as fly shops and specialty stores.

Fisheries, water, climactic, road, and trail conditions, not to mention a range of unforeseen circumstances, can change rapidly in mountainous regions. Fallen trees, heavy runoff, or a hazardous environment, for example, can alter any watercourse. I strongly urge you to contact the federal, state, or local governmental agencies for current information before departing on your fishing trip.

For further information on how to reach waters in this book, obtain the National Forest Recreation and Topographic Wilderness Maps for the region you plan to visit. (Forest Service and Wilderness Maps are available for purchase through the Pacific Southwest Region, USDA Forest Service, 1323 Club Drive, Vallejo, CA 94592.) With the aid of these maps and specific topo maps listed in the Fish Distribution section, you will be able to zero in on a location for premier angling.

California sportfishing regulations frequently change. In recent years, many watersheds have included restrictions on the use of artificial lures and barbless hooks. It is the responsibility of each angler to become familiar with the most current regulations and supplements set forth by the Department of Fish and Game. (Also, each National Park Service may set special regulations for waters in a certain park system.)

Equipment: Fly-Fishing Rods, Reels, Lines, and Accessories

Fly fishing requires a high degree of finesse. A fly rod directing the line in a delicate movement, with an almost weightless fly, is graceful, poetic, and gratifying. Once you enter the world of fly-fishing, the beauty of it can consume you forever.

One important aspect of this sport is the selection of proper equipment. Five basic items make up the fly-fisher's tackle: rod, line, reel, leader, and fly. Selecting a balanced outfit is a perplexing situation. In order to fish with confidence, you must first understand—and then choose—the equipment that is best suited for the waters and species of fish being pursued. These variables dictate the line size, rod length, and reel. Once you select the rod and line for your intended fishing, the next step is to choose a reel to match the outfit.

There are several characteristics to look for when choosing a fly rod: action, length, and material. Basic rod actions consist of fast, medium, and slow. Rods that flex only in the tip section are called fast rods or dry-fly action. The opposite of the fast action is the slow-action rod. Slow-action rods are very supple and they do not have long casting capabilities. The slow-action rod is used mostly for delicate presentations within a designated distance. They are difficult to cast and, generally, result in a bad line loop. For the beginner, as well as the average fly-fisher who spends most of their time fishing for trout and light steelhead, the ideal choice is a graphite 5- or 6-weight all-purpose medium-action rod. This rod will provide smooth, even flexibility, and strength in the tip and butt sections.

Fly reels come in fresh or saltwater models to match line and rod sizes. When selecting a reel, it must have enough capacity to hold the amount of line and backing appropriate for the type of fishing intended. The most appropriate reel is a single-action type. (The reel's simple construction of a one-to-one ratio generates each revolution of the handle to turn the spool one revolution.) It should have a consistent, adjustable drag and an outside rim for palming which serves as a braking system. This is important for stripping line while fighting large fish. Also, a reel with interchangeable spools is convenient for changing from one type of line to another without removing the reel from the rod. It also saves you from buying another reel to accommodate additional lines.

Fly lines are available in a variety of weights, tapers, and functions for use in different water conditions. Each taper design and function has different performance capabilities. There are four basic fly-line constructions: Level (L), Weight-Forward Taper (WF), Double Taper (DT), and Shooting Taper (ST). Level lines have a uniform diameter from one end to the other because there is no taper. These lines have limited performance and versatility. Therefore, the weight-forward, double-taper, and shooting-taper lines are the best choices for success in line performance. A weight-forward taper (WF) line is an excellent choice for making longer casts. These lines carry most of the weight in the forward section for smoother casting. The double taper (DT) line is designed with a level center section that tapers to a finer point at each end. This line is ideal for presenting flies delicately to easily-spooked fish. The other end of the line can also be utilized by reversing it. A shooting taper (ST), also known as a shooting head, is designed with 30 feet of shooting taper. The line is attached to 100 feet of running line. The small diameter of the running line creates a minimum of resistance when it runs through rod guides, making it capable of extremely long-distance casts. (The special running line is less likely to kink and twist as monofilament lines do.)

One of my favorite lines is Scientific Anglers' Weight Forward Wet Cel Monocore Line, also known as a "slime line." The single-strand monofilament core and coating of this clear-tinted blue line feels slippery when wet. The slow sink rate of 1:20-1:80 inches per second serves me well on bright days in clear slow-moving water because it appears invisible in the water. Presenting caddis pupae, scud, or emerger patterns with a 6- or 7-weight Monocore line to wary fish feeding along heavy weedy shorelines is ideal. The most popular and versatile fly line is the floating line (F) for surface or under-the-film presentation. Adding a little weight, 8 to 12 or more above the fly, is ideal for nymphing. A floating/sinking (F/S) is a high-density line with variable sink rates. The front section of the line holds 10 to 30 feet of sinking line and the rear section is a floating line. Sinking (S) lines come in different sink rates to enable anglers to fish below the surface to 40 feet deep from a boat or other watercraft.

With the proper line to match the performance of the rod and reel, you can effectively fish most conditions in Northern California and High Sierra waters. Line size for different fishing conditions ranges from 2- to 9-weight matched with rods 8 to 10 feet in length. I generally load my spools one line size larger than recommended for the rod. The slightly heavier line provides longer casts, better mending control, and allows for smoother casting under windy conditions.

For minimal line disturbances in smaller streams, my 8-foot 2-weight and 9-foot 4-weight graphite rods have been great companions for many angling trips. Fitted with double taper (DT) or weight-forward taper (WF) floating lines, these rod sizes are light and supple, an added advantage in playing large fish with light leaders and tippets. My 2-weight is an excellent choice for using the lightest leader, tippets, and small flies, size 16-22. The 4-weight line with size-14 flies and smaller is ideal in most streams. This line size has enough weight to make delicate presentations and long casts. The rod handles well when playing 3- to 4-pound trout displaying aerial flights. For trout and some steelhead fishing, I use either a 9-foot 5- or 6-weight 2-piece fly rod. Both sizes offer perfect balance of presentation and power fishing with nymphs, small streamers, and dry flies. They are strong enough to handle mild wind conditions in the high country. My 6-weight 4-piece pack rod outfit can effectively fish almost all conditions in the back country.

If you intend to fish larger bodies of water for trout and steelhead, a 9-foot, 7-weight rod will handle all types of nymphs, streamers, and dry flies if delicate presentations are not important. This larger outfit can handle strong winds and powerful long-distance casts. When pursuing summer-run steelhead, large trout, or smaller chinook salmon, a 7-weight rod provides ease in casting for longer periods of time. However, a 9 1/2-foot, 8- or 9-weight graphite rod is my favorite all-around outfit for manipulating shooting-head lines and achieving longer casts in large bodies of water for chinook salmon or large steelhead. I find these lines possess plenty of power for handling large fish. They are also effective in turning over large dry flies and weighted wet flies.

I prefer to use Teeny Nymph T-200 to T-400 as shooting-head lines rather than loading my spools with running monofilament lines and a shooting taper line. These lines come from the manufacturer in one piece combining the shooting head and running line. They are designed with 24 feet of sink-tip and 58 feet of floating line for better control and easier casting in large bodies of water. I load my 5- to 7-weight rod and reel outfit with the T-200. I use the T-300 and T-400 for my 8- to 9-weight rod and reel outfit. For salmon fishing, I use short leaders from two to four feet in length and a 15- or 12-pound-weight tippet.

Leaders and Tippets

Leaders and tippets are vital parts of your equipment. It is the critical link between you and the imitation you are using to fool a fish into striking. The purpose of a properly designed fly leader is to graduate the relatively thick fly line to the small diameter of a tippet. A balanced taper leader gradually transfers power generated from the rod through the line, leader, and tippet to the fly. An improperly designed tapered leader will create casting and knot problems. Therefore, it is essential to use a tapered leader to properly present the fly to the fish.

Attaching a monofilament butt section to the end of the fly line will allow you to change leaders quickly. The butt leader should be about .020 of an inch in diameter. Use a larger diameter if your outfit warrants it. Attach an 18-inch stiff monofilament material onto the fly line with a needle or nail knot. Make a loop at the end of the butt leader. Using a stiff monofilament line will extend the life of the butt leader. If you attach a butt leader to the end of your fly line, it is a simple procedure to loop the end of the leader to the butt leader (loop to loop).

Monofilament material varies between brands. You can make your own tapered leaders by tying sections of monofilament lines progressively smaller. To reduce chances of breakage, each graduated section should not be more than two thousandths of an inch difference. If you wish to tie your leader, there is a leader-tying kit available on the market with material and instruction for each situation. However, you can also buy all-purpose knotless tapered leaders for trout, salmon, and steelhead fishing. These knotless leaders are designed to accommodate a variety of fly-fishing situations. It is a good idea to have a supply of all-purpose leaders in different tippet sizes.

Tippets are the last section of the leader where it joins the fly. For maximum elasticity, tippets should vary in length from 18 to 36 inches. With this practice, fewer lost fish will result. When attaching tippets to the leader, moisten the material before slowly tightening a triple surgeon's knot for maximum strength. Make a habit of checking the tippet and leader regularly and replace damaged sections. Knots reduce the strength of monofilament leaders by 50%. It is simple to ignore flaws. However, anglers who fail to correct any defects may lose a prized fish.

Paraphernalia

Most waters require wading in order to present flies to where fish are holding. Wading in knee-high water with hip waders gives you a feel for the contours and features of the stream bottom. When you feel confident enough to wade in faster and higher waters, wear chest waders with felt soles and cleats if rocks in the streams are slick.

Waders come in a wide range of styles and materials. Among the most popular designs are the hip, waist-high converting to chest-high, and chest-high stocking-foot styles. Wader materials are available in breathable Gore-Tex, neoprene, and nylon. For safety reasons, be sure to wear a belt around your chest waders, and do not attempt to wade in fast or deep waters alone. In many situations, it may be necessary to cross unfamiliar streams. A wading staff is an essential item at all times, especially in fast waters.

Table 1
Matching Fly Size To
Leader-Tippet Size

Fly Size	Tippet "X" Size	Tippet Diameter
2, 4, 6	1X	.010
6, 8, 10	2X	.009
10, 12, 14	3X	.008
14, 16, 18	4X	.007
18, 20, 22	5X	.006
22, 24, 26	6X	.005

Rule of 11: By subtracting any of the above numbers preceding "X" from 11, the result is the diameter in 1,000ths of an inch. For example: Subtract 5X from 11 = .006.

Rule of 4/3: For ultimate presentation, three fly sizes have been given to match a tippet "X" size. By dividing the center bold number in each of the Fly Size groups by 4, the result is the ideal tippet "X" size. For example: In the group of 3 fly sizes 14, **16**, 18, divide **16** by 4 = 4X. You can also use the 4X tippet for fly size 14 and 18.

Exploring Public Lands, Backcountry, and Wilderness Waters

Many public lands in California are easily accessible for recreational use. Public forest lands along the Coast Range and Klamath Mountains provinces span north of San Francisco Bay and west of the Central Valley. In northeastern California, public lands dominate the region. They are scattered throughout the Great Basin, Modoc Plateau, and southern Cascade Range provinces. In the Sierra Nevada Province, government lands extend from Plumas National Forest to the southern tip of California. Linked by thousands of miles of scenic roads, trails, thousands of acres of lakes, and miles of watercourses, these public lands are unlimited resources for outdoor activities. Anglers have a wide range of access to pristine waters from designated roads and trails to cross-country exploration of backcountry and wilderness lands.

Created in 1905, the U.S. National Forest Service has taken on many responsibilities, one of which is to offer outdoor recreation resources in California's public lands. Out of the 19 national forests in California, 18 are in the Pacific Southwest Region. (The exception is Toiyabe National Forest, which is under the jurisdiction of the Intermountain Region). However, six national forests are in Northern California (Six Rivers, Mendocino, Klamath, Shasta-Trinity, Lassen, and Modoc) and eight in the High Sierras (Plumas, Tahoe, El Dorado, Stanislaus, Inyo, Toiyabe, Sierra, and Sequoia). The National Park Service, under the administration of the U.S. Department of the Interior, is responsible for preserving natural and historical features.

Other public recreation areas of interest to anglers are U.S. Bureau of Land Management (BLM), U.S. Army Corps of Engineers, and California State Parks and Recreation lands. The U.S. Bureau of Land Management's primary role is to manage, protect, and enhance valuable resources on public lands. These resources include recreation, minerals, watersheds, fish, and wildlife to name a few. BLM lands offer a variety of challenging fly-fishing resources.

The U.S. Corps of Engineers operates more than 450 water resource and development projects in 43 states. The Corps operates 12 recreation park facilities with dam operations and lake projects throughout northern and central California. These facilities offer a wealth of angling spots in lakes and streams in Northern California, the High Sierras, and the foothills. Recreation areas include Black Butte Lake, Lake Mendocino, Lake Sonoma, Englebright Lake, Martis Creek Lake, New Hogan Lake, and Stanislaus River Parks from Goodwin Dam to the flatlands of the San Joaquin Valley. Other recreation waterways are Eastman Lake, Hensley Lake, Pine Flat Lake, Lake Kaweah, and Success Lake. Except for Martis Creek Lake, most foothill lakes are open to fishing year-round for trout and warmwater fish. Streams below reservoirs are fishable during winter months and early spring. (When fishing below dams and reservoirs, be alert for unexpected water releases.)

A host of recreational areas lies within the California State Park Systems. Through day-use and campground facilities, you can easily gain access to coastal and inland waters. A few state park facilities have excellent access to prime fishing waters, such as Jedediah Smith Redwoods State Park (Smith River), Humboldt Redwoods State Park (Eel River), Benbow Lake State Recreation Area (Eel River), Castle Crags State Park (Upper Sacramento River), and Woodson Bridge State Recreation Area (Lower Sacramento River for shad fishing). In other parts of California, McArthur-Burney Falls Memorial State Park (Pit River, Hat Creek, Baum Lake), Plumas-Eureka State Park (Lakes Basin Recreation Area lakes and streams), Donner Memorial State Park (Truckee River), Calaveras Big Trees State Park (Stanislaus River), and Grover Hot Springs State Park (East Fork Carson River) also provide camping facilities for fly-fishers.

Wild-and-scenic rivers in California offer unique features for various water sports. In 1968, Congress created the National Wild and Scenic Rivers System to preserve certain rivers with outstanding natural, cultural, or recreational features in a free-flowing condition. Federal or state agencies administer and protect these designated rivers.

The Wild and Scenic Rivers Act classifies rivers as wild, scenic, or recreational. "Wild" rivers are rivers, or sections of rivers, free of impoundments. They are generally inaccessible except by trail. Their watersheds are essentially primitive, and their waters are unpolluted. "Scenic" rivers are rivers, or sections of rivers, free of impoundments. These rivers consist of shorelines or watersheds that are still largely undeveloped, but accessible in places by roads. "Recreational" rivers include rivers, or sections of rivers, readily accessible by road or railroad. There may be some development along shorelines, and they may have undergone some diversion in the past. The wild-and-scenic rivers of Northern California's Klamath, Trinity, Eel, and Smith rivers attract the most angling use for anadromous fishes.

Getting to Backcountry Waters

Each year, thousands of outdoor recreational enthusiasts traverse our public lands by motor vehicle to roadside waters. They also use other means of travel—such as foot travel, pack horses, llamas, or mules—to gain entry into backcountry or wilderness waters. Off-highway backcountry travel has become increasingly popular with all-terrain vehicle riders. One of the most popular ways to gain access is by mountain bike. Many fly-fishers enjoy the solitude, beauty, and challenge of nature on their mountain bikes. If you anticipate using a mountain bike in the back country, watch for designated wilderness trails since mountain bikes and vehicles are prohibited in wilderness areas.

Other options for reaching backcountry waters include day hikes for trips close to camp or backpacking for longer trips. Trails range from easy, moderate, to strenuous. When hiking, it is often necessary to ford streams and traverse cross-country. Be prepared with the proper footwear. Faint, infrequently maintained or unmaintained trails are common. Some premium remote waters in the high country are difficult to reach; these destinations usually require long and arduous hikes. When venturing out, bring a compass, U.S. Geological Survey Topographic maps, and U.S. Forest Service maps. They are indispensable for navigating trails and identifying significant landmarks or features in the area.

Pack animals, water taxis, or backpacking are the only mode of transportation to approach primitive areas. There are several options when traveling by pack horse. With spot trips, the packer packs the angler and their gear to designated campsites on lakes or streams, then returns on a predetermined date for the journey back. Dunnage is a service designed for anglers who wish to hike and have their fishing and camping equipment packed and taken to specified locations by the packer. There are options with this mode of service: you can use the packer one way, round trip, or ride one way. On the other hand, the all-expense trip is a deluxe means of travel. It is a full-service trip where packers furnish animals, camping equipment, food, cooking, and they will guide as well.

Using llamas to carry equipment and food into the back country is another luxury for hikers. The demand for llamas on guided trips has increased. These well-trained, surefooted animals are capable of transporting heavy loads over narrow and precipitous trails. Their mountaineering ability, gentleness, and ease of handling are ideal for anglers seeking an alternative to heavy backpacks, mules, burros, and horses. In the past, the Incas of South America used these soft and woolly animals to transport treasures, goods, and other supplies to above 16,000 feet through the Andes Mountains. Besides being friendly, llamas are intelligent, curious, sociable, and will follow you anywhere. By having llamas carry your fly-fishing gear, tents, sleeping bags, and personal items, backcountry fly-fishing adventures are less strenuous.

Water-taxi services are available in the High Sierra. Echo Lake Resort in the Lake Tahoe area offers water-taxi service from Echo Lake to Desolation Valley Wilderness trails. In the Yosemite National Park area, Saddlebag Lake Resort has a water-taxi service from the southern part of the lake to 20 trails in the Lakes Basin Hoover Wilderness. In the southwestern Sierra, Vermillion Valley resort, near Mono Hot Springs, provides ferry service across Lake Thomas Edison. The ferry saves four miles of foot travel to Mono Creek Trailhead, one of the western entries to the John Muir Wilderness.

Backpacking is a favorite means of travel for fly-fishers who wish to enter remote backcountry lakes and streams. It is an economical means of getting there, providing a wider selection of routes and campsites. Being in good physical condition, and careful planning, are priorities to consider before attempting

Llamas are a common mode of backcountry travel.

Cairns (ducks) stacked to identify trail routes.

backcountry treks. Backpackers should also never forget three essential needs while away from their homes: food, insulation to maintain a safe body temperature, and shelter.

Menus for backpacking trips require precise planning. What to bring must be simple, nutritious, substantial, and light in weight. Keep in mind you will prepare all food with minimal equipment. Basic dehydrated foods are available. Do not bring canned or bottled food, they are frequently heavy and you will be required to carry out all empty containers. To save weight, repackage cereal, sugar, powdered fruit drinks, dry milk, instant coffee or tea, and other dry food. (Quick energy foods are great for snacks along the trail.) Also, keep in mind you have fly-fishing tackle and other essential items to carry on your back. Do not load yourself down with unnecessary and heavy items.

Other necessary equipment includes sturdy, comfortable footwear (very important), a backpack, and a sleeping bag. A lightweight sleeping bag and a down or polyester jacket will keep you warm during early mornings and evenings. Some hikers are comfortable sleeping under the stars, but if you opt to go this route, bring a poncho to fill in for an emergency shelter. (I prefer a tent for shelter.) Lightweight tents are ideal for backpacking purposes. For preparing meals in camp, pack along a backpacker's stove and cooking utensils. Other useful items are insect repellent, chapped lip ointments, sunscreen, lotion, flashlight, and personal items. If you take any medications, have an adequate supply with you. Before leaving on your journey, let someone know your agenda. If possible, always hike or backpack with a companion. In the event you become ill or injured, a companion can be a lifesaver.

Some public lands provide more recreational potential than others. Whatever methods you use to gain entry, protect the environment by treading lightly. Many public lands lie next to private lands closed to the public. Obey gate closures and posted signs. Always take precautionary measures to respect the landowners' rights and obtain written permission before traveling across private lands.

Cairns & Blazes

Trails in the back country are usually distinct and easy to follow. However, there are times when trails are not as prominent and frequently become faint or end abruptly. This occurs mostly when crossing over granite slabs or in wooded areas. In this type of situation you will find two different types of markers: cairns (ducks) and blazes. Cairns (ducks) are created by stacking three small rocks of various sizes on top of each other to form a pyramid shape. In some wooded areas, a standard blaze appears on some trees. A blaze is a symbol "i" carved in the bark of a tree approximately six feet above the ground. As you stand near either of these markers, the next cairn (duck) or blaze is visible.

Trail Dangers

Be alert. Stay away from wild animals rearing their young, and avoid spooking any livestock. If you come across animals, don't

Backcountry Food Storage
Counter-Balance Technique

Courtesy U.S. Forest Service

make sudden movements that may startle them. Also, be aware of poison oak and rattlesnakes when fishing from roadside waters, walking along the river's trail access, or other fishing access.

Bears are present in many backcountry areas. They are potentially dangerous. A hungry bear will break into automobiles, damage property at campsites, and pose a threat to those around it. One of the most predominant problems is careless or improper food storage by campers. Bears will eat anything made available to them. This often results in bears rummaging for food they have acquired a taste for, which in turn causes property damage and a safety threat to people.

Take precautionary measures to ensure your safety as well as the bears'. First, bear-proof your food and garbage (it's the law). In bear country, discard all waste in bear-proof garbage cans. Make it a practice to store all food, cans, and ice chests in your car trunk or bear-proof containers, and clean all your dishes. If you do not have a trunk, place all foods (even toothpaste) low and cover them. Keep all windows and vents closed. Cover or hide boxes, packs, or any items that may interest bears. If you are in the back country, pack out your garbage.

Bear-proof food storage lockers are available at some locations along the trail. In areas with bear problems (such as various locations within the Sequoia and Kings Canyon National Parks), you will be able to find a supply of these lockers. The best food storage technique for the back country is the counter-balance, method used to store everything that has an odor. Swing the bundle over a tree branch with a rope. For safety reasons, do *not* bring food into your tent.

Wilderness Permits

Each year, California's rugged mountain slopes, tumbling streams, and placid lakes attract more fly-fishers seeking isolation and new primitive recreational experiences. In 1964, the Wilderness Act established a National Wilderness Preservation System intended to preserve unique wild-and-scenic areas in our public lands. The Wilderness Act of 1964 set aside wilderness areas "where the earth and its community of life are untrammeled by man, where man himself is a visitor who does not remain." Of the 48 wilderness areas managed by California's Forest Service, many of them have access to lakes and streams.

When entering national forest wilderness lands, some areas may require a wilderness permit while others do not. However, there is a quota system during peak seasons in heavy-use areas to reduce adverse impact and to protect wilderness resources. These areas require advance reservations for each date of entry with some openings reserved on a first-come first-served basis. On some wilderness trailheads, permits are available at the point of entry. In most areas, you do not need a permit for day hikes. If you plan to build a wood fire or use a portable stove during your stay, you must obtain a campfire permit from the U.S. Forest Service.

Pacific Crest National Scenic Trail: Shadow of Pristine Waters

Before the construction of railroads and highways, early travelers journeyed by foot, horseback, or wagon. Some of these trails still exist today as a reminder of our rich historic past and for the enjoyment for those who choose to use them. In early 20th century California, outdoor enthusiasts constructed footpaths to gain access to scenic terrain in Northern California and the Sierra Nevada mountains. Trails were the only means of gaining access to remote regions and pristine waters.

The Appalachian Trail on the East Coast was the first interstate recreational trail conceived in 1921 as a national preserve. In 1968, congress passed the National Trails System Act and named the Appalachian and Pacific Crest trails as the first two national scenic trails. The Pacific Crest National Scenic Trail, and countless other trails on national forests, national parks, and other federal lands vary in length, difficulty, type of terrain, and accessibility.

The Pacific Crest National Scenic Trail (PCT) lies along the crest of the spectacular Cascade Range and the backbone of the Sierra Nevada Mountains stretching from Canada to Mexico. Extending over 2,600 miles, the entire PCT passes through National Forests, Bureau of Land Management Resource Areas, and a vast amount of State, local government, and private lands in Washington, Oregon, and California. Elevations range from near sea level to above 13,000 feet in the Sierra Nevada Mountains. The California section of the trail begins at Latitude 42-degree North on the California-Oregon border in the Siskiyou Mountain range. More than 1,600 miles of the trail traverse south through some of California's most scenic lakes and unique streams before ending at the Mexican border south of Cleveland National Forest.

The John Muir Trail: Golden Destinations for Trout

The John Muir Trail (JMT) extends 221 miles along the crest of the Sierra Nevada Province. The trail passes through Yosemite National Park, Ansel Adams Wilderness, John Muir Wilderness, Inyo and Sierra national forests, as well as Sequoia and Kings Canyon national parks. In 1915, the Sierra Club persuaded the state legislature to appropriate funds for initial construction of the John Muir Trail. Completed in 1916, the trail is named in memory of the famous naturalist-conservationist, John Muir, who died the previous year. During the summer months, portions of the trail are like a typical rush-hour freeway.

The best time to travel the PCT in Northern California, and the PCT and JMT in the High Sierra, is July through October. Before July, snow may still be present along the passes and streams may be high and too dangerous to ford. Most trails in the high country are above 7,000 feet in elevation and some sections of trails, including Forester Pass in the southern Sierra, are above 13,000 feet. After October, chances of early snowstorms increase. Even though snowstorms can occur any time of the year, snow usually covers most trails by November in higher elevations. Plan a safe trip by not taking unnecessary risks.

The John Muir Trail officially begins its course from its northern trailhead at Happy Isle, which is located at the upper end of Yosemite Valley in Yosemite National Park. As the trail traverses northeasterly, it unites with the PCT at Tuolumne Meadows off SR 120, Tioga Pass Road. From here, it turns in a southerly direction at Lyell Canyon. Except for a small section in Ansel Adams Wilderness, a major portion of the JMT traverses its course on the PCT. The JMT trail leaves the PCT and heads east at Crabtree Meadows ending on the southern trailhead at the summit of 14,495-foot Mount Whitney. Depending upon your fishing destinations, there is a host of entry trails providing easy connecting access throughout the JMT system.

Planning for a Safe Trip

Weather plays a significant role on outdoor activities in the high country. Sudden and unexpected mountain thunderstorms are common in the afternoon and evening throughout the year. However, they occur more often during the summer months. In late spring or early fall, unexpected snowstorms take place quite frequently. It is essential that you pack the proper apparel because of constant temperature changes.

Take measures to avoid two life-threatening hazards—hypothermia and heatstroke—by wearing adequate clothing. Hypothermia is the condition brought on by the lowering of internal body temperatures due to overexposure to cold temperatures aggravated by wetness, wind, and exhaustion. Symptoms of hypothermia include shivering, low body temperature, drowsiness, memory lapses, exhaustion, as well as vague and slurred speech. (If this occurs, seek medical attention immediately.) One method of preventing rapid loss of body heat is to wear layered clothing, proper footwear, gloves, hats, and rainwear. Heatstroke occurs when the body becomes overheated. This life-threatening situation is characterized by a high body temperature, red, hot, and dry skin, as well as a rapid and strong pulse. (Heatstroke victims should seek medical attention immediately.) Avoid heatstroke by drinking plenty of water. When possible, take frequent rest breaks in shaded areas.

Altitude sickness may affect travelers venturing into the high country. If you take precautionary care you will reduce your chances of being affected. Altitude sickness occurs at high elevations where the air contains less oxygen than at sea level. If you arrive and immediately begin exerted activities, altitude sickness may result. Spend a day acclimating before attempting any strenuous activities. Try to plan your trip to the high country a day earlier before venturing out on strenuous hikes or activities and drink plenty of water to avoid dehydration. (At higher elevations, you need to consume plenty of liquids.)

Other safety concerns include *Giardia* and Lyme disease. An intestinal disorder, also known as backcountry dysentery, *giardiasis* (gee-ar-dye-a-sis) is contracted from drinking untreated natural water from lakes or streams. Caused by a microscopic organism, *Giardia lamblia*, the cystic form of the disease lives in mountain lakes and streams. Most backcountry waters are potentially contaminated even though water flows appear clear, cold, and rapidly running. They may even look, smell, and taste refreshing. However, be aware of its possible danger. *Giardia* thrives in water contaminated with animal or human waste. The discomforts of *Giardiasis* may not show up for several days, to several weeks, after ingestion. Onset of symptoms usually includes: gas, diarrhea, loss of appetite, abdominal cramps, and bloating. This disease causes nausea, headaches, and diarrhea. Make it a rule to never drink untreated water. Several purification methods are available. Most common are boiling water, filter systems, or chemical treatments such as crystals and tablets.

The danger of Lyme disease, caused by a tick bite, exists in some areas of our country. One of the best ways to avoid tick bites is to tuck your pant legs into your socks and tuck your shirt into your trousers. This will keep ticks confined to the outside of your clothing where you can spot and remove them. Wearing light-colored clothing helps in detecting ticks. You can also buy tick repellent at sporting goods stores. Inspect your clothes, head, and body thoroughly at the end of each day. Also, concentrate on areas behind the ears, armpits, and in the groin and navel areas. It takes 12 to 24 hours for ticks to transmit the disease, immediate removal of any ticks will decrease your chances of contracting Lyme disease.

Anatomy of Productive Waters

Fly-fishing is not a battle between anglers, your challenger is the fish. Each encounter is priceless and has its merits no matter who the conqueror. Presenting a fly to fish holding in a lake or stream, waiting for a minute unnatural pause, movement, or other tell-tale sign signing a strike is a heart-thumping affair. When I have plans for a fishing adventure, I greatly enjoy the anticipation. Many times, I envision the exciting moment when a fish will take my presentation.

One of the most important aspects of fly-fishing is understanding where trout, steelhead, and salmon hold in their natural environment. A thorough knowledge of where fish spend most of their time in their underwater world is the key to angling success. A proficiency in reading water is vital to catching fish.

Without polarized glasses, it's difficult to see the characteristics of the fishes' world below the water's surface. Analyzing a fish's survival necessities and evaluating what criteria would satisfy their needs is a great start. They seek areas offering protection from predators, steady current, sufficient oxygen, a comfortable temperature range, and availability of their prime source of food. Security and current speed are two important concerns of fish. Predators such as animals, birds, anglers, and a host of other intruders are the greatest threat to any species of fish.

Prime lies—the premium sections of a stream—require a steady flow of current, broken by boulders, logs, and other obstructions in a streambed deep enough to provide security. A steady flow of current delivers an abundance of food sources, provides sufficient oxygen, and a comfortable temperature level. Where all these elements are available, the largest, aggressive trout will occupy this most advantageous section of the stream. Other areas where fish station themselves include sections that offer food and/or any type of obstruction that interrupts the flow of currents. (These obstacles offer shelter and food sources from current.) Once you've read the water, create a strategic plan on how to entice fish to strike.

Understanding various types of waters will help you better understand characteristics of a body of water. Specific terminology of watercourses is important for identifying features on maps of inland waters. USGS topographic maps, USFS maps, and others, distinguish each flowing water feature as a creek or river. Regardless of whether it is a creek or river, the U.S. Geological Survey classifies the feature as a stream. The U.S. Board on Geographic Names describes the same classification in their Geographic Names Information System (GNIS). GNIS defines a stream as a "linear body of water flowing on the Earth's surface: creek, river, anabranch, distributary, branch, run, slough, bayou, pup, brook, fork, kill, rio." Since a creek or river is classified as a stream, we can, for example, identify Yellow Creek as a smaller stream and the Feather River as a larger stream.

A spring creek, for the most part, consists of flat, slow-moving water. However, runs, pockets, and pools may exist in some sections of spring creeks. The creek's main source of water originates from underground. Its water temperature remains constant; thus creating a perfect environment for aquatic insects and trout. Weed beds and vegetation in these waters harbor enormous populations of insects as well as providing shelter for fish. The spring-fed creek of Fall River, for example, possesses both of these elements—great insect populations and flourishing weed beds.

Kevin Wong fly fishing.

Trout holding in the smooth, slow-moving waters of spring creeks are wary and selective. It is essential you study the various insects living in spring creeks and their hatch schedule. With the combination of gin-clear water and abundant food sources, fly selection and accurate presentations are vital to inducing a trout to take your offering.

Freestone streams are waters moving free and fast over stones, rocks, or other obstructions providing shelter for trout as a resting or holding area. Classic freestone stream structure includes riffles, runs, pools, flats, and pockets. The velocity on a freestone stream depends largely on geological structures and gradient. The headwaters of some freestone streams originate in mountain ranges above 7,000 feet in elevation and often plunge down to lower elevations—traversing through rocks, pebbles, sands, and finally silt in the valley.

Characteristics of Streams

The fastest fishable waters in a stream are **riffles**. These knee-deep choppy waters—created by the effects of broken large rocks and gravel—provide oxygen and rich food supplies to fish. Riffle waters are not deep enough to hold large trophy fish. However,

Anatomy of a Stream: Feeding Areas

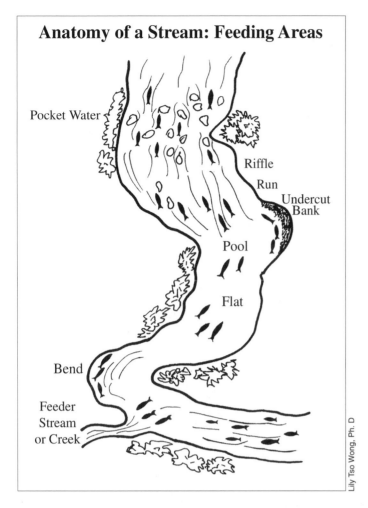

Pocket Water

Riffle

Run

Undercut Bank

Pool

Flat

Bend

Feeder Stream or Creek

Lily Tso Wong, Ph. D

streamer patterns with sinking lines to get flies down to waiting fish at the bottom.

The quiet waters of **flats** move at a slow pace with a minimum amount of surface disturbance. Flats flow quite evenly from bank to bank in shallow streambeds with very little elevation drop. When a hatch is in progress, trout move into this stretch to feed. After the hatch ends, trout retreat to other more sheltered areas. Because the water is smooth and shallow, with an undisturbed surface, casting and presenting flies to wary trout in flats requires an extremely cautious approach.

Streams with odd-shaped rock slabs, huge boulders, and fast waters careening over riverbeds, are home to healthy, hard-fighting trout. Known as **pocket waters**, these are fast waters scattered with emerging boulders and rocks obstructing current flow, creating many mini-pools. These are ideal holding areas because fish can dart out into faster waters to grab food as it drifts by, before returning to slower-moving resting pools. Pocket waters provide oxygen, shelter, and cool water temperatures for the trout on hot summer days. (A few major trout streams in Northern California that provide pocket waters are the McCloud, Upper Sacramento, and Pit River systems.)

Trout are lethargic when water temperatures are in the low 40s and expend very little energy to capture food. At this time, fish find comfort in pools. They will also hold in slower sections beneath an undercut bank gouged by currents. Good feeding activitiy begins when the temperature range is between 57 to 63 degrees. When the temperatures increase to the high 60s, fish seek the cooler, oxygenated water provided by currents. As oxygen decreases and water temperatures rise, trout seek faster currents. Fish hold in sections of streams with riffles, deep runs, and pocket waters. Mouths of feeder streams and springs are also good sanctuaries for the fish.

Finding productive waters where steelhead hold depends upon understanding the many facets of steelhead habitat. Classic steelhead waters include heads of runs, smooth tailouts, and riffles flowing into shallow pools. Look for steelhead in runs where waters are flowing at moderate velocity over gravel bottoms and in transition waters from fast to slow below rapids. Factors such as depth of water, time of day, water clarity, and a sunny or cloudy day play a significant role in where steelhead hold. Early morning and dusk are the best time to fish for salmon and steelhead. However, on cloudy days, fishing opportunities are greater.

Summer and fall steelhead generally hold in more oxygenated water in early morning and late evening. These are prime periods when fish are most active in taking flies. During winter and spring, this can be an all-day affair. When the water level is high, currents with the same velocity and depth provide a resting haven for fish. Migrating steelhead conserve their energy by traveling along edges of streams. This area provides more coverage and currents are less turbulent. Other good steelhead holding waters are in canyons or banks where shade is prevalent most of the day.

Prime lies for salmon are deep pools, below falls, and large bends with deep holes. Other sites for king salmon are obstructions such as large boulders, submerged logs, or fallen trees deflecting waters which provide resting areas. The best water for pursuing chinook salmon are the lower (or midsection) of rivers and mouths of tributaries because the fish are bright and full of strength. When salmon reach the upper stretches of streams to spawn, they are thin, dark, and weak.

the water is shallow enough to allow sunlight to penetrate the bottom to nourish plant life that, in turn, is important to aquatic insects. Some riffle waters also have a slight elevation drop in the gradient of the streambed. This causes flows to accelerate, which is not conducive to holding trout.

Runs are deeper than riffles. Situated between a riffle and a pool, runs are usually about waist deep. These slow, forceful-moving waters flow evenly, with fewer broken surfaces. Trout favor the slower sections, often holding in front of boulders (or other obstructions) resting or waiting for food being swept from riffles. A good quantity of trout hold in the deepest part (and in shallow waters) away from the heaviest current. Since runs are smooth without choppy waters, longer casts and cautious approaches are necessary.

Often located below a run, the area with wide, deep, dark, and slow-moving current is classified as a **pool**. This water type is part of the structure in freestone streams along with riffles and flats. In some pools, waterfalls with a dramatic drop create the deepest part. The pool's structure dissects into three sections: head, body, and tailout. The head of a pool is where food flows from riffles or runs above. Any obstructions slowing the current or providing shelter for the fish make excellent lies. You usually see larger, more wary fish holding in this section of a pool. Depending on the structure of a pool, tailouts range from shallow to swift waters that may not be fishable. Therefore, the head of a pool holds the most concentration of fish. Because of the pool's depth, trout are often reluctant to move to the surface to feed. Success depends upon nymphs and

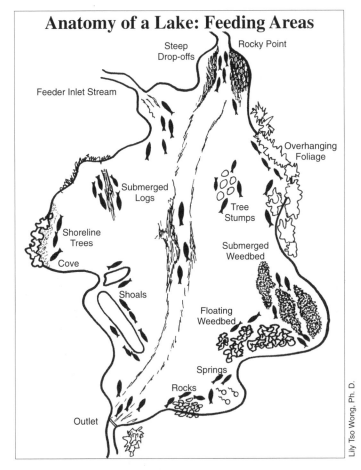

Anatomy of a Lake: Feeding Areas

Steep Drop-offs

Rocky Point

Feeder Inlet Stream

Overhanging Foliage

Submerged Logs

Tree Stumps

Shoreline Trees

Submerged Weedbed

Cove

Shoals

Floating Weedbed

Springs

Rocks

Outlet

Lily Tso Wong, Ph. D.

Characteristics of a Lake

Anglers can unravel the mysteries of unfamiliar still waters by identifying physical features of lakes, reservoirs, and ponds. These waters have characteristics that require another set of guidelines. Reading still waters efficiently is a matter of learning the complexity of the underwater environments and the food sources available that attract fish to these locations.

Where do fish spend most of their time in a stillwater environment? Through observation and continued practice, you will achieve rewarding results by finding out. Binoculars and polarized sunglasses assist in spotting actively feeding fish. Physical features are more difficult to locate in still waters. When you approach still waters, scout the body of water from higher ground. Also, observe seasonal changes and how shade affects the behavior of trout. Protruding and submerged weed beds, for example, are prime feeding zones for cruising fish. Underwater structure provides a host of food sources and security to satisfy the needs of trout. Shoreline structure with vegetation and cliffs is also prime.

One of the reasons most lakes hold larger trout than streams is that lakes have greater potential for harboring aquatic food sources. Submerged plants equal security for most aquatic insects. The plants supply food for insects, as well as a place for fish to hide from predators. When insects emerge, dense areas of weed growth provide a buffet for cruising trout. They hold a rich diet and allow for a leisurely lifestyle so that trout can grow at a faster pace.

Larger trout hold in the shallow waters where they drop off into cliffs, waiting to attack a worthwhile morsel of food. In the early season, shallow shoreline waters are warmer and insect activitity is prolific. Dawn and dusk are prime times to fish these waters. In early spring, fish stay close to the surface along shorelines to feed. When summer arrives, trout seek cooler,, deeper waters next to shallow waters. Fall is the best time to fish for brown and brook trout because they station themselves close to shorelines in preparation for their spawning ritual.

Sunken vegetation, submerged ledges, bushes, tree trunks, fallen trees, rocky or gravel shoals, depressions, and bottom debris are also prime holding waters for trout. These underwater structures provide the comfort of shelter and food. They are also excellent hiding places for crayfish and leeches.

A significant change in the water temperature will indicate the location of springs. These underwater springs are attractive to trout because they provide constant (and consistent) temperature zones and oxygenated water during summer and winter. Locating underwater springs in lakes is to your advantage during warmer months. A good way to locate springs is by taking the water temperature, or by finding spring symbols on the topo map (a small circle with a wiggle tail). Once located, you will find concentrations of fish seeking this cool, oxygenated water.

Float-tubing paraphernalia.

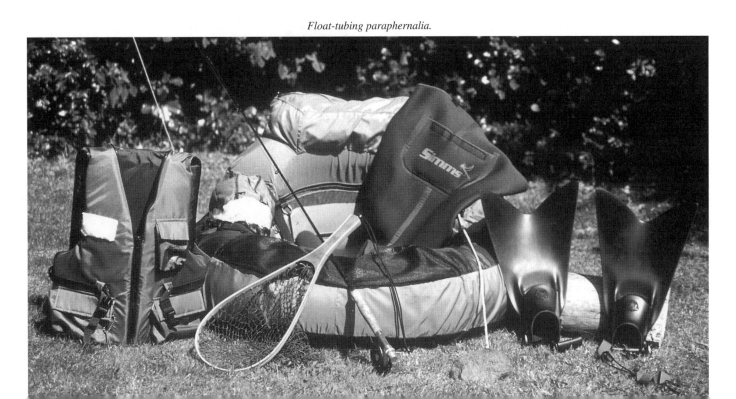

Inlets also provide oxygenated water and drifting food sources for waiting fish. On the other hand, slower-moving waters draw insects to outlets. Trout in inlet and outlet waters are easily spooked unless there are drop-offs or obstructions nearby to offer them shelter.

Regardless of which fish species you are pursing, in lakes or streams, understanding habitat is one of the most important aspects in fly-fishing. It is good practice to approach any watershed cautiously. Analyze and study the characteristics and features of each area. Precipitation, snow run-off, and water releases from reservoirs can alter streambeds. These conditions affect the channels and location of underwater structures. It is to your advantage to always note these changes.

Float Tubes and Pontoon Boats in Stillwater Fishing

Fly-fishing from a float tube or pontoon boat has become increasingly popular for pursuing fish in still waters. These personal fishing crafts offer unlimited access to the environment of the fish.

It is more effective to fly-fish out of a float tube or pontoon boat because it allows you to approach feeding fish in hard-to-reach areas out of casting range for shoreline anglers. Manzanita Lake in Northern California, Martis Creek Lake, and Milton Reservoir in the Lake Tahoe region, for example, are ideal waters for either of these devices. In the eastern Sierra, Mammoth Lake's Upper Twin Lake and Lake Crowley's west shore, are prime float-tubing or pontoon waters. When water conditions are good, you will find a flotilla of colorful watercraft, like a hatch in progress.

Most float tubes consist of a nylon cover encasing a large inner tube. They come in a wedge shape for a more level ride, and an open-ended (open in the front) design for quick entry and exit. This open-ended model eliminates the hassle of attempting to climb into the traditional round type. Depending upon the model and price, features can include zipper pockets, stripping apron, wrap-around backrest, an assortment of D-rings, and adjustable straps with quick-release buckles. Whatever model you choose, be sure to buy one that has a quick-release crotch strap buckle in case you need to get out of the tube quickly. For additional safety when tubing, wear a U.S. Coast Guard-approved personal floating device (PFD), such as Stearns inflatable vest, CO_2 belt, or CO_2 SOSpenders. Also, never fly-fish alone in choppy waters or before impending storms. Fly-fishing with a companion is a good rule to follow in case you run into trouble.

Pontoon-style boats are effective for maneuvering around large lakes, ponds, and moderately moving waters. Fly-fishing out of a pontoon boat will keep you warmer and drier. The craft is more comfortable, sits higher off the water, and positions well for improved sighting of fish activity. Some are even designed to use oars.

I recommend wearing stocking-foot chest-high waders made of nylon, neoprene, or Gore-Tex. My neoprene stocking-foot waders are durable, comfortable, warm in cold water, and flexible when I'm maneuvering around water. One of the most effective fins for use in a float tube or pontoon-style boat is the Force Fin. Its flexible "V" shape directs thrust energy and produces maximum speed, power, and movement without expending much energy. Most of all, the turned-up ends allow you to walk forward as you get in and out of the water. Fin Savers (or Tethers) are accessories worth investing in, these straps keep your expensive fins from being lost in the water.

A 9- to 10-foot rod is ideal for float-tube casting because you ride lower in the water when in a tube. If you use a shorter rod, your backcasts might slap the water. The best solution is to concentrate on making a high backcast. Other useful equipment includes a Double Action manual pump to inflate your pontoon boat or float tube bladder fast and easily. If you intend to hike into remote lakes or ponds, a special backpack strap attached to your float tube makes it easier to carry. However, you may prefer to select a lighter weight backpackable pontoon-style boat with the portability of quick assembly. A float-tube anchor will keep your tube in place with less maneuvering. It fits conveniently in the accessory pocket. Remember to secure your glasses, clippers, pliers, and other accessories with some type of cord. Once these items fall into the water, they sink fast.

Safe float-tube entry.

To Be Free...Catch and Release

To be free is the feeling of complete freedom without the fear of being captured. This is exactly the freedom that I see when I view the many colorful trout gracefully swimming in the depths of serene moving waters. They were created to be free—to roam the watersheds in enchantment. To scurry around with confidence searching for food. We cannot know of this experience until we experience the joy of watching the trout's underwater environment. Oh, how wonderful and relaxed the trout must feel as the flowing water brushes against its body. This is how it feels to be free.

There is no worry when to end this ritual, or when to make the next turn—always in control of its desires. A gentle, responsive creature, it will never hurt a soul. To be stalked and mistreated is to deprive it of survival. Its instinct is to be independent—to swim and roam as it pleases.

Approach its habitat cautiously as you study the activities of the fish within its sanctuary. This should be a treasured heartwarming experience.

Freedom and independence make up the trout's world—surrounded by other underwater creatures sharing their empire. This life form is extremely selective in responding. Catch and release it delicately, and without hesitation. Once you have connected with this living being, you will understand why it will never leave your heart.

You will always be drawn to this life form. Its strange power is overwhelmingly sensitive, exciting, and mysterious. Understand the trout loves its freedom to live and stay free, thriving to survive within its environment. This living creature needs to be protected from predators invading its world. It is a glorious and comforting feeling watching a trout swim away from your hands to be free. When this exquisite trout disappears into the depths of its world, this hard-fighting tireless life form's memory will linger on for you.

A trout's world of freedom and independence.

NATIONAL FORESTS, PARKS, AND WILDERNESS AREAS

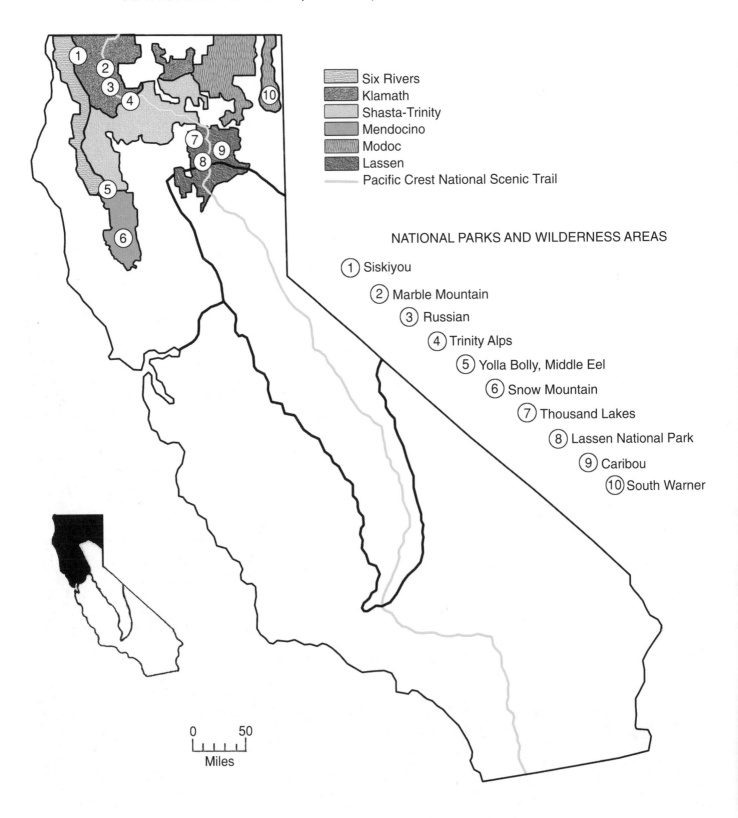

Six Rivers
Klamath
Shasta-Trinity
Mendocino
Modoc
Lassen
Pacific Crest National Scenic Trail

NATIONAL PARKS AND WILDERNESS AREAS

1 Siskiyou
2 Marble Mountain
3 Russian
4 Trinity Alps
5 Yolla Bolly, Middle Eel
6 Snow Mountain
7 Thousand Lakes
8 Lassen National Park
9 Caribou
10 South Warner

0   50
Miles

Northern California
Roadside, Backcountry, and Wilderness Destinations

Northern California's many faces include the notorious Gold Rush, mining, fertile lands, gentle rolling hills, rugged coastlines, vertical bluffs (with the added features of gigantic volcanic formations), and granitic mountain ranges. There appears to be no definite dividing line in the northern latitude of these mountainous ranges. They merge as one great mass of mountain wilderness as far south as Red Bluff, which becomes the northern end of the Central Valley.

For centuries, the cold crystal-clear waters of Northern California tumbled through the remnants of volcanic activity and majestic canyons from the Modoc Plateau, southern Cascade Range, Klamath Mountains, and Coast Range provinces through valley floors to the Pacific Ocean. Many of these large and small coastal streams are home to salmon and steelhead. Each season, anadromous fish return to coastal and inland waters. Trout fishing attracts many anglers to the lakes and streams in this rich historical region.

Hidden away in the northeastern corner of California, the Great Basin Province Empire holds a wide selection of productive trout waters. Anglers seldom visit the many unspoiled breathtaking watersheds in the Warner Mountains and Wilderness areas. The Great Basin provides fly-fishing opportunities for those who wish to explore this remote part of the country.

Many coastal and inland waters have special regulations concerning the use of artificial lures with barbless hooks, size limitations, all-year closures, and opening and closing dates. Check the most current regulations and supplements for the most up-to-date information before venturing out.

Mouth of the Gualala River.

South Warner Wilderness sign.

Coffee Creek sign.

Part 1
The Northwestern Connection

The Northwestern Connection covers waters in the northern end of the Great Central Valley, Coastal Ranges, and Klamath Mountains Province. These mountain ranges dominate the northwestern part of the state. Besides possessing miles of shoreline, wild-and-scenic coastal rivers, and rich inland waters, northwestern California holds a wealth of fly-fishing waters.

From wild coastal rivers, to mountainous lakes and streams, this part of the state includes many volcanic uplands, deep river canyons, cascading waterfalls, dense forests, clear lakes, snow-capped mountains, and towering ridges. These outstanding features also help draw anglers to our fisheries throughout the four seasons.

The ritual begins in early spring with the opening of trout season. At this time though, snow runoff and high water conditions in higher elevations are not conducive to fly-fishing. Therefore, it is best to concentrate your fishing in lower-elevation waters, below 4,000 feet. By early June, lakes and streams in the northwestern part of the state (as well as the Klamath Mountains below 7,000 feet) are usually fishable. However, depending upon winter precipitation, access to fishable waters varies from season to season. Beginning in July and August, head to higher-elevation lakes and streams in the backcountry and wilderness areas for superb angling.

When fall arrives, brook and brown trout move into shallow waters to spawn. I always take advantage of this quality fly-fishing season. In early fall and winter, anxious anglers anticipate prime conditions for anadromous fish in coastal rivers. Salmon and steelhead generally move into lower coastal rivers and migrate upstream after the first heavy rain. The challenge of hooking, playing, and landing salmon and steelhead is an exciting adventure but angling pressure is usually heavy in the larger river systems. However, smaller streams also provide good action when water conditions are good.

Overlooked by many fly-fishers in the winter and early spring, the Sacramento River is an ideal river system in which to pursue exquisite native rainbows. (The Sacramento is rich with prolific caddis hatches.) Low water releases out of Shasta Lake—ranging from 3,000 to 4,000 cubic feet per second (cfs)—offer ideal conditions for fly-fishing. The river within, and below, the city of Redding provides quality waters for wading and boat launching. From Redding to Anderson, the river is accessible by boat for good trout-holding waters.

When heavy flows dissipate—making watersheds suitable again fly-fishing—a knowledge of food sources, as well as fly patterns associated with the various watersheds, will increase your hook-ups. Understand that hatches and water conditions might differ from one season to the next.

"Go where you may within the bounds of California, mountains are ever in sight, charming and glorifying every landscape. Yet so simple and massive is the topography of the State in general views, that the main central portion displays only one valley, and two chains of mountains which seem almost perfectly regular in trend and height: the Coast Range on the west side, the Sierra Nevada on the east. These two ranges coming together in curves on the north and south inclose a magnificent basin . . .This is the grand Central Valley of California, the waters of which have only one outlet to the sea through the Golden Gate. But with this general simplicity of features, there is great complexity of hidden detail. The Coast Range, rising as a grand green barrier against the ocean, from 2000 to 8000 feet high, is composed of innumerable forest-crowned spurs, ridges, and rolling hill-waves which inclose a multitude of smaller valleys; some looking out through long, forest-lined vistas to the sea; others, with but few trees, to the Central Valley; while a thousand others yet smaller are embosomed and concealed in mild, round-browed hills, each with its own climate, soil, and productions."

John Muir
The Mountains of California

Northwestern California

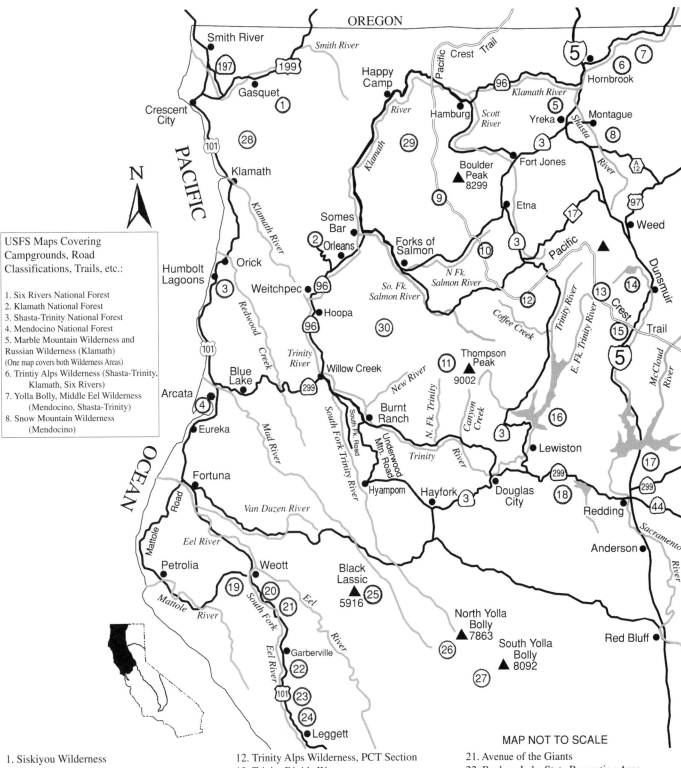

USFS Maps Covering
Campgrounds, Road
Classifications, Trails, etc.:

1. Six Rivers National Forest
2. Klamath National Forest
3. Shasta-Trinity National Forest
4. Mendocino National Forest
5. Marble Mountain Wilderness and
Russian Wilderness (Klamath)
(One map covers both Wilderness Areas)
6. Trintiy Alps Wilderness (Shasta-Trinity,
Klamath, Six Rivers)
7. Yolla Bolly, Middle Eel Wilderness
(Mendocino, Shasta-Trinity)
8. Snow Mountain Wilderness
(Mendocino)

MAP NOT TO SCALE

1. Siskiyou Wilderness
2. Fish Lake Complex
3. Freshwater, Stone, and Big Lagoons
4. Klopp Lake
5. Greenhorn Reservoir
6. Iron Gate Reservoir
7. Copco Lake
8. Shasta Valley Wildlife Area Waters
9. Marble Mountain Wilderness
10. Russian Wilderness
11. Trinity Alps Wilderness

12. Trinity Alps Wilderness, PCT Section
13. Trinity Divide Waters
14. Lake Siskiyou
15. Castle Crags State Park
16. Trinity Lake
17. Shasta Lake
18. Whiskeytown Lake
19. Humboldt Redwoods State Park,
west of U.S. 101
20. Humboldt Redwoods State Park,
east of U.S. 101

21. Avenue of the Giants
22. Benbow Lake State Recreation Area
23. Richardson Grove State Park
24. Smithe Redwoods State Reserve and
Standish-Hickey State Recreation Area
25. Ruth Lake
26. Yolla Bolly, Middle Eel Wilderness
27. Mendocino National Forest
28. Six Rivers National Forest
29. Klamath National Forest
30. Shasta-Trinity National Forest

Northwestern and Central California

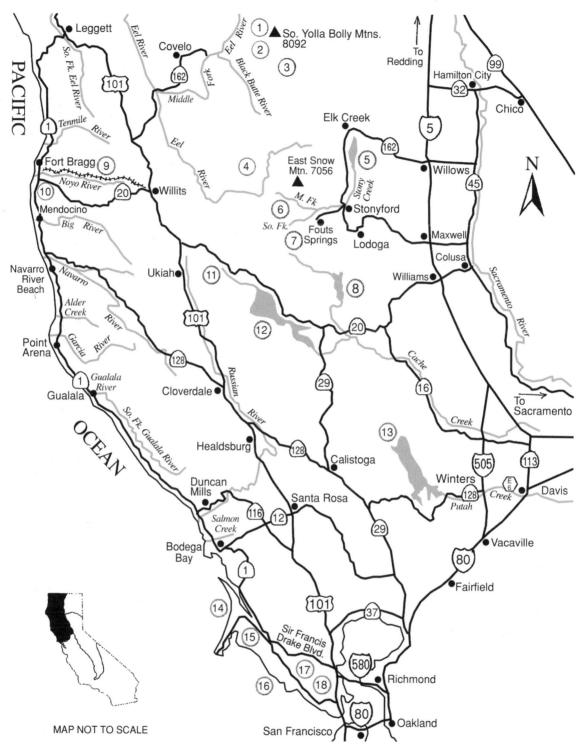

1. Yolla Bolly, Middle Eel Wilderness
2. Hammerhorn and Howard Lakes
3. Mendocino National Forests
4. Lake Pillsbury
5. Stony Gorge Reservoir (Landmark)
   Warmwater Fishery
6. Snow Mountain Wilderness
7. Letts Lake
8. Indian Valley Reservoir
9. Skunk Train Railroad,
   California Western Railroad
10. Jackson State Forest,
    Jug Handle State Reserve
11. Upper and Lower Blue Lakes
12. Clear Lake (Landmark) Warmwater Fishery
13. Lake Berryessa
14. Point Reyes National Seashore
15. Coast Creek
16. Alamere Creek, Crystal and Pelican Lakes
17. Kent Lake
18. Alpine, Bon Tempe, and Phoenix Lakes,
    Phoenix Creek, and Lake Lagunitas

USFS Maps Covering
Campgrounds, Road Classification, Trails,
etc.
1. Mendocino National Forest
2. Yolla Bolly, Middle Eel Wilderness
   (Mendocino, Shasta Trinity)
3. Snow Mountain Wilderness
   (Mendocino)

Spectacular Coastal Salmon and Steelhead Rivers

California's 1,100 miles of coastal waters feature rugged shorelines, pounding surf, and serene beaches. The northern coastal rivers extend over 400 miles north from San Francisco to the Oregon border, and stretch 35 to 60 miles inland from the Pacific Ocean. Known as the Redwood Empire to travelers heading to California's northern coast, the land of the redwoods weaves in and out of spectacular anadromous fishing destinations.

Misty air, ancient towering redwoods, and the timbered banks of coastal rivers characterize the landscape of the north coast. Within this region in the northwestern corner of the state is a treasure in the wild-and-scenic rivers which traverse through the Six Rivers National Forest. (The forest was named by San Francisco author, Peter B. Kyne. The U.S. National Forest accepted this name in December of 1846.) These six major salmon and steelhead watersheds are the Smith, Klamath, Trinity, Mad, Van Duzen, and Eel rivers. The long and narrow national forest which contains them stretches south from the Oregon border through Del Norte, Siskiyou, Humboldt, and Trinity counties.

One of the prime attractions of these rivers is the incredible opportunity to seek anadromous fish. Salmon and steelhead are the most challenging of western game fishes. It can be exciting, frustrating, and rewarding. My obsession with pursuing these fish has led to a mixture of despair and ecstasy. Fall and early winter fishing in Northern California's coastal streams depends largely upon the variable weather patterns. Too much rain, for example, will send the fish straight to their spawning grounds. If there is not enough precipitation, they will remain in the tidewater. However, some fish may find a way to continue their journey. These fish will be wary. On the other side of the coin, one of my best memories was when I was fishing a river holding fresh, chrome-bright, rainbow trout returning home from the sea when a steelhead took my fly. From its wake, I could tell the fish was a powerful fighter. A sudden powerful leap and the most electrifying screeching sound of stripping fly line signaled the contest had begun. Shortly thereafter, I landed and released a 7-pound silver

Aerial view, coastal river meeting the sea.

Trinity River steelhead. Battling these dynamic warriors is a heart-thumping and breathtaking experience. This is the ultimate in steelhead fishing.

A thorough knowledge is necessary when fly-fishing for salmon and steelhead in rivers: skill, perseverance, and a reasonable amount of fly-fishing experience are needed. Understanding runs, salmon, and steelhead environments, water conditions, how to read water, proper tackle selection, an ability to manipulate the fly line effectively, and patience, are key components for success. Each salmon and steelhead river always has distinctive characteristics that are influenced by: the seasons, available river access, stream flow, and turbidity.

On the northern coast, Smith River has some excellent wading water above the U.S. 101 bridge. However, drifting the river by boat has some advantages as well, such as being able to cover more water easily, casting to underbrush areas, and access to waters inaccessible by wading. In early seasons, the lower Klamath River is popular with guide services using jet-boat taxis to transport anglers to premium wading waters. The Trinity River, on the other hand, is an utopia for shore angling. Other, smaller wading streams are Redwood Creek, Mad River, Van Duzen River, Alder Creek, and the Gualala River. Regulations, road access, river access, low-flow closures, and water conditions are all factors to consider before venturing into these waters. Some rivers will also take longer to clear than others. However, when rivers start dropping into fishable conditions, another storm could bring the river up again. Consult with nearby Department of Fish and Game officials, local sporting goods stores, or guides for up-to-date information.

The large coastal river systems of the Smith, Klamath, and Eel rivers are pristine anadromous waters. Depending upon each river system, fall-run salmon start entering most rivers around August and September, followed shortly thereafter by steelhead. The smaller steelhead waters of Redwood Creek, Mattole, Gualala, and Garcia rivers offer good angling when the fish are in and conditions are prime. One of the problems for migrating anadromous fish entering some river systems is frequent closures at the mouths by

Prairie Creek hatchery.

sandbars. With the combination of high tide and significant rain, increased water flow can frequently open channels that can remove the sandbars. This allows anadromous fish to continue their journey to spawning grounds.

Fall-run anadromous fish are the most abundant game fish sought by fly-fishers. The fall fishing season starts with the arrival of small immature steelhead known as half-pounders. In the Klamath River, for example, the fish will usually show up in the lower section of the river around August and will arrive in the Weitchpec area (mouth of the Trinity River) on, or before, Labor Day. Some fish continue their journey upstream on the Klamath while others return to the Trinity River and still others to tributary waters. In November and December, larger steelhead enter many river basins. From December to February, expect fog and rain as constant companions during your fishing expeditions within the north coast, and remember that any substantial storm can blow out most rivers, leaving them unfishable for days. Winter steelhead migration usually continues through March, and toward the end of the season, you may hook into a mixture of new fish entering the river and downrunners (spawn steelhead) migrating to sea.

Fish your favorite water often in order to learn all of its characteristics because heavy winter precipitation can alter the course of the stream. Throughout the years, I have kept a personal log of all major stream flows in the state. This database allows me to keep track of high and low flows, to calculate the time it takes for each stream to recede, and it determines the best water level for superb fly-fishing. The north and central coastal streams are subject to a low-flow closure during the fall and winter months. If a stream's flow does not meet the minimum flow established by the Department of Fish and Game each week, the Department places an emergency closure to protect migrating fish. Other than drought years, other factors contributing to the decline of anadromous fish are the 1964 flood and overlogging in many coastal rivers. Release your catch carefully to protect these fish from extinction.

Current steelhead fly patterns suggest insects inhabiting the stream. It has been theorized that when steelhead return from the ocean, they regain certain feeding instincts imprinted on them when they were juvenile fish before going to sea. During early stages of development in fresh water, their principal diet was aquatic insects and other food sources from the stream. Patterns

imitating salmon eggs are also attractive to steelhead because they return to fresh water after the salmon. In many instances, salmon eggs are dislodged from redds and drift downstream. Steelhead enjoy these morsels and will take fly patterns representing salmon eggs.

When salmon enter a river system, they still have food ingested at sea on their mind. Therefore, salmon patterns similar to food sources from the ocean, such as polar shrimp and ocean baitfish, are more effective in lower river systems.

Once you sample a few coastal streams, you will want to seek out other salmon and steelhead waters. The beauty of the coastal ranges and river canyons, the wildlife, the smell of ocean air, and the sound of pounding surf, make it all worthwhile. I hope you find the beauty and challenge of these waters to be as special as they are for me. However, be extremely cautious when fishing coastal waters. From year to year, many factors can change the personality of your favorite stream. Most streams flow swiftly and torrentially out to sea. Therefore, a wading staff is an essential item when fishing these waters.

Table 2
Fly Patterns for Anadromous Fish

The following table lists the most popular productive fly patterns to accommodate Northern California coastal waters

Steelhead Fly Patterns	Hook Sizes
Brindle Bug	4-8
Glo Bug (Single Egg)	6-8
(Champagne, Orange to Red)	
Mossback	6-8
Silver Hilton	6-8
*Green Butt Skunk	4-6
*Skunk	4-6
**Boss	4-6
**Gold Comet	6-10
**Popsicle	2/0-2
**Thor	4-8

Salmon Fly Patterns	Hook Sizes
Babine Special (Weighted)	2-6
Boss (Weighted)	2-6
Chartreuse Shrimp	4-6
Comets (Orange & Silver)	2-6
Glo Bug, Single Egg	6
(Orange, Champagne)	
Polar Shrimp (Weighted)	4-6
Spey Fly (Orange, Purple)	2-6
Teeny Nymph (Black, Green, Flame Orange, Purple)	2-6
Winter's Hope	4-6

* Summer steelhead flies are not flashy in color.
** Winter steelhead flies are bright and more colorful.

Anadromous Fishes In California Streams
Characteristics and Distribution

Because they are anadromous fishes (sea-going species), salmonids require cool or cold waters throughout the season. These fish spend part of their lives in the ocean but move into fresh water to spawn. Steelhead rainbow trout and chinook salmon—also called king, tyee, and spring salmon—are two major species fly-fishers pursue when the fish return to their rivers of origin. Occasionally, anglers will hook into a coho salmon—also known as silver salmon—when angling for king salmon.

Prolonged temperatures above 70 degrees Fahrenheit (F.) are detrimental to fish, and 80 degrees F. is lethal to most species. Water temperature is even more critical during spawning time because 58 degrees F. is the upper limit in which eggs can survive.

Steelhead Rainbow Trout
Oncorhynchus mykiss

Steelhead rainbow trout are usually referred to as "steelhead" or "metalhead." Small immature steelhead returning after less than a year in the ocean are called "half-pounders." Sea-run steelhead rainbow trout are steel-blue with bright silvery sides and bellies. Black spots are sharply defined on the back, head, sides, dorsal, and caudal fins. When a steelhead enters fresh water, it develops a broad pink or red stripe on each side of its body. After being in fresh water for awhile, the fish takes on the appearance of a resident rainbow. The back gradually turns olive green and its sides and belly become less silvery. Steelhead generally lack red streaks beneath the jaw and the lining of the mouth is whitish. Teeth are on the tip, but not on the back of the tongue.

In many instances, anglers confuse steelhead trout with salmon. When the two are in the same water, it's difficult to tell them apart. One technique to differentiate the two is to count the anal fin rays. The last ray often branches near the base of the fin but should be counted as one. Trout have 9 to 12 rays while salmon occasionally have 12 but generally 13 or more rays.

Steelhead spend at least one year in fresh water before migrating to the ocean, and a majority does not return to spawn for another three to four years. After spawning, steelhead generally do not die. Some fish can even spawn a second or third time.

Fly-fishing for steelhead has historically been one of the greatest attractions on the Klamath and Trinity rivers. Since both streams don't have low-flow closure restrictions during fall and winter months, anglers from California, as well as other states, flock to these river systems during this peak period. When the water is conducive to fishing though, fly patterns are very effective. The Klamath and Trinity both have fall, winter, and summer runs of steelhead. (Steelhead enter practically every tributary of these streams which has sufficient water for spawning.)

Fly-fishing for sea-run rainbow trout is challenging in the Redwood Creek, Mattole, Noyo, Navarro, Alder Creek, Garcia, and Gualala river systems. Mad River has fall, winter, and spring runs of steelhead. Most of the time it will be too muddy to be fishable, but when water conditions are right, it is a great producer. Eel River has a run of half-pounders in late summer and early fall. These half-pounders migrate upstream as far as the mouth of the Van Duzen River. Larger steelhead enter the lower Eel during the fall and are found throughout the river system in the winter. (A spring- or summer-run of steelhead also migrates into the Middle Fork Eel but special regulations are in effect there.)

Spring-run steelhead are often called summer-run steelhead or summer steelhead because they enter the streams throughout spring and summer. They usually stay within the river system throughout the summer, and spawn the following spring.

The Russian River is also a popular steelhead stream from November through February, weather and water conditions permitting. Steelhead fishing usually peaks in January on smaller coastal streams like the Gualala River. During the early season, the river is subject to sandbars and low-flow closures.

King (Chinook) Salmon
Oncorhynchus tshawytscha

Chinook salmon display numerous black spots on their backs, dorsal fins, as well as both lobes of the caudal fin. The high, wide, and oval parr marks, silvery color, and dark margin on the tip of the adipose fin easily identify juvenile kings. Also, the lining of the mouth is dark. At sea, the king's coloration is bluish to gray on the back, and silvery on the sides and belly. When they enter fresh water, salmon gradually lose their silvery color and turn darker. Larger females turn blackish, while males often have blotchy, dull-red sides. Smaller males lean towards yellow rather than red. The jaws and teeth of males become larger at spawning time and they also appear somewhat distorted.

Chinook spawn in cool (or cold) streams with gravel bottoms. They prefer their spawning grounds to be in the lower end of pools where water begins to accelerate, and where you find riffles and long glides.

After spawning, the eggs hatch within a few months. Juvenile king and silver salmon migrate to sea during their first year of life. While in the ocean, chinook stay relatively close to the mouth of their birth river, but many migrate great distances from home. After spending three to four years at sea, chinook return to their river of origin to spawn and die. But, large numbers of males—known as jacks, chubs, or grilse—mature and return at two years of age. Anglers often catch these smaller salmon which, on average, can weigh close to three pounds.

Most fall-run king salmon return to their river of origin in early fall but the exact time varies for each body of water. Kings normally enter a stream when there is sufficient amount of water to migrate to spawning grounds. During migration up the rivers, kings do not generally feed because the stored body fat in their system is reserved for maintenance and gonadal maturation. The purpose of their journey is simply to reach the spawning grounds.

California's largest fall-spawning populations of chinook salmon are in the Smith, Klamath, Eel, and Sacramento-San Joaquin river systems. Smaller streams, such as Redwood Creek, Mad River, Mattole River, and other coastal streams also have a smaller run of kings. Some kings have been stocked in the Russian River and a good number of them are returning to the watershed to Warm Springs Hatchery.

In the Sacramento River system, for example, a winter run of kings usually arrives in the upper river around the Christmas holidays. They remain in the river system until May or June in order to spawn. Some kings enter rivers in the spring. These fish move upstream to their traditional holding areas and remain in the system throughout the summer and spawn in the fall. Timing of spring runs generally corresponds with spring snow melt and runoffs. High stream flows allow the fish to reach upper parts of a stream.

Silver (Coho) Salmon
Oncorhynchus kisutch

The coho salmon is of little interest to fly-fishers. Occasionally, anglers hook onto a coho while pursuing kings or steelhead trout. For this reason, I will include some basic information on the silver salmon.

Distinguishing characteristics of the silver salmon are a dark green head, as well as a black-spotted back, dorsal fin, and upper lobes. The coloration is metallic blue or blue-green, becoming silvery on the sides and belly when they are in the ocean. At spawning time, adults turn dark and dull. Males are characterized by hooked jaws and slightly humped backs. Outstanding features in females are their duller coloration and lack of a lateral red stripe. The lining of the mouth is dark, but the crown of the gums where the teeth project is lighter. A distinguishing characteristic of the silver salmon is the white gum line that differs from the king salmon. During spawning season, mature males become brick red (or brighter red), while females turn a dull bronze.

Between October and February—shortly before spawning—silver salmon return to their birth streams. After spending one to three years at sea, coho salmon will enter a few Northern California streams. Principal populations enter the Klamath, Trinity, Mad, Noyo, and Eel river systems, which include the South Fork and Van Duzen River. A small number also migrates to smaller coastal streams. However, it is rare to find silvers in the Sacramento River drainage. The fish are also not known to enter into the San Joaquin River system either.

Coastal Cutthroat Trout
Oncorhynchus clarki clarki

Coastal cutthroat trout are characterized by a pair of bright red or orange, "cutthroat marks" under each side of the lower jaw. Their coloration is olive green on the back—but it will be lighter on the their sides—and they have silvery bellies. Spots are more prominent in sea-run cutthroats than rainbow trout and because the spots vary in shape (from rounded to irregular), they often appear to cover the entire body—including the fins.

Principal spawning streams for coastal cutthroat trout are confined to the Eel River, Mad River, Redwood Creek, Klamath, and Smith rivers. (Many fish generally return to spawn more than once.) Through the years, coastal cutthroat numbers have declined. However, when these fish do enter their respective river systems, cutthroats begin to migrate upstream in September and October after the first substantial rainfall.

Spawning usually occurs in late winter or spring. Depending upon the number of fish returning each year, fishing for coastal cutthroats is good near the mouth of the Klamath and Smith rivers. The best time to fish for sea-run fish in the Smith River is from late fall through June. And if the coastal cutthroats have not declined substantially, a small run of this species usually enters the Lower Klamath in late summer and early fall. Their food sources consist of: insects, crustaceans, and other fish, while the young (and juveniles), feed mostly on aquatic insects.

The Emerald Waters of Smith River Giants

Situated in beautiful northwestern California—12 miles north of Crescent City on the northern Pacific Coast—Smith River is the gateway to California's first northernmost premier coastal river.

The river is named after Jedediah Strong Smith, the first white man to cross directly overland from Mississippi in order to see the giant redwoods. While leading the first party of white men through the area, Smith's group crossed the river during the summer of 1828. Before being killed by Comanches in 1831, he led many fur trappers West.

Mining and timber harvesting were once popular in the Crescent City, Smith River, Hiouchi, and Gasquet. When visiting the Smith River, food, lodging, and supply services can be found in these areas.

Created by Congress to protect its special scenic value, watershed, wilderness, cultural, and historical attributes, the Smith River National Recreation Area (NRA) provides unique habitat for anadromous and native trout fisheries. Designated as the latest of 12 National Recreation Areas in the United States, the Smith River NRA allows individuals to enjoy a host of recreational activities.

Public access on the Smith is excellent for boaters as well as shore anglers. Jedediah Smith State Park offers fishing access, boat launching, and campsites along the river. Most of the river is easily accessible from paved SR 197, U.S. 199 (Smith River Scenic Byway), or county routes. The major highways run alongside the river, passing through the hamlets of Hiouchi and Gasquet. (Hiouchi is a Native American word meaning "blue waters," while Gasquet received its name for Horace Gasquet, a native of France who established a ranch in a mountain township.)

From serene waters, to violent waves crashing onto its rocky coasts, to cool breezes swishing through mighty redwoods, the Smith River watershed exhibits a potpourri of rich ecological diversity. Long noted for producing the largest Californian salmon and powerful bright-chrome steelhead, the bewitching wild-and-scenic Smith River is the third largest stream for anadromous fish migrating to spawning grounds.

The Smith—lined with towering redwoods and abundant wildlife—is California's last free-flowing river. It receives the heaviest precipitation of all northern coastal rivers, and after a rainstorm, this river is frequently one of the fastest streams to clear in the area. The Smith is an excellent backup stream when all other rivers are out of commission. It clears rapidly because the river bottom consists mainly of rocks and boulders with little sediment.

Depending upon water conditions, one can observe chinook salmon averaging 15 to over 25 pounds entering estuary waters in late August or early September at the Smith River County Park area. (Access to the park is from Smith River Road in the town of Smith River out of U.S. 101.)

As water flow increases, the fish move quickly up to their spawning grounds from the sea. In November, after the first substantial rainstorm, 8- to 15-pound steelhead begin to filter into the

Ship ashore—mouth of the Smith River.

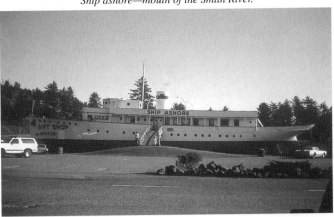

Smith River.

system. Steelhead continue to migrate upriver through March, when water conditions warrant it. When the river recedes after a rainstorm, the Smith is a fly-fisher's dream. The key to locating these fish though is to learn how to read the water well. Through knowledge, experience, or even through the help of guides, one can adapt their own approaches, techniques, and fly patterns in order to entice the fish to strike.

The Smith used to be one of the best cutthroat streams in the area. However, through the years, these delicate fish have been diminishing. A small number of sea-run cutthroats still enter the estuary during September, and continue moving upriver after the fall rains, but the best time to fish for them is during late fall until April. (Some cutthroats are also resident fish and they can be found in the river year-round.)

Originating above 5,800 feet in the Siskiyou Mountains, the Smith flows approximately 45 miles through deep gorges, canyons, forested slopes, and coastal plains before entering into the Pacific Ocean. Between the legal fishing boundaries—from Patrick Creek to the South Fork—the river is narrow and rocky, with shallow pools and pocket waters. Below Patrick Creek, several campgrounds provide access to the river. Many pullouts and short hikes to the river are also accessible between Patrick Creek and the South Fork. At the junction of the South Fork, the Neils Christensen Memorial Bridge near Myrtle Creek provides access to shore anglers and boaters. The paved blacktop Smith River Launching Facility located between this bridge and the confluence of the South Fork provides 12 parking slots for boats and trailers and eight auto spaces. Funded by the State of California Boating and Waterways, Six Rivers National Forest operates and maintains this launching facility.

The river's profile changes at the confluence of the South Fork and Middle Fork. Downstream from the confluence of the forks, a larger stretch of the main stem attracts boaters, as well as shore anglers. Below the forks, the river flows through deep canyons before reaching the hamlet of Hiouchi. Other sections of river with good salmon and steelhead holding waters are from Jedediah Smith State Park to Hiouchi Bridge, and further downstream to the U.S. 101 Bridge. The river's course is a mixture of smooth and flat waters, riffles, and pools. However, be aware of several treacherous rapids below Jedediah Smith State Park if you intend to drift the river from there to Ruby Van Deventer County Park.

The day-use Ruby Van Deventer County Park's large gravel bar and boat launching facility has excellent access for shore fishing. The North Bank Road (SR 197) and portions of the South Bank Road above U.S. 101 provide access to deep pools and long runs along gravel bars. The South Bank Road is accessible from Lake Earl Drive off U.S. 101 (Dr. Fine Bridge). This stretch of river has ample parking and is excellent fly-fishing water.

Below U.S. 101, there are large stretches of deep and slow-moving water that are difficult fly-fishing waters. When fish are in the river system, boaters will line the Bailey Hole area below the Smith River Fishing Access. This boat-launching ramp and access is two miles west of U.S. 101 on Fred D. Haight Drive.

Effective Fly Patterns for the Smith River

Salmon flies representing ocean baitfish and other food sources are the most effective in the Smith River. The most popular patterns are: Nos. 2-6 anchovies, shrimp in green, orange, and black, and lime green Weenies (body tied with green chenille only). Other patterns to have on hand are: Nos. 2-6 Comets in silver, orange, and green, as well as Nos. 2-6 Boss, and Nos. 6-8 Glo Bug and egg patterns. Top steelhead flies are: Nos. 4-6 Halloween, Comet, Brown Shrimp, Winters Hope, Popsicles, and Nos. 6-8 Glo Bug.

Lake Earl

As part of a coastal plan that extends 20 miles to the Oregon border, Lake Earl and the smaller Lake Talawa are two freshwater lagoons located between the town of Smith River and Crescent City. Known as the Lake Earl Wildlife Area, ancient sand dunes surround the fairly shallow lakes and coastlines. An 18-foot-deep channel known as the Narrows connects the two lakes. Before the arrival of early European explorers, this part of Del Norte County was originally home to the Tolowa Indians. Tolowa villages stood near the lakes in the area many centuries ago.

The lakes' main source of water is from Jordan Creek and ground waters. During high tide, ocean waters flood the lakes. High water levels provide opportunities for spawning salmon, steelhead, and cutthroat trout to migrate to and from the ocean. Nutrient-rich water supports the marshland of weeds and grasses necessary for migratory waterfowl. However, these are disastrous for boaters with motors. Most anglers resolve this situation by limiting their fishing to small crafts in the Narrows. Anglers can gain entry to the lakes from the public boat access at the Pacific Shores subdivision south of Kellogg Road and on Lakeview Drive. (Boats with motors are prohibited during duck hunting season.)

Upper Smith River.

A covered bridge near the forks of the Smith.

Song of the Siren: The Elegant Eel River and Avenue of the Giants

The Eel River is a magnificent river system nestled in the northern coastal mountain range amongst spectacular ancient forests. Flowing through portions of Lake, Mendocino, Trinity, and Humboldt counties, the Eel is a complex body of water. The stream has four major tributaries—Middle Fork, North Fork, South Fork, and Van Duzen River—which all feature their own uniqueness. The expansive tributaries are often overwhelming to fly-fishers who are unfamiliar with the watershed. Nevertheless, the North Fork is closed to all fishing.

The wild-and-scenic South Fork and the main stem Eel River, both offer spectacular views to anglers traveling on U.S. 101 from Leggett to Fortuna. If we look past the histories of the beautiful towering redwoods which survived the ice ages, and the geologic upheaval in this coastal region, the river has an interesting historical past as well. The river was named by a Tennessee-born trader named Josiah Gregg who conducted commercial caravans in Missouri and New Mexico. He named it the Eel after he and his men had acquired a large number of eels from a group of Native Americans there. This was no fair trade though because the natives apparently traded the eels for small pieces of a broken frying pan.

Eel River—which is not extremely swift—is one of the coast's premier salmon and steelhead rivers. It flows through narrow canyons in the upper river and opens up into a broad valley as its course reaches the Pacific Ocean. The disastrous flood of 1964, and extensive logging in the area, dramatically affected the Eel as its original deep channel was changed drastically by the buildup of silt and sediment deposits from tributary streams.

After substantial storms, water conditions in the river muddy up rapidly and it usually takes a long time to clear. Dependent upon water conditions, salmon runs usually peak in mid-October to November, and sometimes they last into December. Steelhead enter the Eel River from December through February, with February being the prime month. The last tributary to the Eel River, the Van Duzen River, is usually fishable earlier as this river clears up much more quickly. Large salmon and steelhead arrive in this river system later than in other streams.

Main Stem Eel River

Headwaters of the main stem Eel River drainage originate at RM 197 near 6,739-foot Bald Mountain in Mendocino National Forest.

Flowing south for 24 miles, the river enters Lake Pillsbury (1,818 feet), as well as the Van Arsdale Reservoir (1,493 feet).

Below the Van Arsdale Reservoir, the Eel River flows north and westerly to the Pacific Ocean. However, for over 70 miles from Cape Horn Dam (at Van Arsdale Reservoir) to the mouth of the North Fork, most of the main stem lies on private land. During its northerly course, the river is accessible before reaching Dos Rios, where SR 162 lies perpendicular to the river, from the mouth of Outlet Creek. Steelhead usually congregate at the mouth of tributary streams when they are in the area. Access to the river is from the highway.

From Dos Rios to Alderpoint, the main stem of the Eel winds its way next to the Northwestern Pacific Railroad tracks for 47 miles but no public access is available until Alderpoint. The Alderpoint Bridge and a few spots nearby are the only access points available to anglers. This area requires access through railroad tracks and by working upstream and downstream along the river. However, boaters generally fish the river from Dos Rios to the mouth of the South Fork.

At the Dyerville site, good access is available to gravel bars along the Dyerville Loop and McCann Road. From Pepperwood to Fortuna, fishing is popular with drift boaters. The lower river receives the most angling pressure for half-pounder steelhead, fall-run chinook salmon, and winter-run steelhead from late August through the first part of November. The Fernbridge area, and the 12th Street section of the river south of Fortuna, provide access to the best salmon holding waters in the lower river. These two areas are prime salmon waters.

Yolla Bolly-Middle Eel Wilderness

Situated between the North and South Yolla Bolly Mountains in the rugged country near Mendocino, Six Rivers, and Trinity national forests, the main attraction of the remote 154,000-acre Yolla Bolly-Middle Eel Wilderness is solitude. Elevations range from 2,000 feet at Cottonwood Creek to 8,094-foot South Yolla Bolly Peak.

Yolla Bolly derived its name from the Wintun Native American language. It means "high snow-covered peak." The geologic processes of landslides are evident along the streams and steep mountainsides of North and South Yolla Bolly Mountains. Within the wilderness, headwaters of three major streams—the Middle Fork Eel River, South Fork Trinity River, and South Fork Cottonwood Creek—begin their courses through landscapes covered with dense stands of pine and fir.

A host of spring-fed streams dominates the Yolla-Bolly in Trinity, Mendocino, and Tehama counties. However, some tributary streams of the Middle Fork Eel River are open to fishing with some restrictions. Balm of Gilead Creek, North Fork of Middle Fork Eel River, Middle Fork Eel River, Minnie Creek, Robinson Creek, Rock Creek, Willow Creek, and Yellow Jacket Creek are a few wilderness streams for adventurous anglers.

Several access roads lead to the wilderness trailhead:
1) Trinity County Road 504 from Ruth Lake to Three Forks, thence on Forest Service Route 27N02 to the trailhead.
2) SR 162 from Covelo to Forest Service Route 1N02 (Indian Dick Road) for about 28 miles north to Indian Dick Station area for several trailhead entries.
3) Take SR 36 out of Red Bluff to Harrison Gulch Ranger Station. Then turn left on Wildwood-Mad River Road 30 to Pine

Root Saddle. Thence onto Middle Crest Road 35 to Stuart Gap Trailhead, or continue on Road 35 to Rat Trap Gap Trailhead.

From Corning, in Mendocino National Forest, take County Road A9 to Paskenta. Continue on Forest Service Route 23N01 to Cold Springs Guard Station. At Cold Springs, take right fork 25N01 to road 25N27, which is signed "Ides Cove 5 Miles," then on to road 25N29 to the trailhead.

Middle Fork Eel River

Hidden away in forest and on private lands, the 70-mile Middle Fork Eel River originates from the Yolla Bolly-Middle Eel Wilderness. The Middle Fork meanders south and westerly to its mouth at Dos Rios. This fork is home to a rare spring-run trout, the summer steelhead. These fish exist in few California streams. Due to the scarcity of the steelhead, special fishing restrictions and closures are in effect on the Middle Fork Eel River.

In the past, heavy winter precipitation in sensitive areas, over-grazing, temperature, and logging had depleted most of California's summer steelhead. During the late 1960s, the population of this strain of sea-going trout dropped to a few hundred survivors. The California Department of Fish and Game and the U.S. Forest Service took emergency measures to avoid extinction and they closed a section of the river to conduct extensive studies.

By 1980, the two agencies adopted a joint Management Plan with the purpose of preserving, restoring, and protecting remnant runs of summer steelhead in the Middle Fork Eel. By 1981, the run had improved. California Trout Inc., proposed that a special catch-and-release steelhead season be applied from the mouth at Dos Rios to Bar Creek. The agencies approved the proposal which began in 1982. The intent of the restriction was to provide anglers with a unique sportfishing experience while trying not to impair the steelhead's recovery from near extinction.

It is a privilege for anglers to enjoy these rare and magnificent summer-run steelhead in this section of the Eel River watershed. For this reason, use extreme care and immediately release these rare and fragile treasures.

Summer-run steelhead enter the Middle Fork Eel River during the spring. These scarce fish require special summer holdover habitat in isolated remote headwater streams. The Middle Fork Eel River above Bar Creek offers them these sanctuaries. They remain in the land-locked pools until the following spring to spawn. Very few streams meet the holdover and rearing requirements. It is fortunate the sanctuary waters of the Middle Fork Eel provide them with deep, clear, cool pools, and clean gravel to satisfy their needs because summer-run steelhead have strict habitat requirements for spawning and rearing.

It is imperative that anglers be aware these waters are closed to fishing all year and the waters in the restricted area are heavily patrolled. However, from the mouth of the Middle Fork to Bar Creek, fishing is open on a limited basis.

Access to the Middle Fork Eel River is east of Dos Rios and Covelo along SR 162, Covelo Road. The best fishing access for wild steelhead is at the Eel River Work Center, and there is also a campground nearby. Premium water is near the end of the legal fishing area (mouth of Bar Creek). Weather and water conditions play a vital role in fishing the Middle Fork Eel. (Elevation in this area is less than 2,000 feet.)

Black Butte River, a large tributary to the Middle Fork Eel in Mendocino National Forest, sits in Glenn and Mendocino counties. The headwaters of this large tributary begin at Knee Cap Ridge. Flowing north to join the confluence of Middle

Fork Eel near the Eel River Work Center, Black Butte River and its tributaries, except Cold Creek, have an all-year closure restriction.

Effective Fly Patterns for the Middle Fork Eel River

The water is usually high in the spring and warm during the summer. April or May is the best time to wade the river. Work the waters cautiously with dark Woolly Worms, Woolly Buggers, Pheasant Tails, Hare's Ears, or other dark nymphs. For surface fishing, large dry flies—such as the Steelhead Caddis, Steelhead Bee, Stimulator, and Royal Wulff—are excellent choices.

South Fork Eel River

The largest tributary of the Eel River is the 106-mile South Fork. This body of water has the most angler pressure because of the many walk-in and drive-to river accesses allow for easy wading and shore casting. Therefore, many drift boaters and fishing guides frequent public boat-launching facilities along the South Fork.

The headwaters of the South Fork begin in Mendocino County and flow north to join with the main stem at Dyerville. The long stretch of the South Fork, from Rattlesnake Creek to the mouth, has many miles of river frontage. Due to limited access, angling pressure is low in the upper stretches. The portion of river from Piercy to the mouth receives heavy pressure from shore anglers. State parks and recreation areas along the South Fork—such as Standish-Hickey, Richardson Grove, Benbow Lake, and Humboldt Redwood—provide campsites and river access. In the Standish-Hickey State Recreation Area near Leggett, the park's section of the South Fork has deep pools and shallow boulder-strewn riffles.

Portions of the river from the Cooks Valley-Piercy area to Redway have good river access. This area, situated on the Mendocino-Humboldt County line, has prime riffles, boulders, and tailouts, and shore fishing is great. Five miles north of Richardson Grove State Park, and two miles south of Garberville, fishing access can be found in the Benbow Lake State Recreation area. From Benbow to Garberville, the river swings away from U.S. 101 affording easy access and waters with less angling pressure. This section is reachable from Sproul Creek Road out of Garberville (airport area). The mouth of Sproul Creek, tributary to the South Fork, is one of the best steelhead waters in the area. Boat angling is another means of reaching prime waters. Moving downstream from Redway, the river again parallels Highway 101. Do not overlook the mouth of Dean Creek in this area.

The South Fork of the Eel River traverses along a portion of the 31-mile Avenue of the Giants Parkway which stretches from Phillipsville to Dyerville. The scenic drive continues on the main stem until it reaches the Pepperwood-Scotia area. This segment of the stream is also productive salmon and steelhead holding water. In many stretches along the Avenue, parking and river access is available. Other prime waters are at the confluence of the South Fork and main stem at Dyerville. Anglers can access the water at the Dyerville Loop area.

Sections of the river at Humboldt Redwood State Park (between the towns of Myers Flat and Weott), provide a mixture of deep pools, shallow gravel bottoms, and boulders. When water conditions are conducive to fly-fishing, the Williams Grove Day Use Area and the California Federation of Women's Grove provide excellent river access. However, access is also available from Mattole Road in the Bull Creek area. This area lies on the west side of the river.

Effective Salmon and Steelhead Fly Patterns for the Main Stem, South Fork, and Van Duzen Rivers

Fly patterns for salmon in the main stem and South Fork are No. 6 Lime Hackle Green Weenie, Polar Shrimps, Gold and Silver Comets. Other selections are bright patterns such as Glo Bugs in champagne and orange, and the Thor in No. 6.

Favorite steelhead flies for these waters are Nos. 4-6 Nite Owl, Skunk, Green Butt Skunk, Fall Favorite, Silver and Gold Comets. Silver Hiltons and Renegades can be effective at times. Also, patterns with silver tinsel, red or black are dynamite.

Patterns recommended for the main stem and South Fork of the Eel are just as effective in the Van Duzen. However, flies with orange and red in Nos. 4-8 also work well here.

Van Duzen River

A bank-fisher's paradise for salmon and steelhead, the Van Duzen River is the last large tributary to the Eel River. This river basin sits southeast of Eureka in the north coastal mountains in Humboldt County with elevations ranging from 50 to 5,916 feet.

Currently, a closure restriction applies to the river from the SR 36 Bridge at Bridgeville to (and including) the South Fork Van Duzen. The closure was put in place in order to protect the salmon and spawning grounds.

The headwaters originate near Black Lassic Mountain (5,916 feet), which is one of the most outstanding landmarks within the Van Duzen River Basin. Steep canyons and cliffs are found in many portions of the river, with some of the most prominent cliffs situated in the lower reaches of the river between Cheatham Grove and the mouth of the Van Duzen. Throughout the river, numerous small pools are visible, but an extensive amount of sediment has filled in most of the large ones. The depositing of this large amount of sediment has changed it into a braided stream with the absence of many types of vegetation in many stretches of the river's course. In steep channels, large boulders with bare slope conditions are prevalent from Grizzly Creek State Park to Bridgeville.

The spelling of the name "Van Duzen" differs on various maps, but the Josiah Gregg party of explorers first named the river

South Fork Eel River. Easy access is available from U.S. 101.

Van Dusen's Fork in 1850 after one of its members. In any event, the "Fork" was later changed to "River."

Thirty miles of the 75-mile-long Van Duzen River is open to fishing with special restrictions from the mouth to Bridgeville (originally named Bridgeport). At the turn of the last century, Bridgeville consisted of resorts, stage stops, and overland mail trails. Over time, the area eventually became a lumber-boom community with logging railroads.

The Van Duzen is a narrow river ideal for wading and shore casting. It parallels SR 36 on its way to Bridgeville. One of the best accesses to salmon and steelhead waters in this river basin is at Grizzly Creek Redwoods State Park, located 23 miles east from the mouth. Other river accesses are a few miles downstream at Cheatham Grove (19 miles east from the mouth), and the Van Duzen Redwood County Park (located 13 miles east from the mouth). As salmon and steelhead move upstream to spawning grounds, they congregate near the mouth of tributary streams—such as Yager Creek, Root Creek, and Grizzly Creek—before continuing upstream to their respective creeks.

Due to flooding and extensive logging in the upper river, the Van Duzen River is "dirty" during heavy rainstorms. Once the river clears though, fishing can be fantastic. However, it is important to use light-weight lines, finesse, and water-reading skills. Angling pressure is mild when the South Fork or main stem of the Eel River are fishable.

There is a special tranquility found along the entire Eel River system. In certain areas, views of distant mountain slopes are visible through the immense forest. The drainage basin lies amongst the most impressive giant redwood groves surrounding the area. It is amazing that these ancient trees have survived both fires and floods.

Hidden Treasures of Other North Coastal Rivers

Redwood Creek, Mad, and Mattole rivers are a few of the hidden treasures many anglers often overlook because they do not receive as much publicity as larger streams. Other reasons they are overlooked include: frequent low-flow closures during peak runs, and because access to most water is on private lands. However, several streams are reachable from main, as well as, secondary routes to provide anglers with a unique experience.

The Solitude of Redwood Creek

Thirty-seven miles north of Eureka on U.S. 101, Redwood Creek flows through the town of Orick. Surrounded by redwoods, this small creek is the main attraction because it produces good-sized runs of both salmon and steelhead between November and April. If the cutthroat trout in Redwood Creek have not declined through the years, a fair run provides year-round fishing in the lower section of the stream as well.

Redwood Creek has easy access to prime gravel bar waters above, and below, Prairie Creek near the U.S. 101 Bridge. However, the best steelhead waters are above the bridge. One-half mile further upstream, on Bald Hills Road, an access road leads to a parking lot providing a walk-in trail that runs along the creek to the mouth of Bond Creek. Be aware of angling restrictions and stream closures throughout the various sections of Redwood Creek, and that the stream and its tributaries above the mouth of Bond Creek, are closed to fishing all year. The best time to fish this stream is from December until February.

North coast elk.

Steelhead migrate quickly upstream when there is sufficient water in the river system. However, after a sizable storm, Redwood Creek turns color rapidly and is slow to recover. Hence, timing is of the essence when fishing this stream.

Effective Fly Patterns for Redwood Creek

Fish the moderate, fast-moving waters with weighted Nos. 4-6 Glo Bugs, Bosses, Popsicles, and other bright winter steelhead fly patterns on a floating line. Depending upon the flow, you might want to switch to a sink-tip. This creek is one of the few small streams remaining that sustains a good run of steelhead. Exercise extreme care when releasing the fish.

Humboldt Lagoons State Park

Seven miles south of Redwood Creek, or 30 miles north of Eureka on U.S. 101, you'll find the coastal lagoons. Lying next to the Pacific Ocean, in Humboldt Lagoons State Park, the lagoons offer fly-fishing for cutthroat, rainbow, and steelhead trout when sandbars break open. Parking is plentiful for day-use. Also, there are parking facilities for recreational vehicles and campers on the ocean side of the highway.

Freshwater Lagoon

The smallest of the three lagoons, Freshwater is heavily stocked with rainbow trout. The ideal time to fish this lagoon is from spring to mid-summer with size 10-12 nymphs and emerger patterns. A great number of tourists stop to enjoy the ocean view, so that may create limited parking, nevertheless, you can almost always find a parking spot nearby.

Stone Lagoon

Trophy coastal cutthroat trout over two pounds inhabit Stone Lagoon. For nearly a decade, the Department of Fish and Game, Humboldt State College, and several environmental organizations implemented a restoration program for a trophy cutthroat fishery in this body of water. As a result of this effort to restore the fishery, the first stocking program was in effect during the spring of 1990. The plan was to make Stone Lagoon a strong trophy coastal cutthroat trout watershed. With special regulations placed on this water, fly-fishers can look forward to boundless fishing in the years ahead. (The state's record for a cutthroat caught in this lagoon is now over four pounds.)

Effective Fly Patterns for Stone Lagoon

Stone Lagoon is best fished out of a float tube, small watercraft, or by shore fishing. One of the best approaches is to work the area near its feeder stream McDonald Creek with nymphs and emerger patterns. This often produces exciting results from a good population of fish. Baitfish imitations, shrimp, and crustaceans are excellent choices for fly patterns. Try casting Nos. 8-10 weighted Black Leeches, Nos. 8-10 Green, Black, and Orange Crystal Hair Woolly Buggers, No. 12 Tan and Olive Scuds, or Nos. 4-6 Zonkers and Muddler Minnows to entice these fighting cutthroats to respond. Vicious strikes will often come as you retrieve the fly. A T-200 Teeny nymph, or other fast-sinking line, with a 5- to 6-weight rod is an ideal outfit for the lagoons.

Big Lagoon

This body of water is the largest, and last, of the three lagoons. It has a good run of cutthroat trout and steelhead because during high-water periods in the winter months, the lagoon occasionally breaks open to the ocean. This allows steelhead to enter the lagoon for spawning in tributary waters. Big Lagoon can be fished from shore or from small crafts. Present the same fly patterns as Stone Lagoon for optimal results.

Klopp Lake

F. R. Klopp Lake, situated in the Eureka/Arcata area, is a newly developed, large cutthroat trout pond. To reach Klopp Lake in the Arcata Marsh and Wildlife Sanctuary area, take the SR 255 Exit (Samoa Boulevard) for Samoa. Make a turn on South I Street and then go to the Smallcraft Launching area where a trail leads to the lake. Size 6-10 Muddler Minnow, Spruce, Bucktail Coachman, Cutthroat Yellow, and other streamer patterns will work best.

The Many Faces of the Mad River

In recent years, the amazing Mad River has been a superior steelhead stream. Because of Mad River Hatchery's efficient management, a large number of steelhead return each season. California's Wildlife Conservation Board built the hatchery in 1969 and operation began in 1971. The hatchery's purpose is to increase salmon and steelhead populations in this stream. In addition, there are no permanent barriers to prevent fish from journeying past the hatchery to continue their migration on to spawning grounds.

In December of 1849, members of the Gregg exploration party named the stream Mad River. While Dr. Gregg was conducting a scientific survey work at the mouth of the river, he became angry with his crew because they had not waited for him. As a result of being left behind, the scientist had to wade through the water, carrying his instruments, to catch up with the canoe.

North of Eureka, near Arcata in Humboldt County, Mad River is a medium-sized stream with good access and easy wading when water conditions permit. Although the salmon run is low, a strong run of winter steelhead attracts anglers in December and continues to March. A smaller run of summer steelhead enters the river from April to July.

Situated in the southern tip of Six Rivers National Forest, the river flows through a canyon flanked by South Rock Mountain and Mad River Ridge before entering Ruth Lake. Below the dam in the upper stretches the canyon, water holds steelhead and rainbow trout. When the water is low, adventurous anglers can cross the river below the hatchery and hike miles upstream on a private lumber road into picturesque canyon waters. However, the best stretch of steelhead water is downstream from the hatchery to the Blue Lake Bridge.

This river system has easy access to quality steelhead waters. The river bottom consists largely of sand and gravel, and a large number of steelhead congregate there. Because of this, this part of the stream receives the most congested pressure from anglers. During the peak of the winter season, hosts of anglers line the prolific stretches of the river below the hatchery. When the water level is low, fly-fishers generally wade in from the east bank because the open gravel bars at this point provide less angler pressure for fly-casting. This section of the Mad will definitely put fly-fishers into some good shore fishing and wading waters.

Mad River Hatchery provides excellent parking as well as the best river access. To reach the hatchery, take SR 299 out of Arcata (or Redding) to Blue Lake. Exit at Blue Lake and continue on Blue Lake Boulevard to Greenwood Avenue. Turn right on Greenwood and cross the tracks on S. Railroad Avenue. At the stop sign, turn right onto Hatchery Road. Upon reaching the hatchery, there is a large paved parking lot with trails leading to the river. Walk downstream from the hatchery to prime steelhead waters.

Another stretch of river to fish when water recedes after a storm is the Glendale Road exit from SR 299 west of the Blue Lake exit because this area receives less angling pressure. Travel towards the north bank of the river at Glendale Drive and watch for turnoffs to the river.

The best stretch of steelhead water lies downstream from the hatchery.

Effective Fly Patterns for the Mad River

The Mad River drainage lies in a heavily logged area. After any significant rainstorm, runoff turns the river into a torrent of dark chocolate water. Since the river takes a week to recover, the best time to fish it is when it is spiced with a little coloring. Comet, Popsicle, Skunk, Polar Shrimp, Glo Bug, Silver Hilton, Thor, Nite Owl, and Black Widow flies produce well when steelhead are in the river system. Depending upon water conditions, both orange and chartreuse steelhead flies also deliver great results.

Remote Mattole River Wild Steelhead

Originating at 1,500 feet in elevation—west of Point No Pass near Four Corners in northern Mendocino County—the Mattole River receives less angling pressure than other coastal streams. More than 50 miles of this remote river is one of the few free-flowing streams in Northern California. The name Mattole commemorates a Native American tribe practically exterminated because of their resistance to white settlers.

The sensitive river flows northwesterly through the southwestern part of Humboldt County, and holds some of the strongest-fighting native steelhead in this part of the state. Steelhead will be found congregating in some of the best sections of the river: in riffles, tailouts, and near the mouths of tributaries. Mattole's tributary waters include Stansberry, Mill, Conklin, Clear, McGinnis, Indian, Squaw, and Bundle Prairie creeks, as well as the North Fork Mattole below Petrolia.

Below Petrolia, parking and river trail access can be found along Lighthouse Road in the Mattole Valley. This area will always have good waters when the water levels drop. Access is available whenever the road follows beside the river along Mattole, Conklin Creek, and Lindley roads. Camping—with access privileges—is available at the Arthur W. Way County Memorial Park east of Petrolia. The area between Honeydew and Petrolia has limited lodging though.

Mattole Road goes from Ferndale, along the coastline, to the Mattole. However, from Dyersville (at U.S. 101), the winding Mattole Road is another choice. This route traverses over the coast range through the giant redwood groves in Humboldt Redwoods State Park. But be cautious of dangerous weather conditions. Snow or black ice can be on the road after storms.

Effective Fly Patterns for the Mattole River

Mattole River's aggressive steelhead are not leader shy so use heavy leaders to outsmart these powerful fighters. Silver Hiltons and other winter steelhead fly patterns will provide excellent action on the Mattole.

The Mattole River has a restricted open season with special regulations that vary, such as the use of artificial lures with barbless hooks and zero limits. The prime time to fish for the wild native steelhead is from January to March. Approximately 25 miles of legal fishing limits are found from Honeydew Creek, downstream, and to 200 yards upstream from the mouth. Where the road follows the river in the upper stretches, several areas have public access. However, be respectful of private ownership along some stretches of the river.

Central Coastal Waters... A Tale of Small Rivers

Mendocino County is a land of dramatic, wild, and rugged coastlines. Most central coastal streams from Tenmile River to the Navarro River are brushy. Due to years of drought, overgrown alders have made it difficult to fly-fish in some waters. Also, most portions of these streams have limited public access and anglers must secure permission from landowners.

Before starting to fish on Georgia-Pacific's property at Big River, Tenmile River, and the Noyo River, anglers must first obtain permits from Georgia-Pacific. Permits are available at the Forestry Division, Georgia-Pacific's main office in Fort Bragg. Check with sporting goods stores in Fort Bragg for the most current fishing conditions.

When fishing smaller coastal streams, take extra care when releasing all anadromous fish in order to enhance our future fishery. The most productive steelhead fly patterns in these smaller coastal streams are Nos. 6-8 Silver and Gold Comets, Boss', and Glo Bugs.

Tenmile River

Mendocino County's Tenmile River is 18 miles north of Fort Bragg from SR 1. The small river is a coastal steelhead hideaway stream. (One principal difficulty in fishing smaller coastal rivers is limited access because many streams are on private lands. Remember to obtain a permit from Georgia-Pacific to fish the stream.)

Noyo River

The Noyo River originates west of Willets, in Mendocino County, and is more than 30 miles long. Deriving its name from a former northern Pomo Village near the mouth of Pudding Creek, Noyo River drains into the Pacific Ocean below Fort Bragg. (This river recedes rapidly, in two to three days, after a storm.)

Silver salmon runs occur in the Noyo River from October to December while steelhead enter the river from January through March. But access to the river is difficult because it often flows through private property. The best means of gaining entry to the steelhead waters is to ride the famous Skunk Train that runs between Fort Bragg and Willits. The Skunk Train was originally a logging railroad and dates back to 1885. (The name "Skunk Train" derived from the fumes from the original gas engines.)

The train runs alongside the Noyo River for most of its length and departs daily from Fort Bragg. Crewmembers will drop anglers off at any point along the river's course and pick them up on the train's return trip. Some of the best areas to get off are at the mouths of tributaries, and at other stretches, such as Hayshed Gulch, South Fork, or Camp Three Spur. Before taking the train to fish the river, check the latest access status and obtain permits from Georgia-Pacific.

Other access is in the tidewater section. This area can often be productive when the fish are in the river system. And stretches where the river is productive to a wet line are above, and below, the SR 1 Bridge.

Big River

This river is open to fishing from the mouth to Two Log Creek, but the main stem, and its tributaries (above Two Log Creek), are closed to fishing all year. Big River lies south of Fort Bragg in the town of Mendocino. It originates below Impassable Rocks (2,612 feet), and empties into the Pacific Ocean at Mendocino Bay. The lower river, below the Mendocino Woodlands, is wide, deep, and slow moving with limited access. In the Woodlands section, however, the water attracts steelhead to riffles and pools located in the state park recreation area. (This stream also requires a permit from Georgia-Pacific to fish on private land.)

Navarro River

Navarro River has convenient access and is home to a large run of returning steelhead. Set amongst redwood groves, campsites are available along the river at Paul Dimmick Wayside Campground. Due to heavy logging in the area, the Navarro is often blown out with sediment after a storm, and during these high-water periods, the campground is frequently subject to inundation. State Route 128 traverses west from Dimmick Campground to SR 1. Further upstream from Dimmick Wayside, Hendy Woods State Park is another ideal setting for a base camp. However, keep in mind that the river, and all tributaries above the Greenwood Road Bridge (below the park), are closed to fishing all year.

The prime fishing area is the seven-mile stretch on the river's north bank along SR 128. It stretches from the confluence of the North Fork (at the Dimmick Wayside Campground), downstream to just above the SR 1 Bridge. This stretch has numerous turnouts which will require some walking in order to reach gravel bars. Heavy vegetation dots this portion of the river; therefore, wading is necessary when water conditions permit.

The river, next to Dimmick Campground, is also splendid fly-fishing water. A few other prime sections of the river are located both below and above this section, as well as at the mouth of the North Fork, a major tributary to the Navarro.

The stream is reachable from the coastal route of SR 1 or from inland by traveling on SR 128 west of U.S. 101 out of Cloverdale. Size 8-10 Silver and Gold Comets, Boss', Black Widows, and other winter coastal river steelhead fly patterns will stir up some action.

Alder Creek

Seventeen miles south of the Navarro River is Alder Creek. From the south side of the creek on Highway 1, a road follows the creek for about a mile to the mouth. Alder Creek has a good steelhead run when conditions are prime. Use Nos. 6-10 Silver and Gold Comets and Black Widows when stream conditions are good.

Garcia River

In the southern coast of Mendocino County, 20 miles north of Gualala, the historical towns of Anchor Bay, Point Arena, Manchester, and Elk, surround the small Garcia River. Rich pastureland dominates this river drainage. Access to prime waters requires some hiking. However, the light angling pressure warrants a special expedition to fish the Garcia.

The Garcia can be a moody river, spectacular one day, silent the next. Whenever a storm hits the central coast, this river quickly goes out of commission. Yet, it clears up rapidly as well. However, it does not get as much pressure as nearby Gualala River.

River access stems from several other county roads that branch out of SR 1: SR 1 Bridge area, Windy Hollow Road, and downstream from the Eureka Hill Road Bridge (which is the upper limit for stream closure). However, one of the most popular and productive sections of the Garcia is Minor Hole in the tidal section because steelhead generally enter the tidewater basin through the shallow mouth in the early season.

The Garcia River tidal basin is reachable three miles north of the town of Point Arena, or five and a half miles south of Alder Creek. Access to Minor Hole, in the lower river tidal basin, is from a hard-packed dirt road off SR 1. The mouth of the Garcia lies west of the lighthouse at Point Arena. (Before turning into this road, look for the lighthouse on the ocean side.) The dirt road heads west one mile to a dead-end parking area. To reach the premier fishing area, it is approximately a mile-long walk to the tidal basin. Wading is necessary to efficiently fish the lower river and Minor Hole. Be prepared with heavy shooting head, sink-tip, or Teeny Nymph line because open terrain surrounding the Garcia is vulnerable to wind.

Effective Fly Patterns for the Garcia River

The best fly patterns to get the fly down during high-water periods are Nos. 4-6, Orange Comets and Boss. When the water is low and clear, smaller patterns such as Nos. 8-10 Gold and Silver Comets and green or chartreuse Teeny Nymphs are more effective.

A River by the Sea ... The Gualala

Located along the central coast, Gualala River straddles Mendocino and Sonoma counties. Secluded in forested and heavily wooded terrain, this river is a fly-fisher's paradise. The Gualala (pronounced Walala) has easy river access from the small historical former lumber town of the same name. Lodging, campgrounds, restaurants, and tackle shops are nearby. The Gualala is a Spanish rendering of the Pomo Native American word "Walali" for "where the waters meet." In this case, the Gualala River meets the Pacific

Gualala River Hotel.

Gualala River.

Gualala River

Legend

① Sonoma County Park
② Gualala River Redwood Park
🐟 Fishing Access
⛺ Campground
🚶 Walk-In Access
No Vehicles Beyond Gates

MAP NOT TO SCALE

Ocean. This portion of the central coast traverses along the most scenic route of SR 1. Heading north from San Francisco, the highway skirts the steep ocean bluffs and winds among rolling hills from Jenner to Timber Cove.

Surrounded by beaches, sandbars, and gravel, the Gualala is a challenging steelhead water in December and January. Water conditions and fish returns play a major role each season, and can last through March. However, any substantial rainstorms can blow the river out of shape indefinitely.

The best stretch of fly-fishing waters is less than three miles in length on the main stem. It is reachable from the SR 1 Bridge to the North Fork. The waterway has been one of the most reliable small coastal streams in this portion of the state. The Gualala has dozens of defined pools holding steelhead ranging from 5 to 12 pounds. The fish can inhabit deeper pools from 5 to 12 feet of

water, however, in most pools, the fish hold in waters between 5 to 8 feet deep.

Besides shore fishing, the river has excellent wading possibilities. The Gualala is not a stream for fishing in solitude though. Since this is a favorite bank-fishing steelhead stream, plan to fish it on weekdays. On weekends, and during peak run periods, anglers waltz rhythmically while casting. The art of synchronizing a cast with other casters, or when a fish is on another fly-fisher's line, is a unique experience. It is always a privilege and delight to squeeze into an open slot in the Miner Hole where most fly-fishers congregate in this productive stretch of river.

Entry roads and trails to the stream are easy to locate. Sonoma County Park has camping facilities south of the SR 1 Bridge, but few parking spaces are available along the road into the campground. A short trail of about 350 yards leads upstream to the lower end of the famous Miner Hole on the south bank where heavy fly-fishing pressure is visible. Expect competition though from spin casters on the north bank. When the flow is low, cross the river above Miner Hole along a gravel bar to reach Thompson's Hole and Donkey Hole on the north bank. (Thompson's Hole will always have fewer anglers because there is no competition from the opposite bank.)

Thompson, Donkey, Snag, and Switchville can be reached from River Road 501 (which runs along the bluff on the north side of the river). To reach River Road 501, take 502 Ridge Road north of town. Turn right on River Road 501, go to the Gualala River Redwood Park, and park along the road.

River access to Thompson and Donkey holes is by trail from the Gualala River Redwoods Park. Continue on River Road 501 for access to Snag Hole, Switchville Bar, and upstream, to the mouth of the North Fork at Iron Bridge. Below Switchville, there are several pools in this section of the river.

Below the SR 1 Bridge, Mill Bend can be productive in the early morning along its south bank, but, afternoon winds can hamper casting. During low flow, most anglers congregate in the pools from Miner to Switchville because this stretch is excellent fly-fishing water. When the flow is low, most fish hold in various pools below Switchville. Miner and Thompson holes usually have the most steelhead holding in the river. If Miner Hole does not have room for you, try the Racetrack further downstream.

Gualala River steelhead.

Gualala River's Minor Hole.

Russian River boaters.

The ideal time to fish the Gualala is when the tide is low and water temperatures range from 52 to 54 degrees. During winter months, ice may line the banks in the mornings. Therefore, afternoons are best when water temperatures rise.

One of the essential things to know in order to fish this stream properly is how to choose the correct sink weight so that you can drift the fly to the level where fish are holding. However, be prepared with a variety of different lines, from floating, to extra-fast sink-tip, or Teeny Nymph line. The most versatile line though is an extra-fast No. 2 sink-tip. It is a simple process to add extra weight to it, or to change lines when conditions warrant it.

Effective Fly Patterns for the Gualala River

When the water conditions are high and off color, use heavily weighted size 4-6 patterns (with bright orange and red), and Boss variations. These will get the fly down fast. During low-flow periods, use small green and sparse brown flies representing naturals. The most successful fly patterns are Nos. 8-12 Pheasant Tail Nymphs, Hare's Ears, and Burlap Nymphs.

For most conditions other effective flies on the Gualala include: Nos. 8-10 Gold and Silver Comets, size 10 Nasty

Nymph (olive body, palmered with brown-and-black variegated hackle, and clipped), Nos. 8-10 Black Hackle Peacock, Nos. 8-10 Skunk and Fall Favorites, Nos. 8-12 Olive Marabou Shrimp patterns, and Nos. 10-12 Reddy Teddy (pearlescent body, palmered with yellow ostrich, natural squirrel tail, and red thread).

An excellent fly pattern is a No. 10 pearlescent or light brown Chihuahua Shrimp imitation. This fly consists of a pearlescent, light brown, or burlap body, and a palmered spiral body with peacock herl in the Woolly Worm style. It also has bead eyes at the rear of the hook, a dark brown head, olive marabou, and several strands of crystal hair.

Connecting with Sonoma Coast's Russian River

The first major fly-fishing destination north of San Francisco is the Russian River. This coastal stream, located in Sonoma and Mendocino counties, excites anglers in the fall when anadromous fish begin their journey into the river system. It is accessible from several major highways: U.S. 101, SR 116, and Coastal SR 1. Since the Russian does not get a large run of steelhead, timing is one of the chief factors in order to get outstanding steelhead fishing. Fishing there peaks during the latter part of January and on into February. The Russian River is not subject to low flow closures, so when other low-flow stream closures are in effect, head to the Russian.

The construction of Lake Mendocino's Coyote Dam in 1957 decreased many miles of spawning waters and fisheries. However, the construction of the Warm Springs Hatchery substantially improved the return of steelhead. Each season, hatchery-raised fish are released as smolts into Dry Creek. Because of this, steelhead returns have increased each year.

Downstream in the Healdsburg area, access to the river is—west of the U.S. 101 Bridge—from West Side Road, as well as from the Felta Creek area, below and above Dry Creek. Below Healdsburg, fly-fishing for winter steelhead is accessible at the Hacienda Bridge, and upstream at the Wohler Road Bridge, from West Side Road. Other river access from Guerneville to Duncan Mills is from Vacation Beach in Guerneville, the Monte Rio Bridge, and from Duncan Mills.

Gualala River "Minor Hole."

Bill Schaadt releasing a steelhead.

Gualala River fly patterns.

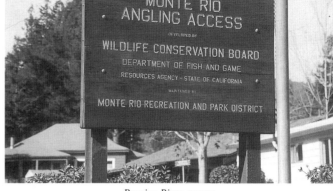

Russian River access.

Fly Patterns for the Russian River

Fly-fishing on the lower Russian River is becoming increasingly more popular because water conditions there are frequently low and clear. A floating line, long leader, and light tippet, coupled with smaller flies, can help you hook into steelhead. After a storm, during high-water conditions, add more weight to the floating line, and switch to a sink-tip or shooting head. Use shorter leaders and larger fly patterns though during high-water conditions. Recommended fly patterns are: a No. 6 Flaming Boss, Comet variations, Green Butt Skunks, Fall Favorites, and Brindle Bugs. (In the upper river, where the waters are clearer, switch to smaller size 8 patterns.)

Salmon Creek

When anglers congregate to fish at this small stream in Sonoma County, it indicates that the sandbar has opened and anadromous fish have entered into Salmon Creek. This stream is open to angling from the mouth to SR 1 Bridge. Size 8-10 Gold, Silver, and Orange Comets, as well as ocean baitfish imitations, are the best patterns for this small stream.

The Russian River.

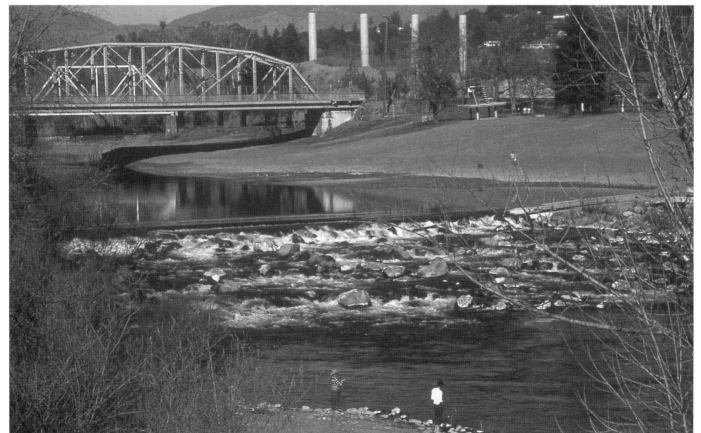

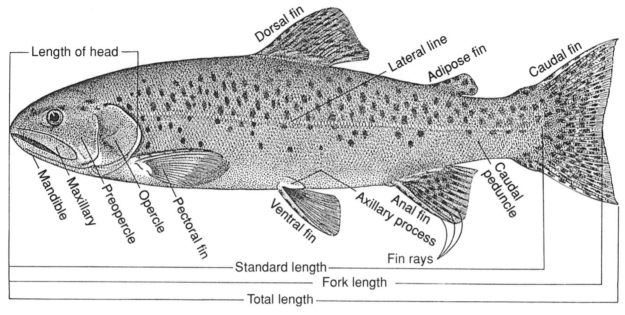

General trout structure

Trout in California Lakes and Streams
Characteristics and Distribution
Genus, Species, Habits, and Life History

A member of the Salmonid family, trout are the most sought-after fish in the Golden State. The sea-going species are referred to as "anadromous" which means that salmon and steelhead trout spend part of their lives in the ocean but move into fresh water to spawn. Rainbow, cutthroat, brook, brown, and golden trout, including subspecies, generally inhabit and spawn in the fresh waters of lakes and streams. The adipose fin is the primary distinguishing characteristic of this family. It is located halfway between the dorsal fin and tail (or caudal fin), on a fish's back.

Trout-spawning fisheries in high-country lakes are important to keep in mind when planning fishing trips. When spawning programs are successful, productive angling continues even after the initial stockings have disappeared because fish subsequently breed naturally producing a supply of fish that various bodies of water will support. However, many high-country lakes have no spawning grounds to maintain fisheries. It is therefore necessary to regularly stock bodies of water, though others require only occasional stockings. Brook trout spawn near shorelines, springs and seepage areas during the fall. Golden and rainbow trout spawn during the spring season but only in running water. Since different trout need different types of spawning grounds, the Department of Fish and Game can stock brook and golden trout in the same water.

Rainbow Trout
Oncorhynchus mykiss

The black spots on rainbow trout are their most predominant feature. The spots are seldom large, or even perfectly round, and can range from pin points to approximately one-eighth of an inch in diameter. These black spots are noticeable on the upper half of the head, the upper half of the body, as well as on the dorsal and caudal fins. The lateral band on rainbows is usually reddish to violet in color. It extends from the head to the caudal fin. Even though the lower side of the head is reddish, there are no red dashes visible on the membrane beneath the jaw. However, similar to those of a cutthroat, some rainbow may show small orange marks in this area. Coloration varies with all trout, but the rainbow portrays the most diversity in the trout family. In some lakes and reservoirs, rainbows may be silvery, except for on their backs, where spots may be few and indistinct and the red on the head, as well as on the sides, may be absent. The rainbow trout is the most widely distributed fish in lakes and streams throughout California.

Redband Rainbow Trout
Oncorhynchus mykiss subspecies

A subspecies of the rainbow trout, *Oncorhynchus mykiss*, the redband rainbow trout resembles the golden trout. The redband rainbow dons a yellowish to golden color along the side of the body, and another characteristic is a wide and vivid lateral red band extending from the head to the caudal fin. The cheeks and opercle are often iridescent red. Other predominant characteristics are the distinct white-tipped dorsal, ventral, and anal fins. Parr marks (dark splotches) along the sides of redbands are distinct and the adults retain these markings. With rainbow trout, parr marks disappear upon reaching the adult stage. Small black spots are visible on the upper half of the head, upper body, and on the dorsal fin.

During the 1970s, Sheepheaven Creek held the only pure population of redbands remaining in California. However, this subspecies is present in a few selected waters in Siskiyou and Modoc counties. Redbands in this basin include the Goose Lake redband, Warner redband, and McCloud River redband. Goose Lake redband trout are confined to the lake and its major tributaries—Lassen, Willow, and Cottonwood creeks. For the past several years, fishing in these tributaries has been closed to protect spawning fish migrating from the lake. Yet, these tributaries have opened recently on a catch-and-release basis.

In the spring, trout enter tributary streams in private and U.S. National Forest lands to spawn. After spawning, adults return to lakes around April. Subsequently, their offspring return the following year or later. Redbands in Goose Lake thrive feeding on the abundance of tui chubs. Several tributaries of the Upper Pit River drainage hold Warner redband rainbows similar to the Goose Lake redband. These fish inhabit waters in the Warner Mountains and South Warner Wilderness. At one time, populations of the McCloud River redband trout were present in a few McCloud River tributary streams, as well as in the river above the Middle Falls. It has been reported that redband trout inhabited the Little North Fork of the Middle Fork in the Granite Basin, a remote pristine tributary of the Middle Fork Feather River drainage in Northern California.

Eagle Lake Rainbow
Oncorhynchus gairdnerii

This rainbow trout subspecies inhabits the high-alkaline waters of Lassen County's Eagle Lake and its tributary, Pine Creek. The lake lies within the Lahontan Basin system, a drainage of the Great Basin of North America.

Eagle Lake trout are stream spawners. Before degradation in lower Pine Creek, trout moved upstream to upper Pine Creek to spawn during the spring. However, because of low flow and stream conditions, the Department of Fish and Game currently traps the trout at the mouth of the Pine Creek Spawning Station for hatchery reproduction. In April or May, offspring reared from hatchery brood stock are stocked in the deepest southern portion of the lake. Most of these trout mature at three years of age. They range in size from 18 to 22 inches. Tui chubs, shrimp, leeches, and snails are their principal food source. Low water and other environmental conditions during the past few years have limited the growth rates for these fish.

Eagle Lake trout still inhabit the lake but their survival is entirely dependent on artificial stocking. The Department of Fish and Game has introduced this subspecies into several lakes and reservoirs in Lassen, Modoc, Mono, Shasta, and Siskiyou counties. This stocking program has been successful. It is unlikely though that the pure strain Eagle Lake trout will naturally reproduce in any waters that have been stocked.

Golden Trout
Oncorhynchus aguabonita

One of the most elusive and brilliant fish in the high country is the golden trout, *Oncorhynchus aguabonita*, crown jewel of the salmonids. Dr. Barton Warren Evermann, Assistant in Charge of Division of Scientific Inquiry, Bureau of Fisheries in 1905, describes the golden trout as the most beautiful of all trout. He noted that the brilliancy and richness of its coloration is not equaled in any other known species.

In the early season, warm hues of yellow and reddish-orange reflect the coloration of goldens at their spawning stage. The cheeks, opercle, pectoral, ventral, and anal fins of the golden trout are red. Other characteristics are distinct white tips—sometimes bordered with black—on the dorsal and anal fins. Parr marks are common in young fish as well as in adults. The golden trout's coloration reflects the glowing pigments of the geologic conditions of decomposed granite, basalt, and volcanic rock that predominate in the stream systems. In recognition of its superb beauty, in 1947, the Legislature designated the golden trout as the state fish of California.

Two subspecies of golden trout are recognized in California: Little Kern golden, *Oncorhynchus mykiss whitei* and Volcano Creek golden, *Oncorhynchus mykiss aguabonita*. Except for the area near the tail, the coloration of the Volcano Creek golden generally lacks spots below the lateral line. A majority of goldens

from Golden Trout Creek show spots only in the tail area and on the dorsal fin. These spots are usually larger than on the Little Kern golden. On the other hand, spots appear profusely on top of the head, back, sides, and below the lateral line of the Little Kern golden. They are recognized as bluish-black blotches between and below the parr marks. The Little Kern golden inhabits the Little Kern River drainage.

Little Kern River originates at 10,000 feet, River Mile 23.5, below Bullfrog Lakes and Farewell Gap, west of the Great Western Divide at the northern tip of Sequoia National Forest. The river cascades south before connecting with the main Kern River (River Mile 117) at the Forks of Kern (4,800 feet).

Because the Little Kern golden is listed under the Endangered Species Act as threatened, several agencies have worked together to restore the pure strain of the fish to its native habitat throughout the Little Kern River drainage. Credit goes to the California Department of Fish and Game, Sequoia National Forest, Kings Canyon and Sequoia national parks, and the U.S. Fish and Wildlife Service. Since 1975, approximately 66 miles of stream and eight lakes have had non-native fish removed and restocked with Little Kern goldens.

The recovery program consisted of constructing many artificial barriers, as well as erosion control structures, in order to restore damaged habitat. Efforts focused on chemically treating the remainder of the non-native trout populations in the drainage. Various agencies will continue to monitor the recovering stream and lake populations of the trout and habitat restoration will continue. During the remained of the restoration process, biologists will chemically treat targeted lakes and streams to remove non-native fish and restock them with pure Little Kern goldens.

Golden trout originated in the high-elevation lakes and streams of the Kern River during the Pleistocene Epoch age. Current theories suggest that the golden trout descended from the rainbow trout that migrated through inland waters of the Kern River drainage during prehistoric times. Through geological changes, barriers isolated the surviving population in the upper Kern River drainage. Glacial actions though subsequently eliminated many of these ancestral trout.

Volcano Creek goldens are native to the upper South Fork Kern River and Golden Trout Creek. This subspecies also inhabits Cottonwood Lakes, Cottonwood Creek, Mulkey Creek, and other tributaries of the South Fork Kern.

Golden Trout Creek (a tributary to the Kern River in Tulare County), was initially named Whitney Creek, and then Volcano Creek. Subsequently, the U.S. Geological Survey applied the name "Golden Trout Creek," because in 1903 Dr. Barton Warren Evermann identified a new species of trout which had been found there—the golden trout.

The first edition of the USGS Olancha 30-minute map of 1907 showed that the Geological Survey had named the creek Golden Trout Creek. However, 2.5 miles of Volcano Creek, originating from Volcano Meadows, is a primary tributary stream to Golden Trout Creek and this is the name that currently appears on 1986 Golden Trout Wilderness and 1987 Inyo National Forest maps. The USGS will add the name Volcano Creek to the Kern Peak 7.5 Minute Topographic Quadrangle map series when the map is revised and updated.

The relationship between Golden Trout Creek and the South Fork Kern River is complex. Golden Trout Creek originates from Big Whitney Meadow (10,500 feet) in the Golden Trout Wilderness, northwest of where the South Fork Kern begins its course. The headwaters of the South Fork Kern River are located above South Fork Meadows at 10,300 feet elevation (River Mile 95). The river flows southwest to Tunnel Meadows, and then almost to a point near Golden Trout Creek.

According to Dr. Evermann, geological activities separated the streams into their present courses. Numerous impassable falls and alluvial barriers in these two streams completely isolated the trout of Volcano Creek from those of Kern River as though a land barrier intervened. Geologic features in the area consist of basalt, lava flow, and cones. At this point, a low alluvial ridge (not exceeding 75 or 80 yards in width) separates the two distinct streams from one another. From here, the South Fork Kern turns in an acute bend eastward while Golden Trout Creek continues to flow west.

It has been noted that Volcano Creek originally was stocked with trout from the Kern River. However, lava flows caused the extinction of all trout in the lower sections of the creek. Subsequently, the trout in the headwaters moved downstream after conditions became suitable. It is possible that at this time the South Fork Kern River trout, which was originally stocked from the Kern River, did not differ from those of Volcano Creek. However, during the period that elapsed since their segregation due to the formation of the alluvial barrier and the numerous impassable falls created by the eruption, there was sufficient proof to allow a separation, which renders the trout distinguishable from one another.

Golden trout adapt well to lakes and streams above 8,000 feet in elevation. As long as they have access to moving waters such as inlets and outlets, they will spawn and reproduce readily, but waters without these elements depend on supplemental aerial stockings. Years ago, many high-elevation lakes and streams were barren. Today, goldens inhabit approximately 300 lakes, 700 miles of streams, and 56 drainages within 13 counties throughout California. Hidden in expansive mountain ranges, the southern Sierra is a rich playground that holds most of the elusive golden trout in the high country.

Pristine golden trout lakes and streams lie in the heart of the remote alpine basins of the John Muir and Golden Trout wildernesses. The greatest numbers of golden trout waters are in Fresno and Tulare counties, followed by Mono and Inyo counties. However, they also inhabit several drainages in the Northern Sierra, Siskiyou County's Golden Russian Lake in the Russian Wilderness, Canyon Creek headwaters, and Morris Lake in the Trinity Alps.

The California Department of Fish and Game has a unique golden trout stocking program. When snow melts in the High Sierra each June, crews from the Department backpack into Cottonwood Lakes 1, 2, 3, or 4 near the southern base of Mt. Langley (14,025 feet). They obtain golden trout eggs from the brood stock population, and transport the eggs to Hot Creek Hatchery near Mammoth for rearing. In September, a DFG airplane gently drops the young goldens into remote high-elevation lakes. These four lakes are vital to the state's golden trout resources because these eggs are the only source of pure strain golden trout offspring in the state.

The Department has been taking golden trout eggs for reproduction purposes from brood stocks out of Cottonwood Lakes since 1918. This process has continued every year, except for during World War II and for three years in the early 1920s. These four Cottonwood Lakes, and their tributaries, used to be closed to fishing year-round to protect the golden trout population, and in order to maintain a renewable source of goldens to stock remote

high-elevation lakes throughout California. However, the Cottonwood Lakes and their tributaries recently opened to fishing with special regulations.

Lahontan Cutthroat Trout
Oncorhynchus clarki henshawi
One of the predominant characteristics of the Lahontan cutthroat trout is the two distinct red stripes on the membrane beneath their jaw. Their coloration is usually yellowish-olive from back to belly, and the entire body is frequently covered with large black spots.

Lahontan cutthroat trout were abundant in Lake Tahoe before becoming extinct during the 1940s. Through the years though, many other kinds of fish entered into the lake's tributaries in the spring to spawn. The introduction of rainbow trout, irrigation dams on the Truckee River, and black-market fisheries may have contributed to their extinction. Some Lahontan cutthroat trout inhabit the Carson River drainage and other watersheds in the eastern Sierra.

Paiute Cutthroat Trout
Oncorhynchus clarki selenirus
Anglers can easily mistake the brilliant color of the Paiute for that of golden trout. And like goldens, parr marks on these fish are also distinct. Years ago, Paiute cutthroats were separated from Lahontan cutthroat in the Carson River drainage below the falls. At the lower end of Fish Valley, the stream has an impassable barrier caused by geological action. Through the centuries, the isolated Paiute cutthroat developed its coloration pattern. The Paiute retains the orange-red cutthroat marks beneath the jaw like the Lahontan.

Paiute cutthroat trout are native to Upper Silver King Creek and its tributaries above Llewellyn Falls. Below the natural barrier of Llewellyn Falls, Silver King Creek flows into the East Fork Carson River. Located within the boundaries of Carson-Iceberg Wilderness in Alpine County, Silver King Creek and its tributaries, including lakes above Llewellyn Falls, are closed to fishing.

Several years ago, a Federal Recovery Plan was implemented to maintain and extend distribution of a genetically pure population of Paiute trout in the Cottonwood Creek drainage in the White Mountain District located east of Bishop. The program was to chemically treat the South Fork and Lower Cottonwood Creek. The stream would then be stocked with Paiute trout. When feasible, the objective of the plan was to transplant fish into unoccupied habitat waters. The proposed Recovery Plan intended to develop and implement other actions to maintain a viable and genetically pure population. By conducting annual surveys, the data collected will document population, size, detect "spotted" fish, and identify unoccupied habitats.

Brook Trout
Salvelinus fontinalis
At spawning time brook trout are almost as colorful as the golden trout. Their bodies are covered with small bright-red spots with light blue halos scattered along the sides. The major characteristic of this beautiful game fish is its prominent yellow to orange-red on the belly which is more pronounced in males. The back and sides of the fish are usually dark olive-green. The dark wavy lines on the back and dorsal fins are the distinguishing feature of the brook. In addition, above the reddish pectoral, ventral, and anal fins is a white and black line. The coloration of brooks may vary from season to season and this can be dependent upon environment. They thrive in waters

above 4,000 feet in elevation in Northern California and the High Sierra.

Brook trout, *Salvelinus fontinalis*, a member of the char family, prefer to spawn in lake bottoms with springs or ground water seepage. If sites are not available, they will use riffles or the tails of pools. Though natural spawning occurs during the fall, once initial stocking of fingerlings are introduced into waters conducive to their habitats, natural propagation will continue.

Brook trout are predominantly a fly-fisher's quarry because they readily succumb to flies. Small spring-fed mountain meadow streams, to larger rivers with cool waters flowing in the summer months, are home to brook trout. Currents within slower moving waters drift food to the fish creating ideal feeding stations. In larger lakes, the fish inhabit areas near springs, in shallower parts of lakes, inlets or outlets, away from deep channels. When fall arrives, schools of brook trout will aggressively forage for food in shallow waters. Once you locate these beauties, catching them on a fly rod with nymphs, streamers, or dry flies is exhilarating. Brooks will trigger rod-bending actions, whiz off with your fly, and head for cover.

Bull Trout
Salvelinus confluentus

The bull trout, *Salvelinus confluentus*, is a species of the char family which is indigenous to western North America. In California, the bull trout used to be only native to the lower McCloud River in northern Shasta and southern Siskiyou counties. Before 1978, it was believed that California's bull trout population was Dolly Vardens, *Salvelinus malma*.

One of the most distinguishing characteristics of the Dolly Varden is that there are no black spots or wavy lines on the body or fins. The back and sides of the fish are olive-green and blend to white on the belly, while the lower sides and back are sprinkled with small red spots. Pale yellow or pinkish-yellow spots are scattered on the body but no marks are visible on the fins except a few light spots visible on the base of the caudal fin rays.

Dolly Varden char are widely disbursed In Alaska, Washington, Oregon, Idaho, Montana, and British Columbia. At one time in California, it was believed this species inhabited the McCloud River below the falls and reservoir. This native char received its name from its resemblance to a popular dress with spots called Dolly Varden at the time scientists removed the fish from the McCloud River. A female member of the party at the time suggested the name.

The difference between Dolly Varden and bull trout is that bull trout have longer and broader heads, with a marked difference in gill raker morphology, and differences in cranial characteristics. Also, bull trout differ from brook trout by the absence of vermiculations on their back or fins. Antoher difference from the brown trout is its complete lack of dark spotting.

Bull trout used to exist only below the Lower Falls in the McCloud River. Due to the opening of fishing in McCloud Reservoir in 1966, and the establishment of Ah-Di-Na Campground, public access to the river expanded tremendously. As a result of these changes, increased over-harvesting by anglers has severely depleted the bull trout's population. By the early 1970s, the population of bull trout had declined drastically, but the introduction of brook and brown trout into the watershed may have also contributed to their decline.

Since the disappearance of bull trout from the McCloud River represents a great loss to California's only population of this native char, there is strong justification for re-establishing them. It is hoped this can be accomplished by introducing stock fish. One possible source of obtaining eggs from a wild bull trout stock is from the headwaters of the Upper Klamath Lake drainage in southern Oregon. Six known populations of bull trout in the Sprague and Sycan rivers, tributaries to Klamath Lake, are also possibilities. These populations may be the closest to the original McCloud bull trout populations. The connections between these fish must have occurred amongst the ancestral Klamath, Pit, and Sacramento River drainages during the Miocene-Pliocene or Pleistocene periods.

Brown Trout
Salmo trutta

Salmo is the Latin name for salmon and *trutta* is Latin for trout. The fish has been referred to as a German brown trout or Lock Leven trout because of its place of origin. The brown trout was first introduced into North America in 1883. In 1884, California received the eggs of the Loch Leven (Scotland) strain to rear here. They are referred to as the Lock Leven brown, or just Lock Leven. However, the most common name used is brown trout.

In most lakes and streams, brown trout can be distinguished by their brown or yellow-brown coloration, but the brown trout varies in color from dark brown or olive brown to golden brown on the sides, with white or yellow on the belly. Dark spots with light halos and red spots on the adipose fin are found on many brown trout. The brown trout is the only trout that possesses both black and red spots on its body. Their pectoral fins are unspotted and may be yellow, amber, or gray. There are few spots, or none at all, on the tail of the browns. In some lakes, the bright colors are difficult to locate because dark spots are few and indistinct. The predominate coloration is quite pale.

Brown trout spawn in fall or winter months which is the ideal time to fly-fish for browns in lakes and streams. Brown trout are abundant in California lakes and streams. These fish hold in swift riffles and large deep pools. Large browns generally station themselves during the day under cover amongst undercut banks, logs, and debris. At dusk, they leave their sanctuaries and aggressively pursue their meals. This is the best time to present your flies to large fighting browns.

Trout Hybrids

In nature, rainbow and golden trout sharing the same waters will readily cross as will rainbow and cutthroat trout. Since these trout spawn at the same time, it is not unusual for them to cross. While some species of trout hybridize readily, some do not.

The tiger trout, hybridized by the Nevada Department of Wildlife, is a cross between the brown and the brook trout. The name depicts the peculiar stripes as well as the voracious eating habit of the "tiger." Despite its rarity, the Nevada Department of Wildlife stocked Topaz Lake with tiger trout and cutbows. Cutbows are a hybrid between a female cutthroat and a male rainbow trout.

Topaz Lake, a bi-state fishery, lies in California and Nevada. An agreement between the two states allows anglers with fishing licenses from either state to fish anywhere in the lake.

Food Sources and Fly Patterns

Quiet dimples, splashy swirls, jumping, and acrobatic acts dominated a stretch of good trout-holding water in Hatchet Creek, one of the Pit River's tributaries. It was an exciting moment as I witnessed a cloud of insects displaying a festive dance. Immediately, I tied on a No. 14 Bi-Visible and presented it to the feeding fish. The moment my fly landed on the water, it vanished before my eyes. Shortly thereafter, the musical sound of line being stripped came from my reel. After a few gratifying moments playing the fish, I landed and released a beautiful 8-inch rainbow. I continued catching and releasing several more rainbows. Within a short time, all feeding activities ceased and the trout returned to their sanctuaries. Success on the water depends largely on the trout's menu and the imitation used to entice a response.

From this exciting experience, I decided to investigate the bread-and-butter diet of trout and other fish by exploring underwater features of streams, lakes, and ponds. During periods of silence, I began turning over rocks, inspecting beds of submerged vegetation, and stirring small sections of gravel and various rocks to uncover the presence and types of aquatic insects inhabiting the waters. The exploration revealed the fascinating world of an insect factory. It is a worthwhile effort to observe the appearance and behavior of aquatic insects in various waters. Once you have identified the food source, its size and coloration, selecting an appropriate fly pattern to best represent the natural will allow you to fish with more success. An important source of food for trout, nymphs make up approximately 85% of a trout's insect diet. And because trout are predominantly subsurface feeders, nymph fishing is very productive in all types of waters.

Other significant aquatic insects in the diet of trout are mayflies (*Ephemeroptera*), caddisflies (*Trichoptera*), and stoneflies (*Plecoptera*).

Mayflies make up the order of *Ephemeroptera*. Their life cycle includes three stages of development: egg, nymph, and adult. As adults, mayflies are the only insects that possess two separate winged stages—dun (subimago) and spinner (imago). With fragile bodies, and two or three slender tails, these aquatic insects live at many elevations in many lakes, streams, and ponds in California. In streams, the greatest population of mayflies is confined to slow- to medium-flowing waters. Their

emergence period takes place during daylight hours from spring to early fall.

The Order *Ephemeroptera* divides into families (or types) of *Siphlonuridae* and *Baetidae* (swimmers), *Ephemerellidae* (crawlers), *Heptageniidae* (clingers), and *Ephemeridae* (burrowers). From each family, they subdivide into genera (or groups). Although mayflies emerge at different times, each genus (group) contains species that will hatch in seasonal successions. Hatching activities peak between spring and midsummer. Mayflies leave the nymphal case as duns with wings. Duns float on the water's surface like sailboats, drying their wings before flying to sheltered resting places. A few species leave the water to hatch by climbing onto rocks or plants. Others rise to the surface film, break the nymphal skin along their back, and dry their wings momentarily before flying to surrounding vegetation. Adult mayflies can live for as little as a few hours, or up to several days, before reaching the spinner stage. The cycle ends though when spinners return to the water to mate, lay eggs, and die.

Tables 3 through 5 (following the description of mayflies, caddisflies, and stoneflies), identify various families and habitats. Mayflies and caddisflies are the cream of the crop in lakes and streams while stoneflies are abundant in streams.

Imitations for all the naturals that are a part of the bread-and-butter diet of trout are too numerous to list. Table 6 lists an assortment of fly patterns to cover a variety of food sources and situations.

The family of **caddisflies** Order *Trichoptera* goes through four life stages: egg, larva, pupa, and adult. They range in color from cream, green, and light orange. These aquatic insects prefer to live in the clean, cool water of lakes and streams which have flows from medium to fast, in all elevations, almost year-round. Their peak emergence period occurs in the summer. As bottom dwellers, some larvae swim freely in currents, while others live in small pebble, or stick-case houses, which they construct.

When these wormlike insects tumble along the bottom, trout are eager to devour them. At the pupa stage, they have soft fleshy bodies and half-formed wings. Their legs and antennae are sheathed along the sides of their bodies. Before hatching, pupae emerge toward the surface. Hungry trout intercept them at this time. Trout generally concentrate in areas

Mayfly: Order Ephemeroptera.

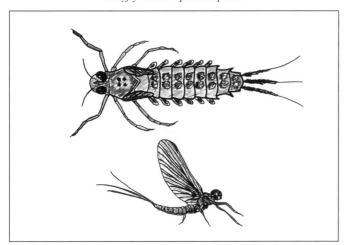

Stoneflies.

Caddis larva with cases and pupa.

Adult - pupa - larva.

where hatches will occur and wait for them. Once the emergence period starts, they eagerly feed on pupae and adults. When a hatch starts in early evening, fluttering adult caddisflies will dominate the scene. With a moth-like appearance, the adult caddisfly features tent-shaped folded wings along its back.

Fast-running water, plenty of oxygen, rocks, and gravel support the lifestyles of **stoneflies** Order plecoptera. The stonefly's life cycle goes through three stages of development: egg, nymph, and adult. Stoneflies inhabit waters holding smooth-faced rocks and boulders. Decaying aquatic vegetation wedged between rocks provides sanctuary from predators for stonefly nymphs and other aquatic insects.

The physical features of stonefly nymphs differ from those of mayflies. Stonefly nymphs have a double set of wing pads, while mayfly nymphs have a single visible wing pad. All stonefly nymphs possess two stiff tails, and two claws, at the end of their legs, giving them the ability to cling to rocks in swift currents. Nymphs crawl out on rocks and vegetation in late evening in order to emerge from nymphs to adults. The adult stonefly folds its wing flat along its back. Oftentimes you can see the dried shucks of stonefly nymphs stuck to rocks above the water line.

Adult stoneflies mate on streamside foliage. After completing the mating ritual, the female releases the eggs into the water by dipping her abdomen on the surface. Adults are vulnerable to feeding fish during this egg-depositing process. If they survive the egg-releasing ritual, the adult stonefly dies shortly thereafter. Being awkward fliers, the adults usually fall into the water, making them easy prey for fish. Presenting stonefly patterns along pocket waters, the edges of streams beneath trees, near overhanging vegetation, and other close to other streamside vegetation are all effective techniques.

Several classifications of stoneflies are significant to flyfishers. Winter stoneflies consist of tiny winter blacks, early blacks, and brown stones. The hatch usually begins in January and February and continues to emerge until late summer, but the most prolific hatches of stoneflies occur during spring and early summer. Emergence of the giant salmonfly (*Pteronarcys californica*) usually peaks during the summer months. These large nymphs dwell in fast riffle waters broken by rocks and boulders in Northern California and the High Sierras. However, large golden stones, and the little yellow stones, are the most abundant summer species.

Stonefly nymph.

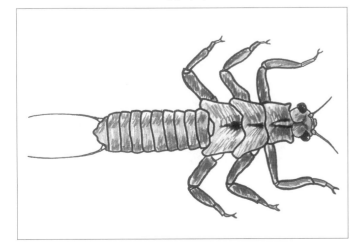

Adult stonefly.

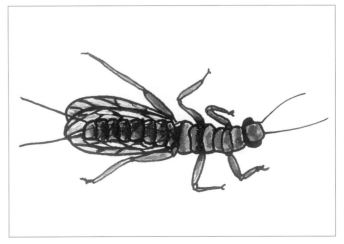

Other food sources rich in calories that trout gorge themselves on are midges, gnats, or mosquitoes (Diptera), damselflies and dragonflies (Odonata), scuds (Amphipoda), leeches (Hirudinea), and terrestrial insects.

Midges, **gnats**, and **mosquitoes** make up a large portion of the diet of trout. Midges look like small worms in the larval stage. During one of my fishing expeditions, I noticed fish ravenously feeding in a cove on a slow stretch of stream. After observing the feeding pattern for a few moments, I noticed that midges were on the menu. I tied on a No. 20 Black Midge Pupa and presented it to a fish that I had been observing. Immediately, another large fish took my fly and the challenge produced a brilliant native rainbow that measured 18-inches.

Midges hatch year-round and so fish are always willing to feed on these tiny morsels. Their life cycle consists of: egg, larva, pupa, and adult stages, of which, trout favor the pupa, followed by the adult. During late fall and early spring at Lewiston Lake, trout are vulnerable to well-presented midge imitations. These insects inhabit lakes and slow stretches of streams where there is an abundance of aquatic vegetation. Midges like to be in weed beds where algae and decaying plants are prolific. During emergence, insects hang in the surface film.

Prepare an assortment of midge pupa patterns in black, brown, olive, and tan, ranging from size 12 to 20. These will provide you with a successful day of fishing when all other patterns fail. In addition, a Blood Midge in No. 16 is an effective fly pattern in most Sierra waters. A Griffith's Gnat, Nos. 20-22, is an excellent imitation for adult midges in still and fast-moving waters. Mosquito patterns can turn an unsuccessful day into a successful one in higher-elevation lakes. After ice-out, in the warm months of July and August, the insects like to live in shallow standing waters. These are great places to seduce fish to strike with well-presented mosquito patterns.

Damselflies and **dragonflies** (Odonata) are also important food sources for fish inhabiting the shallow waters and weed patches of lakes, ponds, and slow-moving pools. Their life cycle consists of three stages: egg, nymph, and adult. The iridescent blue and green coloration of these large insects makes them conspicuous when they are found among aquatic vegetation. If water conditions permit, hatches occur between June and August. If you locate active insects along weed beds, use a floating line with an unweighted dragonfly or damselfly nymph. Impart the fly with variable short and quick retrieves in order to attract the fish's attention.

Water and air temperatures play a vital role when insect hatches occur. Seasonal climate, latitude, and altitude will affect emergence periods. If you are fishing further north, weather conditions in upper latitudes cause hatches to occur later. Altitude of an area is also a determining factor in seasonal hatches since delayed emergence occurs in higher elevations due to the cold water conditions created by snow and snow melts. Therefore, during spring or early summer, seek lower-elevation waters for early seasonal hatches. Emergence periods on a given day will depend on water temperatures. For instance, it is a morning and evening affair during warm summer months. In cooler months, afternoon hatches are common. Cloudy days, however, will induce the fish to feed for longer periods of time.

Scuds (Amphipoda), which are shrimp-like organisms, are excellent food sources for lake trout. High-country and alpine lakes hold scud populations of the genera *Gammarus*. Trout feed so heavily on these crustaceans that their growth weight increases. Scuds inhabit submerged aquatic vegetation in clean waters. Since scuds favor dark shadowy areas, look for shallow waters, shorelines with submerged vegetation, and dark areas around rocks. These prime areas hold large numbers of trout which actively feed on scuds during the early morning and at dusk.

Scud coloration varies in each watershed, ranging from olive, cream, tan, brown, to gray. Match them with slightly weighted (or bead headed) Nos. 12-18 imitations on floating, monocore, or intermediate lines. Vicious strikes often come from a presentation manipulated with a variation of slow, steady, and hand-twist retrieves.

Leeches (Hirudinea) are parasites inhabiting still waters and slow-moving waters. These segmented worms are commonly called bloodsuckers, and range from one to four inches in length. The worms' undulating swimming movement stretches their bodies making them very alluring to feeding fish.

The coloration of leeches ranges from dark olive, brown, cinnamon, black, tan, to gray. Match imitations to the predominant color of the leech in the watershed. When a marabou fly is wet, it undulates in the water like a leech. Woolly Buggers with marabou tails also give the fly the appearance of a leech. Besides using marabou, a few strands of Krystal hair will add some sparkle to the fly. I find that sizes 6 and 8 are good for Eagle Lake, Lake Almanor, and other still waters. Smaller-sized Woolly Buggers with iridescent peacock bodies are also irresistible to trout.

One of the best methods to fish a leech pattern is to use a long leader and floating line. Drift the weighted fly in slow-moving

Mottled leech.

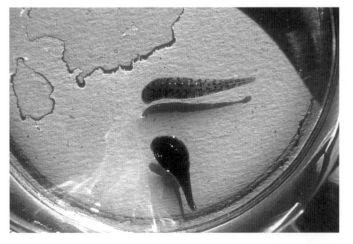

Leech and damselfly patterns.

waters. Monocore and intermediate lines, on the other hand, are very effective in shallow waters and over weed beds. Depending upon the depth and clarity of the water, slow sink-tip or sinking lines with shorter leaders work best, getting your unweighted fly close to the bottom. With a hand-twist retrieve, or a variation of short and long strips, manipulate the fly to create steady lifelike swimming movement, but always be alert for any minute line changes or abrupt strikes.

Ants, beetles, grasshoppers, and ladybugs—which are terrestrial insects—are of great interest to fish. On windy days, these insects are blown from nearby brushes, trees, or rocks into the water. They can also wash into lakes and streams from run-off, or they can inadvertently land on the water's surface, making them easy prey for fish. Grassy banks are ideal places to cast grasshopper patterns in July, August, and September, and flies imitating ants and beetles are often effective at this time.

Large trout will supplement their diet with forage fish. Lakes and streams harbor these small fish—sculpins, tui chubs, lahontan redsides, speckled daces, pond smelts, threadfin shads, sunfishes, and small trout. If you pause along the shallow shorelines of lakes or streams, you will notice forage fish darting through a maze of aquatic vegetation, scurrying from underneath rocks or boulder to logs.

Sculpins inhabit the bottom of fast-riffle waters and in the crevices of streams. The distinguishing characteristics of sculpins are their large flattened heads, large mouths, thin tapering bodies, and large pectoral fins. Yet, you rarely see these fish because they camouflage themselves in their natural environment.

Tui chubs belong to the minnow family. Their coloring is predominantly olive-green on their backs, and white to yellow near their bellies. A tui chub's head is large and conical, but the sides are flat. Traveling in large schools, these forage fish inhabit lakes and the quiet waters of larger streams. There is a large population of tui chub in Eagle Lake and the fish inhabit the shallow area along the shoreline.

Lahontan redsides are a small minnow with dark stripes along their sides. In the spring during spawning season, a pink or red band is prominent. Lahontan redsides inhabit higher elevation streams and lakes.

Speckled dace are small slender minnows with stout tails and small mouths located under pointed noses. Their coloring ranges from brownish to yellowish-green, with dark blotches located along their sides. During spawning time in the spring, their fins have a reddish tint. Speckled dace inhabit riffles in small streams. They feed largely on bottom food sources and small insects.

Pond smelt are small, slender, silvery fish belonging to the smelt family. They have adipose fins, one soft dorsal fin, and they seldom exceed five inches in length. Pond smelt are an important part of the diets of large browns and rainbows in the estuary of Butt Valley Reservoir, a Feather River drainage near Lake Almanor.

A member of the herring family, threadfin shad are small, thin, silvery fish with sawtooth markings on the edges of their bellies. The coloration of these fish varies from yellowish to bluish-green on their backs. A dark spot behind the head is a distinctive characteristic as well. Inhabiting numerous Northern California reservoirs, they tend to travel in schools and are an important forage fish for larger trout. Threadfins like to congregate at inlets and near the faces of dams.

Small sunfish inhabit higher-elevation lakes such as Martis Creek Lake (Nevada County), and Kelly Lake (Placer County).

Effective High-Country Fly Patterns

The short season in the high-country limits the natural food supply, yet midges, in all stages, as well as scuds, comprise the bulk of a trout's diet. Therefore, bring along a selection of adult, pupa, and larva patterns. Size 20-22 Griffith's Gnats, Nos. 16-22 Black Midges and Brassies, and Nos. 18-20 Olive and Chironomid Pupae will increase catches. Scuds are a nutrient-rich food source for high-elevation lake trout. Present Nos. 12-18 Tan and Olive Scud imitation patterns with twitching motions to attract the attention of cruising trout.

Nos. 14-16, with and without bead heads, Pheasant Tail nymphs, Bird's Nests, Hare's Ears, and Zug Bugs, are excellent choices all season. In heavy runs and riffle waters though, use bead heads, add a small split shot 18 inches above the fly, or use sinking-tip lines to get the fly down deep.

Other productive imitations for high-country watersheds include: Black Gnats, Adams, Yellow Humpies, Mosquitoes, small bucktails or streamers, Letort Hoppers, Black Ants, and Muddlers. Caddisfly patterns (pupa or adult) are also effective throughout the season during the afternoon and evening.

For specific watersheds, specialty flies will be included later on in the book in reference to each seperate body of water.

Fishing Strategies

Dimples, bubbles, swirls, splashes, and jumping fish are telltale signs that fish are present. When faced with a school of fish on a feeding

Scuds.

Three scud fly patterns.

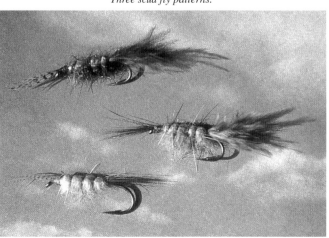

Fly-tying equipment.

rampage, one of the most difficult tasks is to decipher the feeding pattern. Are the trout feasting on the surface, just beneath it, or on the bottom? Understanding the form of rises will be your key to success.

After a surface-feeding fish has risen to the surface, a bubble and ring will be left behind in its stead. That is because when a fish ascends to the surface to take an insect, it opens its mouth to inhale it, and as the fish closes its mouth, water exits through gill openings. After the fish consumes these natural insects, the expelled air creates a bubble. This is an indication that a hatch is on and that fish are feeding. The process occurs when mayflies, caddisflies, and midges emerge as adults. Trout go wild during hatches when insects are under the film hesitating before emergence and when crippled insects are unable to fly away. After emergence, mayflies ride currents until their wings are dry enough for them to fly. During the wing-drying dun stage, mayflies are susceptible to hungry fish. When the wings dry, mayflies will fly to safety and rest in streamside vegetation.

You may see large fish porpoising in slow-moving water or lakes. These fish are usually taking emerging insects from beneath the surface. You may also find trout attempting to dislodge nymphs, scuds, or other bottom-dwellers from aquatic vegetation or weed beds along the bottom. As they feed and move into a vertical position, their tails occasionally break the surface. The best method to use on these trout is to get your fly to the bottom.

Presenting a drag-free fly pattern—like a natural that flows with the velocity of the current—is the best method to induce trout to strike. Feeding trout always face upstream so present your fly with an upstream cast. Mend your line, allowing the fly to drift downstream to a waiting fish. Another presentation to minimize drag is to cast your line downstream, in a series of S-curves, toward fish. In boulder-strewn pocket waters, use short casts above boulders and follow the fly with your rod as the current takes it around rocks to the pocket water.

Cruising lake trout have the advantage of inspecting what you are offering. With this is mind, present your fly with a 12- to 14-foot leader. When approaching a new lake, analyze the water to determine the depth where feeding fish are holding. Allow the fly to sink to the appropriate level with a weighted fly on a floating line or an unweighted fly on a sink-tip or sinking line. When you locate the correct depth, vary the speed of the retrieve until you find the method that works.

Stream nymphing requires another method. Present the fly by dead drifting it to the fish at the water level they are feeding. A trout can intercept your fly at any time during the drift so be alert for the slightest hesitation on your line. In boulder-strewn waters, short-line nymphing is an effective method because they will allow you to present your fly to fish at the proper depth with the added advantage of your being able to detect any subtle takes. Fast waters will require short leaders though, while longer leaders will allow for a wider range of presentation techniques in slow-moving waters. In faster-moving water, high-sticking is used to cast upstream to allow the fly to sink before it passes you. With your rod held high, follow your line with the rod as it floats down stream.

Nymphing with split shot is useful in order to get the fly down in fast-moving water. Depending upon the depth of the water, attach a small split shot (or two) 8 to 12 inches above the fly.

Strike indicators can also improve your strike detection allowing you to keep track of the fly in low-light conditions, still waters, fast moving, and rough waters. Depending upon the depth of the water, attach the indicator approximately 12 to 24 inches above the fly. Wide selections of indicator materials that are available on the market include synthetic, plastic, and foam. However, white, flourescent green, or orange yarns are also useful materials for indicators.

Pristine Waters of the Klamath Mountains Province

The Klamath Mountains Province contain a large number of lakes and streams in the northwestern corner of California. It covers an area of approximately 11,800 square miles in California and southwestern Oregon. This chapter is chiefly concerned with the portion that lies in California.

Bound by Interstate 5 on the east and U.S. 101 on the west, Klamath Mountains Province includes Six Rivers, Klamath, and Shasta-Trinity national forests. Klamath National Forest extends over 120 miles from the Oregon border southward to the Scott Mountains in the Trinity Alps. The national forest borders Six Rivers National Forest to the west. A small portion of the Klamath is situated on the western section of the Cascade Range.

Shasta-Trinity National Forest extends 150 miles between the Salmon Mountains to the west and the southernmost portions of the Cascades to the east. The northern tip of Six Rivers National Forest borders on the Oregon state line. It stretches over 140 miles south along the western slope of the Klamath Mountains in a narrow band. Six Rivers borders Mendocino National Forest between Haman Ridge and Long Ridge south of Zenia.

The Province embraces a host of complex individual mountain ranges. Among them are the Siskiyou, Marble, Scott Bar, Salmon, Scott, Trinity Alps, and Trinity mountains. Alpine glaciations are evident along higher ranges of the Klamath Mountains. The area possesses a distinctively rugged topography whose peaks and ridges range from 6,000 to 9,000 feet. Cirques, bedrock basins, marshy meadows, and U-shaped valleys are common landscape features in higher elevations.

Millions of years ago the area was broad and flat. Violent volcanic activities and the erosive cutting action of ancient glacier movements transformed the Province into a rugged region filled with deep canyons and steep mountainsides. Today, thick forest landscapes dominate the western portion. Swift canyon streams and alpine lakes in the region are dramatic and primitive. Mt. Eddy, at 9,025 feet in elevation, is the highest peak in the vast Klamath Mountains Province. It is the most prominent feature in the Trinity Divide. Mt. Thompson at 9,002 feet and Sawtooth Mountain (8,886 feet) in the Trinity Alps also stand out within the Province.

Ranging from 5,000 to above 9,000 feet in elevation, the rugged mountains in the Klamath Province tower above hundreds of secluded lakes and miles of streams that hold the trout required for outstanding angling. In the fall, angler pressure is heavy on the Klamath and Trinity River basins for the anadromous fish. However, from July to October, trout fishing is a favorite pastime in a network of quality roadside, backcountry, and wilderness waters. Dominant species are brooks, rainbows, browns, and a few of the high-elevation backcountry waters hold golden trout. Waters in the Province provide splendid and remarkable fishing in a spectacular environment.

Waters in the Province offer a wide range of angling destinations. Four major streams provide salmon, steelhead, or trout fishing—the Smith, Klamath, Trinity, and Upper Sacramento watercourses. Besides the Trinity Alps, Marble Mountain Wilderness and Russian Wilderness have readily accessible trails reaching remote lakes and streams. Siskiyou Wilderness receives fewer visitors due to its remoteness and long access roads to trailheads.

Pacific Crest National Scenic Trail Access Klamath and Shasta-Trinity Segments

In Northern California, the Klamath and Shasta-Trinity segments of the Pacific Crest National Scenic Trail (PCT) traverse the Klamath and Shasta-Trinity national forests. These two segments of the PCT trek through three wildernesses in this Province. Fly-fishing can be found along the route within the Marble Mountains and Russian wildernesses, as well as within the Trinity alps.

The Klamath PCT segment starts from the Oregon border southward to the Scott Mountains. Elevations in this segment range from approximately 1,400 feet to above 7,000 feet near Smith Lake (7,684 feet), which is located outside the northeast corner of Russian Wilderness.

The PCT enters California near Donomore Meadows. From the southern tip of the Red Buttes Wilderness, the PCT heads south to Seiad Valley crossing the Klamath River. At Seiad Valley access is at the Lower Devils Peak Trailhead.

As the PCT crosses Seiad Valley, it climbs above 6,000 feet within the Sky High Lakes and Cliff Lakes areas in the eastern portion of Marble Mountain Wilderness. The main features of this section of the trail are Kings Castle and the Marble Mountains. From this area, the PCT heads toward Russian Wilderness to the next trailhead at Etna Summit (5,956 feet). The PCT continues its journey south passing above Paynes Lake in the Russian Wilderness.

The PCT connects about 20 miles with Klamath National Forest near Virginia Lake (6,893 feet) east of Carter Meadows Summit in the Scott Mountains area. After leaving Virginia Lake, the PCT begins its 19-mile journey in a northeasterly direction along the northern portion of the Trinity Alps and the Trinity Divide country.

Pod of salmon.

The Shasta-Trinity segment enters the Trinity Alps country at Carter Meadows Summit Trailhead (6,146 feet), southwest of Callahan. This segment extends 154 miles in a west to east direction across Shasta-Trinity National Forest. From Carter Meadows, the PCT traverses along Scott Mountains to the Scott Mountain Trailhead at SR 3, northeastern entry into the Trinity Alps.

The trail leaves the Alps east of Black Rock (7,486 feet) and crosses SR 3. It then continues along the Scott Mountains, passing Masterson Meadow Lake at 6,205 feet. The trail then climbs more than 6,400 feet above Kangaroo Lake (6,020 feet) in the Trinity Divide country.

The next trailhead entry is at Parks Creek Summit Trailhead on FSR 17 west of Weed. From the summit, the PCT travels south for approximately 21 miles along The Eddys, passing through Deadfall Lakes, the Seven Lakes basin, and other lakes in the Trinity Divide country. After leaving the Basin, the PCT continues its nine miles to the ridge of Castle Lake before beginning a 13-mile descent to Castle Crags State Park at Interstate 5. The PCT crosses Interstate 5 and continues east to the McCloud River District in the southern Cascade Range.

The Wild and Scenic Klamath River System

The Klamath River is one of the largest streams in California. Except for the Colorado River in southern California, the Klamath is the only major stream in California that originates out of state. Its headwater arises from Oregon's Williamson River above the swampy country of Klamath Marsh. The Williamson, as well as Wood and Sprague rivers, flows into Upper Klamath Lake and Lake Ewauna above 4,000 feet at the eastern slope of the Cascade Range near Klamath Falls, Oregon. From Lake Ewauna, the Klamath River traverses in a southwesterly course before crossing the California border at Latitude 42 degrees. From the California border, Klamath's 209 river miles (RM) flow through Siskiyou, northern Humboldt, and southern Del Norte Counties before reaching the Pacific Ocean.

Many prime anadromous waters are inaccessible from roads in the Klamath River Basin due to steep rugged canyons or private ownership. However, there are stretches on the Klamath where anglers can reach salmon and steelhead holding waters for shore fishing, wading, or boating. Lodging is available at numerous locations on SR 96 from Interstate 5 to Orleans. Most campgrounds west of Interstate 5 to Aikens Creek above Weitchpec are open year-round. They are available on a first-come, first-served basis. Besides being a prime source of anadromous fish, the Klamath River system also boasts beautiful sites for resident trout.

Historical Significance

Klamath River country is rich in history, as are the people who inhabited the area. In the past, there were several names applied to the river: Clamitte, Klamet, Indian Scalp, and Smith. The name Klamath derived from the Chinook word Tlamatl, which was the name for a sister tribe of the Modocs (Maklaks).

For many years, Klamath River served as special fishing grounds for the Karok, Yurok, and Shasta Native American tribes. The tribe caught thousands of anadromous fish each year. At Ishi Pishi Falls near Somes Bar, Native Americans used dipnet fishing for salmon extensively. They constructed fish weirs from logs, poles, and brush across the Klamath and Trinity rivers to spear or net upstream-migrating salmon, steelhead, and other species of fish. Each season, the Yuroks constructed these weirs across the Klamath

according to strict rituals and procedures, and they removed them at a specific time. However, some weirs remained in the Trinity as impassable barriers until the first heavy rains washed them out.

The Karok or "Karuk" (meaning "up the river"), are residents that live above Thompson Creek on the Klamath River. They are neighbors to the Yurok tribe (meaning "down the river"), who are a slightly larger group. The Yuroks' home is from the mouth of Bluff Creek to the coast. Three principle towns in the Kurok's territory include the mouth of Camp Creek, Salmon River, and Clear Creek. These two tribes have similar cultures except for their languages. When fishing for chinook salmon, the Karok's special technique is by dipping and lifting their nets. The Karoks continue to practice all of the traditional customs and ceremonies of their ancestors. Clear Creek (Inam) and Somes Bar (Kota-mein) are sites of the tribe's restored sacred ceremonial grounds.

A smaller Shasta Tribe inhabits the area along the Klamath between Indian and Thompson creeks including a few miles above the mouth of Fall Creek. The Scott and Shasta rivers are within their territories. What is incredible about these people are their fishing customs. They built fish dams across the Klamath River at the mouths of Shasta River, Scott River, and Indian Creek. Each family holds property to a dam. All salmon caught in the willow fish traps belong to the head of the household. This individual is at liberty to give away as many fish to anyone requesting them. However, there is no restriction for spearing fish at the dam. When fishing in Native American Tribal lands, please respect their heritage and surroundings.

More historical information involves a party of miners in the 1800s. They traveled along the entire Klamath River from its mouth to the Shasta River. The party stopped along every bar panning for gold. Therefore, many bars above Somes Bar to the confluence of Shasta River received geographic feature names, such as Ti Bar, Rattlesnake Bar, Woods Bar, Oak Bar, Kanaka Bar, and Woodrat Bar to name a few. With the violence that occurred during the Gold Rush days, Salmon River's Murderers Bar acquired its name for the killing of three persons by Native Tribes who lived on the opposite side of the creek. Other bars were named after specific pioneers like John Scott, who discovered gold in 1850 along the Scott River. The river, mountain, and valley received his name.

Remnants of the Gold Rush days in the are evident within the communities along the Klamath and its major tributaries. Due to the extensive mining at this time, sediment from mining operations in the river disturbed rocks that contain dykes of serpentine that were embedded in many portions of the Klamath. Where the clear waters of the Trinity River converge with the Klamath at Weitchpec, a vast difference in water coloration is apparent.

Anadromous fish were able to migrate upstream to spawn before the 1900s. Near the Oregon border, dramatic changes occurred on the Klamath River. A significant portion of the river blocked salmon and steelhead from returning to their spawning grounds in California and Oregon. Problems stemmed from the construction and completion of Copco Dams No.1 and 2 (California Oregon Power and Light Company), hydroelectric developments in 1922 and 1925 respectively, and the completion of Iron Gate Dam in 1962. The projects and fluctuations of river flow hampered their upstream migrations. With major alterations to the river, stranded fish were below the dam. Consequently, Copco regulated the flow to allow fish to migrate to their respective home waters. To mitigate the loss of spawning habitats, Pacific Power and Light Company constructed Iron Gate Hatchery, operated by the Department of Fish and Game, to protect runs of Klamath River salmon and steelhead. The hatchery provided an excellent artificial propagation program for the return of salmon and steelhead.

To protect Klamath River's anadromous fishery, several other measures were put into effect. In 1924, an initiative act adopted by the State of California prohibited the construction of dams in the river downstream from Shasta River (RM 177). To protect and ensure sufficient breeding stock of fish, legislation abolished commercial net fisheries in the estuary in 1934. The state spent several hundred thousand dollars purchasing canneries and equipment from commercial industries to preserve the river as a sport-fishing stream. In 1950, they implemented a program to remove abandoned mining dams that blocked migratory fish. As a result, miners eventually discontinued their activities.

The Department of Fish and Game monitors fish screens placed on numerous irrigation diversions in the drainage and the placement of fish traps on intermittent and heavily diverted streams to prevent losing juvenile salmon and steelhead. With all these stream adjustments, most spawning grounds meet environmental requirements for migratory and holdover spawner fish in the Klamath River drainage. As an additional measure, Klamath River is now a free-flowing, Wild and Scenic river unencumbered with dams in the lower stretches. Three other large tributaries in the drainage—Scott, North Fork Salmon, and Trinity rivers—are also Wild and Scenic rivers. As a result of drought and extensive water usage for agriculture and domestic purposes, there has been a decline in anadromous fishery in the Klamath and its tributaries.

Timing of Runs

Fly-fishing for anadromous fish during peak periods in the Klamath is sensational. Success depends largely on timing of the run, weather, and water conditions. Once anglers are aware of these conditions, there is a greater chance of hooking on to these fish. Two well-defined spawning runs of adult chinook salmon enter the river system from the Pacific Ocean. Smaller spring runs generally start in late March, peak around Memorial Day, and dimish by June. This schedule may vary each season. High water from spring run-off is not conducive to fly-fishing. Fall is the best time to pursue the larger Chinook salmon run. In most seasons, fall-run fish enter the Klamath in July and gradually increase in August and September. The run peaks in mid-October to November when they reach the upper rivers. Late August and September are the best time to fish the lower river. By the end of October to mid-November, chinook fishing ends as steelhead trout filter into the river. Traditionally, prime time to fish the Klamath and Trinity is September, October, and November, water conditions permitting.

The Klamath River hosts a great number of salmon and steelhead. However, one of the greatest attractions for fly-fishers is the pursuit of wild steelhead trout. These fighting fish filter throughout the river and most tributaries that hold a significant amount of water. Known as the summer run, steelhead usually enter the Klamath River system in the spring or early summer. However, through the years, there is a possibility they have declined. When the steelhead arrives in the system, they remain in the river until the following spring to spawn.

A large number of late-summer or early fall-run steelhead known as "half-pounders" arrive in the river system in late August or early September. These immature steelhead attack flies aggressively, providing excellent action for fly-fishers. Generally, the half-pounder steelhead reach Orleans on the Klamath and the Trinity in Hoopa Valley around mid-September, and the upper reaches of both rivers around October and November. As the winter season

approaches, a small run of larger steelhead enters the Klamath as well as the Trinity. The fish are lethargic and congregate in deeper water during high and cold water periods. Larger winter-run fish require different angling techniques and heavier fly lines. Winter conditions hinder a fly-fishers ability to offer flies effectively. Therefore, alter the set up and approach for changing conditions by adding more weight or by switching to the proper sink-rate line that will get the flies down to the fish.

Some prime spots for holding fish are near the mouth of tributaries. Salmon and steelhead usually congregate in these holding areas before entering major tributaries. Besides the Shasta, Scott, Salmon, and Trinity rivers, smaller tributaries such as Clear, Elk, Indian, Thompson, and Beaver creeks also have good spawning grounds for salmon and steelhead.

Upper Klamath River

Below Iron Gate Dam, 190 miles of the river's course flows in a southwesterly direction through precipitous rapids, fierce currents, riffles, wide smooth pools, and runs before reaching the Pacific Ocean. In the upper Klamath River, anglers seldom visit a stretch of nutrient-rich productive waters between Boyle Powerhouse and Copco Lake. When water conditions are favorable to fly-fishing, one can expect 16- to 20-inch native rainbows succumbing to well-presented flies. To fish these waters effectively, it is essential to keep track of the river flow from Boyle Powerhouse by calling the Pacific Power & Light Company in Portland, or at 1-800-547-1501. After 5:00 P.M. on Fridays, they will announce an estimated weekend flow. Ideal conditions are 600 to 700 cfs. Be extremely cautious when river flows increase. Successful fly patterns during the early season in this stretch of river are Nos. 8-10 bead head Caddis Pupa and Pheasant Tail Nymph. Do not overlook salmonfly hatches in early summer. When these occur, use a No. 4 salmonfly pattern.

Primary spawning beds in upper Klamath River proper are from the legal fishing area below Iron Gate Dam to the mouth of the Shasta River. West of Interstate 5, SR 96 parallels the Klamath River offering access to the river except for steep canyons and properties in private ownership. Between the confluence of Shasta and Scott rivers, this stretch of the Klamath provides some excellent angling waters. Access to above and below the confluence of Shasta River west of Interstate 5 is on the south side of the Klamath. The stretches of river near the mouths of tributaries such as Humbug, Beaver, and McKinney creeks are good producers. Also, the river from Ash Creek Bridge down stream to Horse Creek is productive water when the fish are in the river system. Concentrate on the bars from the south side of the river.

Salmon and steelhead usually congregate above and below the mouths of the Scott River near Hamburg. This area provides an excellent stopover before these fish continue their journeys to the Scott or upper Klamath. Do not overlook the waters near the mouths of Horse Creek, Sambo Gulch, and Kinsman Creek. However, some productive holding waters are below the mouths of Scott River and Tom Martin Creek. Cover the mouths of tributaries such as Macks and Jim creeks by walking downstream or by boat.

Middle Klamath River

River approach is impossible in the Klamath River below Hamburg to Happy Camp because it winds in and out of steep canyons between National Forest and private lands. However, some waters are accessible above and below the bridge at Happy Camp, Indian Creek, and Elks Creek. Limited road entry is at Thompson Creek. However, county roads along Indian and Elk

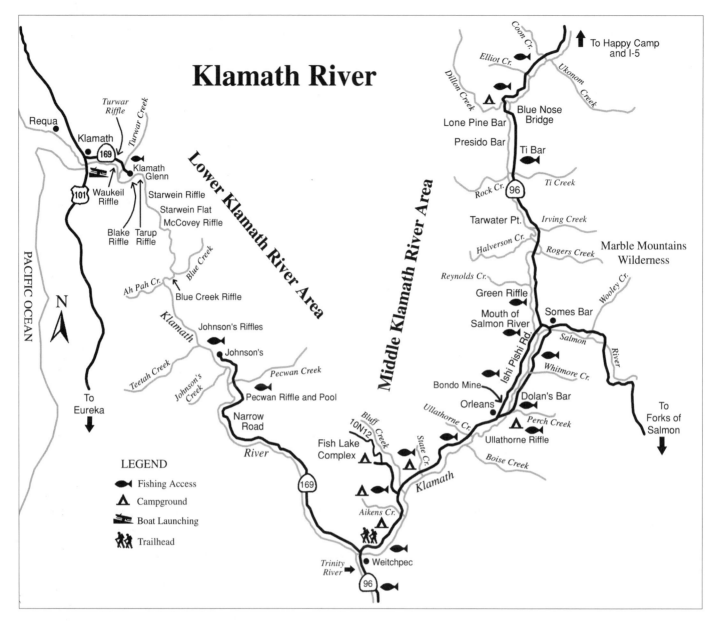

Klamath River

creeks provide some entries. Other productive waters near Somes Bar are Coon Creek, Dillon Creek, Lone Pine Bar, Presidio Bar, Ti Bar, Tarwater Point, Halverson Creek, Rogers Creek, the Green Riffle, Reynolds Creek, and mouth of the Salmon River.

Above Weitchpec, the best waters are in the Somes Bar area and downstream to Aikens Creek. High bluffs or south banks where shade provides sanctuary for the fish are ideal fly-fishing waters. However, canyon waters are best for boaters to get to because they provide cover for the fish. Drifting the Klamath by boat allows anglers to effectively cover waters that are difficult to reach. Bondo Mine, Dolan's Bar, and Pearch Creek in the Somes Bar and Orleans area provide excellent results when the fish are in the river system. At Orleans, there are several roads to reach the river. Most anglers favor the Orleans Bridge. One can wade and cover more waters in this area. Entry to the famously productive Ullathorne Creek Riffle, for example, is from a road out of SR 96. Work the waters above and below the mouth of the creek as well as downstream to the mouth of Boise Creek. From Slate Creek to Aikens Creek, several campground facilities next to the river provide excellent river access. The campgrounds accommodate many anglers during the peak fall

season. Take advantage of this prime fishing water on the Klamath. Because of high bluffs, river access between Aikens Creek and Weitchpec is difficult except for a few steep trails

Hidden Trout Waters: Fish Lake Complex

The Klamath River drainage offers many roadside and backcountry fishing destinations. Hidden away north of SR 96, between Weitchpec and Orleans near Bluff Creek, a group of lakes in Six Rivers National Forest offers several drive-to and hike-to lakes. Fish Lake Complex, in Humboldt County, is example in that it features both brook and rainbow trout.

The Fish Lake Complex includes Fish Lake, Blue Lake, and Red Mountain Lake. What is astonishing about Fish Lake is that it is in a beautiful wooded setting and angler pressure is light. Twenty years ago, sparse landscapes provided openings along the shoreline. However, upon my return years later, dense vegetation limited fishing from shore. Therefore, it is a good idea to bring a float tube or other craft to cruise around the lake to reach feeding brook and rainbow trout. There is a USFS full-service tent and RV campsite at Fish Lake. The facility for camping is usually open from April 1 to November 1. This is the largest natural body of fresh water in the complex and the Department of Fish and Game stock it frequently during fishing season. The best time to fish the complex is late spring, early summer, and again in the fall.

To reach Fish Lake, take Bluff Creek Road, FSR13 (13N01). Then turn east on FSR 10N12. Drive directly to the lake and circle around it. However, Blue Lake and Red Mountain Lake offer easy access and solitude with a little hiking in a charming setting. Blue Lake and Red Mountain Lake are approximately nine miles from SR 96. Forest Service Route 13N01 from SR 96 will also reach Blue and Red Mountain lakes. Keep an eye out for road pullouts. The hike to Blue Lake for brooks and rainbows is easier than the steeper climb to Red Mountain Lake.

Lower Klamath River

The lower Klamath Rive,r from Weitchpec to the mouth at Requa, traverses in a northwesterly direction. It is difficult to gain entry to the river below Weitchpec. State Route 169 heads west from Weitchpec to Johnsons. This steep, narrow canyon road can cause traffic pains because of residents traveling between these points. In late October, the 20-mile drive on this narrow canyon road through the Yurok Indian Reservation provides productive waters in the island area one-half to three-quarter miles below Johnsons. Between Johnsons and Starwein Flat, there is no road to this stretch of the Klamath.

Klamath Glen River Access

When anadromous fish enter the Klamath River from the sea between August to late September or early October, anglers congregate in the lower river. During the peak of the run, boating is the prime mode of transportation to reach migrating fish as they pass through the lower river. Access is from the coastal town of Klamath on U.S. 101. From the U.S. 101 Bridge, take SR 169 and head east to Klamath Glen and the public boat-launching ramp sites. When you come to a junction at Klamath Glen, turn right at Turwar Riffle Road, pass Mo Beth Way and the residential area, and head toward the river. At River Mile 7, this launching site at Turwar Riffle has a large gravel bar. However, the river is deep and swift in this lower reach. Therefore, if anadromous fish have arrived in this section of the river, be extremely cautious of rapid currents.

Boaters generally go upriver to the mouth of Blue Creek and other sites in search of migrating fish. Jet boat taxi guide services also transport anglers upstream so they can fish the lower river. Fly-fishers can chose to either fish from the boat, or else they are dropped off so they can wade the stream. Early morning is the best time to fish because of the prevailing winds during the afternoon. Be cautious though of the heavy currents which dominate a major portion of the wide and deep lower river. In this area, Glo Bugs, other egg-sac imitations, and chartreuse-green shrimp fly patterns are effective.

Out of Scott River

Scott River, east of Hamburg, is the second largest tributary to the Klamath. West of Fort Jones, Scott River Road serves as an entrance to the Marble Mountain Wilderness which contains: Shackleford Creek/Campbell Lake and Canyon Creek/Sky High Valley trails which depart from Lovers Camp. The Scott is a superb free-flowing river fed by snow melts from Scott Bar and the Marble Mountains. Kidder, Shackleford, Boulder, Canyon, and Kelsey creeks, which are all tributaries to the Scott, originate from the wilderness. The terrain in the area is dotted with granitic rocks, semi-arid rocky canyons, and alpine meadows.

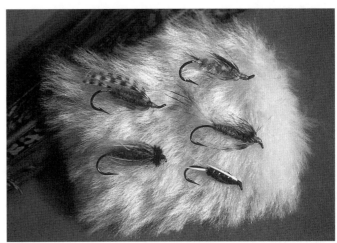
Steelhead fly patterns.

The South Fork of the Scott River begins its course at South Fork Lakes (6,748 feet) near the Salmon Mountains in Siskiyou County. The headwaters lie near the northern border of the extremely rugged Trinity Alps Wilderness. As lakes and streams in the Trinity Alps are accessible only by trail, angling information is covered in the Trinity Alps section under Trinity River. Wherever entry is available in the upper river, the Scott is an excellent trout stream. Some hydraulic operations, old ruins, and hard rock mines are still visible in the Sugar Hill area.

On the east side, the headwaters of East Fork Scott River tumble down the Scott Mountains from springs and tributary creeks located near 5,000 feet west of the China Mountains. This area is part of the Trinity Divide, and is across from the southern end of the valley. Access to the East Fork Scott is difficult though because a significant portion of the river, and its tributaries, flows over private ownership lands.

Miles of tributary streams provide spawning gravel for steelhead and salmon. Both the South Fork and East Fork of the Scott River merge with the main stem at RM55, and this stretch of river passes through the town of Callahan. For more than 36 miles, the main stem continues its flow through Scott and Quartz valleys. Once a flourishing mining industry populated with gold miners and mining camps, the rural community is now home to ranch owners.

Surrounded by high and extremely steep mountain ranges sprinkled with snow, a number of these prime recreation lands are privately owned. Paper and timber companies, as well as fruit growers, now own most of the land in the area so please respect all posted signs.

Below Quartz Valley, you can gain access to the Scott River from the Jones Beach Picnic Area until the Kelsey Creek Ranger Station. Several campgrounds are also available within this 4-mile stretch. The Scott River (RM 14) is also accessible near the Kelsey Ranger Station from the Bridge Flat Campground. The Kelsey Creek area is one of my favorite sections of the Scott because it is excellent steelhead water during the late fall, as well as early winter, when the fish are in the Scott River system.

There are high diorite cliffs and sharp escarpments which change dramatically from the Indian Scotty Campground, down to Scott Bar (an early mining town). This area has deep canyon walls and wild Class V waters (advanced whitewater runs). It is interspersed with riffles, and deep serene pools, where anadromous fish swim in during fall and winter. Anglers though should not attempt to maneuver the swift-flowing, demanding, and challenging rapids of this river without proper training.

The next river approach is at Townsend Gulch which is located near the mouth of Tompkins Creek and Gold Flat, between RM 10 and 11 on the Scott. From Townsend Gulch to Scott Bar, the river lies nearly 400 feet below the steep canyon road which slowly veers away from the river. Four miles from the mouth, the Scott Bar area also provides river entry. However, it is difficult to approach the river between Scott Bar and the mouth because of the road is at least 40 feet above the river's edge.

A Passport to the Salmon River

Situated in the rugged Klamath National Forest, the Salmon River is the third largest tributary to the Klamath. From Somes Bar, Salmon River Road follows the course of the river to the Forks of the Salmon. The narrow scenic road rises from 80 to up to several hundred feet above the river.

South Fork Salmon River (RM 39) begins its course below Sawtooth Ridge (8,282 feet) and Black Mountain (8,038 feet) which are in the northern sector of the rugged Trinity Alps. (Lakes and streams that originate in the Alps are also covered under the Trinity Alps in the Trinity River section). When steelhead enter the system in late summer and early fall, waters in the South Fork are cool and clear because its source is located near 8,000 feet. Characteristics of the river consist of everything from classic pools to torrent rapids. There are some unique waters situated in the lower section of the South Fork, from Matthews Creek Campground to the Forks of Salmon, and near Cecilville, you can see the sites of century-old gold camps and mines. In addition, wild native trout inhabit the smaller tributaries of this famous steelhead river.

The headwaters of the North Fork of the Salmon tumble from English Lake (5,828 feet), at RM 36 on the southern sector of the Marble Mountain Wilderness, out of the snow-capped Salmon Mountains. Flowing quickly, tributaries and intermittent streams feed into the North Fork before reaching the small community of Sawyers Bar at 2,162 feet (RM 15).

The narrow Sawyers Bar Road lies in the heart of a rich mining region. And except for a few river accesses below Sawyers Bar, which is next to the road, generally, portions of the river are wide with heavy flows.

Floating the river below the Forks is one of the most popular modes of steelhead fishing in the Salmon. (Located at RM 19, the Forks is the name given to the area where the South and North forks merge with the main stem of the Salmon.) By staying at a resort near the Forks of the Salmon, you can also gain entry to the river in an area that provides excellent steelhead fishing.

Near other sections of the river, narrow roads descend and pass through high cliffs and canyons. Surrounded by the glistening marble and granite formations of the region, canyon waters consist of series of luminous green pools with boulders and riffles.

Effective Fly Patterns and Tactics for the Klamath River

In the upper section of the Klamath, a 5- to 6-weight floating or sink-tip line is ideal for half-pounders, while a 7- to 8-weight line is required for larger steelhead trout and salmon. But fishing for anadromous fish in the lower river requires larger outfits, such as a 6- to 7-weight line for steelhead and a heavier 8- to 9-weight line for salmon. Since the lower river is deep and wide with swift currents, have several sink rates on hand. Type II to V sink-tip,

uniform sinking, shooting taper, or Teeny Nymph T-Series shooting lines will work well. Another Teeny Nymph line, the TS-Series, works well with longer casts, or when the wind makes casting extremely difficult.

In low-water conditions, floating lines, leaders and tippets with small diameters, and sparsely tied small flies work best. Use enough weight to allow the fly to sink near the bottom of the drift. Some outstanding fly patterns to work drainages with are Nos. 4-8 Brindle Bugs, Nos. 6-8 Glo Bugs, Silver Hiltons, Mossbacks, Assassins, Carey Specials, and Weitchpec Witches. Other anadromous flies to work the waters with are Nos. 4-6 Green Butted Skunks and Fall Favorites, Nos. 2-6 Purple Speys, Nos. 6-10 Dark Stone Nymphs, No. 6 Burlaps, and Nos. 6-10 Orange Stimulators and Elk Hair Caddis.

The Klamath is similar to many other large western rivers. It is a treacherous body of water filled with fast currents and slippery rocks. The swift currents of many sections of the river can be easily overlooked because of water discoloration. First-time visitors to the Klamath should be extremely cautious when fishing these waters, but most importantly, wading staffs, cleats over wader boots, and PFDs (personal floatation device) are essential equipment.

Shasta River Connections

The little Shasta River—a tributary to the Shasta River—is located east of Yreka in the Klamath National Forest. A rainbow and brown trout stream, the upper stretches of the Little Shasta lie in the Goosenest Ranger District of the Klamath National Forest. Little Shasta River begins its course from springs located in Little Shasta Meadow. Surrounded by Ball Mountain (7,786 feet), Panther Rock, and Willow Creek Mountain (7,830 feet), the spring-fed stream of the Little Shasta flows west toward Yreka. As it enters Little Shasta Valley, the stream enters the confluence of the Shasta River near Montague. Other waters entering into the Shasta River begin in the Trinity Divide country. (They are covered in the Trinity Divide country in the Trinity River section.)

Nestled in the Shasta Valley Wildlife Area east of Yreka near Montague, fishing is permitted in Bass and Trout lakes with special imposed regulations. In order to manage and protect the area and its wildlife resources, visitors are permitted to enter the grounds only through the main headquarters. Policies set forth for use in this wildlife sanctuary should be followed, one rule being that parking is only available in designated areas. However, during critical phases of the nesting season, public entry in some areas may be completely closed and signs will be posted where applicable. Only electric motors are allowed for boat users, but float tubes and pontoon boats are ideal for these two lakes.

Fifteen- to 18-foot-deep Bass Lake is one of two lakes in the Wildlife Area open to the public. Fishing season for trout in Bass Lake lasts from February 1 until September 30. During the warmer months, weed growth surrounds the shoreline. Therefore, spring is the best season to fish Bass Lake for planted trout. (The lake also holds a population of bass and red ear sunfish.)

Do not overlook ideal fly-fishing opportunities for wild rainbows and Eagle Lake-strain trout in 135-acre Trout Lake. Fishing season for this 30- to 35-foot deep lake, is from the Saturday preceding Memorial Day through September 30, on Wednesdays and weekends only. Plan your trip accordingly for a superb experience fly-fishing for trout ranging in size from 12 inches to 6 or 7 pounds. Bass and red ear sunfish reside in Trout Lake as well. But other special regulations include the use of artificial lures only.

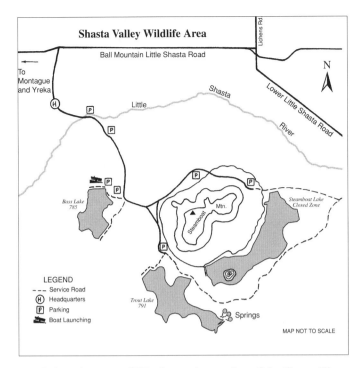

Shasta Valley Wildlife Area

Lichens Rd.

Ball Mountain Little Shasta Road

N

To Montague and Yreka

Lower Little Shasta Road

Little   Shasta   River

H

P

P

P

P

P

Bass Lake
785

Steamboat
Mtn.

Steamboat Lake
Closed Zone

P

P

Trout Lake
791

Springs

LEGEND
- - - Service Road
H Headquarters
P Parking
Boat Launching

MAP NOT TO SCALE

Below the town of Weed, a major portion of the Shasta River lies on privately owned lands.

Below Hawkinsville, the river traverses through Shasta River Canyon along SR 263. The river is accessible near the Pioneer Bridge on U.S. Bureau of Land Management (BLM) land. Look for spur roads near Pioneer Bridge in order to gain entry to the river. But don't forget to first review the latest sport fishing regulations for the Shasta River under the Klamath River system.

Upper Klamath River Drainage

Other upper Klamath River drainages offering stillwater trout waters are Juanita, Orr, and Indian Tom lakes. Greenhorn Reservoir is an exceptional fishery located along the outskirts of Yreka.

Juanita Lake

At 5,160 feet, scenic Juanita Lake is hidden below Ball Mountain (7,786 feet). This 40-acre lake lying east of Interstate 5 and west of SR 97 near MacDoel, has campsite facilities with piped water, vault toilets, grills, and tables next to the lake. This Siskiyou County lake receives trout plants regularly during trout season. The best method to fish this serene lake is by non-motorized boats, crafts, or float tubes. Cast popular nymphs with and without bead heads and dry flies to attract trout.

Access to Juanita is from Interstate 5 to Weed. Exit at the junction of SR 97 for approximately 35 miles to MacDoel. A spectacular view of the north slope of Mt. Shasta is visible from the highway. About one-half mile before reaching MacDoel, turn left at a sign and travel on West Butte Valley Road to reach Juanita Lake.

Orr Lake

Orr Lake, at 4,643 feet, lies south of MacDoel and east of SR 97. This Butte Creek drainage should not be overlooked if you are planning a trip to Juanita Lake. From MacDoel, head south on Old State Highway to Bray. Follow directions at Bray to the lake.

Patterns such as Pheasant Tail Nymphs, Bird's Nests, Hare's Ear Nymphs, Damselfly Nymphs, and Caddisfly Pupae are excellent flies to fish Orr Lake.

Indian Tom Lake

Situated near Dorris at the Oregon border east of SR 97, Indian Tom Lake should not be overlooked if you are in the area. For stream fishing, anglers can venture into Antelope and Butte creeks.

Greenhorn Reservoir

Superb fishing for trout up to 18 inches is possible in the town of Yreka. Situated between Upper and Lower Greenhorn Park off Greenhorn Road west of Interstate 5, Greenhorn Reservoir (2,754 feet) is an exceptional watershed. The reservoir is fed from springs at 5,249 feet in the headwaters of Greenhorn Creek (Klamath National Forest).

In early spring, before weed growth peaks and again in the fall when the weeds are decreasing, fish in the reservoir in the upper Greenhorn Park area are more prolific. However, when the water warms and weed growth increases, it is best to fish the lower Greenhorn Park area. The best entry to upper Greenhorn Park is from Greenhorn Road. To reach lower Greenhorn Park, take Ranch Lane.

Through the years, Greenhorn has had some repairs due to a mineshaft below it. The latest restoration increased the capacity of the reservoir. Rainbow trout are the dominant species in the reservoir. However, occasional brook trout are stocked in this 27-surface-acre, 30- to 35- foot deep body of water. Crappie and largemouth bass also reside here.

Effective Fly Patterns for Greenhorn Reservoir

Float tubes, pontoon boats, or other water craft are the best means to fish Greenhorn. Shore fishing is also possible, but not as rewarding. Best fly patterns are Nos. 14-18 Pheasant Tail Nymphs, Hare's Ears, and Bird's Nests, with or without bead heads, and Midge patterns. Size 10-12 Olive Woolly Buggers or Olive Leeches work well in this drainage. The pulsating action created by the marabou feathers will entice larger trout to strike.

Remote Siskiyou Wilderness

West of Happy Camp, 153,000-acre Siskiyou Wilderness consists mainly of rugged mountains and dense vegetation. Elevations range from 1,000 to 7,000-plus feet with Preston Peak (7,309 feet) as the dominant peak in the wilderness. For those wishing to hike into this lightly traveled wilderness, Clear Creek National Recreation Trail, also known as Forest Service Trail 5E01 "No

Steelhead flies.

Mans to Youngs Valley," traverses 21 miles along Clear Creek. "No Mans to Youngs Valley" derives its name from "No Mans Creek," located at the trailhead and the trail destination at Youngs Valley.

Clear Creek, a tributary to the Klamath River, holds a small summer run of steelhead. Anglers can reach the Clear Creek trailhead from the steep, narrow canyon FSR 15N32 west of SR 96 near Happy Camp. Several access points are available near the end of the road. Buck and Devils Punchbowl lakes feature rainbow and brook trout fisheries. These lakes are reachable by foot from Clear Creek Trail.

Lying below Bear Peak (5,740 feet) in Little Bear Valley is the Bear Lakes Basin. A rainbow and brook trout fishery, the Basin drains into Clear Creek. Small Hare's Ears, Pheasant Tail Nymphs, and emergers are great patterns to get the trout's attention. To reach the Bear Lakes, take the South Kelsey Historical Trail at the end of FSR 15N19 west of SR 96. The best time to travel into the wilderness is from late June to mid-October.

Marble Mountain Wilderness Shangri-La

Besides the great anadromous and trout fisheries in the Klamath Mountains Province, there are three other wilderness areas offering superb trout fishing to anglers who are looking for solitude and remote fly-fishing adventures. These three wilderness areas are within close proximity of each other: Marble Mountain Wilderness, Russian Wilderness, and the Trinity Alps Wilderness. The Pacific Crest National Scenic Trail (PCT) traverses through these three wilderness areas that accommodate anglers with an abundance of pristine waters.

Surrounded by Scott River on the east and Salmon River to the south, 242,500-acre Marble Mountain Wilderness lies in the heart of Klamath National Forest within the Klamath Mountains Province. Originally established in 1931 as the Marble Mountain Primitive Area, and reclassified as Wilderness in 1953, the Marbles became one of the original wildernesses in the National Wilderness Preservation System.

Originally the Marble Mountains underwent violent volcanic actions that caused the erosive cutting of rivers and glaciers. Named for a high monolith of white limestone standing at 6,880 feet, the Marble Mountains are composed primarily of prehistoric marine invertebrates. The majestic white of the Marble Mountains, lush green meadows, the 175-foot-deep blue Cliff Lake, and sheer rock cliffs epitomize wilderness. Most lakes in the wilderness lie amongst sheer rock cliffs and densely timbered mountainsides. This Siskiyou County wilderness is comprised of mountainous terrain, diverse vegetation, and over 70 pristine lakes varying in size from one-half acre to 67 acres.

All streams in the wilderness are tributaries to the Salmon, Scott, or Klamath rivers. Tributary streams such as Canyon Creek, Shackleford Creek, Kelsey Creek, Kidder Creek, and Elk Creek, support a population of wily trout. In addition, Grider Creek, Granite Creek, Bridge Creek, Ukonom Creek, Haypress Creek, North Fork and Little North Fork Salmon River are also excellent trout waters. With active fish stocking programs, the lakes and streams primarily support brook, rainbow, or Eagle Lake trout. Fly-fishing in these waters is productive in July and again in September and October before inclement weather begins.

Anglers can cover many waters in a trip no matter which entry is selected, due to the fact that the majority of lakes are situated in three distinct groups. These areas are the northwestern (Ukonom Lake-Haypress Meadows) sector, northeastern and eastern sections (Boulder Peak-Marble Mountains area), and the southern portion surrounding English Peak.

Roads to trailheads are from SR 96 between Hamburg to Somes Bar, Scott River Road, Fort Jones-Etna-Sawyers Bar Road, and Salmon River Road. The most heavily-used entry is from the eastern portion of the wilderness out of Scott River Road. Canyon Creek Trail from Lovers Camp and Shackleford Creek Trail serve the majority of wilderness travelers. This location holds over 18 lakes ranging in elevation from 5,000 feet to above 7,000 feet.

Canyon Creek Trail covers seven miles of moderate difficulty through spectacular wilderness lakes and streams, lush meadows, wildflowers, and wildlife. On the trail, scenic views of Marble Mountains are visible.

The PCT enters the wilderness at the northern sector east of Huckleberry Mountain (6,303 feet). The trail traverses the entire wilderness north to south passing through Marble Valley and the Marble Mountains. It passes above the Sky High Lakes and Campbell and Cliff lakes, to name a few. A host of connecting trails allow anglers to visit other lakes and streams. Since the PCT's route is on ridges, the trail is subject to lingering snowfields in the early season. The PCT leaves the Marble Mountain Wilderness at the southeast corner near the Salmon Mountain Summit and continues its route through the Russian Wilderness.

Canyon Creek Lakes

One of the most popular wilderness entry routes is the Canyon Creek Trail out of Scott River. Located in the northeastern corner of the Marbles, the first of the high-country lakes in the Scott River drainage is 12.5-acre, 56-foot-deep Lower Sky High Lake (5,765 feet). Sky High Lakes Basin has good campsites that can serve as base camp. Nearby 4-acre, 38-foot-deep Upper Sky High Lake (5,780 feet), a few feet above the lower lake, also has good campsites. Located near the top of the ridge above Lower Sky High Lake, the fish in small, 14-foot-deep Shadow Lake are subject to winter kill during severe winters. This lake is accessible following a faint trail from the PCT.

A chain of lakes in the Scott River District, such as 26-acre, 90-foot-deep Lower Wright Lake (6,930 feet), 5.5-acre, 58-foot-deep Aspen Lake (7,100 feet), and 2-acre, 25-foot-deep Buckhorn Lake (6,800 feet) are beautiful lakes to explore. Other adventurous lakes in the district are 3.5-acre, 25-foot-deep Chinquapin Lake (7,150 feet), 16-acre, 68-foot-deep Deep Lake (6,350 feet), and 4-acre, 25-foot-deep Dogwood Lake (7,250 feet). Also, small 1.5-acre, 11-foot-deep Wolverine Lake (6,800 feet) sits in the Boulder Peak (8,299 feet) area.

Trailheads to other waters in this district are located at Bridge Flat Campground. The Kelsey Creek Forest Service Facility provides entrance to the Kings Castle area. Two isolated brook trout lakes situated below 7,405-foot Kings Castle contain brook trout: tiny 2-acre, 8-foot-deep Bear Lake (5,950 feet) and 5-acre, 15-foot-deep Paradise Lake (5,430 feet). While the PCT traverses through Paradise Lake, Bear Lake is best reached from Happy Camp on the Kelsey Creek Trailhead. During the summer months, algae growth dominates Paradise Lake.

Situated below Boulder Peak (8,299 feet), the highest peak in the wilderness, several trails provide means of entry to Deep and Wright Lakes in this rugged granite country. Steep, challenging trails offer miles of scenic views, wooded country, and plush meadows before reaching 26-acre, 90-foot-deep Lower Wright Lake (6,930 feet). From Canyon Creek Trail, one can arrange a car shuttle trip returning by way of Shackleford Creek Trail.

Shackleford Creek Lakes

Another group of lakes in the Scott River District is Shackleford Creek Lakes. Shackleford Creek Trail is another favorite eastern entry into the wilderness. This popular trail provides stream fishing along the route to Campbell, Cliff, and Summit Lakes. Being surrounded by precipitous cliffs, the deepest lake in the Marbles is the 175-foot-deep, 52-acre Cliff Lake (6,109 feet). Summit Lake at elevation 6,300 feet, on the other hand, is a smaller 5-acre, 15-foot-deep lake containing a large population of brook trout. Campsites are available at Campbell, Cliff, and Summit lakes.

Isolated from other lakes in the area are 5.5-acre, 43-foot deep Shelly Lake (6,710 feet) and 2-acre, 15-foot-deep Kidder Lake (5,900 feet). These lightly fished bodies of water are reachable from the Kidder Lake Trail before branching into separate trails.

North Fork Salmon River Lakes

Lying below English Peak (7,322 feet), the North Fork Salmon River begins its course at RM 36 from the English Lakes. This area, in the Salmon River District, hosts several lakes with campsites for visiting anglers. At 5,828 feet, 6.5-acre, 28-foot-deep Lower English Lake, 8-acre, 20-foot-deep Abbott Lake (5,663 feet), and 13-acre, 25-foot-deep Lake of the Island (5,682 feet) lie below the Marble Mountains. A short distance above Lower English Lake, Upper English Lake (5,847 feet) is a small 1-acre, 5-foot-deep lake. Although this upper lake holds a population of brook trout, it is subject to winter kill.

Trailheads to the English Peak complex are accessible from the southern and southeastern part of the wilderness. The closest access road to Little North Fork Campground trailhead is from Sawyers Bar Road out of Etna or Forks of Salmon.

The other route is from Idlewild Campground located east of Sawyers Bar. A shuttle vehicle between Little North Fork Trailhead and Idlewild Trailhead at Sawyers Bar Road will cover more lakes and streams. This loop trip is another favorite backcountry hiking destination in the Marbles. Both routes run along the Little North Fork and North Fork Salmon River.

The trail from Little North Fork Campground primarily follows the Little North Fork Salmon River in most part. From Idlewild Campground, FSR 41N37 stretches along the North Fork River to the English Lakes. This is a great opportunity to fish the river along the trail before reaching the first lake in the area. Both trails are popular for horse packers. While in the English Peak complex lakes, anglers can take side trips to nearby lakes in the southern drainage of Wooley Creek.

Wooley Creek-Haypress Meadows Trail Complex Lakes

Haypress Meadows trail in the Ukonom District has spectacular panoramic views of the Marble and Salmon mountains to the east as well as the Siskiyou Mountains to the west. This trail attracts a host of hikers and horse packers entering from the west side of the Marbles. Somes Bar, on FSR 88, holds a trailhead sigh limited parking. The complex has a network of interconnecting trails to lakes and campsites in the wilderness. Elevations range from 4,000 to 6,000 feet. Haypress receives its name from a machine located in the area that presses hand-cut hay for supply ranches along the Klamath River.

In the southwestern sector of the wilderness, from Wooley Creek north to Elk Creek, the area is surrounded by granitic rock. In this area, past stream erosion has created many radiant pools in the granite along Wooley Creek. These exsquisite formations are a beautiful sight. Rugged landscapes with sparkling lakes dot the steep terrain in this remnant glacier basin. Wooley Creek, tributary to the Salmon River, lies on the northwestern slope of Marble Mountain Wilderness. Miles of stream from the mouth of Wooley Creek serve as a summer habitat for steelhead and spring salmon.

Headwaters of North Fork Wooley Creek begin its course in the Salmon Mountains from springs and the chain of four Cuddihy Lakes. The largest lake of this group is 7-acre, 20-foot-deep Cuddihy No. 3 (5,700 feet) followed by 3.5-acre, 18-foot-deep Cuddihy No. 1 (5,650 feet), and 2.5-acre, 20-foot-deep Cuddihy No. 4 (5,700 feet). Smallest 1-acre, 5 feet deep Cuddihy No. 2 (5,650 feet) is stocked with brook and Eagle Lake trout, but subject to winter kill. Other lakes flowing from the headwaters are 9-acre, 25-feet-deep Deadman Lake (5,680 feet), 9-acre, 37-foot-deep Pleasant Lake (5,520 feet), 5-acre, 17-foot-deep Hooligan Lake (5,160 feet), and 3.5-acre, 41-foot-deep heavily fished Spirit Lake (5,920 feet).

Two other small headwater lakes flow into Bridge Creek before connecting with Wooley Creek. At elevation 5,750 feet, 3.5-acre, 11-foot-deep Meteor Lake (5,750 feet) is stocked with rainbow and Eagle Lake trout. South of Meteor, a trail goes directly to nearby 3-acre, 13-foot-deep Monument Lake (5,780 feet) that holds brook, rainbow, and Eagle Lake trout.

Lying above Hancock Creek, tributary to Wooley Creek on the northern face of English Peak, Hancock Lake at elevation 6,345 feet is the third largest lake in the wilderness. Its 44-acre, 56-foot-deep lake holds sizeable trout; therefore, bring along different line types from floating to sinking. This is an ideal lake to tote along a lightweight float tube. Further north, below Hell Hole Ridge in the Big Meadows area, the lightly fished 5-acre, 13-foot-deep Lake Katherine (5,741 feet), 9-acre, 22-foot-deep Lake Ethel (5,697 feet), and 3.5-acre, 24-foot-deep Wild Lake (5,888 feet) are other lakes to consider venturing into.

Further east, a few South Fork Wooley Creek headwater lakes situated in rocky terrain require cross-county scrambling through brush and rough landscape. Above the ridge from Cliff Lake is 14-acre, 112-foot-deep Man Eaten Lake (6,200 feet). Lying below the Marble Mountains, anglers need to take either the Summit Lake or Kidder Lake trails to join the PCT. From the PCT, where the Kidder Lake trail meets, hikers need to continue on the PCT to locate the best route to cross-country down to Man Eaten Lake. This superb deep-blue lake does not receive many visitors; you may be surprised with some excellent fighting trout.

Another lake requiring a cross-country trek is 6.3-acre, 84-foot-deep Wooley Lake (6,676 feet) which holds rainbow and Eagle Lake trout. There are several small lakes in this rugged country subject to winter kill, such as Blueberry, Heather, and Osprey lakes. The steep and rocky terrain of 2.5-acre 17-foot-deep Kleaver Lake (6,450 feet), reached cross-country from Wooley Lake, is home to rainbow, brown, and brook trout. During severe winter seasons, the lake may have occasional winter kills however. Situated over a steep rocky ridge to the north of Wooley Lake is 2.5-acre, 39-foot-deep Milne Lake (6,750 feet), a brook trout fishery.

The 22-acre, 32-foot-deep Onemile Lake (5,700 feet) that flows into Ukonom Creek, thence joining the Klamath River and the chain of four angelic Cuddihy Lakes, receives the most angler traffic because of several highly-accessible trails. Rugged landscapes with awe-inspiring lakes dot the steep terrain in this remnant glacier basin.

Lying west of Onemile Lake a short distance from the same drainage is 8.5-acre, 43-foot-deep Secret Lake (5,300 feet). Near the outlet of Onemile Lake on the western side, a trail skirts over the ridge before dropping down to the valley of Secret Lake. Other major trails to gain entry into Onemile Lake and other waters are from southwestern Marbles out of Haypress Trail from Somes Bar. The Elk Creek-Granite Creek Trail from the north is another route to gain entry.

The largest lake in this northwestern part of the wilderness is 67-acre, 68-foot-deep Ukonom Lake (6,080 feet). Ukonom Lake flows into Ukonom Creek before entering the Klamath River near Clear Creek located between Happy Camp and Somes Bar. There are more than a dozen lakes surrounding Ukonom Lake on the northwestern section of the wilderness. A host of trails lead to this well-populated lake from Elk Creek to the north and Marble Valley from the eastern entry. Trails heading east and south pass through many lakes and streams within the wilderness.

Elk Creek-Granite Creek Trail Complex Lakes

Situated in the northwestern corner of Marble Mountain Wilderness is a group of lakes located in the Happy Camp Ranger District. These lakes lie north of the Haypress Meadows Complex and are also accessible from Onemile Lake along Haypress Trail. Elk Creek-Granite Creek Trailhead is accessible from Happy Camp to Sulphur Springs Campground.

Other trails between Ukonom Lake and the Cuddihy Lakes connect Tichnor Creek and Granite Creek. These trails provide many angling destinations from base camps at Granite Meadow, Granite Creek, Blue Granite Lake, and a large campsite at Ukonom Lake. From these base camps, moderate hiking is necessary to reach the Cuddihy Lakes, Onemile Lake, or Ukonom Lake. A steep and rocky spur trail leads to 12-acre, 28-foot-deep Blue Granite Lake (5,255 feet), while small 4-acre, 11-foot-deep Green Granite Lake (5,350 feet), and 2-acre, 14-foot-deep Gold Granite Lake (5,600 feet) are reachable from a gentle trail through several meadows. Water sources are available along the trail on Granite Creek.

The Marble Mountain Wilderness offers a host of angling experiences in this part of the Klamath Mountains Province. Regardless of which part of the Marbles you choose to visit, splendid memories of the beauty and scenic country will never be forgotten.

Solitude in the Russian Wilderness

Small and secluded, the lightly used 12,000-acre Russian Wilderness sits in rugged slopes and U-shaped glaciated valleys between the remote back country of Marble Mountain Wilderness and the steep forested jewels of Trinity Alps. Most of the landscapes in the wilderness consist of granitic rock formations. Russian Peak (8,196 feet) is the most prominent peak in the wilderness. Established in 1984 by the Wilderness Act, the wilderness is sandwiched between Scott River and Salmon River drainages of the Salmon Mountains in Klamath National Forest. Several roads lead to trailheads in the Russian Wilderness. However, SR 3 out of Interstate 5 from Yreka or SR 3 from Weaverville to Etna and Callahan are two routes that reach other adjoining county and designated Forest Service roads to trailheads.

This high granite country possesses over 20 lakes and miles of streams offering secluded fly fishing excursions. The many shimmering lakes ranging in elevation from 5,800 feet to 7,400 feet are typical cirque lakes resulting from glacial activities in the past. The steep and rocky trail systems serve most of the lakes and streams in this small Siskiyou County wilderness. However, to reach a few pristine lakes, some cross-country knowledge, USGS Eaton Peak 7.5 Minute Topo map, and a compass are good aids for this wilderness angling adventure.

The Pacific Crest National Scenic Trail (PCT) runs the entire length of the wilderness, traversing north and south, passing through a host of lakes, and offering panoramic views. Since the PCT route traverses through high ridges across the wilderness, patches of snow usually linger longer than on other trails. The only lake accessible from the PCT is 17-acre, 50-foot-deep Paynes Lake (6,450 feet). There are numerous campsites at this lake. However, the PCT skirts two lakes lying above the trail.

The cross-country scrambling requires climbing steep and rough terrain covered by dense and brushy landscapes, large boulder-strewn moraine, and massive granitic canyons. One of the lakes lying on the southern section of the wilderness is 8.5-acre, 55-foot-deep Bingham Lake (7,080 feet). This lake holds rainbow, brook, and Eagle Lake trout. Further north, the small brook trout watershed of 0.7-acre, 15-foot-deep, 7,200-foot elevation Statute Lake lies several hundred feet above the trail.

Taylor Creek and Hogan Creek Lakes

Taylor Lake Trailhead, located south of Etna Summit, is the route most travelers use to enter the northern tip of the wilderness. An easy, short hike to reach 35-foot-deep, 12-acre Taylor Lake (6,492 feet) is ideal for day trips or overnight camping. From Taylor Lake, one can take side trips to 7-acre, 26-foot-deep Hogan Lake (5,950 feet) and Upper and Lower Twin lakes by taking a faint trail at the upper end of Taylor. To reach Twin Lakes, the faint trail leads to the ridge at the southwest end of Taylor Lake. Following a left turn at a blaze, small 0.6-acre, 15-foot-deep Lower Twin Lake (6,700 feet) and shallow Upper Twin Lake, situated about 125 feet from Lower Twin, are visible.

The 6,836-foot Big Blue Lake is the deepest lake in the Russian Wilderness. Situated in granite country, this 17-acre, 96-foot-deep lake has loose talus and no trail into the lake. Therefore, anglers need to cross-country from Albert Lakes or Hogan Lake. Small Pheasant Tail Nymphs, Hare's Ears, emergers, and small streamers are excellent patterns to arouse the rainbow, Eagle Lake, and brown trout to strike.

Scott River Lakes

The central part of the Russian Wilderness holds a group of lakes below Eaton Peak (7,638 feet) offering brook or rainbow trout fishing and a wide range of trails to reach its destination. The largest lake in this part of the wilderness is 26-acre, 27-foot-deep Big Duck Lake (6,700 feet). Trailhead entry is out of the eastern wilderness boundary.

Other wilderness lakes in the Scott River system are 6-acre, 21-foot-deep Horseshoe Lake and 13-acre, 27-foot-deep Eaton Lake (6,610 feet). Small 3.5-acre South Sugar Lake in the Sugar Creek drainage receives an abundance of waters from springs in the headwaters.

Russian Creek Lakes Complex

On the western slope, one of the trailheads entering the magnificent Russian Lakes complex is from the North Fork Salmon River along South Russian Creek. Sitting at 7,100 feet, the 5-acre, 72-foot-deep blue waters of breathtaking Russian Lake has magnificent rainbow and Eagle Lake trout fishing. Within the complex, small 1.5-acre, 8-foot-deep Golden Russian Lake (6,080 feet) is the only lake in Siskiyou County hosting a golden trout fishery. Golden Russian Lake periodically receives plantings of golden-trout fingerlings by the Department of Fish and Game. However, if the proper weather conditions prevail at other lakes of this county, they may also receive plantings of these fingerlings. Since there is no trail to the lake, you need to trek cross-country from Lower Russian Lake. The best direction is to head northwesterly over the ridge and into the adjoining canyon. Within this group of lakes, 4-acre, 16-foot-deep Waterdog Lake has good fishing for brook, rainbow, and Eagle Lake trout.

Other accessible trailheads are from the western and southern portion of the wilderness. The western entry into the wilderness is from Idlewild Campground at the confluence of North Fork Salmon River and South Russian Creek. The campground is located on Sawyers Bar Road between Sawyers Bar and Etna. The trail follows South Fork Russian Creek to Lower Russian Lake. The southern entry is from Trail Creek Camp trail located on the East Fork of the South Fork Salmon River. The campsiteis situated on the Cecilville Road between Cecilville and Callahan.

Effective High-Country Fly Patterns

The short season in the extreme elevations of the high-country limits the natural food supply. Midges in all stages and scuds comprise the bulk of the trout's diet. At the larval stage, midges look like a small worm. However, during emergence periods, insects hang in the surface film. Therefore, bring along a selection of adult, pupa, and larva patterns imitating midges. Size 20-22 Griffith's Gnats, Nos. 16-22 Black Midges and Brassies, and Nos. 18-20 Olive and Chironomid Pupae will increase catches in most waters. Scuds are a nutrient-rich food in the diet of high elevation lake trout. Present Nos. 12-18 Tan and Olive Scud imitation patterns with twitching motions to attract the trout's attention.

Nos. 14-16, with and without bead heads, Pheasant Tail nymph, Bird's Nest, Hare's Ear, and Zug Bugs, patterns are excellent choices all season. In heavy runs and riffle waters, use bead heads, add a small split shot about 18 inches above the fly, or sink-tip lines to get the flies down deep.

Other productive imitations for high-country watersheds include Black Gnats, Adams, Yellow Humpys, Mosquitoes, small bucktails or streamers, Letort Hoppers, Black Ants, and Muddlers. Caddisfly patterns (pupa or adult) are effective in the afternoon and evening throughout the season.

Specialty flies for specific watersheds will be included later in the discussion of each body of water.

Trinity River Serpentine Express

Extensive roadside access and trails to backcountry and wilderness waters offer spectacular fly fishing excursions throughout Trinity River Basin. The vibrant sounds of swiftly-flowing freestone streams holding salmon, steelhead, and trout permeate the Basin. A fly fisher's paradise for wading and boat drifting, Trinity River is one of the most prestigious anadromous stream in Northwestern California. The largest tributary to the Klamath River, the Trinity is controlled by cold-water releases from Trinity and Lewiston dams.

In many sections of the river, it is seldom necessary to trek very far to reach prime holding waters or wade very deep to connect with the fish. Most of the river has adequate access points for boat entry and egress. Therefore, boat-drifting the river is an alternative to cover waters difficult to reach by other means. Optimum range of flow levels for portaging is important in each river reach that has boating access. When it is too high, control becomes impossible and the danger that boaters may be swept into willows, rocks, or fallen trees is high. However, at low-water levels, portaging may cause tiring delays, or exposed rocks in rapids may be too dangerous to maneuver around. The U.S. Bureau of Reclamation

regulates flows at Lewiston and Trinity dams. Tributary waters play a major role in influencing increased volume flows of water which flow down the river.

Some excellent holding waters for boating are in the upper river or lower reaches of the Trinity. In the upper river, 17 river miles of flows are between Lewiston to Douglas City. The ideal section of river to float is from Douglas City to Junction City. This scenic and serene 14 river miles receives minimal angler pressure. It is inaccessible to traffic as the river's course bends away from the highway. In some sections of the river, it is floatable from Junction City to the North Fork. The flow along this length of river begins to increase due to major changes in the river's characteristic.

In the lower reaches of the Trinity, more experience is required to float the 8 miles from Willow Creek to Tish Tang, and another 8 miles from Tish Tang to Hoopa Valley. However, the last 8 miles of float from Hoopa Valley to Weitchpec can be a wet and rugged trip. For safety, I strongly recommend you get in touch with a guide before venturing out on your own. This will give you the opportunity to know the temperament of the water before attempting new challenges. At the same time, you will learn where some of the best riffles, runs, and pools are located.

Serene alpine lakes and clear streams in the Trinity Alps and Trinity Divide country also offer excellent fly fishing trips for adventurous anglers. Spectacular views of sharp ridges and serrated peaks of rugged granite slopes of Trinity Alps are visible when traveling along portions of SR 299.

Occupying over 2,550 square miles of Trinity County and more than 400 square miles of Humboldt County, the terrain in the Trinity River Basin is mountainous with a host of surrounding peaks, deep gorges, canyons, small valleys, forests, brush lands, and flood plains in the lower river. Elevations range from 200 feet at the mouth in Weitchpec to 9,025-foot Mt. Eddy, the headwaters of the Trinity River. The Basin is relatively remote. The majority of the population in Trinity County centers on Weaverville, Lewiston, Hayfork, Hoopa, Willow Creek, Trinity Center, Hyampom, and hamlets located along the main stem and tributaries of the Trinity River. Weaverville, known as Weaver by old-timers, is the largest community in the Basin. Named in 1850 for John Weaver, a gold prospector who arrived in the area in 1849, this mining town was the center of prolific mining activities during 1849. The following year, it became the county seat.

Kevin Wong with a steelhead.

Buckhorn Snow Summit in Trinity County.

Floating on the Trinity River near Big Flat.

Weaverville, an old mining community, has a few historical buildings and museums. Of historical value, the Joss House State Historic Park, located along SR 299, was originally built in 1850. The Joss House is currently a Chinese Taoist temple of worship, however, in 1873 the building was destroyed by fire, only to be rebuilt in 1874. In 1848, Major Pierson B. Reading discovered gold at Reading's Bar. The discovery site is located near the current Douglas City Bridge on SR 299. In various areas of the Trinity, gold seekers are still actively mining and panning in some sections of the river system. The northern Wintu, Chimariko, Chilula, Whilkut, and Hupa Native Americans once lived in this Basin. They were primarily hunter-gatherers. One can still find remnants of their existence along the river.

Trinity River, mountains, Alps, counties, and National Forests of the region received their names from an error made by Pierson B. Reading. When Reading arrived in 1845, he named the river Trinity, the English version of Trinidad, a mistaken assumption that the stream flows into Trinidad Bay.

The hydrographic boundary of Trinity River Basin follows the ridges separating the Trinity River drainage from adjacent watersheds. Klamath, Salmon, Scott, and Shasta rivers lie to the north while the Sacramento River, Cottonwood Creek, and Clear Creek are in the southeast. To the southwest are two anadromous watersheds, Mad River and Redwood Creek.

In this part of Northwestern California, the 203,500-acre Whiskeytown-Shasta-Trinity National Recreation Area (NRA) offers many recreational opportunities. Established in 1965, the NRA consists of three separate units: Whiskeytown Lake, Shasta Lake, and Clair Engle-Lewiston Lakes. Clair Engle-Lewiston Lakes are part of the Trinity River drainage. However, both Shasta and Whiskeytown lakes are within the Sacramento River drainage. The objective of the NRA is to recognize many opportunities provided by the four reservoirs created by the U.S. Bureau of Reclamation's Central Valley Water Project.

The second largest National Forest in California, the Shasta-Trinity National Forest was created in 1954 by merging Shasta National Forest (established in 1905) and Trinity National Forest (established in 1907).

Situated in the rugged Klamath Mountains of Trinity Divide country between the Scott Mountains on the northwest and The Eddys to the east, approximately 150 river miles of the Trinity River begins its journey. It flows south and west 35 river miles before entering Clair Engle Lake (also known as Trinity Lake) and Lewiston Lake. From Lewiston Lake, the river traverses 111 river miles in a generally westerly course to Big Bar where it turns northwest and north, finally reaching its confluence with the Klamath River at Weitchpec.

The flow of the picturesque stream from the headwaters to Weitchpec resembles a long, graceful serpent winding its way to the mouth at Weitchpec. Tributary streams flowing into the main stem remind me of a dragon performing a ritual dance. Major tributaries of the Trinity include Coffee Creek, Swift Creek, East Fork, Stuart Fork, Rush Creek, Browns Creek, Canyon Creek, North Fork, Big French Creek, New River, and South Fork. Hayfork Creek is the largest tributary to the South Fork.

Each stretch of the Trinity from its headwaters to the confluence with the Klamath at Weitchpec has its own personality and geographic features. Many prolific lakes and smaller streams above Clair Engle Lake lie within a combination of the heavily forested, gentle and rugged terrain of Trinity Alps Wilderness and the Trinity Divide country. This part of the country possesses some easy drive-to, long and strenuous hikes that reach various destinations. Below Lewiston Dam, premium angling is found in the upper, middle, and lower Trinity River because the highway traverses and hugs major portions of the river with easy access. Three major tributaries flow south from the Trinity Alps into the main stem: Canyon Creek, North Fork Trinity River, and New River. They provide angling opportunities for catching resident trout and anadromous fish with special restricted regulations in most parts.

In this beautiful mountainous setting, gravel bars and flood plains are prominent in various sections of the river below Lewiston Dam. The characteristics of each segment of the river changes from upper, middle, and lower. Heavy-forested vegetation dots the upper river. Streamside willows and other brush provide an abundance of insect life. Steelhead and resident trout respond to surface action during mayfly, caddisfly, and stonefly hatches. Therefore, wading and roll casting are necessary in brush-lined sections of the river to reach holding fish. However, beginner as well as advanced fly fishers can cover most of the Trinity without difficulty. As you reach the middle Trinity, the terrain opens into wider, expansive water with less vegetation. Notably, canyon walls and deep gorge waters begin to surface. However, upon arrival at the lower river in Hoopa Valley, this serpentine river transforms into a large, wide, and distinct profile of flood plains before entering the last gorge.

In the middle and lower reaches of the Trinity, from Cedar Flat to Weitchpec, the river snakes like a dragon through the most hauntingly beautiful, yet unforgiving sections, of the entire Trinity River. The length of the unique gorges here is six to seven miles, but these narrow and unique corridors are made of precipitous cliffs that rise several hundred feet straight up from the river to the highway. Sheer rock faces, treacherous rapids, waterfalls, various species of pine trees, wildflowers, whirlpools, and astonishing swirling waters are found inside of these gorges. These three gorges are the Burnt Ranch Gorge (Cedar Flat to Burnt Ranch), Tish Tang Gorge (Tish Tang to Hoopa), and the Weitchpec Gorge (Hoopa Valley to Weitchpec). During early morning in the winter months, you can see beautiful mists rising out of Tish Tang Gorge when traveling along SR 96 from Tish Tang to Hoopa Valley. You can get a glimpse of these gorges from the highway along pullouts or from the river at the entry of these gorges. However, steep trails down to the river are another alternative.

Rugged terrain limits transportation in the Trinity River Basin. However, the heaviest used route is SR 299, the major east-west route from Redding west or Arcata east through the town of Willow Creek. Winding through evergreen forests and scenic Buckhorn Summit (3,626 feet), SR 299 is the principal connection to Interstate 5 in the Central Valley and U.S. 101 out of the coastal region for travelers entering the Basin. Much-developed public fishing access, public campgrounds, and other recreational sites are available near various sections of the river. The is accessible from pullouts and campgrounds that are nearby or adjacent to the river. State Route 96 from Willow Creek to Weitchpec is another heavily used route. This lower Trinity River route passes through the Hoopa Valley Indian Reservation.

In the Trinity Alps and Trinity Divide sections of the Trinity, portions of the river are accessible from SR 3 before reaching Clair Engle Lake. Lewiston Lake is accessible from SR 299 to Trinity Dam Boulevard. Other limited access routes within the Basin are on logging and mining roads.

Trinity River-Central Valley Project

Authorized by Congress in 1955 and completed in 1964 as part of the Central Valley Project, surplus water from the Trinity River Basin (known as the Trinity Division) is stored, regulated, and diverted through a system of four dams and reservoirs. The project included four power plants, two tunnels, and one siphon into the Sacramento River for deficient water supplies of the Central Valley Basin. The Trinity River Division is a multi-purpose project. It improves recreational opportunities and increases minimum flows in the Trinity River. In addition, waters diverted from the Trinity River combined with that of the Sacramento River provide irrigation services to landowners in Northern California.

Snowmelt from the Alps and Divide provide waters that ar stored in Clair Engle Lake behind Trinity Dam. Water releases from the reservoir are used to generate power and re-regulate Lewiston Lake located seven miles downstream. Waters are diverted from Lewiston Lake to the Trinity River and through Clear Creek Tunnel to Judge Francis Carr Powerhouse. Subsequently, water is released to the Sacramento River from Whiskeytown Lake out of Clear Creek, a tributary of the Sacramento River. With the completion of the Trinity and Lewiston dams, spawning areas above the construction sites of these dams became inaccessible to anadromous fish. They were unable to continue their journeys upstream. Therefore, the Trinity River Fish Hatchery was built to mitigate for the loss of salmon and steelhead spawning grounds.

Recently, a new open and closed season for the main stem of the Trinity River went into effect. Portions of the river affected are from the Old Lewiston Bridge to the mouth of the South Fork located between Salyer and Willow Creek at the James G. McCart Bridge. However, the main stem Trinity is open all year from the confluence of the South Fork to the mouth at Weitchpec. The entire river has a special regulation for anglers requiring barbless hooks only. Check the latest Sports Fishing Regulations for any changes before venturing out.

When on the Trinity River, check with local businesses for where in the river system the fish are concentrated. It was interesting and informative to hear reports on how local residents anticipate and calculate the estimated arrival time of anadromous fish reaching each destination point in the lower river and other sections. As soon as word is received from sources at Weitchpec as to the exact time a school of anadromous fish enters the mouth of the Trinity, locals would calculate their approximate arrival time at Red Rock, located at the upper end of the Weitchpec Gorge. The locals can also predict how long they will be in each area for successful hookups, when they would continue their journey, and estimate arrival times at Tish Tang, Grays Fall, Burnt Ranch Gorge, and other access areas. Generally, most locals are able to estimate how long it takes the fish to reach each destination. This allows them to intercept the fish upon their arrival at each designated stretch of the river system. Timing is of the essence in locating anadromous fish. During the time when fish are on the move, they are not interested in accepting any flies.

In recent years fish populations have declined dramatically in the Trinity River. Due to periodic closures of several coastal rivers until substantial rains warranted their re-opening, the Trinity received heavy angling pressure. Therefore, it is a good practice to release the fish immediately.

Along its length of the Trinity River below Lewiston Lake to Weitchpec, the river shows a variety of characteristics. For the purpose of this book, the Trinity is divided into five sections: 1) Headwaters from Trinity Divide Country and Trinity Alps Wilderness, 2) Upper Trinity River from Clair Engle Lake to Junction City, 3) Middle Trinity River from Junction City to Cedar Flat, 4) Lower Trinity River, 1: Cedar Flat to Willow Creek, and 5) Lower Trinity River, 2: Willow Creek to the confluence of Klamath River at Weitchpec.

Miners boat.

Section 1 Headwaters of the Trinity Divide Country and Trinity Alps Wilderness

Explore the Inner Depths of Trinity Divide Country

Hidden within the Klamath Mountains in northwestern California, numerous lakes and streams lie in various types of terrain between Pacific Coast ranges and the Southern Cascades. Cirques, bedrock basins, marshy meadows, and U-shaped valleys are integral parts of the landscape found in higher elevations.

Known to many as the Trinity Divide, the watersheds of the Shasta-Trinity National Forest offer diverse angling destinations. Numerous drive-to and hike-in lakes and streams can be found near Scott and Trinity mountains. In the Trinity Divide, where it is possible to explore vast sections of trout and steelhead water, cascading waterfalls and stately mountains await anglers.

The northern border of Trinity Divide country lies southwest of Gazelle-Callahan Road between the hamlets of Gazelle and Callahan. On the western slope, it runs from SR 3 (at Callahan) to East Side Road and its junction with Dog Creek Road. The southern sector of this region lies at Dog Creek Road, between East Side Road and Interstate 5 at Delta. On the eastern slope, the Divide borders Interstate 5 from Gazelle to Delta.

Besides the Gazelle-Callahan Road, there are three U.S. Forest Service roads that traverse the Trinity Divide between Interstate 5 and SR 3: Forest Service Routes (FSR) 17, 26, and 25. In this part of the country though, the condition of access roads can vary a great deal because the terrain ranges from well-graded trails to rocky and rugged cross-country scrambles, and the myriad of side roads is in a state of disrepair. Therefore, use caution and reduce the speed of your vehicle. Be aware of narrow rocky spur roads that require high-clearance vehicles, and the fact that trail and road conditions can change rapidly. Consult with local Forest Service District Offices for up-to-date information before you departure.

On weekdays, travelers will most likely share some roads (such as SR 3 and FSR 17), with logging and haystack trucks. Access routes to other watersheds though will require driving through rough roads before you will have to take a short or long hike to your angling destination. For the more adventurous angler, day hikes, backpacks, horseback, or llama services will get you to remote amazing back country waters.

One of my most unforgettable experiences took place while I was traversing FSR 25, the Castle Creek-Mumbo Creek-Ramshorn Road. The condition of the road abruptly changed several times. I began at Castle Crag State Park and before I had reached Whalen Summit, the road had narrowed to a one-lane gravel road which abruptly switched to an unimproved one-lane road and there were sparse gravel chuckholes covering most sections of the route. When I was traveling from east to west, I was in the inside lane because if the vehicle had been on the outside lane, I would have been angling toward the vertical cliff. At this point, I began to notice that the vehicle was hugging the mountainside next to the unimproved road too tightly. Fortunately, it was during the early part of November and we were the only ones traveling on the road at that time, nevertheless, it took over two hours to traverse 25 miles.

Most of the waters in this area lie within U.S. Forest Service land. However, some section are either privately owned, or are inaccessible. And although meadow ponds frequently average 10 feet in depth, many are too shallow to sustain fisheries. One example is Masterson Meadows Lake. Situated on the eastern slope of Scott Mountain, it is a shallow lake that is subject to winter kills. Yet, because of supplemental aerial stocking, the lake has good populations of brook and brown trout.

The Department of Fish and Game stock numerous waters in this region on a regular basis with catchable, subcatchable, and fingerling brook, rainbow, Eagle Lake, and brown trout. In Trinity Divide country, there are over 50 lakes for anglers to explore. These waters range in elevation from 5,000 to above 7,500 feet. They vary in size from one-half-acre shallow tarns, to 47-acre Castle Lake, the largest body of water in the Divide. At many of these lakes and streams, anglers practically have the entire watersheds to themselves. If you are an adventurous individual, you can spend years exploring the country's awe-inspiring lakes and streams and return year after year to your favorite ones.

In the Trinity Divide, lakes lie along the crest of the rugged mountain range that separates Trinity, Siskiyou, and Shasta counties. The rugged and majestic Trinity Mountain Ranges separate two major river courses as well. Streams on the western slope of the range flow into the Trinity River, while those on the East Side drain into the Sacramento River. In addition, several small streams flow northward from the Trinity Divide into the Scott and Shasta river systems.

The Trinity River begins its course on the western side of the Divide and flows into Clair Engle and Lewiston lakes. Anglers often overlook the vast selection of lakes and tributary streams in this country. Boundless breathtaking waters and hungry trout await fly-fishers in this area. A variety of easy to strenuous hike-in locations in the Divide region are worth exploring, especially if you enjoy solitude.

Headwaters Trinity River: Deadfall Lakes Basin

One of my favorite hikes is Deadfall Lakes on the western slope of Mt. Eddy (9,025 feet). At 7,259 feet in elevation, the 40-foot-deep Middle Deadfall Lake is more productive during early and late seasons. This 25-acre body of water is the second largest lake in the Divide. The lake receives its water supply each season from snowmelts. Surrounded by heavy vegetation and brushy landscapes in most parts, Middle Deadfall is best fished from a float tube or pontoon-style boat. I recommend you tote along a lightweight apparatus to get into the waters. You will be rewarded with plenty of action.

Bordered by a grassy meadow, the smaller Upper Deadfall Lake is worth the extra 500-foot-climb. Upper Deadfall also receives its water supply from snowmelts. The 7,790-foot, 2.5-acre tarn, 15-foot-deep Upper Deadfall Lake lies very close to timberline. Use a smaller sized fly (Nos. 16 to 20) with little disturbance of the water when fishing Upper Deadfall.

The 5-acre, 25-foot-deep Lower Deadfall Lake (7,139 feet) is a short walk from Middle Deadfall Lake. Many visitors bypass Lower Deadfall and head for Middle Deadfall. This lower body of water has some open shoreline. However, most of the fish usually congregate near the outlet area of the lake. Do not overlook fishing Deadfall Creek for rainbow and brook trout at Deadfall Meadows off FSR 17.

The best route to the Deadfall chain of lakes is by an easy 4-mile hike on the Pacific Crest National Scenic Trail (PCT) at Parks Creek Summit where the PCT crosses FSR 17. The scenic trail on the ridge passes through wooded and expansive open areas. Psychologically, this hike creates an unforgettably tranquil experience for me.

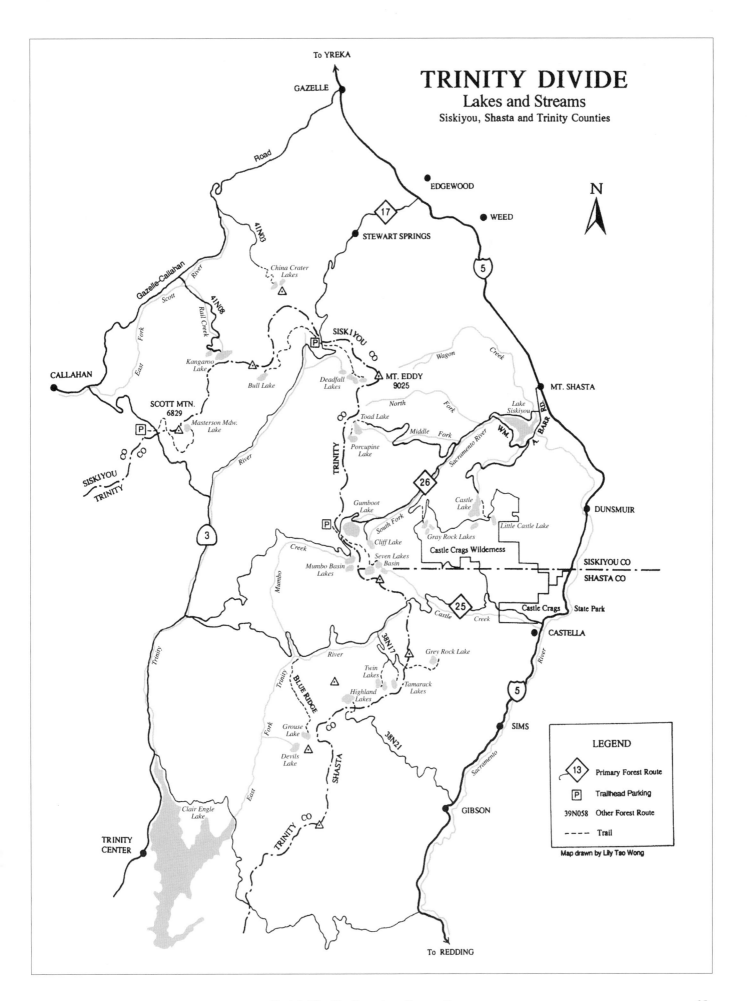

TRINITY DIVIDE
Lakes and Streams
Siskiyou, Shasta and Trinity Counties

N

To YREKA

GAZELLE

EDGEWOOD

WEED

17

STEWART SPRINGS

5

41N03

China Crater Lakes

SISKIYOU

Wagon   Creek

MT. SHASTA

Gazelle-Callahan   Road

Scott   River

Rail Creek

41N08

East   Fork

CALLAHAN

Kangaroo Lake

Bull Lake

Deadfall Lakes

MT. EDDY 9025

North   Fork

Lake Siskiyou

W.M.

A. BARR RD.

SCOTT MTN. 6829

Masterson Mdw. Lake

Toad Lake

Middle   Fork

Sacramento River

DUNSMUIR

P

Porcupine Lake

SISKIYOU   CO

TRINITY

26

Castle Lake

Little Castle Lake

SISKIYOU
TRINITY

Trinity   River

Gumboot Lake

South Fork

Gray Rock Lakes

Castle Crags Wilderness

SISKIYOU CO

3

P

Cliff Lake

Seven Lakes Basin

SHASTA CO

Creek

Mumbo Basin Lakes

Mumbo

25

Castle   Creek

Castle Crags   State Park

CASTELLA

38N17

Grey Rock Lake

River   River

Twin Lakes

Tamarack Lakes

5

Trinity

Trinity

BLUE RIDGE

Highland Lakes

SIMS

East   Fork

Grouse Lake

SHASTA

38N21

Sacramento

Devils Lake

Clair Engle Lake

TRINITY   CO

GIBSON

TRINITY CENTER

LEGEND

13	Primary Forest Route
P	Trailhead Parking
39N058	Other Forest Route
- - -	Trail

Map drawn by Lily Tao Wong

To REDDING

Deadfall Lakes trailhead sign.

Hiker on Lower Deadfall Lake.

Another nearby trail to the Deadfall Lakes, with limited parking facilities, starts at Deadfall Meadows. Approximately a mile west of Parks Creek Summit the road descends a switchback to Deadfall Meadows. The trail crosses Deadfall Creek in several areas before the steep climb. This trail to the Deadfall Lakes is shorter. However, in less than two miles, there is almost 1,000 feet in elevation gain. The PCT scenic trail, on the other hand, has an approximately 300-foot elevation gain in less than 4 miles.

Another scenic route to the Deadfall Lakes is out of Lake Siskiyou. The Sisson-Callahan National Recreation Trail starts at 3,500 feet in elevation near Lake Siskiyou and parallels most of the North Fork Sacramento River. The trail crosses over 8,000-foot Deadfall Summit (above the Deadfall Lakes). Spectacular views of the lakes, with Castle Crags to the south and the Trinity Alps to the west, are to be had from the summit. The trail descends to the Deadfall Lakes before continuing downhill 7,200 feet to connect with the PCT. It then plunges to Deadfall Meadows.

Depending on which trail you opt to travel, it is possible to hike in and out of these lakes in one day with a backpack. You can also choose to travel with commercial horse pack or llama outfitters if you have a lot of gear to transport. Since the elevation of the Deadfall Lakes is over 7,000 feet, be cautious of snow on the ground when traveling into the high country early in the season.

Picayune Lake

Situated over the ridge of The Eddys Mountain range along the Trinity Mountains, 27-foot-deep, 11.5-acre Picayune Lake (6,080 feet) lies in private ownership lands. Access to Picayune is from FSR 26 and several other routes crossing over the ridge. Upon reaching one of the downhill roads, a private road heads south. However, there is an all-year locked gate less than one-half mile from the lake. It is an easy hike from the gate to the lake. Picayune Lake is also accessible from the ridge out of the Pacific Crest National Scenic Trail. According to the Forest Service, please bypass fishing Picayune if there are guests present at the cabin. However, before venturing into Picayune, check with the Forest Service for current regulations or changes. By returning to FSR 26, you can explore nearby Mumbo Basin Lakes.

East Fork Trinity River

Through a combination of driving and hiking, you can reach the East Fork of the Trinity River drainage which hosts an abundance of watersheds worth exploring. They include the Mumbo Lakes, Tamarack and Twin lakes, Highland Lakes, and the Devil's Lake Complex.

The headwaters of the East Fork Trinity River begins its course from springs below Whalen Summit. The East Fork weaves in and out of rugged Forest Service terrain and privately owned properties. A major portion of the stream is inaccessible because of steep canyons, heavily brushed landscapes, or private ownership. The most accessible areas are below Whalen Summit near Horse Heaven, along portions of FSR 25 and where FSR 38N17 turns south to the Tamarack and Twin lakes basins. The inlet area where the East Fork Trinity empties into Clair Engle Lake is also accessible.

Mumbo Basin Lakes

Mumbo Lake (6,100 feet) with depths of 16 feet is easily accessible from a short spur road off FSR 26 out of Lake Siskiyou or Castle Crags State Park. This 5.5-acre lake is home to regularly stocked catchable rainbow, brook, and rainbow fingerlings.

Shallow Upper Mumbo Lake (6,150 feet), located several hundred yards to the east, has also been stocked with brook trout fingerlings. The lakes are best fished with a float tube or other craft due to fallen logs and trees lining the shorelines. Along the route, spectacular views of the area are available from Gumboot-Mumbo summit.

Tamarack and Twin Lakes Basin

Access roads to Tamarack and Twin lakes basin traverse through rough rocky terrain and should not be attempted by passenger or low-clearance vehicles. One way of reaching access roads is out of FSR 26. The other route is from Interstate 5 to Castle Crags State Park on Castle Creek Road and FSR 25. Also, another route connecting with FSR 25 is SR 3 from Clair Engle Lake.

From FSR 25, turn south onto FSR 38N17 and travel about three miles on this rocky terrain road. Upon arrival at a junction, take the right fork to Twin Lakes Meadow where camping is available. To reach the lake, take Trinity Divide Trail 5W12 to Lower Twin Lake. Sitting at elevation of 5,773 feet, 14-foot-deep, 8.5-acre Lower Twin Lake holds a population of rainbow and brook trout. However, it is difficult to fish from shore because heavy growth of vegetation surrounds the lake. On the other hand, 12-acre, 40-foot-deep Upper Twin Lake (5,776 feet) has more open area.

If you wish to travel into the Tamarack Lakes Basin, take the same turnoff road to the Twin Lakes Basin (FSR 38N17) from FSR 25. Upon arrival at the same junction, continue on FSR 38N17 crossing Tamarack Creek. This portion of the road to Tamarack Lake is extremely rocky. Do not attempt to travel on this road with a low-clearance vehicle. A favorite destination for visitors is 21-acre, 16 foot-deep Tamarack Lake (5,862 feet). Size 12 or 14 Gold Ribbed Hare's Ear, Pheasant Tail, and Prince Nymphs are excellent searching patterns in this basin for brooks and rainbows.

Nearby Little Tamarack (5,862 feet) is only a short hike from the lower end of Tamarack. This small 2-acre, 9-foot-deep lake is best fished from a float tube. It also has a population of brook and rainbow trout. If you are camping at Tamarack Lake, it is possible to trek less than a mile to Upper and Lower Twin lakes.

Highland Lakes and Devils Complex Lakes

The terrain and landscape surrounding the secluded Highland Lake and other nearby lakes is a mixture of steep, rough, boulder-strewn, thick timber, brush, and meadows. Access to the 7-acre, 15-foot-deep Highland Lake (5,726 feet) is from FSR 25, thence through Highland Lakes Road 38N21. Surrounded by three shallow ponds, Highland Lake has excellent waters for fly-fishers. Pond Lily Lake, Grouse Lake, and Devils Lake, on the other hand, provide angling opportunities for those seeking off-the-beaten-path waters through long arduous journeys in the back country. They are accessible by hiking through easy, but rough terrain out of Highland Lakes Basin.

Shallow 2-acre, 10-foot-deep Pond Lily Lake (5,817 feet) is an attractive lake surrounded by heavy timber and brush in a meadow setting. It is accessible from a poor logging road or by way of Trinity Divide Trail 5W12 out of Highland Lake. Three-acre Grouse Lake (5,888 feet) with a depth of 15 feet is accessible by hiking from Pond Lily Lake over the ridge of Gozem Peak (6,240 feet). Below the peak at 6,120 feet in elevation, a spur trail goes west and south about a mile to the lake.

A Trinity Divide lake offers sanctuary for rainbow, brook, and Eagle Lake trout.

Situated below 6,805-foot Red Mountain, the seldom-visited shorelines of 15-foot-deep, 2.5-acre Devils Lake (6,112 feet) involve trekking cross-country from Grouse Lake. It entails traveling through extremely steep and rugged terrain with large boulders strewn throughout the area. Both Grouse and Devils Lake hold brook and brown trout.

Scott River Watersheds

In the northwestern corner of the Trinity Divide country, the East Fork Scott River hosts several trout-producing waters: Kangaroo, Lily Pad, Rock Fence, Upper and Lower Crater, and Grouse Creek lakes. In this part of the Divide country, anglers frequently overlook many smaller streams. Where public access is possible, small rainbow trout are present in the East Fork Scott River, and tributary streams of Mtn. House, Houston, Rail, Kangaroo, and Grouse creeks. Besides rainbow trout, the East Fork Scott River drainage holds some steelhead rainbow trout.

Before venturing out on any hiking trips within the Divide or other waters, check with the local Forest Service Ranger District to find out whether these waters are accessible to the public or are on private land. Through the years, ownership and accessibility can change. Please respect private property in posted waters of any river system.

Kangaroo Lake

One of the most accessible and productive lakes in the Scott Mountain Range area is 21-acre Kangaroo Lake (6,020 feet). The 110-foot-deep Kangaroo Lake flows into Rail Creek before joining the confluence of East Fork Scott River. No motors are allowed on the lake, so in order to reach prime locations, a rubber raft, float tube, or pontoon boat works best.

Campground facilities at the lake have been expanded with the addition of 13 new sites. As a developed recreational area, an extensive renovation program of the original campground included facilities suitable for the moderately handicapped, barrier-free parking, and toilets. Construction improvements include approximately one-quarter mile of paved access trail terminating at a stone fishing pier at the lakeside. The USFS campground season runs from June through October. The lake is extremely popular for day-use at no charge. In addition, there are a number of sites that are suitable for recreational vehicles or camper trailers.

To reach Kangaroo Lake from Interstate 5 near Weed, take the Edgewood/Stewart Springs exit to Gazelle. Continue northwest to Gazelle along Old 99 Highway. In Gazelle, turn left on the Gazelle-Callahan Road and continue southwest for about 15 miles. Turn left when you see a sign for Kangaroo Lake. Follow the signs for seven miles on Rail Creek Road to the lake.

Other Scott River Drainage Lakes

A short distance from Kangaroo Lake, shallow 2.5-acre, 9-foot-deep Lily Pad Lake in Siskiyou County (5,940 feet) holds brook and rainbow trout. The road to Kangaroo Lake passes by Lily Pad Lake. Nearby Rock Fence Lake, on the other hand, is larger than Lily Pad Lake. However, some walking is necessary along a jeep road to reach the lake.

A couple of secluded lakes lie below 8,551-foot China Mountain: Upper and Lower Crater lakes. At 7,505 feet, larger 5.5-acre, 50-foot-deep Lower Crater Lake is isolated in this forested mountainside. Just over the rocky ridge, smaller Upper Crater Lake (7,508 feet) is a 2.5-acre, 26-foot-deep body of water. In recent years, Upper Crater Lake has been stocked with Eagle Lake trout.

Access to Upper and Lower Crater lakes require trekking through many switchbacks and a steep climb. The main route is out of the Gazelle-Callahan Road from either Gazelle or Callahan to FSR 41N03 near Mountain House. From there, follow the road until you pass Crater Creek to Section 24, Township 41 North (T41N), and Range 7W (R7W). Within a short distance, the steep switchback trail begins. In over three miles, expect more than 1,800 feet in elevation gain.

In this drainage, 12-foot-deep Grouse Creek Lake at 6,182 feet can be tremendous for some surprisingly hefty sized brook trout. This small 3-acre lake is reachable from trails out of Grouse Creek or the summit of Scott Mountains Road (SR 3).

Shasta River Drainage

Situated on the eastern slope of the Trinity Divide, out of Scott Mountains Range, several bodies of waters offer solitary spots for fishing. These small hike-in Siskiyou County treasures, such as West Parks Lake, Caldwell Lakes, Dobkins and Durney lakes, offer spectacular activities when venturing into the Basin. A few small creeks in this drainage, such as Parks, Eddy, and Dale creeks, are worth stopping en route to other destination waters.

West Parks Lake Basin

West Parks Lakes support a limited number of trout. Depending on water and environmental conditions, two-acre, 12-foot-deep Lower West Parks Lake (7,232 feet) and larger 2.5-acre, 22-foot-deep Middle West Parks Lake (7,435 feet) could provide some fishing activity. However, one-acre, 12-foot-deep Upper West Parks Lake is subject to winter kill and is usually barren. Access to the West Parks Lake Basin is from logging roads and trails from FSR 17, the Stewart Springs/Parks Creek Road. Upon reaching West Parks Lakes Creek, the bridge has been removed. However, if the water level is low enough, cross the creek and continue on this route to Road 41N73A. At the end of the road, a faint and steep trail goes to the lower lake.

Caldwell Lakes Basin

Nearby, spring-fed Caldwell Lakes Basin provides better fishing conditions in this drainage. Although the Caldwell Lakes drain into Parks Creek, they are often mistaken for the West Parks Creek Lakes. According to information from the Department of Fish and Game, the Caldwell Lakes received their name in honor of John Caldwell. Caldwell was a pioneer hunter of Edgewood in Siskiyou County, who fished and hunted in the area during the early years.

Upper, Middle, and Lower Caldwell lakes provide brook trout fishing in a secluded setting. The 7,100-foot, 2-acre, 13-foot-deep Upper Caldwell and 1.5-acre, 8 foot-deep Middle Caldwell (7,100 feet) are situated next to each other. Lower Caldwell (6,835 feet), on the other hand, is a 2-acre lake with depths of 12 feet. Both Upper and Middle Caldwell have more open shorelines than the lower lake.

Access to the Caldwell Lakes Basin is also from the FSR 17, the Parks Creek/Stewarts Springs Road. After traveling approximately 5 miles on FSR 17, turn right on FSR 41N74. At the end of the road, travel the rest of the way on Caldwell Lakes Trail 6W01 to Lower Lake. Elevation gain hiking to Upper and Middle Caldwell lakes is less than 300 feet.

Mount Eddy Lakes

Lying below 9,025-foot Mt. Eddy southwest of Weed, Dobkins Lake (6,788 feet) and Durney Lake (7,045 feet) provide ideal conditions for fly-fishing. Do not overlook fishing above the falls along Dale Creek and the outlet stream of Dobkins. Brook, rainbow, and brown trout inhabit 3.5-acre Dobkins Lake.

A rugged 4WD road and some foot travel are required to reach Dobkins and Durney lakes. Dobkins Lake is accessible from Dale Creek Road, located west of Interstate 5 near Weed. High-clearance and 4WD vehicles are advisable. At the end of the road, take Trinity Divide Trail 5W03 to Dobkins Lake. Durney Lake is a short distance from Dobkins. It should take less than an hour by foot to reach 15-foot-deep, 3.5-acre Durney Lake, a brook trout fishery. The open shoreline provides an ideal setting for fly-fishing.

In this drainage, 20-acre Little Crater Lake (7,581 feet) is situated in a deep rocky crater. The lake is not visible from the trail because it lies in a depression and has no outlet. However, Little Crater Lake has ideal conditions for casting from shore because it is practically void of vegetation.

To reach Little Crater Lake, take the same route as for Dobkins and Durney lakes. Upon reaching the junction to Dobkins and Durney, turn left on a spur road. At the end of the road, take Trinity Divide Trail 5W02 in a westerly direction. The strenuous hike has a 2,200-foot elevation gain in nearly three miles before going downhill about 20 feet to the lake. Because of this, Little Crater may not receive as many visitors as Dobkins and Durney.

Other Information

Before venturing on any routes—gravel spur or unimproved dirt roads—it is essential to obtain USGS 7.5 Minute Topographic maps to study the contour of the land and USFS maps to locate other information. The topographic map quadrangles are indispensable for detailed information not covered in other maps.

Whichever lake or stream you visit, Trinity Divide country will leave you with spectacular memories of the Scott and Trinity Mountain ranges within the Klamath Mountains Province.

Adventurous Treks into Trinity Alps

The Klamath Mountains Province possesses a distinct country of rugged topography and forests of fir and pine. This characteristic is most predominant in the Trinity Alps. The Alps is one of the most rocky, dramatic, and primitive areas in the Province. Established in 1984, the 513,100-acre Trinity Alps Wilderness, formerly known as the Salmon Trinity Alps Primitive Area, is the second largest wilderness in California. Surrounded by Trinity River (Trinity and Siskiyou counties) to the east, south, and west, the Alps range in elevation from 7,000 to 9,000 feet. Spectacular mountain ridges, swift deep canyon streams, and alpine lakes are prevalent in the region.

Over 2,500,000 years ago, the mountainous area consisted of gentle slopes. However, a global cooling of the earth caused an abrupt change in the area. Accumulations of snow turned to ice. These glaciers tumbled down stream valleys leaving behind jagged peaks and cirque lakes above 6,000 and 7,000 feet. Through the years, glaciers advanced and retreated several times. Remnants of small glaciers are still visible around Thompson Peak (9,002 feet), highest peak in the wilderness, Wedding Cake (8,569 feet), and Sawtooth Mountain (8,886 feet) in the Sawtooth Ridge range area.

Abandoned mines, cabins, buildings, and other gold mining structures left behind are visible in the Alps. One notable area is Hardscrabble Creek in the Coffee Creek drainage. Besides its historical features, breathtaking views, mountain landscapes, wildlife, wildflowers, and excellent fly-fishing waters abound in many lakes and streams within the wilderness. A host of tributary streams to the Salmon, Scott, and Trinity rivers maintain suitable habitat for excellent trout holding water. Surrounded by scattered timber stands, large meadows, barren rock cliffs and peaks, more than 50 lakes and miles of streams host several species of trout to accommodate anglers throughout the seasons. Lying between the Trinity and Salmon mountains, more than half of the lakes in the wilderness support brook trout. With the exception of golden trout inhabiting two lakes, rainbows and browns occupy other lakes. Rainbow trout inhabit most streams in the wilderness.

Situated in portions of Shasta-Trinity, Klamath, and Six Rivers national forests, many waters in the Trinity Alps are seldom visited. However, in recent years, the Alps received moderate to heavy use during the season from mid-June to mid-October. Upon entering this luxurious pristine wilderness, the vibrant sounds of rushing streams originating from the Alps can be heard. Among them are Tangle Blue Creek, Bear Creek, Coffee Creek, Swift Creek, Stuart Fork, Rush Creek, Canyon Creek, North Fork Trinity River, New River, South Fork Salmon River, and South Fork Scott River.

Visitor's permits are required to enter Trinity Alps Wilderness for both day hikes and extended trips. Most of the lakes in the Alps

The Trinity Alps tower over the Trinity River basin.

are easily reached by several main roads before branching into Forest Service Routes to trailheads. The majority of the lakes in the Alps lie on the eastern side. The most heavily used trails are accessed from Swift Creek, Stuart Fork, and Canyon Creek trailheads. Lesser used trails south of Coffee Creek Road are through Big Flat Campground. Big Flat is below Preachers Peak (7,202 feet) and near the headwaters of South Fork Salmon River.

In the northern sector, one can enter the wilderness within the Klamath National Forest from SR 3 at Scott Mountain Campground or Callahan in the East Fork Scott River area. The south side entry to the wilderness lies in the Shasta-Trinity National Forest, while the west side entrance is from Six Rivers National Forest. On the northern sector of the Alps, the main routes are approached through Salmon River Road from Somes Bar, and the Cecilville Road out of Callahan. State Route 3 is the main thoroughfare to reach other routes to the wilderness trailheads on the eastern slope.

Waters in the Trinity Alps are divided into their respective drainages. The northern portion of Trinity Alps Wilderness waters flow into the Salmon and Scott river systems. All other waters on the eastern, southern, and western slopes from the Alps drain into the Trinity River.

East Slope Lakes and Streams
Upper Trinity River

The majority of large and smaller tributary lakes and streams on the eastern slope of the Trinity Alps Wilderness in Trinity County are accessible from SR 3. Waters originating from the Alps flowing into Upper Trinity River include: Tangle Blue Creek, Bear Creek, Coffee Creek, Swift Creek, Stuart Fork, and Rush Creek.

Tangle Blue Creek Drainage

Tangle Blue Creek, tributary to the Upper Trinity River, lies on the northeastern slope of the Alps. This tributary has four magnificent lakes for hikers to explore: Big and Little Marshy lakes, Tangle Blue, and Log Lake. Headwaters of Big and Little Marshy lakes and Tangle Blue Lake originate from springs. Mosquito Lake (6,613 feet), fifth lake in the drainage, is a privately owned lake with signs posted.

Situated below the Scott Mountains, 5.5-acre, 15-foot-deep Big Marshy Lake (6,297 feet) and nearby 1.5-acre, 6-foot-deep Little Marshy Lake (6,196 feet) have lower visitor usage. Tangle Blue Lake (5,746 feet), on the other hand, has more frequent visitors. Both lakes are accessible from the PCT or the Tangle Blue Creek Trailhead. It is approximately a 5-mile moderate hike from Tangle Blue Creek Trailhead at the wilderness boundary.

Surrounded by forests stands and meadows near the base of Scott Mountain (6,829 feet), large campsites make it an ideal place for families visiting Tangle Blue Lake. Day-use hikers frequently visit this easy to moderate 4-mile hike from the Tangle Blue Creek Trailhead. The 12-acre, 17-foot-deep Tangle Blue Lake is a productive fly-fishing lake. Use light gear and small nymph patterns to lure action from brook and rainbow trout. Inflow into the lake is open but sandy. Any accessible segment paralleling Tangle Blue Creek is great water in which to wet your line.

Bear Creek Drainage

Situated in a granite basin, Bear Creek drainage hosts three lakes, Big Bear, Little Bear, and Wee Bear. Big Bear Lake, with an elevation of 5,844 feet, is a 28-acre, 73-foot-deep lake. Big Bear is one of the largest scenic lakes in this deep granite basin. This brook and rainbow trout lake is a 6-mile moderate hike from Bear Creek Trailhead off SR 3.

Another deep granite basin lake with towering landscape is Little Bear Lake (6,220 feet). This smaller 6-acre, 74-foot-deep body of water requires some cross-country scrambling through rocky granitic terrain from Big Bear Lake. Wee Bear Lake, at 6,220 feet, is a tiny 0.5-acre, 14-foot-deep lake fed by Little Bear. Located 100 yards below Little Bear, it is an easy walk from the upper lake.

Coffee Creek Drainage

Approximately 30 miles of Coffee Creek originates from the Salmon Mountains below Packards Peak (7,828 feet), Coyote Peak (7,680 feet), and Adams Lake. Seldom visited, Adams Lake is a 1-acre, 16-foot-deep lake located at 6,143 feet. The rough 2.5-mile hike passes through extremely steep terrain, yet Adams is a popular trail for equestrians.

Trailheads entering the Alps are accessible from Coffee Creek Road. The road originates in the hamlet of Coffee Creek

Coffee Creek—the gateway to the Alps.

(2,485 feet) on SR 3 and follows the creek to trailhead entries. Early in the season, roadside fishing along Coffee Creek can be stupendous.

Situated below Red Rock Mountain (7,853 feet), south of Coffee Creek, are Union and Foster lakes. The 14-foot-deep, 3.5-acre Union Lake (6,023 feet) is accessible by an easy, to moderate, 9-mile hike through a combination of forest and meadow landscape along the creek. The creek supports rainbow and Eagle Lake trout, however, Union Lake is a rainbow and brook trout fishery.

Lying east of Union Lake, flowing into Union Creek, is 5.5-acre, 20-foot-deep Foster Lake. At 7,245 feet, Foster Lake received its name from a pioneer Trinity Center family. Above the lake, on the high saddle (7,400 feet), is one of the best views of Mt. Shasta visible from this area. At the junction of Union Lake Trail, the steep trail through brushy landscape and open terrain gains 1,500 feet to reach Foster Lake. Below this saddle, to the east, it is possible to connect with Boulder Creek trails that go to lakes in this drainage—Lion, Conway, Boulder, and Little Boulder.

This group of lakes holds a combination of brook, rainbow, and Eagle Lake trout. The area is an ideal setting for rock climbing, scrambling, and day hikes to Lion and Conway lakes which are situated along the western arm of Boulder Creek. Foster Lake is also accessible from nearby Lion Lake. It is possible to make a loop trip between these waters from several different trailheads. The moderate, to difficult, 7- to 10-mile hike to these lakes starts from the Goldfield Trailhead and Campground located on the south side of Coffee Creek.

The route from Coffee Creek Road to the Boulder Lakes Trailhead is 11 miles of good grade. The trail enters from the east side of the wilderness. It is very important not to leave any food in your car at the trailhead because bears inhabit the area and will smash into automobiles to seek food.

If your destination is the Lion Lakes group, the best lake for base camp is 1-acre, 3-foot-deep Conway Lake (6,838 feet). Of the two lakes, this one is situated at the lowest elevation. Although it is very shallow, Conway is able to sustain a brook trout fishery due to a constant flow of water entering the lake. During the summer months, waterlilies dominate the lake. Above Conway Lake, 3-acre, 37-foot-deep Lion Lake (6,996 feet) supports a brook trout fishery.

From the Boulder Lake Trail, anglers are able to venture into Found, Tapie, Boulder, and Little Boulder lakes. From this trailhead, connections can be made to the entire Lion Lakes group. Found, Tapie, and Boulder lakes flow into the eastern arm of Boulder Creek. The highest of this group though is 2.5-acre, 9-foot-deep Found Lake (6,866 feet). Below this lake is 1.75-acre, 15-foot-deep Tapie Lake (6,501 feet). Be aware that there is no trail between Found, Tapie, and Boulder lakes so it is necessary to climb cross-country from Boulder Lake on steep and rocky terrain to reach Found and Tapie lakes.

Larger 8-acre, 27-foot-deep Boulder Lake (6,070 feet) is an easy 2-mile hike from the Boulder Lakes Trailhead and fly-fishing is good in its inflow area. Located east of Boulder Lake, branching off from the Boulder Lake trail, is 4.5-acre, 19-foot-deep Little Boulder Lake (6,318 feet). Little Boulder is also an easy 2-mile hike from the Boulder Lakes Trailhead. These lakes are also accessible from the North Fork Swift Creek Trailhead.

Located in the headwaters of Sugar Pine Creek, 9-acre, 43-foot-deep Sugar Pine Lake (6,579 feet) is surrounded by granite

peaks and ridges. The lake is accessible from a difficult 5.5-mile hike following the creek. Plenty of potential day hikes to Sugar Pine Lake can be found from Union, Foster, and the Boulder Creek lakes.

North of Coffee Creek Road is a host of lakes lying in the tributary waters of Coffee Creek. Amongst the first in this group is 6.3-acre, 12-foot-deep Granite Lake (6,446 feet) which flows into North Fork Coffee Creek. The 9-mile hike is an easy to moderate climb mostly along the North Fork. Granite Lake supports a superb brook, cutthroat, and Eagle Lake trout fishery.

Several lakes situated in the headwaters of East Fork Coffee Creek are productive fly-fishing destinations. One of the first lakes in the group is 4.5-acre, 15-foot-deep Doe Lake (6,992 feet). The difficult 7-mile hike to Doe will reward anglers with solitude and seclusion. For additional trips, the trail continues northwest to Granite Lake.

On the eastern side of the East Fork, 25-acre, 84-foot-deep Stoddard Lake (5,832 feet) is one of the most frequently used lakes in the wilderness. Lying north of Coffee Creek, this East Fork Coffee Creek headwaters lake is best fished from float tubes or other light craft. The Stoddard Lake Trailhead is accessible from a Forest Service Route out of SR 3 at Eagle Creek Campground. The trail is an easy to moderate hike to Stoddard Lake.

Nearby is 4-acre, 15-foot-deep McDonald Lake (5,896 feet). It contains a population of brook and rainbow trout. This lake attracts plenty of mosquitos; be prepared to bring repellent to deal with these bothersome insects.

Swift Creek Drainage

Within the spring-fed Swift Creek drainage, there are several lakes that receive low to moderate usage, and the trails to reach these lakes range from easy to moderate difficult. The Swift Creek Trailhead begins at Preachers Meadow near the wilderness boundary. The heavily-used trail passes through mixed conifer forests and Parker and Mumford meadows as it winds its way to the headwaters of Landers, Ward, and Horseshoe lakes.

Other lakes in the drainage can be reached from the Lake Eleanor or North Fork Swift Creek trailheads. Lying one-half mile outside of the trailhead, brook and brown trout are present in the 3-acre, 10-foot-deep Lake Eleanor (4,950 feet). The largest lake in this group though is 18-acre, 64-foot-deep Granite Lake (6,000 feet). It supports brook, rainbow, cutthroat, brown, and Eagle Lake trout. Fishing along Granite Creek is also productive for rainbow and brook trout.

In the headwaters of Granite Creek (the Swift Creek drainage), 6-acre, 17-foot-deep Landers Lake (7,042 feet) lies below Red Rock Mountain (7,853 feet). The 7- to 9-mile hike to Landers is an easy to moderate climb from the trailhead. The 5.5-acre, 23-foot-deep Ward Lake (7,118 feet) has rainbow, brook, brown, and Eagle Lake trout. Bears are frequent visitors in this area so be cautious and store food at all times. Yellowjackets can also be bothersome near 6-acre, 22-foot-deep Horseshoe Lake (6,850 feet). Use great caution and store food in tight containers.

Dipping, or swimming, in shallow 1.5-acre, 10-foot-deep Shimmy Lake (6,300 feet) could result in some painful experiences. Giant water bugs in this body of water can inflict painful bites. The lake gets rather warm in the summer and is subject to winter kills during severe winters because it is situated in open terrain.

Stuart Fork Drainage

Heavily-forested terrain, rushing mountain streams, spectacular views, and a well-maintained trail into the Stuart Fork drainage make it a worthwhile journey into the Alps from Bridge Camp Campground. Excellent fishing abounds along the trail that runs beside Stuart Fork, the outlet, and the surrounding cove area of Clair Engle Lake.

To reach the Stuart Fork Trailhead, take SR 3 out of Weaverville and head north or south from Callahan. Upon reaching the Stuart Fork arm of Clair Engle Lake, turn west on the road to Trinity Alps Resort. The road leads to Bridge Camp Campground located near the wilderness boundary. From the trailhead, the Stuart Fork Trail is about 15 miles of easy to moderate hiking along a heavily used trail that travels beside the Stuart Fork, eventually reaching the lakes lying below Thompson Peak (9,002 feet).

Known as the crown jewels of the Trinity Alps, Mirror, Sapphire, and Emerald lakes offer some of the finest wilderness waters for anglers willing to make the long journey. Situated in a setting of permanent snowfields and glaciated granite terrain just below Thompson Peak (9,002 feet), 14-acre, 25-foot-deep Mirror Lake (6,600 feet) is the first lake in the headwaters area. Downstream from Mirror Lake is 43-acre, 200-feet-deep Sapphire Lake (5,882 feet), the deepest lake in the Trinity Alps. A steep climb from Sapphire to Mirror is a difficult trek through rough terrain and this trip is only for hikers in good physical condition with lots of experience in cross-country travel. The best place to camp is at Morris Meadows, which allows campers to take day trips to Sapphire. Both of these lakes are reachable from Morris Meadows camp, but it takes approximately six hours of steep climbing over mountainous granite country to cover the two-mile distance.

Another headwaters watershed is 21-acre, 68-foot-deep Emerald Lake (5,500 feet). It is surrounded by granite and has a rock and concrete dam that holds in its water. Sapphire and Emerald lakes support rainbow, brook, and Eagle Lake trout, while Mirror Lake holds rainbow and brook trout. Stocked with golden and brook trout, 3.5-acre, 31-foot-deep Morris Lake (7,350 feet) and the 24-acre, 167-foot-deep brook and rainbow trout fishery of Smith Lake (6,950 feet), should only be attempted by anglers experienced in cross-country travel. Lying south of Smith Lake is 14-acre, 26-foot-deep Alpine Lake (6,112 feet). Alpine is reachable from the Stuart Fork Trail; thence connect with the Boulder Creek Trail to the west. However, for the last mile or so before arriving at Alpine the terrain is extremely rocky and rugged.

Other lakes to visit below Siligo Peak (8,143 feet) in the Stuart Fork drainage are 4-acre, 56-foot-deep Lake Anna (7,550 feet) and scenic 13-acre, 34-foot-deep Summit Lake (7,700 feet). Sparse vegetation and broken boulders are dominant the landscape in these areas. Smaller lakes in this drainage include 4.5-acre, 19-foot-deep Deer Lake (7,150 feet), 2.5-acre, 13-foot-deep Luella Lake (6,950 feet), 2.5-acre, 13-foot-deep Diamond Lake (7,250 feet), and 2.5-acre, 17-foot-deep Echo Lake (7,250 feet).

Rush Creek Lakes and Streams

Lying on the southeastern slope of the Alps are the remote Rush Creek lakes. Isolated from other lakes in the Alps, the Rush Creek lakes are lightly fished. These seldom-fished lakes form the headwaters of Rush Creek which flows into the Trinity River below Lewiston Dam.

Upper, Middle, and Lower Rush Creek lakes support rainbow and brook trout. Set deep between high granite walls below Monument Peak (7,763 feet), Upper Rush Creek Lake (6,900 feet) is rocky and occasionally has heavy lingering snow into the summer months. However, Middle (6,479 feet) and Lower (6,250 feet) Rush Creek lakes are surrounded by meadows.

The Rush Creek Trailhead is accessible from Rush Creek Campground near SR 3 north of Weaverville. From Lewiston, take Rush Creek Road to SR 3 and from there, travel to Rush Creek Campground.

South Fork Salmon River

The headwaters of South Fork Salmon River begin their course below Caribou Mountain (8,525 feet) from Josephine Lake (5,818 feet) in Siskiyou County. Although this 17-acre, 47-foot-deep lake is stocked with rainbow and brook trout, a major portion of it is privately owned. Josephine Lake, and the headwaters of the South Fork, are reachable from the Big Flat Trailhead out of Big Flat Campground at Coffee Creek. From Big Flat Campground, there are also trails leading to lakes and streams on the eastern slope of the Alps, such as the Caribou Lakes, the headwaters of Stuart Fork, and the Swift Creek drainage.

In the headwaters section of South Fork Salmon River, a cluster of three lakes is situated in the Caribou basin below Sawtooth Ridge. In this basin, 72-acre, 72-foot-deep Caribou Lake (6,822 feet) is the largest glacier lake in the Trinity Alps. Breathtaking, spectacular views of the entire basin are visible from the Caribous. Located at the lower end of the Caribou basin is 22-acre, 83-feet-deep Lower Caribou Lake (6,520 feet). Surrounded by steep towering mountains and sheer granite cliffs, this deep lake holds some large rainbow, brook, and Eagle Lake trout. The third lake in this basin is 10-acre, 42-foot-deep Snowslide Lake (6,640 feet). Store all food well to keep it safe from invading mice and other animals.

Three-acre, 16-foot-deep Little Caribou (7,165 feet) is a smaller lake situated away from the basin. Lying west of the Caribou lakes is 9-acre, 21-foot-deep Little South Fork Lake (5,959 feet). No trail is accessible to reach this Little South Fork Creek headwater lake. Between the Caribou basin and Little South Fork Lake, the terrain is extremely rough. Therefore, cross-country trekking through brushy terrain is necessary from where the trail ends at the creek in order to reach Little South Fork Lake.

East Fork South Fork Salmon Waters

The headwaters of a lake group of the East Fork South Fork Salmon River lie below Deadman Peak (7,617 feet). Situated below Scott Mountains, between the East Fork South Fork Salmon River and South Fork Scott River drainages, 3-acre, 15-foot-deep Hidden Lake (6,658 feet) is reachable from the trailhead at Carter Meadows Summit out of Cecilville Road east of Callahan.

Trailheads for Long Gulch Lake and Trail Gulch Lake trailheads are out of the Carter Meadow area. Beginning at different locations, both trails follow the creek for the most part. However, as the climb swings away from the creek, be prepared for steeper rocky terrain near 10-acre, 47-feet-deep Long Gulch Lake (6,406 feet). The 14-acre, 21-feet-deep Trail Gulch Lake (6,436 feet), as well as Long Gulch Lake, supports rainbow and Eagle Lake trout. Both Long Gulch and Trail Gulch are surrounded with talus and rocky landscapes.

South Fork Scott River

A number of lakes and streams in the northeastern sector of the Trinity Alps flow out of the South Fork Scott River drainage.

Lying below Deadman Peak (7,617 feet) in Siskiyou County, head-waters of the South Fork Scott originate from 6.4-acre, 34-foot-deep Upper South Fork Lake (6,748 feet) and 4.4-acre, 23-foot-deep Lower South Fork Lake (6,689 feet). These two lakes are accessible from the trailhead where the PCT crosses Cecilville Road between Callahan and Cecilville.

In this northern section of the Alps, a group of lakes are accessible from SR 3 at the Scott Mountain Campground Trailhead. The PCT crosses this portion of the wilderness connecting to other trails leading to East Boulder Lake and the Fox Creek lakes.

Fed from springs, 32-acre, 60-foot-deep East Boulder Lake (6,676 feet), the largest lake in this area, and 7-acre, 29-foot-deep West Boulder Lake (6,963 feet) are easily accessible from the PCT. Within the Fox Creek lakes, 9.5-acre, 38-foot-deep Fox Creek Lake (6,571 feet) has fairly heavy equestrian traffic, while smaller 3.5-acre, 16-foot-deep Mavis Lake (6,686 feet) receives less usage. Both lakes have readily accessible trails from the PCT. Three-acre, 16-foot-deep Virginia Lake (6,893 feet) supports rainbow and Eagle Lake trout.

Isolated from the Boulder lakes, 11-acre Washbasin Lake (7,022 feet) is an 85-foot-deep lake set in a crater-like depression without an outlet. This brook trout fishery is accessible from trails out of scenic 3-acre, 16-foot-deep Mill Creek Lake (6,590 feet) or East Boulder Lake.

Trinity River Streams

Most lakes from the Trinity Alps flow into the tributary waters of the Trinity River. However, a few lakes lying on the eastern side of the Alps flow south into Canyon Creek and North Fork Trinity River. Trailheads to reach Canyon Creek lakes are out of Canyon Creek Trailhead which is accessible north of Junction City. Entry to the North Fork Trinity River headwaters is from Hobo Gulch Trailhead located north of Helena.

Canyon Creek Lakes

Tumbling waterfalls, granite spires, and scenic alpine lakes dot the headwaters of Canyon Creek. Towering Thompson Peak (9,002 feet), Wedding Cake (8,569 feet), Sawtooth Mountain (8,886 feet), Mount Hilton (8,934 feet), and glaciers in this region provide one of the most awesome views of the Alps in Trinity County.

To reach the Canyon Creek Trailhead, turn north from Junction City (SR 299) onto the narrow Canyon Creek Road to Lower Canyon Meadows, which is followed by Ripstein Campground. The trailhead is a short distance from the campground. An easy to moderate 8-mile hike along Canyon Creek passes through a landscape of spectacular waterfalls and meadows before reaching Upper and Lower Canyon Creek lakes. Rainbow and golden trout are found above the falls in upper Canyon Creek.

Lying below towering granite peaks and permanent snowfields, 25-acre Upper Canyon Creek Lake (5,688 feet) features brook, rainbow, and golden trout. All species thrive well in this 86-foot-deep

lake. A short distance from the upper lake, smaller 14-acre, 56-foot-deep Lower Canyon Creek Lake (5,606 feet) has a brook, rainbow, and Eagle Lake trout fishery. A day hike to "L" Lake is an option from base camps out of Canyon Creek lakes.

Isolated northeast of Upper Canyon Creek Lake, 2-acre, 29-foot-deep "L" Lake (6,562 feet) is mostly frequented by day-hikers camping at the heavily populated Canyon Creek lakes. This L-shaped lake supports a brook trout fishery. Further north of Upper Canyon Creek Lake is 1-acre, 13-foot-deep Kalmia Lake. Kalmia received its name from the "mountain laurel" vegetation growing along its shoreline. Lying below Wedding Cake (8,569 feet), and other unnamed peaks, during most of the summer it is a difficult and strenuous cross-country trek to Kalmia due to extremely deep snowfields. This small lake supports a brook trout fishery.

Another small lake situated downstream from the Canyon Creek lakes is 1.5-acre, 18-foot-deep Forbidden Lake (6,168 feet). Forbidden Lake lies below a glacier moraine at the headwaters of Boulder Creek, a tributary to Canyon Creek. Further downstream from Forbidden is the larger 5-acre, 17-foot-deep Boulder Creek Lake (5,709 feet). Situated in a meadow below the base of mountainous terrain, these two lakes can also be side trips for day hikes that originate from the Canyon Creek lakes. While Forbidden Lake holds brook trout, Boulder Creek Lake supports brooks and rainbows.0

North Fork Trinity River

North Fork Trinity River is closed to fishing year-round. However, this large tributary to the Trinity River hosts several lakes in the Alps. The long 19-mile hike from the Hobo Gulch Trailhead to Grizzly and Lois lakes passes through splendid forests and views of towering peaks. Be cautious when approaching the last portion of the trail though because it is extremely steep, difficult, slippery, and unmarked.

Lying below the base of Thompson Peak (9,002 feet), at the headwaters of Grizzly Creek, is 42-acre, 173-foot-deep Grizzly Lake (7,105 feet). It is the second-deepest lake in the Alps. More than several hundred feet of cascading waters tumble out of Grizzly Lake down to Grizzly Meadow.

Lois Lake, at 7,600 feet, is the highest lake in the Alps. The 2.5-acre, 40-foot-deep remote brook trout lake is seldom fished. For possible day trips, it is a challenge to climb the very difficult 1,200-foot steep chute from Grizzly Meadow to the lake.

An adventurous lake in the Rattlesnake Creek drainage of the North Fork is 28-acre, 70-foot-deep Papoose Lake (6,653 feet). This journey is an extremely strenuous 14-mile hike from the Hobo Gulch Trailhead through rattlesnake country. However, once you're there, your reward is the opportunity to connect with large rainbow, brook, and Eagle Lake trout.

The Hobo Gulch Trailhead sits at the end of the road at the wilderness boundary. From SR 299 at Helena, turn north on Hobo Gulch Ridge Road to reach Hobo Gulch Campground and Trailhead. This entry to the wilderness has high visitor usage. Be prepared for heavy traffic during the peak seasons.

Wild, Rugged, and Remote New River

The New River drainage encompasses approximately 144,000 acres of mountainous forestland. Some of the New River's primary characteristics are its virgin forests, rugged mountainous terrain, and remoteness, which attract visitors seeking solitude. Although this southwestern sector of the wilderness lacks high alpine lakes and glaciated landforms—a characteristic of the Alps—New River has been recognized as off-the-beaten-path by most backcountry visitors.

In contrast to other major trails in the wilderness, the New River trails are more diversified. Currently, the main stem of New River is closed to fishing all year. However, these trails enable travelers to enter the Alps from one trailhead to fish lakes and streams in other drainages in the Alps and have the option of making loop trips without backtracking.

The New River drainage was one of the major gold-mining settlements in the early 1850s. Shortly after gold was discovered in 1848 in the Trinity River drainage, prospectors and miners came from all over the country to seek their fortune. By 1851, mining operations spread into the New River drainage. Due to its rugged mountainous terrain, access was a major obstacle for early settlers. The ruggedness and remoteness of the area was the reason the New River received its name. Eventually, the explorers and miners discovered the New River. It has retained its name since that time. (This area is now known as the Burnt Ranch Gorge).

Access to the main stem below the East Fork is out of Denny Road. It is a 17-mile paved and winding road north of SR 299 near Hawkins Bar. This route leads to the historic community of Denny. Anglers entering the Alps by way of the New River back country above the closed fishing area, have three nearby trailheads at the wilderness boundary. Early settlers and miners constructed these trails as a means of connecting mines and their facilities.

The three trailheads are accessible about six miles beyond the Forest Service station and campground from a gravel road near Denny. New River Trailhead, at 2,200 feet in elevation, is located on County Road 402 and Route 7N15 from Denny. This trailhead has a stock corral and public toilets. The East Fork Pony Buttes Trailhead (2,000 feet) is situated at the end of roads 402 and 7N01. Public toilets and a stock corral are available here also. The third entry is Jim Jam Trailhead. Sitting at 3,400 feet, this trailhead is accessible at the end of Road 7N03. It can be reached from roads 402 and 7N01.

Effective Fly Patterns, Tactics, and Other Trinity Alps Information

When fishing in the Divide, Alps, and other waters in the Trinity River Basin, I recommend using a very light-weight rod, matched with a floating line. Attach a micro shot 12 to 18 inches above the fly if the flow is moderate or the fish are feeding at a lower level. A sink-tip line will also lend itself well here.

My favorite patterns are small nymphs and pupa imitations that include Pheasant Tails, Hare's Ears, Birds Nests, and Zug Bugs in Nos. 14 to 18, and the LaFontaine Sparkle Green Pupa, No. 14. If the fish are actively feeding during insect activity, they will readily take emergers and dry flies. Adams, Adams Parachutes, Comparaduns, Yellow Humpys, Bi-Visibles in olive, dun, black and brown, Nos. 16 to 20 and olive Elk Hair Caddis in Nos. 14 to 16 are effective flies during this period. Also, the Madame X in size 8 to 10 is an excellent attractor pattern when drifted naturally or manipulated with a few twitches to dance the fly along the surface. Using a 6X tippet on 12- to 14-foot leaders is an indispensable technique for still waters.

The fly patterns and techniques mentioned are just as accommodating on other waters in the Trinity Basin. However, during the early part of the season, larger flies in Nos. 10 to 14 are more effective in lower-elevation waters. Also, have on hand a variety of flies representing *Callibaetis* and caddisflies in all stages of development, plus damsel nymphs, midges, ants, grasshoppers, and baitfish.

One of the rewards of fishing these backcountry alpine waters is that they often hold a large concentration of various species of trout. Do not overlook the inlet and outlet areas of many lakes and streams. In addition, trout residing in backcountry lakes are prone to being exceptionally spookable. They will take cover immediately upon any sign of threat to them. Therefore, approach alpine lakes and stream waters cautiously. In still waters and streams, keep a low profile as much as possible. The key to success is approaching each watershed quietly and fooling the trout with long and delicate presentations. The most effective fly patterns are small nymphs and dry flies representing mayflies and caddisflies.

At times it is difficult to wade or cast from shore in backcountry waters because of drop-offs or forested shorelines. It is advisable to tote along a float tube and a four-piece travel rod. My Buck's Bag has a backpack system for hooking tackle and other paraphernalia onto my tube.

Regardless of which lake or stream you select in the Trinity River Basin, a variety of surrounding forested landscapes, spectacularly scenic views, and fishing opportunities make each trip a worthwhile journey.

Author toting a float tube.

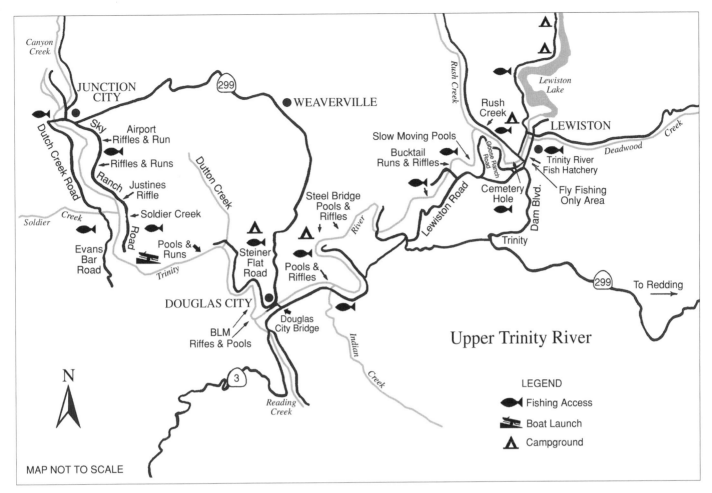

Upper Trinity River
Wild and Secluded Gems from
Clair Engle Lake to Junction City

The spectacular views of majestic granite peaks, emerald alpine lakes, and sparkling streams from the Trinity Divide country and Trinity Alps have inspired fly-fishers to seek exciting adventures in this part of the state. Anglers can sample the solitude of backcountry and wilderness waters or they can opt for other challenges in Clair Engle Lake, Lewiston Lake, or the main stem of the Trinity River.

The BLM administers 47,500 acres of land along the Trinity River below Lewiston Lake. Major portions of this acreage are in Trinity County, situated between Lewiston and the confluence of the North Fork Trinity at Helena and Hayfork Valley in the South Fork drainage. The Bureau administers nearly half of the 40 miles of the Trinity River between Lewiston and Helena as well as 21 miles of tributary streams. BLM lands provide public access to overnight camping and day use in the upper and middle river.

BLM operates three unimproved sites near Lewiston, and three improved campgrounds in the Douglas City and Junction City area. The three BLM campgrounds are open on a first-come, first-served basis with river access along the Trinity River. The Steel Bridge Campground located at the north end of Steel Bridge Road between Lewiston and Douglas City is generally used as an overflow area for the Douglas City and Junction City campgrounds. The improved campground at Junction City is open all year. However, due to freezing temperatures, the water is turned off in mid-winter. Douglas City Campground receives heavy usage for eight to nine months of the year. Other BLM lands with fishing access between Lewiston to Douglas City are:

- Cemetery Hole, one mile southwest of Lewiston.
- Rush Creek, located two miles northwest of Lewiston.
- Hog Hole, upstream from the mouth of Rush Creek.
- Bucktail Pool, several miles northwest of Lewiston below the bridge at Browns Mountain Road.
- Steel Bridge at the end of Steel Bridge Road.
- Steiner Flat, below the Douglas City Campground.
- Douglas City, one mile southwest of Douglas City.
- Junction City, one mile west of Junction City.
- Mouth of Oregon Gulch and Cooper's Bar.
- Mouth of the North Fork River on SR 299 at Helena.

Clair Engle Lake

At 2,370 feet, Clair Engle Lake lies at the base of Trinity Divide country and Trinity Alps Wilderness. Before the construction and subsequent filling of waters into Clair Engle and Lewiston lakes, the area was known as Trinity Valley.

Clair Engle Lake, located nine miles above the town of Lewiston, is over 20 miles long and boasts a 145-mile shoreline when full. The 465-foot-deep Clair Engle Lake, also known as Trinity Lake, was formed when Trinity Dam was completed in 1961 and filled in 1963.

One of the best trout concentration areas in Clair Engle Lake is the Stuart Fork Arm. The Stuart Fork and the East Fork of the Stuart Fork extend west from the lake. Numerous campgrounds are available along the arm. However, the best fishing is at the inlet arms in the Pine Cove and Covington Mill where the East Fork of Stuart Fork enters the lake. Another excellent area to fish is along the East Fork Trinity River Arm. If you are traveling in the vicinity of Trinity Center along SR 3, do not overlook various waters near the inlet of Swift Creek.

Lewiston Lake

Situated below Clair Engle Lake, regulated coldwater releases from Trinity Dam into Lewiston Lake (1,910 feet) provide a constant lake level throughout the year. With more than 15 miles of weedy shoreline, the 70-foot-deep, narrow 8-mile-long lake is surrounded by forested landscape. Noted for its excellent brown trout fishery, Lewiston Lake also features rainbow and Eagle Lake trout.

The consistently low water-surface temperatures, resulting from deep-water inflow out of Clair Engle Lake, make it unsuitable for water sports. The approximate yearly water surface temperature of 40°F. to 65°F. degree and the slow river movement makes it an ideal trout fishery. However, be cautious of water releases from Trinity Dam when the horn sounds a warning. Warning signs are posted along the shorelines of the lake. When waters are discharged from the dam, currents and rising waters in the upper lake resemble a stream. Anglers in lightweight craft, pontoon boats, or float tubes should retreat to safer locations.

Due to the narrow width of the lake, and to ensure quality fishing, there is a 10-mile-per-hour speed limit for boaters. Located in the upper section of the lake, the Pine Cove Boat Ramp provides a quality wheelchair fishing access. This day use area has several decks built over a prime fishing section of the lake. Forest Service and private campgrounds and lodging are available in several locations along the west shore of the lake.

Sawmill burner.

The most productive areas to fish are the flats below the dam, Pine Cove, and the island flats located below Lakeview Terrace Resort. The island flats are accessible by electric motor, pontoon boat, or other light craft. Do not overlook the flats in these areas as they usually hold larger trout.

In less torrential waters, present fly patterns above the fish waiting for morsels flowing downstream. If the flow is heavy, try switching to a weight-forward sink-tip or sinking line with a short leader.

Effective Fly Patterns and Tactics for Lewiston Lake

An incredible insect population, including excellent midge and *Callibaetis* hatches, occur in this watershed. The prime winter attraction for fly-fishing is from November through March. Most important during this period is the midge emergence. They will draw the trout up. Midges and *Callibaetis* emerge when the sun warms the water. For a short period before noon, hatches cloud the air, prompting trout to display aerial flights, thus producing excellent action. The trout's main food item at this time is midges, so small midge patterns work best. Spring is another prime time for consistent *Callibaetis* hatches.

I recommend using a floating line with 5X to 6X tippets on 10- to 12-foot leaders. Superior fly patterns to use at Lewiston are Black Midges, Griffith's Gnats Nos. 20 to 22, Parachute Adams, Callibaetis, and Tan Paraduns Nos. 16 to 18. Another terrific method is nymphing under an indicator—to detect light hits from the fish—with caddis-type patterns, Hares Ears, Pheasant Tails, All-Purposes, and Bird's Nest Nymphs in Nos. 16 to 18. Whenever the indicator deviates from the normal float, gently set the hook. On the other hand, Woolly Buggers and other streamer patterns in Nos. 8 to 10 are alternative producers. However, a No. 18 midge pupa is the best pattern for consistent strikes.

Upper Trinity River

It is no secret that the 111 river miles of the mainstem Trinity River, from Lewiston Lake to Weitchpec, are one of California's major (anadromous) streams. It is at the top of the list for many fly-fishers pursuing resident trout and steelhead in this upper river. When the fly-fishing season opens during spring and summer, heavy angler pressure is concentrated in this upper stretch of the river, especially in the fly-fishing-only section.

The primary flow of the Trinity below Lewiston Lake commences from a computerized controlled release operation structure at Lewiston Dam. It is controlled according to energy demands. The flow ranges from 300 cfs to 800 cfs. During heavy precipitation, it usually rises much higher. Generally, during the fall and winter months, it flows around 300 to 400 cfs. However, during spring and early summer snowmelt runoffs from the Alps and Divide country, the release may reach a torrential flow of over 4,000 cfs. As we head downstream, the flow increases at Cedar Flat and significantly more at Hoopa. The lower Trinity receives more water from the South Fork and other tributary waters. The lower river increases flow two to three times more than the upper river. Based on my collection of data for several years, flows have been consistent. On the other hand, flows can change and vary from year to year.

One of the principal reasons for the release of water from Clair Engle Lake and Lewiston Lake Dams is to control the flow of the Trinity. The project provides water for irrigation, power, recreation, fish and wildlife conservation. As part of the Bureau of Reclamation Trinity River Division and Central Valley Project, water from the Trinity River Basin is stored, regulated, and diverted through a system of reservoirs, dams, power plants, and tunnels to water-deficient areas of the Central Valley.

The regulated water releases influence more of the upper river from Lewiston to Junction City because this stretch receives lesser inflow from smaller tributaries. Between Junction City to the North Fork at Helena, for example, the main stem of the Trinity gains significant unregulated natural flows from larger tributaries, such as Canyon Creek and the North Fork.

The terrain surrounding the 18.2 river miles between Lewiston and Douglas City ranges from moderate to rugged mountains and wooded landscapes of ponderosa pine and Douglas fir. Most of the river system in the upper river has been dredged for gold. Between Steel Bridge Road and two miles upstream to Poker Bar, the area is a narrow V-shaped valley.

There are many residential developments and subdivisions set on relatively level flood plains, recreational and environmental settings, as well as rugged terrain in this portion of the river. Therefore, river access for the most part is limited. Most river access is from main or secondary roads, including two miles of SR 299 near Douglas City. However, the stretch of water from Douglas City to the Junction City area is accessible by boat only.

Trinity River Fly-Fishing-Only

An excellent body of water for fly-fishers is 250 feet below Lewiston Dam to the old Lewiston Bridge. The rich and placid waters of the Trinity River are near the town of Lewiston, approximately 50 miles west from Redding. Heading west from Redding on SR 299, after passing Buckhorn Summit, a sign will indicate a turn north onto Trinity Dam Boulevard. Parking is available at the Trinity River Fish Hatchery area or on the west side of the river after crossing the Old Lewiston Steel Bridge. There are several access sites to the river: Lewiston Hatchery, New Bridge and Old Bridge. Campgrounds are available in the vicinity of Lewiston and Trinity lakes. Resorts and trailer parks are available in Lewiston.

Throughout the summer, coldwater releases in this upper river sustain runs of steelhead, salmon, native rainbow and brown trout. Resident brown trout and planted juvenile steelhead (for out-migration) also populate this stretch of the river. A host of deep pools interspersed with excellent riffles are great candidates for fly-fishers. Look for sections of the river where flows bounce against large boulders or rock embankments. These stations provide excellent current flow and depth to meet the needs of fish. From the fish hatchery to the new bridge, this section of the stream hosts man-made spawning riffles providing excellent morning and early afternoon dry-fly and small-nymph fishing.

River access on USFS lands between the hatchery parking area to the New Bridge provide anglers opportunities to gain entry in several areas. The Trinity River Fish Hatchery Parking Area, overlooks the river just below the dam. Although there is a 30-foot slope to reach the river, the long pool in this stretch flows into a man-made shallow spawning riffle consisting of cobbles and gravel.

Another means of reaching the river is the Mary Smith access on the opposite side of the hatchery. To reach the site, make a sharp right turn at the Mary Smith Campground on Lewiston Lake and travel one-half mile of dirt and gravel road to the river. This area has good wadable waters at the tailwater near the dam. The streambed in this stretch consists mainly of cobblestones since it has been restored as a salmon spawning area.

In the New Bridge area, parking is available near the fish weir above the bridge. The flow is heavier in this part of the river. River

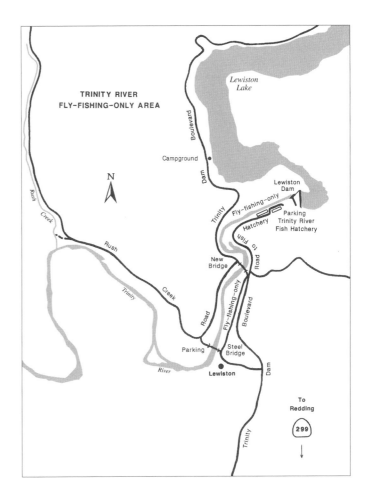

access is available behind the Lewiston Hotel and Lewiston Inn. Lewiston received its name from B. F. Lewis who settled in the town in 1853. He operated a ferry and trading post along the Trinity River.

The season for this superb fly-fishing stretch of the Trinity runs from the last Saturday in April to September 15 with special regulations unless changes occur. During spring and summer, heavy angler pressure is concentrated in this upper river.

Effective Fly Patterns for Trinity River Fly-Fishing-Only
A large population of wild resident brown trout will readily take well-presented dry flies, streamers, and nymphs. Although these wild

Trinity River.

browns are wary and apprehensive, the brilliant coloration of these beauties is displayed when they are feeding. For superb fishing, use small dry flies and nymphs in the morning and mid-afternoon.

It is a breathtaking experience to observe a trout take a fly in a subtle, graceful, deliberate manner. As soon as they're hooked, wild rainbows or browns will engage in a battle with plenty of wits and extreme strength. They start stripping line, shaking their heads violently, and searching for rocks, debris, or anything to tangle the line.

During one of my fishing escapades, the rod nearly lept from my hand when I drifted a No. 16 beaded PT Nymph. These thrilling moments gradually led to my netting a 15-inch brown. Casting small Nos. 16 and 18 dry flies, No. 16 Olive Green (brown hackle palmered, ribbed with gold wire), or Beadhead Pheasant Tail Nymphs from Lewiston Hatchery to the New Bridge will fool the larger brown trout.

For some exciting action, try casting a small Olive Pheasant Tail Nymph over a suspected trout lie from the New Bridge downstream to below the Old Lewiston Steel Bridge. Nymphing (with San Juan Worm and mayfly pattern) with an indicator is also productive in this one-and-one-half-mile stretch. Another method is to dead drift emergers in the tail outs.

The section of river above the Steel Bridge holds more riffles and faster water. Pheasant Tail, Hare's Ear, Brassie, and other nymphs representing caddisflies are excellent patterns to work the stream in this area.

Old Lewiston Bridge to Douglas City

Downstream from the Old Lewiston Bridge, the Trinity provides excellent fly-fishing for salmon and steelhead, rainbow, and brown trout. Beginning late spring to November, streamer patterns imitating small fish will generate some activity. During the fall and winter months of November through February, mayfly hatches provide excellent dry-fly fishing for brown trout.

Large pools, riffles, and runs—such as Cemetery, Hog, Bucktail, and Steel Bridge—are popular places for anglers pursuing salmon and steelhead when they are in the river system. There is a recreation site at Cemetery Hole, maintained by Trinity County near Lewiston, has parking and excellent trails for river access. In this area, commercial campgrounds and lodging are available along the river. It is located approximately one mile downstream from Lewiston on Goose Ranch Road. From the gravel parking lot, a one-quarter- to one-half-mile trail leads to the river at Cemetery Hole. This section of the river holds long series of riffles, runs, and pools. It is an excellent area to try a few casts when steelhead are holding long enough to be interested in taking a fly.

Fisheries restoration efforts were made by the Department of Water Resources with the Trinity River Task Force to improve fish habitat, and it appears these efforts produced significant results. Reconstructed pools and spawning riffles in the Lewiston area have produced a substantial increase in fish. Also, the habitat-restoration project above Grass Valley Creek over the last several years greatly increased natural spawning success. However, in

Trinity River—Bucktail pool.

recent reports, silt has presented some problems. Grass Valley Creek is accessible to a large valley area from Lewiston Road to a dirt road a short distance from the waters.

BLM Hog Hole Fly-Fishing Access

Approximately three-tenths of a mile from the mouth of Rush Creek and next to Rush Creek Road, or a mile from the Steel Bridge, Hog Hole is a popular river access location for spin fishing. A dirt road heads slightly downhill 20 feet to a grassy terrace near the river. Willows surround this BLM parcel of land except for a couple of clearings, the largest one known as Hog Hole.

The pool derived its named locally because of competition from anglers for shore fishing space. It appears there is room to accommodate four to six anglers. There can be some scrambling within the area once a fish is on. When the flow is low, anglers can wade further upstream in the riffles section. However, fly-fishers use the Hog Hole access area for boat launching to fish this 15-foot-deep, slow-moving section of the river. To effectively fish this stretch of water, use a sink-tip line with an olive green or brown Crystal Woolly Bugger or Woolly Worm. Try casting close to the willows and tules using a medium retrieve. Brown trout inhabit this area. Toward late afternoon and early evening, larger brown trout will succumb to your flies.

Bucktail Pool Access

A long stretch with pools and riffles runs along the BLM recreation site in the Bucktail Pool of the river. It encompasses approximately 80 acres of area where Brown's Mountain Road (off of Lewiston Road) crosses the Trinity River. It is approximately two miles downstream from the mouth of Rush Creek. This segment of the stream has a combination of steep, rugged rocky areas and brushy willow terrain surrounding portions of the river.

At Bucktail Pool, one side of the bank is a gravel bed with little vegetation. From Brown's Mountain Road, access to the river is not difficult. Most anglers fish bucktail pool and the small bridge area. However, the current is swift until it drops off into the pool. Near Bucktail Pool, there is evidence of an abandoned mineshaft, which has been closed off with rusty iron bars.

When the fish are in this section of the river, angler pressure is heavy. To get to upstream steelhead riffle waters from Brown's Mountain Road, you need to make a right turn onto a dirt road before the river. The dirt road traverses through a gravel terrace that had been dredged at one point. This access route takes you through dense brushy willows and other vegetation, old vehicle bodies, plus rocky, gravel, dirt, and weed patches. There is less angler pressure in this section of the river.

Steel Bridge Area

Although there are many roadways in the Lewiston area, river access is limited by private ownership and some difficult terrain.

Author casting to riffle water on the Trinity River.

Old cabin near Steiner Flat.

Within the Steel Bridge and Poker Bar area, over two miles of river flow through BLM land. There are also small BLM segments throughout the area. At the end of Steel Bridge Road, there is a BLM campground and parking for river access.

Indian Creek Access

From SR 299, one and one-half miles above the Douglas City bridge and downstream from the mouth of Indian Creek, the riffles and pools should not be overlooked. Parking is available near the motel. River access is a short walk along the banks. In this section of the river, anglers can pursue steelhead and salmon when they are in the river system.

Douglas City to Junction City

Douglas City was originally called Kanaka Bar in the early mining era. This area was a typical stagecoach stop with a general store, blacksmith shop, saloons, hotel, and a trading post. Of importance in the Douglas City area is Reading Bar, the site where gold was found. The site is located upstream from the Douglas City BLM Campground. Reading Creek is named after Major Pearson B. Reading who discovered gold in 1848. This is the period that triggered the gold rush in the Klamath Mountains.

Salmon eggs (roe).

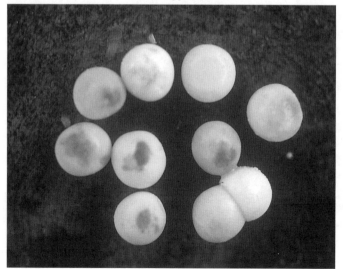

Upon reaching Douglas City from Indian Creek, fly-fishers can sample the shallow waters above the Douglas City bridge. However, below the bridge, access to riffle water is rather difficult. Head further downstream for better river access.

One of the major access sites to the Trinity River in the Douglas City area is the Douglas City Campground. Its location is approximately one-half mile from Douglas City off Steiner Flat Road. Rather than continuing on SR 299 north, turn left after crossing the bridge. Parking is ample for day-use visitors. Several worn paths lead down to the river.

Steiner Flat and Other Access Sites

Further downstream, Steiner Flat Road offers other access sites to the Trinity. However, steep terrain hinders some river access. Sand and gravel bars and a stretch of flood plains are evident in this area. Flattened gravel tailings with sand pits are scattered near the river.

The length of the Steiner Flat County Road is approximately four miles. It follows the Trinity River from SR 299 at Douglas City through a steep hill with a 25- to 30-foot elevation above the river. Several passable access spur roads to the river are hidden amongst heavy shrubbery vegetation. Several sites are opened for camping. However, it is difficult for trailers to enter the area from Steiner Flat Road due to steepness, heavily grown shrubs, and tall grass. The public usage road ends at the locked gate shortly after Dutton Creek. The land along the river is administered by BLM. However, through the years, home sites have increased throughout the area.

Secluded Floating Waters

Between Douglas City at Steiner Flat Road and Junction City, most fishing is by floating the river that allows access to a considerable amount of steelhead riffle waters. These nine river-miles of quality water hold some excellent opportunities for fly-fishers to hook up

Salmon egg-fly pattern (Glo Bug).

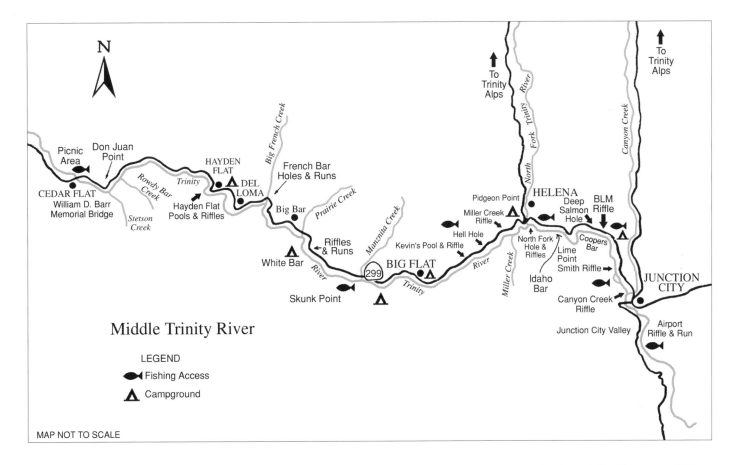

Middle Trinity River

LEGEND

🐟 Fishing Access

⛺ Campground

MAP NOT TO SCALE

with steelhead when the run is in. Although river access is limited due to private ownership of local and no-access roads, many wading sites are in the Douglas City and Junction City area.

Salmon Egg Imitations and Glo Bugs

During the months of November and December, keep an eye out for steelhead feeding on salmon eggs and following the activity of salmon throughout the river system. These fish tend to lay in shallower edges of major riffles and tailouts, intercepting floating eggs and other aquatic food disturbed by spawning activities. Therefore, when you encounter this type of water, do not overlook the area. It is essential that you present a natural drift of your egg patterns with the same depth and speed of flow to the area where the fish will intercept your offerings. Before casting, observe the lanes where other items are drifting.

Determining what color of egg pattern to use depends on how long and at what stages the eggs has been deposited. In the early stages of the spawn, the eggs tend to be a clear orange tone. As it progresses into later stages, the color will appear lighter and opaque, a milky pink or light peach with an orange dot near the center. The best pattern to use when steelhead are feeding on salmon eggs are Glo Bugs in orange or pink and light peach with a darker orange dot near the center.

Middle Trinity River
Awe-Inspiring Waters from Junction City to Cedar Flat

The Junction City area is one of the gateways to a host of roadside accesses to riffles and long runs for steelhead fishing. The access road to the trailhead into the Trinity Alps by way of Canyon Creek Road is out of Junction City. The terrain surrounding Junction City Valley is bountiful with vegetation. For the most part, wading is required. An abundance of river access is found along SR 299

from Junction City to Willow Creek, and SR 96 between Willow Creek to Hoopa.

Junction City Valley Waters

Excellent steelhead waters are scattered throughout the Junction City area. One reason for fishing the Trinity is that you can be on the move, covering many miles by vehicle that require only short walks to the river. The further away from the main route you walk, the better your chance to get into some prime, undisturbed waters. Plan to cover waters upstream as well as downstream from Junction City. Most sections of water in the area are a mixture of swift runs, riffles, and pools. Therefore, as a safety measure, a wading staff is essential to cover the varied types of water you'll encounter. You don't want to be surprised with a brisk plunk into a cold bath.

Several excellent waters are located downstream from Junction City by taking the west side Dutch Creek Road. When you reach the Trinity River or Soldier Creek sign, select the left Evans Bar Road. Evans Bar Road heads down the hill to the river near the mouth of Soldier Creek.

To reach the east side of the river, take Sky Ranch Road from Junction City. Do not turn onto private roads. Continue until you reach a large gravel parking area to find some nice riffles and runs. There may be trucks with trailers parked at the bars, as this is a boat-launching site. En route, you can also take spur roads to the river. This section is heavily covered with brush and timber, therefore, wading is necessary.

One of my favorite stretches in the Junction City area is the Smith riffle. This section receives angler pressure during the weekends when steelhead are in. Located one-half mile east of the Junction City Campground, only a few spots are available for parking. If you find a parking space, it is only a short walk to the river. You need to climb up a mound of dirt, rock, gravel and

Other recreational opportunities are available in the middle Trinity River.

maneuver down through thickets and shrubbery. Upon reaching the river, tree roots line the bank. Wading is necessary in order to reach fish hiding beneath tree roots and other obstacles on the opposite bank.

Other roadside access to the rivers is ample along the stretch of the Trinity between Junction City and the North Fork. Look for pullouts and parking spots along the road to reach premium steelhead waters.

Pigeon Point and the Mouth of the North Fork

At the confluence of the North Fork and main stem of the Trinity River, Helena, originally called Bagdad, is the southern entry of the Trinity Alps Trailhead. The river and surrounding area become more expansive and broad with large gravel bars. The river plains resulted from gold dredging in the early 1900s, leaving extensive tailings, debris, and litter behind. Hydraulic mining washed away and scarred many of the mountainsides. It is even more noticeable in the Junction City area.

Prime steelhead fishing at Helena is found by working upstream from Pigeon Point Campground to the confluence of the North Fork. This is an excellent stretch of fly-fishing water when steelhead are approaching the mouth of the North Fork. These fish stop to rest before entering the large tributary waters.

River access is from USFS Pigeon Point Campground and the North Fork Bridge. The nearly one-mile-long segment of the river contains pools, rapids, and deep channels. Several footpaths from the campground lead to the river. In some sections of the river, large gravel bars are clear of vegetation. In order to cast to holding steelhead, you need to wade in some sections of the river.

Hell Hole and other Access Waters to Cedar Flat

From Pigeon Point to Cedar Flat, this section has many pullouts and steep canyon wall waters. Hell Hole is a popular salmon hole with heavy angler pressure. The fish usually stop and rest at the pool below the fall before continuing up stream. If you intend to fish Hell Hole, parking is on the opposite shoulder of the road. River access is by descending from a steep zigzag trail through a mixture of small, medium, and large boulders. It is the only means to reach this stretch. This is an excellent deep pool for getting your fly down to the fish. Drop your line below the fall and let it drift to holding fish. It is essential to use a correct sink rate to get the fly down to the level where the fish are holding. They will succumb to Nos. 8 to 10 bright orange or chartreuse salmonfly patterns.

Further upstream from Hell Hole, the river is accessible by driving down a short dirt road to the river. In most instances, the water is clear and the fish are extremely wary. You can wade cautiously and cast to a few steelhead. However, most of the fish are salmon. In extremely clear water you can see pods of them milling around.

Other accessible waters with pullouts or campgrounds and limited or day-use parking include Big Flat, Skunk Point Picnic Area, near the mouth of Manzanita Creek, Big Bar, White Bar Picnic Area, French Bar, Mouth of Big French Creek, Hayden Flat, Sandy Bar, Cedar Flat, and before the William D. Barr Bridge area. As you are traveling along SR 299, watch for other pullout sites offering roadside parking, short walks, or other means to reach the river.

Steelhead Holding Waters and Effective Fly Patterns

When in search of steelhead holding waters, look near obstacles such as large rocks, boulders, tree trunks, limbs, riffle waters, flows with moderate speed currents, and the heads of runs or tailouts.

If you notice one fish rolling, chances are there is a large school of them nearby, usually 15 or more steelhead in the same area. They stack up like a cord of wood. During this period, use a floating line and a 6-foot leader with a strike indicator for an even drift. Add a split shot to get the fly down quickly.

On one of my trips to the Trinity, I tried several steelhead flies without much success. Then I noticed a tempting black rubber-leg fly pattern I had purchased and tied for use. Materials needed to tie the fly include a combination of heavy lead wire, thin black rubber strips, and black chenille. Use 3X-long Nos. 2 to 6 hooks wrapped with heavy lead wire, and attach 5 thin strips of black rubber (available at fly shops) to serve as three pairs of legs in the upper body, two short tails, and two long antennae.

Next wind a strip of medium to large black chenille to finish it off. I also substituted the plain black chenille for silver tinsel black chenille. Both nymph-style patterns will generate some vicious action when used with pulsating movements to tease the fish.

Another favorite pattern of mine is a No. 6 Babine Special. The fly has a white tail, two double dark pink chenille Glo Bug style body, red hackle between the two Glo Bugs, and white hackle at the eye.

Refer to Table 1 and other steelhead fly patterns I mentioned in sections pertaining to anadromous fish.

Black rubber-leg flies are a great enticer.

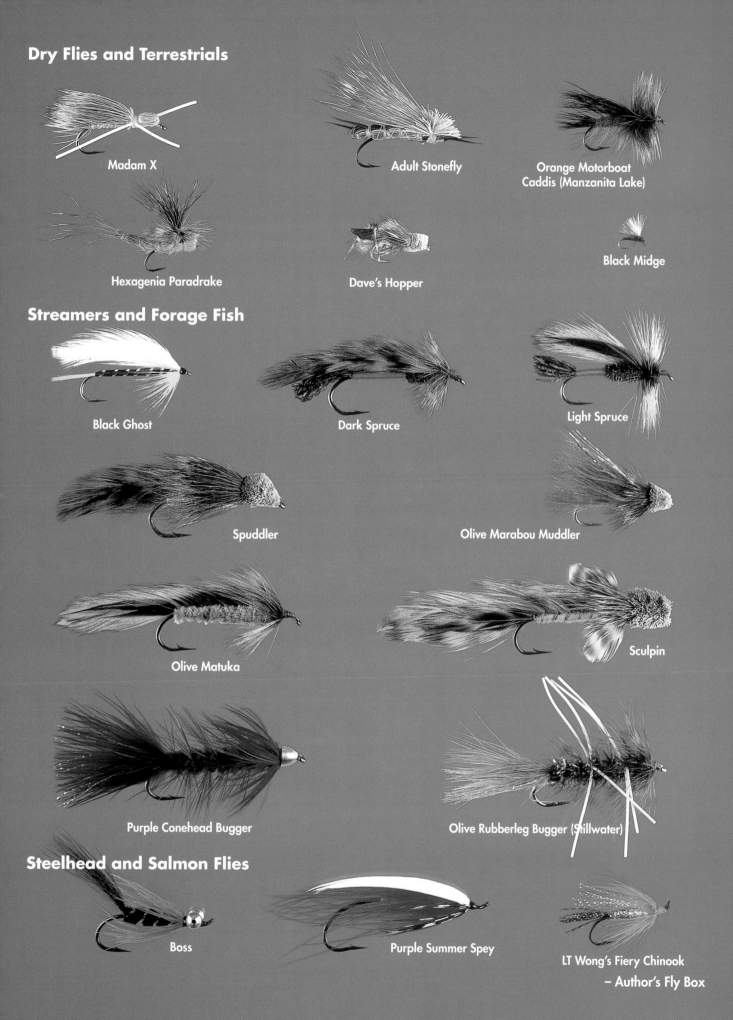

Dry Flies and Terrestrials

Madam X

Adult Stonefly

Orange Motorboat Caddis (Manzanita Lake)

Hexagenia Paradrake

Dave's Hopper

Black Midge

Streamers and Forage Fish

Black Ghost

Dark Spruce

Light Spruce

Spuddler

Olive Marabou Muddler

Olive Matuka

Sculpin

Purple Conehead Bugger

Olive Rubberleg Bugger (Stillwater)

Steelhead and Salmon Flies

Boss

Purple Summer Spey

LT Wong's Fiery Chinook
— Author's Fly Box

Wet Flies

Damsel Nymph

Golden Stone Nymph

Brassie

Bird's Nest

Caddis Larva

Gold Ribbed Hare's Ear

Peeking Caddis

Emergers, Dry Flies, and Terrestrials

Midge Pupa

Caddis Pupa

Renegade

Sparkle Dun PMD

Adams Parachute

Black Gnat

Streamers and Forage Fish

Leech

Muddler Minnow

Steelhead Fly

Brindle Bug

Wet Flies

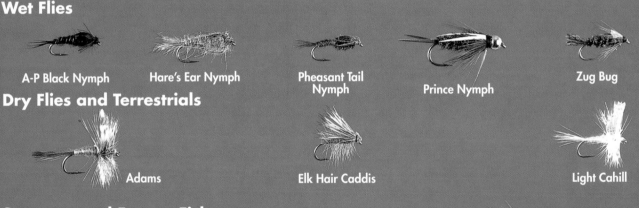

A-P Black Nymph

Hare's Ear Nymph

Pheasant Tail Nymph

Prince Nymph

Zug Bug

Dry Flies and Terrestrials

Adams

Elk Hair Caddis

Light Cahill

Streamer and Forage Fish

Woolly Bugger

Matuka

Steelhead and Salmon Flies

Glo Bug Single Egg

Silver Hilton

Wet Flies

Black Rubberlegs

Hexagenia Nymph

Kaufmann's Dragon

Mercer's Z-Wing Caddis

San Juan Worm

Fox's Poopah

Bead Head Fox's Poopah

Bitch Creek

Perfect Scud

Yellow Stone Nymph

Emergers, Dry Flies, and Terrestrials

CDC Caddis Emerger

LaFontaine Sparkle Pupa

October Caddis Poopah

Hex Poxy Back Emerger

Watters Foam Hex

Lawson's Paradrake (Green Drake)

Transparant (Ant)

Humpy

Stimulator (Golden)

Stimulator (Yellow)

Trico Spinner

Streamers and Forage Fish

Crystal Woolly Bugger

Milt's Pond Smelt

Hot Flash Minnow (Threadfin Shad)

Clouser Minnow

Steelhead and Salmon Flies

Bead Assassin

Babine Special

Orange Comet

Green Butt Skunk

Polar Shrimp

Fox's Fertilizer

Skunk

Popsicle

Estuary Shrimp

Hot Shot Comet

– Flies courtesy of The Fly Shop, Redding, CA

Typical golden trout.

Cascading waterfall.

Redband trout from Sheephaven Springs.

Middle Deadfall.

Wildflowers.

Justine Wong with steelhead.

White Crystal Hair "Tui Chub"

Red Rock, Trinity River.

Ash Creek.

Wagon Creek.

Tish Tang Gorge misty morning.

Castle Crag.

Hell Hole.

Fall River rainbow trout.

Eagle Lake osprey nest.

Lily with guide Jay Fair.

Lower Trinity River, Part 1
Cedar Flat to Willow Creek

The lower section of the Trinity from Cedar Flat to Willow Creek receives less angler pressure due to its canyons, precipitous gorge, difficult access, and private ownership lands. This stretch of the river is the most rugged of the entire river system. Access to the 7.5-mile Burnt Ranch Gorge is by foot trails from Gray Falls and Burnt Ranch campgrounds. From a pullout along SR 299, you can view the confluence of New River tumbling into the Trinity. Steep slopes and dense vegetation block most of the views from SR 299 before and after the gorge.

Boating is unsafe in the torrential waters from China Slide to Hawkins Bar. However, at Hawkins Bar and downstream the river is more conducive to fly-fishing. Camping is available at Burnt Ranch and Gray Falls campgrounds.

Hawkins Bar River Access

One attraction to the Hawkins Bar area is the legendary Bigfoot. Through the years, sightings of this humanoid creature have been reported in the area. The legend has attracted many visitors hoping to get a glimpse of Bigfoot. Access to the river is opposite the Big Foot store. Turn right and head downhill to a wide flood plain for excellent steelhead waters.

South Fork Trinity River

Years ago, the South Fork Trinity River offered spectacular fishing for trout and anadromous fish. However, through the years, like many of the other waters in this drainage, the South Fork has suffered from sedimentation, pollution, environmental activities, and overharvesting of anadromous fish. It has crippled this once-great fishery. With new regulations imposed along the South Fork as well as other waters in this drainage, this stream can return to being one of the finest in the basin.

Winter precipitation and spring runoff contribute to streambed destruction in this sensitive areas. During this period, the heavy flows from the South Fork and the confluence of the main stem Trinity near Willow Creek become heavily discolored. It may take days before the main stem clears up. However, the fall months are the best time to visit the South Fork.

Headwaters of the South Fork originate in the northwest sector of Yolla Bolly Middle Eel Wilderness below Chicago Rock (5905 feet), North Yolla Bolly Mountains (7,863 feet), Black Rock Mountain (7,755 feet), and Black Rock Lake (6,250 feet), which is a brook trout fishery. This Trinity and Humboldt county stream flows northwest through thick forest landscapes, canyons, meadows, flat lands, and crossing Forest Glen at SR 3 before reaching the community of Hyampom (1,285 feet) in Hyampom Valley.

This entire segment of the South Fork above the bridge near Hyampom is closed to fishing all year. However, approximately 35 miles of the South Fork Trinity from Hyampom to the confluence of the Trinity has special regulations and open season for trout and anadromous fish. These regulation affect the open season of the South Fork at the mouth of Grouse Creek between the two points.

A large portion of the Wild and Scenic South Fork River is situated in Six Rivers and Shasta-Trinity national forests. River access is

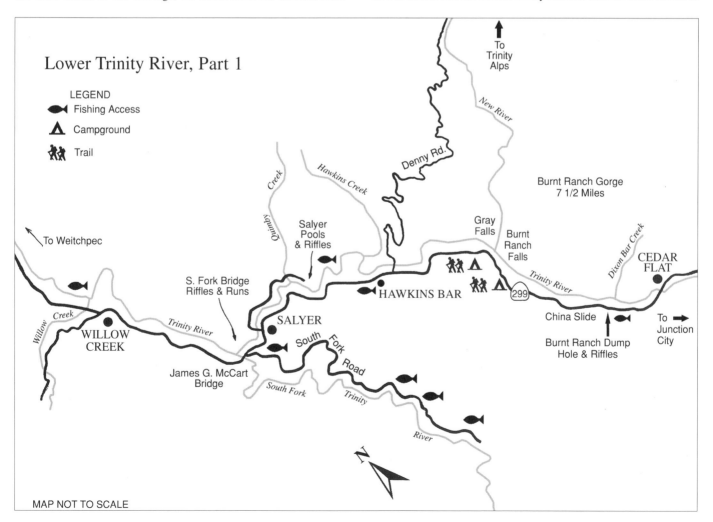

Old cabin near Steiner Flat.

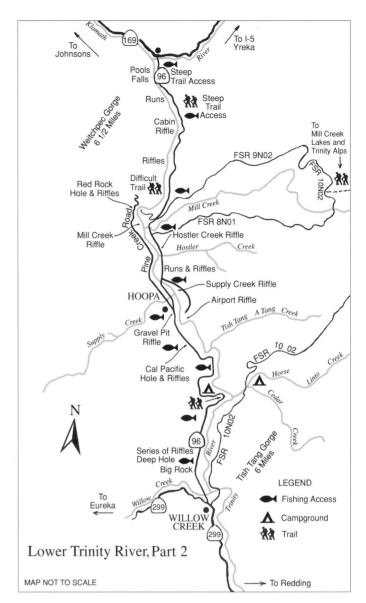

Lower Trinity River, Part 2

MAP NOT TO SCALE

To Redding

available from several campgrounds and picnic areas near Hyampom. The river is mostly surrounded by steep canyons ranging from 80 to 500 feet. However, in some sections, steep rough dirt roads lead to the river.

At the mouth of the South Fork and confluence of the Trinity, several river accesses east of the James G. McCart Bridge (South Fork Bridge) require hiking down steep, faint, brushy trails to the river. During periods of low flow, this section of the river has expansive gravel bars. From the gravel bars, you can fish the main stem or work yourself up to the South Fork.

From the mouth to the SR 3 Bridge in Hayfork, Hayfork Creek, the largest tributary to the South Fork, is a catch-and-release stream with other special regulations. The best river access is a short distance downstream from Hayfork or at the mouth near Hyampom. Other sections of the stream veer away from the road making access difficult. However, there are few steep access trails out of County Route 301 from Hyampom to Camp Trinity near Grassy Flat and Miners Creek.

Lower Trinity River Part 2
Willow Creek to the Confluence of Klamath at Weitchpec

A series of riffles, runs, and deep salmon pools are accessible throughout various sections around Willow Creek, Tish Tang A Tang Creek, and Hoopa Valley Indian Reservation waters, including Red Rock. In Hoopa Valley, Red Rock is the last river access before entry into the final gorge waters to Weitchpec. This lower section of the Trinity is reachable by turning north from SR 299 at Willow Creek onto SR 96. From Willow Creek, it is 23 miles to Weitchpec, and 12 miles to reach the flood plains of Hoopa Valley. When traveling on SR 96, the 25 river miles of the lower Trinity River are a combination of steep canyons, Tish Tang Gorge, flood plains in Hoopa Valley, and finally the last gorge before the meeting of the torrential giant, the Klamath River.

Willow Creek Access

River access to the Trinity is from several points at Willow Creek. Camp Kimtu is a fee-charged area managed by the Willow Creek Community Services District. Vehicles are not allowed on the river bar. A short walk offers approximately one-half mile of river access. To reach Camp Kimtu from Willow Creek, turn into Country Club Drive to Kimtu Drive and follow the signs. Known locally as the "Big Rock," this day-use river access is situated across SR 96 from the Lower Trinity River Ranger Station. From SR 96, take the turnoff onto a county road through a gravel pit mining area to the river's edge. Series of riffle waters and deep salmon holes are accessible

downstream from Big Rock Beach. This is one of the more heavily used accesses by swimmers as well as anglers. Therefore, early morning hours are your best bet to get away from swimmers.

Horse Linto, Tish Tang A Tang, and Mill Creek Lake

Several small tributary creeks in the lower Trinity that are reachable by foot offer trout fishing. Horse Linto, Tish Tang A Tang, and Mill creeks are reachable from its mouth. However, the mouth of Mill Creek is within the Hooper Valley Indian Reservation.

The lower section of Horse Linto Creek offers excellent habitat for steelhead, chinook salmon, and resident rainbow trout. During the months of November and December, the creek is filled with spawning salmon splashing and jumping while conducting their rituals. According to the diaries of early explorers, when they crossed the creek on horses, the abundance of fish along the creek spooked their horses. Today, the creek is still a rearing and spawning ground for salmon and steelhead trout. Through the years, various factors such as flood, drought, logging, mining, heavy angling, and grazing have led to the decline of the fish population. The Six Rivers National Forest built structures along the creek in an attempt to restore the fishery. The national forest has devoted considerable effort and expense to ensuring habitat management for stream improvement. So release all anadromous fish carefully when fishing Horse Linto Creek.

Kevin Wong with a salmon.

Lower Trinity waters.

Weirs and gravel bars along the lower segment of the creek allow the salmon to spawn. Horse Linto Creek got its name from a group of local Native Americans watching and listening to the roaring noise of the stream during cool and dark evenings. It was the immense sound of the waters that created the creek name Has-Len-Din (the sound of cascading water tumbling over rocks). Through the years, the pronunciation evolved into Horse Linto.

Excellent riffle waters along the mouth of Horse Linto and Tish Tang A Tang, both tributaries to the Trinity, are ideal sections of the river to intercept the fish when they are in the river system. These tributary waters are a challenge to fish.

If you wish to venture further by foot from Tish Tang A Tang Creek for trout, continue the trail at Mill Creek to the western entry of the Trinity Alps to Lower Mill Creek and Blacks Lakes. However, when the trails end, prepare to do a little cross-country scrambling. To reach Horse Linto, take Country Club Drive to Patterson Road. Follow FSR 8N03 to the campground and trailhead. Further downstream from Horse Linto Creek is Tish Tang A Tang Creek. Mill Creek, on the other hand, is situated in the Hoopa Valley Reservation.

Tish Tang A Tang Access

Situated 8 miles north of Willow Creek on SR 96, Tish Tang Campground and Day Use area offer easy access to the gravel bars. This stretch has open areas and the mouth of the creek has excellent riffle waters. However, a 4WD vehicle is recommended to travel on the gravel bars.

The Tish Tang section of the Trinity includes the 6-mile second gorge (Tish Tang Gorge), an entry to Hoopa Valley. It includes the established area around Willow Creek, and another V-shaped valley upstream. Inflows from the South Fork of the Trinity significantly increase the flow of the main stem, broadening and flattening the channel with gravel deposits into open flood plains at Hoopa Valley. This portion of the Trinity has a gentle river gradient with few rapids. However, steep slopes, dense vegetation, and a host of private owner-ship land prevents river access except for a few areas.

The Trinity's river course from Tish Tang to the confluence with the Klamath flows north through Hoopa Valley. Broad flood plains and some agriculture land in the lower 16 miles of the Trinity are evident. You can see the color contrast of the blue-green water of the

Trinity merging with the milky green water of the mighty Klamath at Weitchpec.

Throughout its reach in Hoopa Valley, the river's gradient is low. However, during the early season until May, the flow reaches its high peak, making wading more difficult. In most sections of the river's course, SR 96 runs along it. Hoopa Valley offers the most river access within the lower Trinity.

Hoopa Valley Indian Reservation Waters

The Hoopa Indian Reservation encompasses approximately 87,000 acres of land within the Six Rivers National Forest in Humboldt County. Access to the reservation is from SR 96 north at Willow Creek to Hoopa. Most of the reservation is situated within the Trinity River Basin. The lower 16 miles of the Trinity River in Hoopa Valley and the Weitchpec Gorge lie within the Hoopa Valley Indian Reservation. The northerly boundary is at the confluence of the Trinity River and Klamath River at Weitchpec.

Established in 1876, the reservation includes the town of Hoopa. The town was founded in 1864. The U.S. Bureau of Indian Affairs holds the reservation in trust for the Native Americans. Recreational use of the land lies under the jurisdiction of the Hoopa Valley Indian Tribal Council. When fishing in access waters, please respect all rules and regulations as set forth by the Department of Fish and Game.

With the advice and consent of the U.S. Bureau of Indian Affairs (BIA), the Hoopa Tribal Council has general jurisdiction over all resource uses and management of the reservation land, as well as river access for recreation. Recreational use is officially encouraged on tribal land. However, there are sections of the river where owners restrict access. The Tribal Council controls all access within the boundaries of the reservation. Check with the U.S. Bureau of Indian Affairs for the latest access information before venturing out.

According to some residents of the Hoopa Valley Indian Reservation, it takes the salmon seven to eight days to reach Hoopa from the ocean (less than 80 miles). Depending on water conditions, it usually takes them four days from Hoopa to reach the South Fork of the Trinity.

Hoopa Airport Road Access

A magnificent fly-fishing section of the river, with gravel bars and large pools, is accessible from a dirt road at the end of Hoopa Airport

Road. The gravel area provides space for parking at the river's edge. It is important that wherever you come across evidence of ritual functions displayed by the Native Americans, you do not disturb their sites. It is a privilege to fish in this exceptional portion of the Trinity. Please leave the area in the same condition as you found it.

State Route 96 Highway Bridge Access

Access to the river downstream of the SR 96 Bridge at Hoopa is from several routes heading directly to the river. However, my favorite route is from the Jolly Cone Hamburger stand. From SR 96, turn left after passing the Jolly Cone stand and head west for the river. If you pass the Security Pacific Bank on SR 96, you missed the turnoff road to the river. All the roads lead to the flood plain within 100 yards of the river. From there, rough spur roads head closer to the river. I refer to this area as the Oak Tree Riffle because there is a large oak tree near the river.

Trinity River at the Mouths of Supply, Hostler, and Mill Creeks

Some productive sections of the Lower Trinity near the mouths of several tributaries include Supply, Hostler, and Mill creeks. Situated in flood plains, this portion of the Trinity has excellent fly-fishing waters. Long pools, riffles, and runs are typical in the lower Trinity within the Hoopa Valley Indian Reservation. In most sections of the river, access is a short distance from the road. The entire stretch of the gravel bar at the mouth of Mill Creek on the Trinity is open. It is an excellent area for boat and fishing access.

Red Rock Access

Accessible from SR 96, the open expansive bar of Red Rock is the final access to the Trinity River before it enters Weitchpec Gorge. This last river entry site is an undeveloped area. When the salmon and steelhead reach Red Rock, it is evident because they splash, jump, and are in a playful mood. During this period, food is the last thing on their mind. It is a resting place for them after traveling upstream along the gorge through the waterfalls. When anglers have knowledge of their arrival, the area can become a circus. So the best time to attempt fishing the Red Rock area is on weekdays during early morning hours or evenings. There is a deep pool in front of Red Rock where salmon rest. Further downstream are nice riffle waters where steelhead congregate.

Access to the river at Red Rock is a little difficult to locate. Once there you'll see huge rock on the opposite side of the river with a reddish tint to it, hence, the name Red Rock. From SR 96, just before the grade climbs to Weitchpec, turn left onto a road paralleling SR 96. After

Flood plains, gravel bars, long pools, and runs—typical lower Trinity waters.

Red rock in the Trinity River.

Steelhead flies.

making the left turn, veer right and pass a group of houses on the left. Then turn left and head toward the river.

Scenic Weitchpec Gorge Waters

Red Rock is the last access before the river enters the Weitchpec Gorge. The terrain in this section of the river is quite steep and brushy. The narrow Weitchpec Gorge below Red Rock in Hoopa Valley is scenic and rugged. As you enter the gorge, steep mountainsides make river access difficult. In most stretches, the descent from SR 96 to the river is a 200- to 300-foot drop through thick trees and brushes. There are a few steep trails as well as cross-country routes along SR 96 to the river. However, finding a place to park on this two-lane road with narrow shoulders is difficult.

The gorge is a popular run for fishing from canoes and kayaks to Weitchpec. However, anglers willing to travel by foot along the mountainsides during low flow are rewarded with fishing solitude. In some reaches, prepare to scramble over large rocks, boulders, and around heavy brushy banks. This is the typical pattern along the 6.5-mile stretch of the gorge from Red Rock to its confluence with the Klamath at Weitchpec.

Purple-orange Spey fly.

Large open gravel bars, riffles, and long runs are found in the secluded gorge waters. If you wish, camping is possible on open gravel bars. It is a splendid experience to get away from the crowd during peak season.

The last access to the Trinity is from the mouth at Weitchpec. The trail, located behind the general store at Weitchpec, drops more than 200 feet to the gravel bar at the confluence of the Trinity and Klamath rivers. This is one of the most beautiful sites around, the meeting of these two impressive bodies of water.

The gravel bars along both the Trinity and the Klamath rivers are open and wide during periods of low flow. During low flow, it is a wonderful experience to see the large number of anadromous fish arriving in the area. They either continue upstream on the Klamath or enter their home waters of the Trinity. This is one of the most widely known river access sites, resulting in competition amongst anglers.

The feeling of remoteness is strong as the landscape crops the mountainsides. This area is also the last exit for boaters from the river. Although it is a difficult chore to climb the steep trail with canoes and kayaks, I hear that the unforgettable memories of traveling through one of the most scenic and secluded sections of the river make it a worthwhile trip.

Effective Fly Patterns and Tactics for the Trinity River

Productive fly patterns to work the drainage include Brindle Bugs Nos. 4 to 8, Glo Bugs, Silver Hiltons, Mossbacks, Assassins, Carey Specials, Red Ibes, and Weitchpec Witches Nos. 6 to 8. Other effective flies are Green Butted Skunks, Fall Favorites, Popsicles Nos. 4 to 6, Purple Speys Nos. 2 to 6, Dark Stone Nymphs Nos. 6 to 10, Burlaps in No. 6, Orange Stimulators, and Elk Hair Caddis' Nos. 6 to 10. Dry-fly fishing is prolific during spring hatches. Small stonefly and mayfly hatches occur during midday. To handle steelhead and trout in the Trinity use a 5- to 7-weight rod with matching floating line loaded with 150 to 175 yards of backing. The greased line technique is appropriate in many stretches of the Trinity that have medium depths, moderate current, and resting and holding places for steelhead.

The greased-line technique, also known as dry-line application, is the art of controlling or mending your line after casting across or slightly downstream as the fly hits the water. This method is to prevent the fly from sinking quickly. Mending means to lift the belly of the line in a loop to keep the current from dragging the fly down.

Part 2
Great Basin, Modoc, and Cascade Range Waters

Amidst a variety of vegetation from grasslands to high alpine terrain, a growing sport fishery has attracted adventurous anglers to the premier, secluded waters in northeastern California. Most lakes and streams situated north of the Sierra Nevada are within the Great Basin, Modoc Plateau, and Cascade Range provinces. In this region, canyons, meadows, and quaking aspens surround roadside, backcountry, and wilderness watersheds that hold quality fly-fishing waters. Miles of backcountry creeks tumble through rocky terrain, steep falls, and extravagant wildflower meadows, providing anglers with great pleasure as they fish the sparkling streams and tranquil lakes in this part of the state. Serene creeks, turbulent pocket waters, deep pools, riffle waters, flats, and still water provide an abundance of mayfly, caddisfly, stonefly, and other insect hatches to sustain a healthy trout population.

The Great Basin's principal source of angling opportunities are in the Warner Range. Other waters in the Great Basin lie in Mono Lake and the Owens River watershed in the southern juncture of eastern Sierra to the Nevada Stateline. The Modoc Plateau Province extends into Oregon and eastward into the State of Nevada. As part of the Modoc Plateau, the Warner Mountains join it on the eastern side.

The division between the Great Basin and Modoc Plateau is vague; both regions have similar characteristics. The most prominent features of this Province are typically sagebrush, volcanic rock formations, lava beds, rolling hills, forest meadows, and open range lands.

In the seldom-visited and small, mountainous terrain of the Warner Mountains and the Great Basin Province Empire's lush country, one can find many productive cold lakes and trout streams. The tributary waters of the Pit River in the Warner Mountains have ideal habitat for small rainbow, brook, and native redband trout. One can find brown trout in lower-elevation waters.

From California, the Cascade Range Province extends in a northerly direction through Oregon, Washington, and into British Columbia. Volcanic rocks dominate the Southern Cascade Range in Northern California, mostly scattered throughout Lassen National Park and Pit River country. Situated 40 miles south of the California-Oregon boundary, beautiful double cone Mt. Shasta is one of the principal attractions in the Cascade Range Province. Mt. Shasta is the largest of the Cascade volcanoes. Approximately 17 miles in diameter at its base, Mt. Shasta rises to an elevation of 14,162 feet, the highest peak in Northern California. Mud Creek, the deepest canyon on the southeast portion of the cone, produces mudflow deposits. When spring runoffs occur, mud flows from Mud Creek empty into the McCloud River. The muddy river hampers fishing during early season.

Mt. Shasta.

"Less recent craters in great numbers roughen the adjacent region; some of them with lakes in their throats, others overgrown with trees and flowers. Nature in these old hearths and firesides having literally given beauty for ashes. On the northwest side of Mount Shasta there is a subordinate cone about 3000 feet below the summit, which has been active subsequent to the breaking up of the main ice-cap that once covered the mountain, as is shown by its comparatively unwasted crater and the streams of unglaciated lava radiating from it. The main summit is about a mile and a half in diameter, bounded by small crumbling peaks and ridges, among which we seek in vain for the outlines of the ancient crater."

"Nearer the coast are the giant forests of the redwoods . . . Beneath the cool, deep shade of these majestic trees the ground is occupied by ferns, chiefly woodwardia and aspidiums, with only a few flowering plants. But all along the redwood belt there are sunny openings on hill-slopes looking to the south, where the giant trees stand back, and give the ground to the small sunflowers and the bees."

John Muir
The Mountains of California

Great Basin, Modoc, and Cascade Range

OREGON

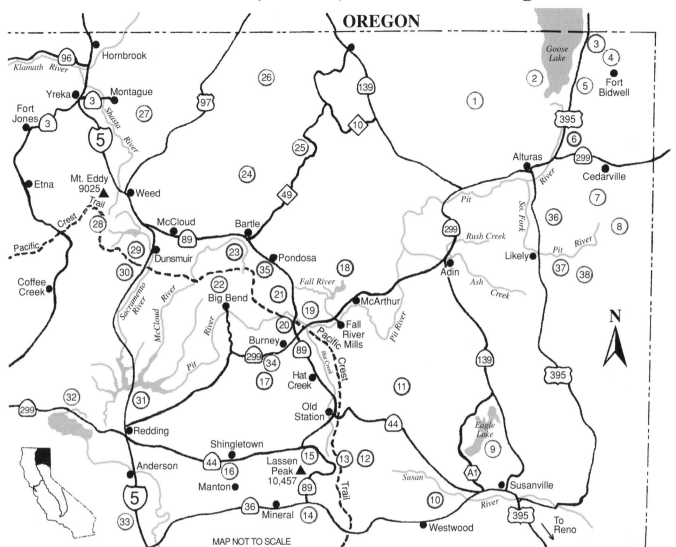

1. Modoc National Forest
2. Goose Lake
3. Cave and Lily Lakes, Dismal Creek
4. Lake Annie, Eightmile, Twelvemile, Bidwell and Mill Creeks, Fee Reservoir
5. Willow and Lassen Creeks, Briles Reservoir
6. Davis Creek, Thoms and Cedar Creeks (Cedar Pass Area SR299)
7. Warner Mountains Waters
8. South Warner Wilderness
9. Eagle Lake
10. Bizz Johnson Rail Trail
11. Lassen National Forest
12. Caribou Wilderness
13. Lassen National Park - See Lassen NFS map for detail
14. Mill Creek
15. Manzanita Lake
16. Grace and Nora Lakes
17. Thousand Lakes Wilderness - See Lassen NFS Map for Detail

18. Ahjumawi Lava Springs State Park, Big Lake and Horr Pond, Eastman Lake and Tule River
19. Shasta County Rest Area (Parking - Fishing Access)
20. McArthur-Burney Falls Memorial State Park, Burney Creek
21. Lake Britton
22. Iron Canyon Reservoir, Kosk and Nelson Creeks
23. MCloud River Loop
24. Shasta-Trinity National Forest
25. Medicine Lake Highlands - Medicine, Little Medicine and Bullseye Lakes
26. Klamath National Forest
27. Shasta Valley Wildlife Area Waters - Bass and Trout Lakes
28. Trinity Divide Country Waters
29. Lake Siskiyou
30. Castle Crags State Park
31. Shasta Lake

32. Whiskeytown Lake
33. Battle Creek
34. Hatchet Creek
35. Bear Creek
36. Fitzhugh Creek
37. West Valley Reservoir, East Creek
38. Blue Lake

USFS Maps Covering Campgrounds, road classification, trails, etc.
Northwestern Connection
Great Basin, Modoc, and Cascade Range
Northern California
1. Modoc National Forest
2. Lassen National Forest (Includes Thousand Lakes Wilderness, Caribou Wilderness, and Lassen Volcanic National Park)
3. Shasta-Trinity National Forest
4. Klamath National Forest
5. South Warner Wilderness

The southern Cascade Range offers some of the most magnificent fly-fishing waters in this region. Known as the Intermountain Region, the Cascade Range holds a self-sustaining trophy trout population as well as regularly stocked trout. Superb fishing, abundant wildlife, and the awesome beauty of the Intermountain Region will leave a fly-fisher's dream fulfilled in many ways. A host of roadside, backcountry, and wilderness lakes and numerous streams are easily accessed from one watershed to the next. One can visit several bodies of waters in a weekend and more on longer stays. Nearby camping facilities, motels, resorts, lodges, and fly and tackle shops make it convenient for anglers visiting the area.

One of the largest drainages in northeastern California is the Pit River watershed. The Native American Achomawi tribe lived along the Pit River and the Atsugewi tribe made their home along the Hat Creek and Burney Creek watersheds. The Pit is fed by a host of tributary waters from the Warner Mountains and South Warner Wilderness. It also receives flows from Rush Creek, Ash Creek, Fall River, Hat Creek, Burney Creek, Rock Creek, Clark Creek, Hatchet Creek, Nelson Creek, Kosk Creek, and other smaller feeder streams.

The Pit River, McCloud River, Upper Sacramento River, and their tributary waters provide exquisite fly-fishing waters. These major tributary waters enter Shasta Lake at the northern end of the Sacramento Valley. Lakes and streams from these river systems host a wide variety of trophy, native, and stocked rainbows, as well as anadromous fisheries in the Lower Sacramento River. Early season anglers can wet their appetite in many lower-elevation waters. Throughout the summer, springs supply cool waters to this river system to sustain excellent angling opportunities. The varied topography and species of fish in the watersheds offer many challenging opportunities for novice as well as experienced fly-fishers.

Fishing opportunities do not end with the waters in this part of the state. The lesser-known lakes and streams also provide a selection of premium trout waters in the Pit, McCloud, and Sacramento River drainages. By taking advantage of these waters, angling pressure can be diverted from overused streams.

Quaking aspen.

Mill Creek falls.

Gateway to Great Basin Empire and Surrounding Waters

Fascinating geological formations are prominent in northeastern California. The Warner Mountains in the Great Basin Province merge with the Modoc Plateau Province in the eastern border of Modoc National Forest. Rock formations in the Cascade Range include beds of debris and sediment from early eruptions in the Cascades. Hot springs are abundant as volcanoes once dominated the area. Significant Gold Rush activities occurred in Modoc County from 1905 to 1912. This is the period when the Native Americans valued obsidian. The most notable area is the Highgrade Mining District near the north end of the Warner Mountains.

The Great Basin Province Empire includes water of the Warner Range east of Alturas and Surprise Valley. Portions of Nevada, Oregon, Idaho, and Utah are part of the Great Basin Province. The species of fish vary in the Great Basin in northeastern California, ranging from brook, redband, and rainbow trout. However, Eagle Lake trout inhabit the basin's southern surrounding waters of Eagle Lake in the Lahontan Region.

Eagle Lake trout become hefty trophy trout by foraging on tui chubs. The coarseraker tui chub (*Siphateles bicolor obesus*) is abundant along shorelines of lakes. Their principal locations are in the east slope of the Sierra Nevada drainages north of Mono County. These members of the minnow family frequently travel in large schools and can attain lengths over six inches. During spring and fall, trout move and congregate along the warmer shorelines feeding on tui chubs. As the water warms during summer months, trout move offshore and retreat to deeper and colder waters. Spring and fall months are the best time to fish along the shorelines.

Exploring the Intimate Warner Mountains

Situated in the extreme northeastern corner of California, Modoc National Forest offers a host of opportunities for anglers to sample many lakes and streams. Bounded by Surprise Valley to the east and the headwaters of the Pit River drainage to the west, the Warner Mountains are the main geographic features. A double fault created the Warner Mountains and Surprise Valley

The Warner Mountains and Cascades are home to red-band trout.

when the mountains rose and the valley dropped. Moderate slopes encompass the western portion of the mountains while the eastern slope is extremely steep. The Warners extend 80 miles from north to south and are 10 miles in width.

State Route 299 (Cedar Pass) divides the mountain ranges into two sections, north and south. Situated in the southern portion of the Warner Mountains, secluded South Warner Wilderness provides adventurous opportunities for fly-fishers. Elevations range from 5,805 feet at Clear Lake to 9,892 feet at Eagle Peak.

Below the Warner Mountains at the eastern border of the forest, the setting in Surprise Valley is a rich, fertile farmland with cattle ranches. In earlier years, the entire valley was a huge lake. Through the years, the lake became three small lakes known as Upper Lake, Middle Alkali Lake, and Lower Lake. They stretch from Fort Bidwell south to the Modoc-Lassen County line. Having no outlets, these lakes are called playas. Waters remaining in a playa contain minerals and salts that have dissolved. These lakes receive waters from creeks flowing out of the eastern slope of Warner Mountains.

U.S. 395 south from the Oregon border, U.S. 395 north from Reno, Nevada, and SR 299 east out of Redding are the principal routes to reach the Warner Mountain lakes and streams. Some prime waters require 4WD vehicles to reach destinations. In many instances, it is advantageous to hike along streams to locate the best trout holding waters. Please check with the Forest Service Ranger offices for road conditions during early and late season.

This wild country, located in the eastern portion of Modoc National Forest, is filled with historical areas where pioneer settlers, fur trappers, immigrants, and Native Americans crossed paths. The Warner Mountains, for example, received their name in memory of Captain W. H. Warner of the U.S. Army Corps of Engineers. In 1849, Captain Warner was killed while examining routes from Humboldt Valley in Nevada to the Sacramento River. At the height of hostilities between the immigrants and Native American tribes (Pits, Modocs, Wintuns, and other tribes from the region), immigrants were massacred on their journey to Oregon and California during the Gold Rush days.

One famous incident that occurred in Modoc County during the early 1850s was the Fandango Massacre. According to the story, as the weather grew terribly cold one night in a small valley, the immigrants danced a Spanish fandango to keep warm. While they were dancing and celebrating their success in crossing Lassen Pass, a band of Native Americans surprised and massacred the immigrant party.

News of the devastating massacre reached the commander stationed at Fort Bidwell. Fort Bidwell was a safe haven for the settlers. A Calvary was sent to the encampment and the attack against the Native Americans was successful. The site of the massacre occurred in Fandango Valley near the headwaters section of Willow Creek. In 1849, members of the "Wolverine Rangers," named the valley Fandango Valley. Fandango Peak (7,732 feet) and Fandango Pass (6,155 feet) also received their names from the same incident.

Upper, Middle, and Lower Alkali lakes in Surprise Valley receive waters from the eastern slope of North Warner Mountains. However, the gentle rolling topography of the western slope holds an abundance of streams draining into Goose Lake and the Pit River. The lush, forested creeks flowing around aspen trees and winding through canyons and meadows are laced with scurrying mayflies and stoneflies. Caddis activity is visible in the clear waters fed by springs. It is a challenge to lure rainbow, brown, and brook trout from out behind strewn boulders, underneath logjams, and undercut banks scoured by heavy runoffs.

The wild, pure, and indigenous redband rainbow trout that inhabits the Great Basin is distributed in tributary waters of Goose Lake drainage and the Pit River in the North and South Warner mountains. In the Goose Lake drainage, the three major tributaries holding Goose Lake redband trout are Lassen, Willow, and Cottonwood creeks. These spring-fed creeks have been closed to fishing for several years. Recently, these three streams opened with a special regulation of zero limits and the use of artificial lures with barbless hooks. The longest stream with the best access is Lassen Creek.

The rainbow palette of the pure Warner redband trout is similar to the cutthroat's except it lacks the red slash marks beneath the jaw. Also, the red stripe on the side is wider. These beautiful rainbows can be found in Clear Lake, Mill Creek, which feeds the lake, and East Creek, to name a few.

Headwater streams originating out of the South Warner Wilderness flow into South Fork Pit River at Jess Valley. The wilderness also holds some of the most rewarding fishing experiences in this northeastern corner of the state. However, do not overlook roadside lakes and streams west of the Warner Mountains in the Pit River drainage.

North Warner Mountains Lakes and Streams

An amazing variety of lakes and streams lie within the North Warner Mountains north of SR 299. Countless mountain streams worthy of pursuit drain into Surprise Valley and the Pit River. Lakes and streams scattered in this northern sector include Twelve Mile Creek, Pine Creek, Lily and Cave lakes, Bidwell Creek, Mill Creek, Briles Reservoir, Buck Creek, and Davis Creek. Most waters in the northern Warner Mountains receive very little angler pressure. Campgrounds along South Fork Davis Creek and Lily and Cave lakes offer excellent access to other waters in the region.

The 7- to 12-foot-deep Lily Lake (6,000 feet) and Cave Lake (6,450 feet) with depths ranging from 14 to 21 feet are accessible from Highgrade Road near the Oregon border. Motorboats are not allowed on these two lakes. Lying 80 to 120 feet in a depression, Cave Lake may have dangerous underwater currents. Be cautious and practice safety measures when fishing Cave Lake. The lake received its name because a large cave is visible on the water's edge at one end of the lake.

South Warner Mountains Lakes and Streams

Below the peaks of Squaw, Warren, and Eagle of the South Warner Wilderness and surrounding mountains outside the wilderness are many tributary waters of the South Fork Pit River. Lakes and streams in this region are accessible by vehicle, hiking, horseback, or llama services. As tributary waters tumble through this mountainous region and into the valley floor south of Alturas, fly-fishers have many opportunities to fish most trout waters. A few sample waters anglers can explore in the South Warner Mountains outside the wilderness area are Parker Creek, Shields Creek, Pine Creek,

Fitzhugh Creek, East Creek, Blue Lake, and South Fork Pit River. The South Fork Pit and its tributaries offers excellent fly-fishing waters before flowing into the main stem near Alturas. As the main stem continues its course through agricultural lands west of Alturas, it accumulates additional water before entering Shasta Lake north of Redding.

Unspoiled South Warner Wilderness

Lying along the Warner Mountains of the Modoc National Forest, 70,400-acre South Warner Wilderness contains a mixture of rolling hills, expansive vistas, and mountain meadows. Some unique features include rugged topography, clear streams, and several of the highest peaks in northeastern California. Eagle Peak (9,892 feet), Warren Peak (9,710 feet), and Squaw Peak (8,646 feet) are visible landmarks in the wilderness. The South Warner Wilderness, an isolated spur of the Cascade Range, situated in the eastern portion of Modoc National Forest, is located 23 miles east of Alturas off U.S. 395.

The South Warner Wilderness offers a broad landscape of high-desert sagebrush and massive cliffs. Past glaciations are evident in higher elevations and Patterson Lake is one example of a glaciation-formed lake. The wilderness is filled with many species of trout inhabiting glacial lakes along grassy meadows and small enchanting streams.

Lakes and streams in the wilderness are accessible from seven major trailheads. These trails range from flat and open to steep and challenging terrain. Pepperdine, Pine Creek, Mill Creek Falls,

East Creek—Great Basin waters.

East Creek, Patterson, Emerson, and Bear Camp Flat trailheads are primary entry points for wilderness travelers.

Patterson Lake

The second most heavily used trailheads in the South Warner Wilderness is Pepperdine. This trailhead is accessible from the northern sector of the wilderness. It is equipped with a staging area and camping facilities. Within an hour's drive from Alturas out of County Road 56 and Parker Creek Road, the trailhead offers limited parking facilities and an area with horse corrals. The Pepperdine Trailhead has a campground for those who wish to camp the night before making an early start along the trail to Patterson Lake. This long, moderate west side Summit Trail traverses through flat open country before reaching 9,040-foot Patterson Lake located below Warren Peak. One can continue south and west by joining the Pine Creek Trail from Patterson Lake to enter the Pine Creek Basin.

Pine Creek Basin

The Pine Creek Basin Trailhead is the third most used facility. It is reachable by traveling east from Alturas on County Road 56 and West Warner Road. The moderate trail traverses alongside the creek. It enters the large expansive Pine Creek Basin. The basin provides an opportunity for anglers to fish for wild redband, rainbow, and brook trout. Small spring creek nymphs and dry flies are the most effective patterns to entice the trout to strike in this spring-fed stream.

Fitzhugh Creek

A tributary to the South Fork Pit River, Fitzhugh Creek originates from springs west of the Warner Mountains. The North Fork begins its course out of South Warner Wilderness above 8,000 feet. A major portion of Fitzhugh Creek meanders through steep, brushy, vegetated canyons and descends approximately 20 miles before flowing into the South Fork Pit River.

Three access routes from U.S. 395 south of Alturas lead to Fitzhugh Creek located in U.S. Bureau of Land Management (BLM) areas. At each destination, short hikes down the canyon will reward anglers with rainbow and brown trout inhabiting the cool waters of this spring creek. This secluded stream offers excellent fishing destinations for those willing to hike down the canyon for large brown trout. Sagebrush, grassy meadows, ponderosa pine, and willows heavily line most of the banks. The best method to fish Fitzhugh is to follow the streambed from access trails. Because paths are rough and muddy during early season, four-wheel-drive vehicles are recommended to gain entry.

The best means of reaching this BLM meadow watershed within a canyon rim of Fitzhugh Creek is from Little Juniper Reservoir Road. The second access route out of U.S. 395 is the French and Payne reservoirs roads. Upstream water in this section of Fitzhugh Creek lies in deep, rocky canyons with heavy vegetation. Another entry location is out of Pine Creek Boulevard to Pine Creek Reservoir. After passing the reservoir, continue on this route until you reach the end of the BLM property. Work the stream with small nymphs and dry-fly patterns, keeping in mind smaller insects are typical residents of these spring creeks.

Clear Lake

The Mill Creek Falls Trailhead is a short, moderate hike to Clear Lake (5,805 feet). This hike is breathtaking, and one can observe spectacular Mill Creek Falls by taking a side trail to the falls area.

The trailhead is accessible by heading east from Alturas, Likely, Jess Valley, and the West Warner Road. If you wish to opt for a short, one-day hike to Clear Lake, parking facilities are available at Mill Creek Campground near the trailhead. This is convenient for an early start.

It is worth hiking the moderate one-half mile to Clear Lake from the trailhead at Mill Creek Falls Campground. This lake, with upright, fallen, and flooded timbers, offers sanctuaries for the trout. It is situated in a remote section of the South Warner Wilderness east of Likely. Clear Lake is a 150-year-old lake formed when a landslide filled part of a deep canyon. The brushy shorelines and dropoffs make it difficult to cover the waters effectively, so a pack-in float tube is the best method to fish the lake. This small lake, surrounded by forested mountains, holds resident redband rainbow, rainbow, brook, and brown trout.

Emerson Lakes

Emerson Trailhead to North Emerson (7,740 feet) and South Emerson (7,950 feet) lakes is accessible near Eagleville from the eastern side of the wilderness. It is approximately one and a half hour's drive from Alturas on SR 299 to Cedarville and County Road 1 (Surprise Valley Road) south to Eagleville. The final several miles of dirt road to the trailhead are steep and rough. It is extremely slippery when wet. North and South Emerson lakes are also accessible from the southern entry at Patterson Meadow. The access road to this trailhead is out of Blue Lake. The Emerson lakes hold brook, rainbow, and Eagle Lake trout. However, rainbow and brown trout dominate Emerson Creek.

Hike-in Clear Lake.

Caribou Sanctuaries and Eagle Lake's Elusive Trout

The varied topography of Caribou Wilderness, Pine Creek Valley, and Eagle Lake Basin of Lassen County provides a wide spectrum of sparkling fly-fishing waters amongst gentle, rolling, forested plateaus and desert-like landscapes. Limited white and red fir on slopes and lodgepole pine on flat lands are outstanding features surrounding lakes and streams in this part of the country.

Known as the "cold desert," areas lying east of the Cascade Range experience hot, dry summers and cold winters. Upon arrival in the Lahontan Region, sagebrush is the predominant plant of the region. This plant is prevalent when one is driving along SR 299 East from Fall River Mills and U.S. 395 north of Susanville. Eagle Lake and other nearby waters lie within the region.

Caribou Santuaries

Wilderness, Backcountry, and Roadside Waters

Forested landscapes fringe the serene lakes of volcanic and glacial origin in the Caribou Wilderness. One can see crater peaks, cinder cones, and numerous depressions scattered throughout the region. The most prominent peaks are Red Cinder (8,375 feet), North Caribou (7,793 feet), South Caribou (7,767 feet), and Black Cinder Rock (7,760 feet). Other surrounding volcanic peaks above 7,000 feet are Black Butte, Bogard Buttes, Swain Mountain, Mt. Harkness, Red Cinder Cone, and Ash Butte.

Mill Creek below Clear Lake.

Headwaters of Pine Creek and the Susan River originate from the northern sector of Caribou Wilderness. However, lakes and streams located in the southern part of the wilderness are in the North Fork Feather River drainage. Brook, native, and stocked rainbow trout provide quality fishing to those willing to hike in to the wilderness. The 55-foot-deep Triangle Lake (7,100 feet) and Feather River drainage lakes such as Eleanor, Jewel, Gem, Emerald, and the five Hidden lakes are the most popular waters frequented by anglers. Other distant lakes are reachable by horse pack or foot travel if one wishes to set up base camp inside the wilderness. Turnaround Lake, (7,000 feet) with a depth of 38 feet, is another watershed to explore.

Three entry points with well-maintained trails provide access into Caribou Wilderness: Northern, eastern, and southern entries. The eastern entry has camping and parking facilities at the wilderness boundary. This is the best route to reach a group of nearby lakes. Inside the wilderness, anglers can head north to Triangle and Turnaround lakes or south to other Feather River drainage watersheds.

At the eastern entry, Caribou and Silver lakes—headwaters of the Susan River—are two roadside waters outside the wilderness providing a variety of trout species. Regularly stocked with brown, rainbow, and Eagle Lake trout, eight-foot-deep Caribou Lake (6,620 feet) offers a variety of excellent fishing opportunities for boaters and shore anglers. For the best results, boaters should concentrate along the northern part of the lake. Silver Lake (6,480 feet) with a maximum depth of 72 feet, is a windy and moody lake. When heavy winds come up during midmorning, fishing activity ceases. Therefore, anglers should fish the lake from 6:00 to 9:00 a.m. with dark Woolly Buggers and other streamer patterns. Silver Lake, one of the 10 lakes with the same name in California, holds a large brown trout fishery. Be prepared to also battle with Eagle Lake trout that have been stocked here.

Secluded Pine Creek

Flowing 38 miles from its headwaters in the Caribou Wilderness, Pine Creek empties into Eagle Lake near Spalding Tract. However, during summer and fall, no amount of water flow in the lower portion of Pine Creek ever reaches its destination. Review the Department of Fish and Game regulations for stream closure in lower Pine Creek flowing into Eagle Lake. Fly-fishing for brook trout in the upper stretches of Pine Creek is at its best in the early season. The most accessible route to reach Pine Creek is at Upper Stephens Meadows and Pine Creek Valley. Work the stream for brook trout with dark nymphs and olive pupae in Nos. 12 to 14 near Bogard Campground at Pine Creek Valley west of SR 44. Mayflies and caddis are prolific in this small stream. Present these fly patterns to fish hiding behind rocks, fallen tree limbs, or other obstructions.

Crater Lake

One extraordinary brook trout impoundment anglers may wish to visit in this lava-strewn country is Crater Lake (6,852 feet). The 45- to 73-foot-deep lake drops several hundred feet in elevation from its highest point into a depression. This small lake is best fished from a float tube or boat. However, when the water level drops in the fall, one can cast from shore to spawning brook trout cruising near the shorelines.

Be on the lookout for early-season snow. I recall a fall trip to Crater Lake during the latter part of October, shortly after unexpected precipitation and found snow on the road and shore-lines. I had difficulty tying on a fly with frozen fingers (left my gloves at home). It was quite an experience hooking onto a couple of 10-inch fish. Early fall is the ideal time to visit Crater Lake. A Forest Service campground next to the lake is a convenient facility for longer stays. Crater Lake is 7 miles east of SR 44 north of Pine Creek Valley.

Nearby 5- to 17-foot deep Long Lake (5,692 feet), located off SR 44, is a great early season watershed. Situated along marshland, wading is limited. However, anglers will have more success with the use of float tubes or small watercraft. This lake holds brook and Eagle Lake trout.

Elusive Eagle Lake Trout: A Fly Fisher's Aspiration

Eagle Lake, known to the natives as Lake Acapsukati, was once a sleeper in the fly-fishing world. However, that has changed through the years. This highly alkaline freshwater lake with over 100 miles of shoreline is a popular haven for fly-fishers as they stalk the strong football-shaped rainbows. The special species of Eagle Lake rainbow trout (*Oncorhynchus gairdnerii aquilarum*), a sub-species of the rainbow trout, is native only to Eagle Lake and Pine Creek in Lassen County. In 1917, J. O. Snyder described the trout, and it was named *aquilarum* after the Latin name for eagle.

Ancient Acapsukati, or Eagle Lake, is a remnant of the prehistoric inland sea formed in the Lahontan Lake System. Hinga Sim Mohm Dohnim is another name for Eagle Lake in the Maidu language meaning the Forbidding Lake.

Irregular in shape, Eagle Lake is divided into three bodies of serene crystal waters connected by channels. Bordered by sagebrush hills in semi-arid desert, the northern section averages six feet in depth and the middle section has a depth up to 10 feet. The southern section, situated in lush pine forest, reaches a maximum depth of 92 feet.

Lying in an isolated valley 17 miles north of Susanville, road access to the lake is from SR 139 and County Road A1 north of SR 36. At 5,100 feet, Eagle Lake is the second largest natural body of water lying entirely within California, Clear Lake in Lake County being the largest. Sea snails—which date back to Prehistoric times—and tui chub minnows up to 18 inches, are found in this basin. Pine Creek, the primary tributary stream, provides most of the water supply into Eagle Lake.

In the past, fishing in this much-abused lake has not always been up to par. During the late 1940s, the Eagle Lake trout nearly became extinct. In the early 1950s, poaching, water diversions, poor water quality, among other things pushed the exotic fish to near extinction. As a result of the efforts of the California Department of Fish and Game's management program, a few female spawners were collected at the mouth of Pine Creek. An artificial propagation program was undertaken by establishing an egg-taking station at the creek. Through the years, the department managed to rear the trout at the Crystal Lake Hatchery. When the trout attained the weight of one pound, they were annually released into the lake. The trout grew up to 20 inches or more, weighing four pounds in less than a year. The rehabilitation of Eagle Lake trout has been very successful. In recent years, the

Eagle Lake.

Eagle Lake rainbow.

fishery has increased from near nothing to one of California's and the West's most outstanding trophy trout fisheries. However, in recent years, the fish have begun to decline again due to various environmental factors.

The native rainbow is the only trout known to survive in this highly alkaline freshwater lake, which lies within a closed basin. However, much of the Eagle Lake trout has been successfully introduced into waters of Butte, Del Norte, Humboldt, Lassen, Modoc, Mono, Plumas, Shasta, Siskiyou, Tehama, and Trinity counties.

Although Acapsukati's season runs from the Saturday preceding Memorial Day through December 31, fly-fishing can be tough and frustrating. Catching these rainbows is a challenge in this complex body of water. When hooked, they will speed off like a runaway truck and fight like a steelhead fresh from the ocean. However, an understanding of the diversity of the water, its temperament, and habitat will enhance one's chances of success. From mid June to late September, trout move to deeper waters at the southern end. In the fall, trout return to shallower water at the northern sector of the lake. This area hosts from 15 feet to over 100 feet of tule patches, providing excellent coverage for the fish.

Fly-fishing reaches its peak in October and tule beds are prime areas for productive fishing. Voracious and elusive rainbows are often seen cruising along shorelines in early evening foraging for food in this quality stillwater fishery. Early morning and late afternoon to dark are best bets when trout are concentrating on schools of tui chubs, particularly along the outer perimeter of tule beds. The most productive boating areas are in the upper lake between Rocky, Buck, and Troxel points. Best shore fishing areas are along the coves above Wildcat Point, between Christie and Merrill campgrounds.

Wading or float tubing along the western shoreline where tule patches are thick, from the airstrip at Spalding Tract to Pelican Point, is very productive. One can also hike toward Pelican Point in the early evening for hungry trout cruising the shorelines in search of tui chubs, shrimp, leeches, and snails.

Stillwater fishing is generally at its best when the mercury dips and the weather is inclement. During this period, trout usually inhabit the shallows to attack the chubs by the mouthful. Cold, overcast, breezy days or when skies threaten rain are the best time to expect blockbusting action. Acapsukati can be moody and treacherous when strong winds appear. It is essential to head for shore, or the nearest shelter at the first hint of oncoming wind. We were surprised by one of these squalls. Fortunately, we were close to shore escaping any type of disaster. A nearby grove of trees provided excellent shelter for us until the heavy winds subsided.

Fifty-five percent of the basin surrounding Eagle Lake is administered by the BLM. The lands lie primarily on the east and north shores of the lake. Camping, a resort, lodging, food, guides, and boat rental services are available at the lake. The U.S. Forest Service and BLM also provide camping facilities at both the north and south shores of the lake. Boat launching is located at Stone's Landing (north shore), Spalding Tract (west shore), and the southern end of the lake at Gallatin Beach.

Food Sources, Flies, Tackle, and Presentations

To successfully fly-fish for native trophy trout averaging two to six pounds, a variety of gear is needed to accommodate most situations. The most critical component of your outfit will be the selection of lines. Although floating lines in six- or seven-weights work well along the tule beds, I have experienced productive results with Scientific Anglers Wet Cel Weight Forward Monocore line in slightly deeper water. This slow sink-rate line has a clear, slick finish that becomes invisible in the water. Long 12-foot leaders tapered to 3X or 4X tippets are ideal setups.

The best stillwater presentation for these large rainbows is to have a direct connection to the fly without slack in the line. Use a

Eagle Lake general store.

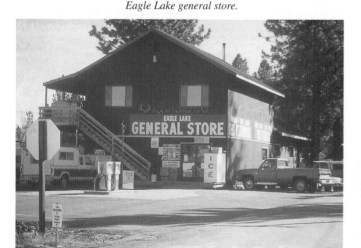

Gulls in search of fish.

Casting to tules in Eagle Lake.

to Lassen Youth Camp area, and sections of the eastern shore on SR 139. Fly-fishing selections of stillwater should revolve around principle trout food sources such as minnow and leech imitations. Woolly Buggers, and leech patterns in olive, brown, dark and light cinnamon, purple, white, and black are effective. I suggest that you modify several deadly Woolly Bugger patterns with palmered hackles, sizes 4 and 6 (3X long):

- White crystal chenille body with white marabou tail.
- White crystal chenille body with rust or dark brown marabou head and tail.
- Rust or burnt orange crystal chenille body with rust marabou head and tail.
- Olive crystal chenille body, palmered with olive hackle and olive marabou tail.
- Add a few strands of rust-colored crystal hair to all marabou tails.

Susan River and Bizz Johnson Rail Trail

Northeastern California has other exciting trout waters that make the pilgrimage a worthy adventure. Hardy anglers will find many challenging attractions along various sections of Upper, Middle, and Lower Susan River. The Susan River holds a population of native fish. However, during early season the river receives occasional supplemental plants of brown, rainbow, and Eagle Lake trout from the Department of Fish and Game. Spring and early summer are prime times to fish the Susan River before water temperatures rise during the summer months.

slow erratic retrieve to imitate a leech's swimming movement to attract the trout's attention. Another action used to imitate a tui chub minnow is to strip the line in slowly with an overhand movement and pump the rod up and down. Always be alert to detect strikes because the take is usually very subtle.

With a boat you can successfully cast to edges of tule beds with a T-200 or T-300 Teeny Nymph line. In addition, an extra-fast sink-tip and Scientific Anglers Uniform Type IV sinking line will sink fast to eliminate any slack during periods of wave action in deeper waters. This will increase your chances for more hookups. Use the countdown method to locate the depth of feeding trout. When the fly lands on the water, start to count slowly to a designated number and begin to retrieve. If there are no hits after several casts, let the fly sink deeper and count to a higher number until strikes begin to occur. Another alternative is to change to a different sink-rate line to locate the correct feeding depths. Once found, recast several times and continue the counting process. When the feeding level is verified, vary the retrieve technique for consistent strikes.

Tules, along the western shore in the northwest corner below the Cinder Pits between Pine Creek and Rocky Point, hosts abundant trout food sources. Other areas providing rich food sources are Troxel and Little Troxel on the northeast side of the upper lake

Susan River.

Jeff Blunden with an Eagle Lake trout.

Susan River originates from springs out of Cooper Swamp near Silver Lake, Caribou Lake, and continues its course through valleys, forests, rugged Susan River Canyon, Susanville, and empties into alkali Honey Lake. Except for a stretch of stream in the Clover Valley area, portions of Susan River are accessible by vehicle from Caribou Lake to Westwood Junction.

Middle Susan River features one of the nation's most successful Rails to Trails projects. The 26-mile-long hiking, biking, and equestrian Bizz Johnson Trail crosses the Susan River 11 times on original railroad bridges and trestles. It also passes through two tunnels, 450 and 800 feet long—quite an interesting and unique trail for fly-fishing excursions.

The trail received its name in honor of Harold T. "Bizz" Johnson who served in the U. S. House of Representatives from 1958 to 1980. As a former Member of Congress, Johnson was instrumental in the establishment of this project. It follows the old Westwood railroad line along the scenic Susan River Canyon from Susanville to Westwood. Most trails pass through forested woodlands, adjacent rivers, and rugged canyons, providing views of the remnants of the railroad and logging days. Along this stretch, a variety of trailheads with shuttles are accessible without backtracking.

Upstream from Susanville, the Susan River has remarkable fishing. Near the Bizz Johnson Trail, it has 11 miles of stream frontage access. The best fly-fishing waters are within the six miles of river flowing through flats and canyons between Goumaz and Devils Corral. The river is accessible at Goumaz (four miles from SR 44 on Forest Service Road 30N03) and Devils Corral off SR 36 (10 miles west of Susanville).

In Susanville, spring and early summer are also the most productive times to fish for native rainbow and brown trout in the Susan River. Fly patterns such as Hare's Ears, Cream Caddis Pupas, emergers, and Elk Hair Caddis, Nos. 10 to 14, work well throughout the Susan River.

Hiking, horseback riding, backpacking, and mountain biking are also popular means of travel for reaching fishing destinations. The trail surface consists of a three percent grade composed of aggregate material. Regardless of your mode of travel along the trail, exercise caution when crossing planks and decked bridges and when traveling through unlighted tunnels. If you wish to avoid the tunnels, trails along the river provide alternative routes.

Located southeast of Clover Valley, Susan River's McCoy Flat Reservoir offers excellent fly-fishing opportunities when conditions are right. This little-known productive reservoir, with depths of 9 to 13 feet, is subject to periodic low or diminished water supplies making it unfishable at times. When the reservoir is fishable, the trout's principal diet consists of caddisflies, callibaetis mayflies, shrimp, and damselflies. Large and strong-fighting Eagle Lake rainbow and brook trout will succumb to fly patterns representing the rich food sources of McCoy Flat Reservoir. Small boats or float tubes allow anglers to cover productive waters.

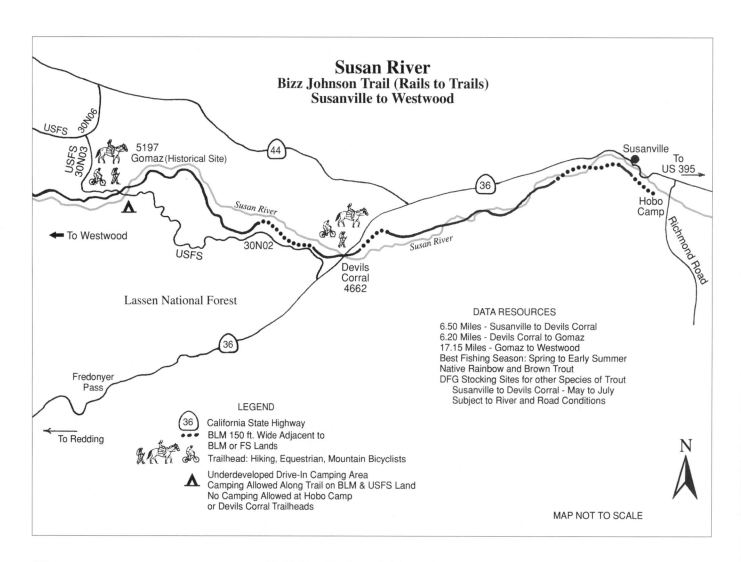

Susan River
Bizz Johnson Trail (Rails to Trails)
Susanville to Westwood

USFS 30N06

USFS 30N03

5197 Gomaz (Historical Site)

44

Susanville

To US 395

36

Hobo Camp

Richmond Road

Susan River

30N02

Devils Corral 4662

Susan River

To Westwood

USFS

Lassen National Forest

36

Fredonyer Pass

To Redding

DATA RESOURCES
6.50 Miles - Susanville to Devils Corral
6.20 Miles - Devils Corral to Gomaz
17.15 Miles - Gomaz to Westwood
Best Fishing Season: Spring to Early Summer
Native Rainbow and Brown Trout
DFG Stocking Sites for other Species of Trout
    Susanville to Devils Corral - May to July
    Subject to River and Road Conditions

LEGEND
36 California State Highway
••• BLM 150 ft. Wide Adjacent to BLM or FS Lands
Trailhead: Hiking, Equestrian, Mountain Bicyclists
▲ Underdeveloped Drive-In Camping Area
Camping Allowed Along Trail on BLM & USFS Land
No Camping Allowed at Hobo Camp
or Devils Corral Trailheads

N

MAP NOT TO SCALE

Adventurous Modoc and Cascade Province Waters

Native Americans and pioneer settlers are all part of the history of the wild volcanic rock landscape of Pit River Country. Fur trappers and early homesteaders opened up California's fertile valleys and gold fever land in the Modoc Plateau and Cascade provinces. They traveled from the north and east by following several trails through northeastern California. The Lassen Trail and Noble Road were among the two best-known routes. Immigrant Danish pioneer Peter Lassen blazed the hazardous Lassen Trail, scene of many Native American ambushes. Lassen Volcanic National Park received its name from Peter Lassen.

The Modoc Plateau and Cascade provinces, known as the Intermountain Region, hosts one of the largest river systems in northeastern California, the Pit River. Located east of Redding in Modoc, Siskiyou, and Shasta counties, this region is one of the most unspoiled areas in this part of the country. Winding through prime agricultural, timber, and wilderness country, the Pit River drainage is home to a wide selection of premier trout waters ranging from small intimate streams to a large raging river. This drainage offers irresistible natural and man-made lakes and countless miles of coldwater streams for fly-fishers in pursuit of prime trout waters.

Modoc and Cascade country holds plenty of wild and stocked trout in upper- and lower-elevation waters. During low and average water flows before snow runoffs, and again late in the fall, the streams are easy to wade. However, some sections are hazardous and difficult to wade, demanding the use of staff. The bottom is mostly gravel with slippery rocks and boulders.

Treasures of Modoc and Pit River Country

Modoc and Pit River country holds one of the wildest streams of the west, providing pristine angling paradise throughout the region. East of Fall River, the upper basin is a broad, semi-arid plateau with lava beds situated below isolated mountains rising from the east. Elevations vary from 4,000 to 5,000 feet. In the lower basin, the region consists of steep ridges, heavy pine, and fir forests.

On early maps, the Pit River was mistakenly named Pitt's River for the British Prime Minister William Pitt. In the early years, the English companies commonly financed fur-trapping expeditions in this area. However, its true name probably derived from the Pit River Native Americans. They were the only tribe to dig pits for trapping game. According to California poet Joaquin Miller in the 19th century, the traps were dangerous because they were 10 to 15 feet deep and small at the mouth. It was impossible for anything to escape once it had fallen into the trap.

The Pit River winds through Modoc, Lassen, and Shasta counties for nearly 200 river miles, interspersing with flatlands, rugged country, scenic and impassable canyons, and several PG&E hydro projects before entering Shasta Lake. To the northwest, Mt. Shasta (14,162 feet) dominates the horizon while Mt. Lassen and its range serves as a scenic backdrop.

A number of delightful lakes and streams of the Pit River country in the Intermountain Region offers a diversity of intimate settings for beginners as well as experienced fly-fishers. This part of the state holds some of the best waters within close proximity of each other for fly-fishers of various abilities. Beginner fly-fishers can sample the waters of smaller tributaries and lakes, such as Burney Creek, Hatchet Creek, Upper Hat Creek, and year-round stillwater fishing at Baum Lake. Experienced fly-fishers can select the Manzanita Lake, the fast pocket waters in the canyon of the Pit below Lake Britton, meadow stretches and riffle waters of Hat Creek, or the deep runs of Fall River. A variety of trout species: rainbow, brown, brook, and Eagle Lake trout thrive in these waters.

Other tributary waters providing excellent trout waters should not be overlooked. Rush Creek, Ash Creek, Kosk Creek, Clark Creek, Nelson Creek, and Iron Canyon Reservoir, to name a few, also support a unique trout population.

Wild and Challenging Pit River

The Pit is known as one of Northern California's most treacherous trophy trout waters. Swift water—wide in most sections—large crevices between rocks, sharp edges on some, and fast waters flowing around huge boulders make wading extremely difficult. While landmarks such as rocks and boulders break the flow, they provide plenty of holding and sheltered pocket waters for healthy wild robust rainbows and browns. Keep in mind that fast, torrential waters, slippery boulders of varied sizes, and heavy vegetation growth are a few of the rough features to consider when wading in this river system. Do not attempt to wade the Pit without understanding the anatomy of a stream, fast-water wading, and the potential danger of the deep and swift pocket waters in this freestone river.

In many sections of the Pit, anglers must have a good sense of balance, physical endurance, chest-high waders, felt-sole wading boots or stream cleats, and an extra-strong wading staff or metal ski pole with the bottom rubber gasket removed to maneuver around rock formations on the river. Think of the wading staff as a third leg to help you balance in strong fast-moving currents. With its limited access in most parts, geological features, and difficult wading around the swift currents in the Pit, angler pressure is light.

Pit River is the longest arm of the Sacramento River flowing into Shasta Lake. The drainage is known to be a rewarding and demanding river for fly-fishers. Originating on the western slope of the Warner Mountains near 4,800 to 5,000 feet, the Fork Pit River begins its course from springs, Russell Slough, and other nearby waters south of Goose Lake and the hamlet of Davis Creek. The North Fork meanders south until it merges with the confluence of the South Fork at Alturas. The South Fork Pit River gathers its waters from tributaries out of the western slope of the South Warner Wilderness Mountains and tumbles down into Jess Valley before being diverted into channels to Alturas.

The prime time to fish the Warners is from mid-June to early October. Pheasant Tail and A.P. Black nymphs, Hare's Ears, and Zug Bugs in Nos. 14 to 18 are my most consistent producers. The deadly combination of pheasant fibers and peacock herl tantalizes the trout into striking.

South Fork Pit River

Lakes and streams in the South Fork Pit River drainage provide excellent trout waters with little angler pressure. Situated east of Likely near Jess Valley, the South Fork Pit River has a population of browns and rainbows. This section of the stream offers fishing en route to the Warner Mountains.

The South Fork holds a variety of water from deep, wide slow-moving to meandering shallow riffles. However, its flow is regulated from water releases out of West Valley Reservoir. Depending on the winter, in some years the water may get muddy in the early season. In this area, many watercourses lie within private ownership lands, so pay attention to where you access the waters.

Blue Lake

Lassen County's exquisite 160-acre Blue Lake (6,067 feet) is located approximately 15 miles east of Likely in the South Warner Mountains. Jess Valley and Blue Lake roads provide access to reach this natural lake. Blue Lake Campground is a convenient stayover for anglers to also fish nearby East Creek outside or inside the wilderness.

Other Lakes and Streams

Lying at the base of the Warners within the Modoc National Wildlife Refuge east of Alturas, Dorris Reservoir, at 4,400, offers anglers the opportunity to sample large rainbow trout. Access to Dorris Reservoir is out of Parker Creek Road.

Known as the Devils Garden, several secluded lakes north of Canby in the central part of Modoc National Forest are accessible by vehicle. Duncan Reservoir, Reservoir "C", Janes Reservoir, McGinty Reservoir, Reservoir "F", and Sibley Reservoir are easily accessed by County and Forest Service routes. The geological features of the area consist mainly of high rocky plateaus surrounded by grass, sage, and juniper. Pine trees cover the higher elevation terrain.

Secluded Ash Creek and Rush Creek

Situated east of Adin, out of Ash Valley Road (County Route 88, 527, and FSR 39N08) to Ash Creek Campground in Modoc National

South Fork Pit River.

Forest, Ash Creek is one of my favorite streams in the area. When you come to a fork in the road, watch for a left turn at FSR 39N08 to the campground and stream. This stream is a great candidate for drive-to roadside angling from shore or wading. In some stretches, the stream has excellent open terrain for fly casting.

The best fishing section in this secluded Lassen County stream is from near the campground to above Dan Ryan Place. Working both upstream and downstream from the campground along this beautiful creek will reward you with rainbows and browns. However, one needs to be cautious when presenting flies to wary trout. The best technique to outsmart the rainbows is to drift your flies to trout lying in wait to intercept bits of food as it floats by.

Upper and Lower Rush Creek, located north of Adin off SR 299, has a mixture of rainbows, brooks, and occasional browns. To reach the creeks and campgrounds, access to this small stream lying east of SR 299, is from USFS Road 22 and County Road 198. To reach the creeks and campgrounds, a sign will provide mileage information to Lower Rush Creek (one-half mile) and two and one-half miles to Upper Rush Creek. Campgrounds are available at Lower and Upper Rush Creek.

Untamed and Magnificent Pit: Alturas to Lake Britton

Situated between Alturas and the Cascade Range, the Pit River flows west through miles of lush agricultural lands, then drops into Lassen County, and plunges through deep whitewater canyons west of Fall River Valley in Shasta County. This lush valley provides wild-trout fishing opportunities in Fall River's spring creek.

Surrounded by Ahjumawi Lava Springs State Park to the north, Tule River, a tributary of the Fall River, also provides fishing on Big Lake, Eastman Lake, and Little Tule River. Eastman Lake receives its waters from Lava Creek and continues its flow to Little Tule River and Tule River.

A tributary to Fall River, Tule River's Ahjumawi Lava Springs State Park waters in 15-foot-deep Big Lake (3,305 feet) and Tule Lake (3,300 feet)—formerly Horr Pond—with maximum depth of 20 feet, are accessible by boat only. A large open canoe is the best craft for exploring these waters. Ahjumawi was once a large camp for the Pit River Native Americans. Nine campgrounds are located in various areas of the park.

Ahjumawi is part of the Native American's ancestral homeland and remains an integral part of their culture. In their native language, Ahjumawi means, "where the waters come together." The Native American's village, ceremonial sites, and prehistoric old stone fish traps are still in use today. Recent lava flows broken by faults, lava tubes, deep cracks, and craters have been preserved, be on the lookout for rattlesnakes in the meadow area. These rattlers are dark and blend well with the coloration of lava.

Access to the park or to float downriver to the confluence of Fall River is from the Rat Farm public boat-launching site. The site is located near McArthur Swamp from Rat Farm Road. To reach the launching site, turn north at McArthur (after passing Fall River Mills) onto Main Street. Continue on Main Street, past the Inter-Mountain Fairgrounds for approximately 0.7 mile to a fork in the road, turn north onto Rat Farm Road as the road follows a canal. After crossing the canal, you'll reach a gate—be sure to close it behind you. Proceed on this road for three miles to reach the Rat Farm car-top boat ramp. Once in the water, unlimited access is available on the Fall River from the confluence of the Tule River above Glenburn.

Rat Farm is the site of an old, long-abandoned muskrat ranch. PG&E allowed the public to use it for access to fishing, duck hunting, and other recreational purposes on Big Lake and the Tule River. They provided public bathrooms because recreationists heavily use the site.

From Ahjumawi, the river captures water from Eastman Lake and Little Tule River as it heads south, converging with lower Fall River. Thence, the stream continues its course until converging with the Pit River near Fall River Mills.

When snow packs thaw in the spring, rivulets, brooks, creeks, and streams in the high country are swollen with billions of gallons of torrential waters gushing through the drainages. With nine power houses, Pacific Gas and Electric Company (PG&E) borrows water from watersheds of the Cascade Range and Sierra Nevada to generate power for Northern and Central California. After using the stored water to generate hydroelectric power, PG&E releases the water downstream through its plants for municipal use and irrigation purposes. Stored water serves many purposes: recreation, diminishing the threat of floods, maintaining stream flow when it is low or dry, and for perserving water supplies.

In 1921, the first two powerhouses in the Pit River system were built on Hat Creek, Hat Creek 1 Powerhouse and Hat Creek 2 Powerhouse. Through the years, other powerhouses were built along Pit River. Pit 1 Powerhouse is situated between Fall River Mills and Lake Britton. Pit 3 to 7 powerhouses are located from Lake Britton to below the mouth of Montgomery Creek and Fenders Ferry Bridge.

Both the Pit and McCloud rivers are ideal candidates for power generation. Since rocks deposited by ancient lava flows are highly porous, they absorb rainwater when saturated; and release the water in an even flow. Also, the Pit is closely regulated below Lake Britton by PG&E dams and powerhouses.

The section of river along Pit 1 Powerhouse, located east of Hat Creek, has brush lined banks and a swift current surrounding the boulders scattered throughout. Wading is difficult due to the fluctuating flows released from the powerhouse upstream. However, it is possible to hook on to some large trout, though it requires some work. Access to this segment of the Pit is off of SR 299 heading east to Fall River Mills from the junction of SR 89 (four corners). After crossing the Pit River Bridge, continue for several miles, and look for a sign on the south side (Powerhouse Road) for directions to Pit 1 Powerhouse. On the north side of SR 299, you can see the penstocks on the mountainside. As the Pit River races from Pit 1 Powerhouse in a northwesterly direction under the SR 299 Bridge, it flows into Lake Britton.

Burney Creek
Originating from below Clover Mountain (6,806 feet), Dan Covey Butte, Howard Springs, and other springs above and below 5,000 feet, Burney Creek is one of Pit River's smaller tributary waters. Do not overlook upper Burney Creek wherever access is available. The creek flows through the town of Burney and on to McArthur Burney Falls Memorial State Park. This quality trout water offers many opportunities for fly-fishers to explore. The best sections are above and below Burney Creek Falls in the state park. Fish the base of Burney Falls and near the bridge above the falls. Also, a section of water along SR 89 outside the park is a good bet for spring and early summer fishing before flows decrease. During the height of summer from June to September, Burney Creek is dry between the park and the town of Burney.

The spring-fed waters of Burney Creek below the falls keep the flow constant during the summer. However, Burney Falls and the spring above the falls continue to flow all season. It is interesting to note that Burney Creek and other streams in the region flow in and out of underground reservoirs.

Rock Creek and Clark Creek
Rock Creek and Clark Creek are tributaries to the Pit River. Rock Creek merges with the Pit River below Pit 3 Dam while Clark

Creek flows into Lake Britton. It is worth a trip to explore these two creeks when you are in the vicinity of Pit 3 Dam. Most sections of these two creeks have heavily brushed terrain. However, on small pools, short line nymphing with low side-casts upstream and letting your line drift to holding fish will get you into some interesting action.

Shasta County's Rock Creek has a special all-year closure regulation approximately one mile upstream from its confluence with the Pit River to Rock Creek Falls. Upstream from the falls, most of Rock Creek is heavily lined with trees and brush.

The best route to Rock Creek is from FSR 11, near Pit 3 Dam. As you are going west on FSR 11, you will cross the small Rock Creek Bridge.

One of the accesses to Clark Creek is west of Lake Britton on FSR 37N05. Head north on FSR 37N05 until you reach the Clark Creek Bridge. From here work upstream along small riffles and pools. Be extremely cautious treading alongside the stream. You will either see the fish or your presence will send them scurrying around, spooking all other fish in the area because of the gin-clear water. This is true with all small crystal-clear streams.

Another access route to Clark Creek is to turn west onto FSR 38N01 from SR 89. Continue west on this route until you reach upper Clark Creek.

Pit 3 Dam to Pit 3 Powerhouse Reach
One of the most productive reaches of the Pit River is below Lake Britton Dam (Pit 3 Dam) to Pit 3 Powerhouse. In this 5.6-mile reach,

Burney Falls.

Pit River.

Pit River at Big Bend.

As the river's course continues in a westerly direction through Pit 5 Reach, the canyon walls become steeper. The river is more expansive and access is more difficult, so the fly-fishing is unpredictable. The river stretches more than 30 miles from Pit 7 Reservoir near Fenders Flat before its final destination to Shasta Lake and the confluence of the Sacramento River.

Pit River Fly Patterns

Suggested Flies	*Hook Sizes*	*Best Months**
Nymphs and Emergers		
Bird's Nest	10-14	April to November
Golden, Black, Brown Stone Nymph	4-10	April to June
Gold Ribbed Hare's Ear	10-12	April to November
Hare's Ear Nymph	10-12	April to November
A.P. Black Nymph	10-12	April to November
Bead Head Emerging Caddis	14-16	May to August
Kaufmann's Dark Stone Nymph	4	June to October
BH Pheasant Tail	14-16	April to November
Red Fox Squirrel Nymph	8-12	April to November
Black Rubberlegs (Heavily Weighted)	2-6	April to November
Prince Nymph	10-12	April to November
Cream, Olive CDC Caddis Emerger	12-16	May to August
Tan Caddis Larva, Pupa	12-14	May to August
Olive LaFontaine's Deep Sparkle Pupa	12- 14	May to August
Tan, Olive Emergent Sparkle Pupa	12-14	May to August
Yellow Caddis Larva	8-10	September to October
Orange Caddis Pupa	8-10	September to October
Streamers		
Brown, Olive, or Black Woolly Bugger	8-12	April to November
BH Olive, Crystal Bugger	8-12	April to November
Muddler Minnow	8-12	April to November
Olive, Brown, Cinnamon Marabou Leech	2-4	April to October
Dry Flies		
Golden Stone	6-8	April to June
Yellow Humpy	12-14	June to September
Pale Morning Dun	16	May to November
Tan and Olive Elk Hair Caddis	14-16	May to July
Goddard Caddis	14-16	May to July
Improved Sofa Pillow	6-8	September to October
Orange Bucktail Caddis	8	September to October

* Timing of hatches and activity may vary each season.

the canyon road drops 240 feet at a steep grade and has easy river access. From Pit 3 Powerhouse to Pit 4 Dam, the road parallels the waters. This is one of the reasons this reach attracts angler traffic. The reach has rich insect habitat that provides the trout with lots of food for rapid growth rate and strength. A special regulation of barbless hooks and a restricted possession limit has been set from Pit 3 Dam downstream to the outlet of Pit 3 Powerhouse.

Nymphing with sink-tip lines, Teeny Nymph Line, or a full-sinking line is the best method to fish the Pit effectively. It is important to drift the nymph to the bottom near the fish. Although the Pit is best fished with large, heavily weighted nymphs, nymphing with a two-fly system or dry-fly patterns such as Elk Hair Caddis can work quite well.

Look for fish rising in tailouts during evening hours. *Dicosmoecus* (giant orange sedge or October caddis) hatch around late September to early October. Use a yellow caddis larva, LaFontaine's Brown and Orange Sparkle Pupa, Orange Bucktail Caddis, or Orange Elk Hair Caddis.

Pit 4 Reach, Pit 5 Reach, and Fenders Flat to Shasta Lake

Although there are some good holding waters along the Pit 4 Reach, access becomes more difficult. Within this 7-plus-mile reach, steep contours ranging from 40 feet to 400 feet through the canyon walls make access more difficult as the road heads away from the river. A series of waterfalls and rapids dominate the reach from Pit 4 Dam to Pit 4 Powerhouse. As the river heads toward the Big Bend area, access is also available from Big Bend Road north of SR 299. The fall months may be a more productive time to investigate this reach of the river.

Hatchet Creek.

Hatchet Creek

A tributary to the Pit River, the 18 miles of Hatchet Creek begins its course below Snow Mountain (6,814 feet) and drops down to 3,811 feet near Fuller Flat. Hatchet Creek got its name when an emigrant refused to hand over his hatchet to a Native American. Subsequently, he cleverly gained possession of it.

Situated 45 miles east of Redding in Shasta County, Hatchet Creek crosses two major paved roads, at SR 299 and downstream at the Big Bend Road. Upstream from the SR 299 Bridge located southwest of Burney, several roads provide access to intimate dry-fly-fishing for small rainbow, brown, brook, and Eagle Lake trout.

Kosk Creek.

However, nymphing is just as productive. This section of stream meanders through open and brushy landscapes. The property belongs to a lumber company and is subject to closure upon discretion of the owners.

Another access to the creek is downstream from the SR 299 Bridge where Hatchet Creek crosses. This stretch of stream is a little more difficult to maneuver. It lies in rough, rocky terrain surrounded by brush and willows. However, the best stretch to fish is below the bridge. Further down stream, it picks up speed before entering canyon waters. It is a challenge to connect with the trout in this type of water.

As the stream flows toward Big Bend near Hillcrest, the creek cascades down several magnificent waterfalls (Lion Ash Falls and Lion Slide Falls) and steep canyons (1,400 feet) before merging into Pit 7 Reservoir (between Pit 6 Dam and Pit 7 Dam).

Nelson Creek, Kosk Creek, and Iron Canyon Reservoir

If you are in the Big Bend area of the Pit River during late spring, take the time to explore Nelson Creek, Kosk Creek, and Iron Canyon Reservoir. Nelson and Kosk creeks offer rainbow trout while Kosk Creek has yielded some nice large browns. The easiest access to Nelson Creek is near the mouth at Big Bend. However, Kosk Creek is accessible if you travel north on a Forest Service route into Shasta-Trinity National Forest. The route follows the creek for the most part.

Iron Canyon Reservoir, (2,664 feet) with 15 miles of forested shoreline, is a beautiful 500-acre lake situated in the gentle mountainous terrain of Shasta-Trinity National Forests. Boat ramps, campgrounds, and campsites are available at Iron Canyon Reservoir. Access to Iron Canyon is five miles from Big Bend.

Along Fall River's Serene Watercourse

If any trout in northeastern California were to be designated as "clever," the fish of Fall River would top the list. Situated 70 miles east of Redding, Fall River is sandwiched between the Cascade Mountain Range and the Sierra Nevada Province at Fall River Mills. John C. Fremont named Fall River in 1946 because of the numerous falls and cascades that break the river's course.

Fall River is one of Northern California's richest with the most fish per river mile. From its headwaters at Thousand Springs (3,330 feet), Spring Creek, Bear Creek, and other unnamed creeks near Dana, the stream winds through lush green meadows of Fall River Valley to the confluence of Tule River.

Fall River rainbow trout.

Pasturelands, hay fields, large oak trees, modern mansion-type homes, old barns, and farmhouses provide fantastic views as you float down the river. The miles of cool, glistening water in the upper river are filled with fertile aquatic vegetation to support incredible insect production, thus providing ideal habitat for trophy trout. The lower reaches of Fall River receive additional sources of water from Tule River before flowing into the Pit River.

The 12-mile stretch of quality water has a barbless hooks restriction and other special regulations. There are no special regulations on Fall River from the mouth of Tule River downstream. This classic meadow stream also has a restriction against using electric-powered boats.

Fly-fishers who regularly fish this river can attest to the trial-and-error needed in this superb, wide and slow-moving serpentine spring creek. An abundance of submerged weed beds and undercut banks provide excellent holding water for trout and their food chain.

Most fish inhabiting the stream have learned their lessons well after being deceived and spooked so often. In fact, some trout have scars and hooks on their lips. Therefore, they are inclined to reject an imitation more often than not. With this in mind, long leaders, light tippets, fly-pattern selection, and accurate presentations are key factors in arousing the fish to strike. For the most successful results, observe stream flow and currents carefully, make the proper fly selections, maintain slack line, use mending tactics, and a delicate presentation.

Shasta County's largest spring creek is best known for its prime dry-fly fishery with mayfly patterns during the morning. From late afternoon to dusk, do not overlook fishing with caddisfly patterns when these hatches prevail.

Throughout the season, mayfly and caddisfly hatches dominate this river system. In some instances, one can see mayfly and caddis hatches blanket the air and waters. Pale Morning and Olive Duns in Nos. 14-16 and other standard patterns are effective during this time period. The peak period for green drake action occurs in May and again in October. When this occurs, use a No. 12 imitation. However, nymphs such as Pheasant Tails, Bird's Nests, Hare's Ears, and Zug Bugs in Nos. 10-24. Matuka, leech, and small trout imitations also allow fly-fishers to connect with Fall River's trophy sized native rainbows and browns. When you have sampled the incandescent beauty and fighting ability of these native trophy trout, the serenity and exquisite beauty of this spring creek will haunt you year after year.

Anglers can fish Fall River throughout most of the season. Other than the annual spring snow runoff, the river level does not rise quickly as most streams do. Generally, by late May, the water

Hex fly on a green leaf.

becomes crystal clear. Therefore, long leaders with light 6X tippets produce the best results.

The average depth of the stream is three to four feet and it averages around 75 to 80 feet in width. However, in some areas, the stream can drop more than 15 feet. Heavy aquatic vegetation covers many sections of the stream, creating excellent cover for the fish and providing good anchorage for boats.

As you float the river, it is quite a sight to observe large trout darting in and out the carpets of vegetation nestled in the sand, gravel, and rocky bottoms. Current speed and dense weed patches distract them from the depth of the river.

Fish are concentrated in the thick weed cover during the early season, awaiting the prolific hatches of mayflies. May through June is one of the most impressive periods to fish Fall River. This is the time of year to experience the spinner fall, the last stage of the mayfly's life cycle. The pale morning dun (PMD), either submerged, emerging, or dancing on the surface, is the most consistent fly. Drifting a No. 16 Pheasant Tail Nymph with a strike indicator, and allowing the fly to float in a natural fashion, will account for many strikes.

The famous "Hex" hatch emerges at dusk beginning in mid-June and lasting through early July in the middle and lower section of Fall River. The stream-bottom mud-burrowing *Hexagenia limbata* (big yellow mayfly) inhabits the river above and below the Island Drive Bridge. The nymphs emerge from their burrows in the bottom of the stream and rise to the surface film, burst free of their shuck and hatch into adults. The duns float several seconds on the surface before becoming airborne. The best method to fish the "Hex" hatch is to be prepared with rod, line, tippet, and flies ready for action before the hatch commences. The trout become frenzied and go into a feeding spree during the hatch for 30 minutes to an hour.

Time is of the essence during this short period of darkness. Be prepared to fish without having to constantly tie or change flies. Begin with nymphs using a 4X tippet before the hatch. During the hatch, switch to big yellow adults. At times, it is frustrating to spend this premium time fumbling in the dark, but its well worth it if you can do it. The best fly patterns to use are Hexagenia Nymphs, Cripple Emergers, and Paraduns in Nos. 6-8. Other productive patterns in the same sizes include the yellow humpy, Yellow Goofus Bug, extended body Parachute flies, and other large yellow mayfly imitations. From September to mid-November, use a No. 8 orange October Caddis when these large caddisflies emerge.

For many years, private ownership of the land on both banks prevented access to the river. It was closed to public fishing until the Sierra Club and other individuals filed a suit proclaiming the river a navigable stream. In the early 1970s, the Superior Court in Redding, California ruled the river as navigable, thus all fences and other obstructions across the river and obstructions were ordered removed. This allowed access for anglers with boats and crafts to float the river. However, the riparian lands still hold a no trespassing restriction subject to prosecution of violators.

Boat-Launching Facilities

Access to Fall River is limited to several first-come, first-served access sites because of private land holdings along both banks. The only means of access to the river is by boat from designated launching facilities. Three public boat-launching facilities provide access to upper Fall River: Cal Trout site, the old PG&E dredge site area, and the Rat Farm site at Big Lake. Guests of Rick's Lodge in the upper Fall River near Dana can use their boat-launching facility. Also, access for guests at Lava Creek Resort to Little Tule River and Fall River is available through Eastman Lake.

The Cal Trout public launching access site is located near the end of the quality water at Island Road Bridge, approximately six miles north of Fall River Mills. Because of limited parking, no more than 10 vehicles carrying car-top boats are allowed. Trailers are not permitted. Plan to arrive early to get a parking space and also allow time to moor upstream and float the river. With the current moving around three miles per hour—maximum traveling speed is five miles an hour—figure in advance the amount of time you wish to spend during the float. Be prepared to transport your boat from the parking facility for 150 feet to the launch site. For individuals using the parking and launching facilities, only electric motors are allowed. For newcomers to Fall River, hiring a guide to fish this spring creek will be extremely rewarding.

Another public launching facility, down river from Cal Trout's launching site is near the old PG&E dredge site. This facility offers limited parking for car-top boats only. Trailers are not permitted at this site. Developed by the California Wildlife Conservation Board, this launching site is located north of County Road A19 (MacArthur Road) between McArthur and Glenburn off SR 299. Anglers must carry their boats 20 to 30 feet to the river for launching.

The Rat Farm public boat-launching facility located north of McArthur from Big Lake offers another alternative to reach lower Fall River. Once in the water, unlimited access is available to fish Fall River from the confluence of Tule River to Glenburn.

Bear Creek—a Pit River drainage.

Fall River Fly Patterns

Suggested Flies	*Hook Sizes*	*Best Months**
Nymphs and Emergers		
A.P. Nymph	14-16	April to November
BH Brassie	10-12	April to November
Golden Stone Nymph	10-12	April to June
Yellow Stone Nymph	4-10	May to June
Bird's Nest	12-16	April to November
Hare's Ear Nymph	12-16	April to November
Hexagenia Nymph and Paradun	6-8	June to July
Bead Head Emerging Caddis	14-16	May to August
Pheasant Tail	16-18	April to November
Paranymph (Tan, Olive, Sulphur)	16-18	April to November
Prince Nymph	10-12	April to November
Cream, Olive CDC Caddis Emerger	12-16	May to August
Caddis Larva, Pupa (Tan)	12-14	May to August
LaFontaine's Deep Sparkle Pupa (Olive)	12-14	May to August
Emergent Sparkle Pupa (Tan and Olive)	12-14	May to August
Zug Bug	12-18	April to October
Yellow Caddis Larva	6-8	May to June
Orange Caddis Pupa	6-8	May to June
Streamers		
Brown, Olive, or Black Woolly Bugger	8-12	April to November
Wool Head Sculpin (Olive and Black)	4	April to November
Olive Matuka	8-12	April to November
Muddler Minnow	8-12	April to November
Olive, Brown, Black Marabou Leech	2-8	April to November
Dry Flies		
Trico Spinner (Black Body/White Wing)	18-22	August to September
Deer Hair Spider (Olive)	18	June to September
Golden and Yellow Stone	10	May to June
Green Drake	12	April to May, October
Pale Morning Dun	16-18	April to November
Brown Olive Spinner	14-16	April to November
Hexagenia Cripple Emerger	6-8	June to July
Hexagenia Paradun	6-8	June to July
Yellow Goofus Bug	8	June to July
Yellow Humpy	8	June to July
Elk Hair Caddis (Olive, Green)	14-16	May to August
Improved Sofa Pillow	8	May to June
Orange Caddis Bucktail	8	May to June
Orange Elk Hair Caddis	8	May to June

* Timing of hatches and activity may vary each season.

Bear Creek

Bear Creek provides early season fishing near Pondosa off SR 89 east of Dead Horse Summit (4,505 feet). The creek originates near 5,000

Hat Creek country.

feet above Kemp Flat in Shasta-Trinity National Forest in Shasta County. The creek continues its course, flowing north into Siskiyou County. Upon reaching SR 89, it flows east and finally south to the confluence of Fall River at Thousand Springs.

Situated between Burney and McCloud, this small stream has two different open seasons, one in late April and the other in late May. The Pondosa Way Bridge splits Bear Creek into two opening seasons. Anglers can fish upstream of the bridge during the early opening season. Upstream from the bridge, anglers have the choice to park their vehicles for a little roadside fishing.

Another option is to hike or drive a short distance upstream (truck or 4WD vehicle) for secluded fishing from the bank or wading in areas where dense landscape shorelines predominate. Another access to Bear Creek is three miles north from Pondosa off SR 89. Turn south on a gravel dirt road and continue for a short distance before reaching Pondosa Dam. Certain portions of the road are rugged. It is best to work your way up stream on foot.

Captivating Hat Creek and Wilderness Waters

Crystal-clear wild-trout water, serene, magnificent, delicate, splendorous, challenging, demanding, self-sustaining, exceptionally strong-fighting trout, and plenty of insect hatches are key words for this Shasta County stream—known as Hat Creek. What more can you ask of a stream?

Hat Creek country offers many premier waters for fly-fishers to explore. Upper and Middle Hat Creek, the Cassel area, and Baum Lake below Hat 1 Powerhouse are a few examples. Lower Hat Creek, below Hat 2 Powerhouse, is a fly-fisher's dream. These waters are great for early season angling as they are below 3,000 feet.

Hat Creek received its name when a party of Shasta citizens was blazing the trail for an emigrant road, the Noble Route, to the northern mines in 1852. During this trip, D. D. Harrell, a member of the party, lost his hat in the stream.

East and West Fork Hat Creek begins its course in Lassen Volcanic National Park below Lassen Peak (8,929 feet) and Reading Peak (8,714 feet). Located in Lassen National Volcanic Park, east of the headwaters of Hat Creek, is Hat Mountain (7,444 feet). It is interesting to note that Hat Mountain was named because it resembles a creased hat. According to a Native American legend, a god sat on Hat Mountain all night after having brought fish to Honey Lake after the destruction of Mt. Tehama.

As the two forks flow north, they merge into a single stream— the main fork flowing out of Lassen National Park into Lassen National Forest. The creek parallels the highway for the most part,

but, it crosses the roadway back and forth in several locations. Along SR 89, public fishing access is not a problem since there are several campgrounds and pullouts throughout this stretch of Upper and Middle Hat Creek.

Pacific Crest National Scenic Trail Access: Lassen Segment
Within the Cascade Range, the Lassen segment of the PCT begins at McArthur Burney Falls Memorial State Park located south of Lake Britton. The trail continues south along the ridge of Hat Creek and crosses Baum Lake. It then follows Hat Creek Rim down to the trailhead near the Subcave and Old Station along upper Hat Creek. From here, the PCT heads toward Lassen National Park. It passes through the entire national park, crosses SR 36 and extends 120 miles to the Feather River canyon of the Northern Sierra Nevada Mountains Province.

If you wish to travel by foot to fish along the route, PCT trailheads or other areas are accessible from McArthur Burney Falls Memorial State Park, SR 299 west of Hat Creek crossing, Baum Lake, Crystal Lake Hatchery or PGE Powerhouse, and Cassel Campground. Other PCT accesses are near Old Station along Hat Creek, Lassen National Park, and Humboldt Summit near Humboldt Peak (7,087 feet), near the headwaters of Butt Creek. This trailhead is accessible from Humboldt Road. Turn west from SR 89 to Humboldt Road, which is located southwest of Lake Almanor.

Upper and Middle Hat Creek
The stretches of Upper and Middle Hat Creek are stocked principally with rainbow, brook, and brown trout. Except for a small section of the creek in the Old Station area, the upper 20 miles in U.S. forest lands provide excellent access from Lassen National Park to Hat Creek Valley.

You can reach one of the first stream accesses at Big Pine Campground by making a right turn at SR 89. Follow the creek in a southerly direction on FSR 32N13 toward the mouth of Lost Creek at the junction of FSR 32N12. This route continues for a distance to various spots where access to the creek is available. Several Forest Service campgrounds are also spread out along SR 89. The last campground along SR 89 on Hat Creek Valley is Honn. This is a small campground away from the crowds. However, the creek is small and brushy in this section.

Upon reaching Hat Creek Valley, the river meanders in a northeasterly direction away from SR 89 to the community of Cassel. Many quality waters abound in the stretch below Hat 1 Powerhouse. There is a PG&E Campground in Cassel. The flats in Cassel Forebay are another alternative in which to cast your line in the evening for

Hat Creek power house.

Rainbow trout.

some surprising action. The stretch of water in the Cassel area is regularly stocked by DFG above and around the forebay.

The access road to Cassel is from SR 89. After passing Honn Campground on SR 89, make a right turn and head east on Cassel Road to the community of Cassel. Another route to Cassel is out of SR 299. At the junction of SR 89 and SR 299, continue east until you reach the Cassel Road turnoff. Turn south and continue on the road until you reach the same area.

Throughout the summer, Hat Creek receives cold spring waters year-round, providing continued action. Because of easy roadside access and the excellent waters for all levels of fly-fishers, upper Hat Creek receives intense fishing pressure, particularly on weekends. Campgrounds along the creek are usually full during the height of the season. Therefore, early or late season is the best time to visit Hat Creek and nearby waters. However, the special regulations area below Hat 2 Powerhouse receives heavy angler pressure during early season.

Baum Lake

Located in the Hat Creek drainage near the Crystal Lake Hatchery, 15-foot-deep Baum Lake (2,978 feet) is essentially a small body of water that is part of Hat Creek. However, fed by the springs of Rising River, the average depth of Baum in most sections is seven feet. The weed beds in the lake provide excellent insect habitat. Baum Lake offers excellent winter and spring fly-fishing. Large, active rainbows cruise around the lake in late February, March, and April. During cooler weather, the entire shoreline can be productive.

The fish are vulnerable to size 16-18 or smaller Pheasant Tail Nymphs, Black Midges, and Callibaetis on floating lines from shore or small watercraft. The Black Midge in Nos. 18-20 is one of my most consistent flies during March and April. However, during later season, No. 16 works best. During late spring, I have also had great success with dark Sparkle Midge Pupas and Griffith's Gnats in No. 20.

Other excellent fly patterns to have on hand are Nos. 14-16 Elk Hair Caddis, Bird's Nests, Zug Bugs, and LaFontaine's green and reddish brown Caddis Pupa. Black or olive Woolly Buggers and Light Olive Leech patterns in Nos. 8 to 14 also work well during spring. During the months of July and August, Callibaetis Cripples and Pheasant Tail Nymphs No. 18 are top-producing patterns. In October and early November, the best flies are caddis pupa and Callibaetis mayflies. Entice the fish to take your mayfly offerings (mahogany duns) late morning to midday.

Access to Baum Lake is from SR 299 or SR 89. On SR 299, continue east for approximately two miles. Then make a right turn onto Cassel Road and drive approximately two miles. Make a left turn on Crystal Lake Hatchery Road. Drive another mile and turn left toward Baum Lake. The other route is from SR 89. After passing Honn Campground, turn right on Cassel Road. Upon reaching Cassel, turn left to Crystal Lake Hatchery Road. Make a right turn and follow the same directions as above to Baum Lake.

Thousand Lakes Wilderness

The heavily-used 16,335-acre Thousand Lakes Wilderness in Lassen National Forest was established in 1964. During the Ice Age, the valley was carved by glacial action. After the glaciers receded, many lakes and ponds were formed in the valley. The wilderness is dominated by Crater Peak (8,683 feet), the highest peak in this wilderness and Lassen National Forest. Magee Peak (8,549 feet) is the second highest peak in the wilderness. In the midst of the trophy and wild-trout waters in this fabulous country, an ideal short day-trip or backpacking trip from nearby Hat Creek provides good fishing for various species of trout, such as colorful brook trout, rainbows, and Eagle Lake trout.

The moderate to strenuous hike into Thousand Lakes Valley is for the adventurous angler willing to trek-in a couple of miles and traverse lush forestlands. Laced with lots of vegetation, open and barren mountains, and clear lakes, Thousand Lakes Wilderness is a land of contrasting topography throughout its valleys and high peaks. Within the wilderness, you can find lava and granite formations, majestic peaks, dense lodgepole pines, with a mixture of open meadows and thick brushy surroundings.

Eiler, Magee, Everett, and Barrett lakes receive the most visitors. However, my favorite watershed is Lake Eiler. In most years, snow remains on the ground until June. The best time to venture into Thousand Lakes is mid-June through September. Fly-fishing in the sheer beauty of this wilderness and the tranquility of its waters is an unforgettable experience. While trekking along the trail, remnants of volcanic and glacial formations, rocky ravines, and open terrain will appear.

There are four trailheads into Thousand Lakes Wilderness. The Tamarack Trailhead is located on the eastern side of the wilderness. This is the easiest trail to take to Lake Eiler for day trips.

Heading north from Lassen Park on SR 89 before reaching the Honn Forest Service Campground, turn west and follow the unimproved road toward the Tamarack Swale. It is approximately seven miles of driving on FSR 33N24 and 33N25 to reach the trailhead. When you come to a junction, make a right turn to the trailhead. From this trailhead, destination lakes are Eiler, Box, Barrett, and Durbin. These lakes are also accessible from the western entry. Extended trips take from this trailhead, take you to are Everett (7,181 feet) and Magee (7,198 feet) lakes.

The Cypress Camp Trailhead is located on the northwestern parcel of the wilderness. The 10-mile ride to the trailhead on FSR 34N22 takes you to the western side of the wilderness. Although the hike is more strenuous and on steeper terrain, this trail also takes you to Lake Eiler.

The third trailhead is the Magee Trailhead located on the southwestern sector of the wilderness. Although this route is one of the most scenic trails in the wilderness, only experienced hikers with great physical ability or on horseback should negotiate the rocky and steep terrain. This trail takes you to Magee and Everett lakes.

To reach the Magee Trailhead, FSR 16 is accessible from SR 89 north of Lassen Volcanic National Park. From FSR 16, take FSR 35N17 and 33N48 to the trailhead. This trail is the shortest to reach Magee and Everett lakes.

The fourth trailhead entry to the wilderness is the Bunchgrass Trailhead. Take FSR 16 to FSR 32N45 to the trailhead. It is less than 10 miles to SR 89. The scenery is breathtaking on this trail.

Lake Eiler, Box Lake, Barrett Lake, and Durbin Lake

One of the largest lakes in the wilderness is 21-foot-deep Lake Eiler (6,403 feet). The lake was named for Lu Eiler who discovered Thousand Lakes Valley. He was credited for guiding the McGee surveying party to it. Depending on the level of the lake, you can fish from shore or tote a float tube to cover more water. Other lakes you can trek to are 12-foot-deep Barrett Lake (6,430 feet) and 7-foot-deep Box Lake (6,408 feet). Durbin Lake (6,460 feet) with a depth of 11 feet is a little further away. Lying south of Durbin Lake is 26-foot-deep Hufford Lake (6,749 feet). From Durbin you need to cross-country to Hufford Lake with less than 300 feet in elevation gain.

Wild-Trout Waters of Lower Hat Creek

Lower Hat Creek's wild-trout water is known to be one of California's prime fisheries. Prior to 1968, it was a quality trout stream. However, the increase of rough fish population in the creek endangered the trout fishery. Faced with this problem, Cal Trout, PG&E, and the California Department of Fish and Game implemented a project to eliminate the rough fish. In addition, a fish barrier at the mouth of Lower Hat Creek was built to block re-infestation by squawfish, suckers, and other non-game fish. In order to manage the creek exclusively for wild trout, Cal Trout persuaded the Department of Fish and Game to adopt a Wild Trout Program. Thus, the Hat Creek Wild Trout Project was created to continue improving trout habitat on these waters. The stretch from Hat 2 Powerhouse downstream to Lake Britton has proven successful in supporting a self-sustaining fishery.

As one of Northern California's premium bodies of water, Lower Hat Creek holds an immense population of highly selective trout. The beauty, serenity, and rewarding waters of this stream beckon the fly-fisher to return year after year to experience new challenges. However, prolific weed patches line the pristine slow-moving meadow waters of this lower stretch.

Generally on opening day and early season, most experienced fly-fishers concentrate fishing the riffle waters below Hat 2 Powerhouse. Access to Hat 2 Powerhouse is from SR 299 east. After crossing the junction of SR 89 and Cassel Road, the next road is the Hat 2 Powerhouse Road. Take this turn off and head south. At the junction of the road, turn left and continue through mountainous terrain until you reach the powerhouse parking lot.

Below Hat 2 Powerhouse, you'll find open fields and beautiful scenery. Beyond the hills, the hamlet of Carbon is a popular area. One difficult segment of freestone water on Lower Hat Creek is downstream from the powerhouse to the Carbon Bridge. This stretch is full of lip current and riffle waters with undercut banks. Interspersed with tumbling riffle and pocket waters, this glassy spring creek can be difficult for those unfamiliar with this type of water. To reach the Carbon Bridge, there are two accesses from the SR 299 Hat Creek Bridge, by walking or driving. If you wish to follow the creek by foot, parking is available at the Hat Creek Day Use Picnic area off SR 299. Walk across the SR 299 Bridge on the east side of the creek and follow a trail. A little more than a mile upstream is the old Carbon Bridge, which is the site of an old way station for freight wagons that traveled from Redding to Alturas. All that is left in the area is pilings of Carbon Bridge.

The other route is to drive directly to the site by turning south from SR 299. After crossing the SR 299 Hat Creek Bridge for a short distance, make a right turn on a dirt road. Initially, the road will make a bend in an easterly direction, then it curves back heading south, and then makes a turn in a westerly direction down to the Carbon Bridge site.

Carbon (coal) was a toll station established and named by Fred Knox because of the contrast between the white cliff of nearby Chalk Mountain. In the same vicinity, the Carbon Hatchery was built in 1885, and in 1888, Shasta Hatchery replaced it.

As the creek flows toward SR 299 from the Carbon Bridge section to the Hat Creek Day Use Picnic Area, the slower sections with more vegetation and overhanging branches are some great waters to explore. However, there are some good waters below the park if you do not mind walking downstream. Be cautious when walking along the banks of the creek to avoid falling into muskrat holes. They are scattered throughout and can easily be missed.

Access from the park to Lake Britton is about two miles on an old road on the east side of the bridge heading downstream. To reach the old road, walk across the SR 299 Bridge to the east side of the creek. Continue by foot on the road following the east side of the creek to reach the Fish Barrier and Lake Britton.

This spring-fed creek has plenty of deep holes, moss, rocks, and a vast amount of insects to match all style's of fly-fishing—providing excellent habitat for wild native trout. As one of the top fly-fishing streams in the country, Hat Creek has a special regulation from Lake Britton upstream to Baum Lake, excluding the concrete Hat No. 2 Intake Canal between Baum Lake and Hat 2 Powerhouse—only barbless hooks may be used. Also, aquatic invertebrates of the orders of Plecoptera (stoneflies), Ephemeroptera (mayflies), and Trichoptera (caddisflies) may not be taken from this body of water. Because of this special regulation on three of the most important foods in the trout's diet, the fish become healthy and robust wild trout. Abundant aquatic vegetation supports a diversity of insects and provide excellent sanctuary for the robust wild trout. Caddisflies, mayflies, stoneflies, and terrestrials make up the bulk of insect hatches.

Although the majority of hatches occur in the spring, they can be found throughout the season. Trico Spinners, Nos. 18-22, or Yellow Stonefly patterns, No. 14 will match Stonefly hatches April through June. During mayfly emergences, small mayfly patterns, Nos. 18-22 work best. For the best results matching the evening hatches from May to September, cast Elk Hair Caddis or Royal Wulff patterns, Nos. 14-16.

The clear, flat waters are best fished with a floating line, 10-foot or longer leaders with 7X tippets, imitating the hatch with the correct fly patterns of each emergence cycle, and accurate drag-free presentations.

Hat Creek Fly Patterns

Suggested Flies	Hook Sizes	Best Months*
Nymphs and Emergers		
A. P. Nymph (Olive)	14-20	April to November
BH Brassie	10-12	May to November
Golden Stone Nymph	10-12	April to June
Little Yellow Stone Nymph	14	May to June
Black Rubberlegs, (Heavily Weighted)	2-6	April to October
Gold Ribbed Hares Ear	10-12	May to November
Bird's Nest	10-14	May to November
Hare's Ear Nymph	10-12	May to November
Hexagenia Nymph and Paradun	6	June to July
Bead Head Emerging Caddis	14-16	May to September
Pheasant Tail	16-20	May to November
Prince Nymph	10-12	May to November
Cream, Olive CDC Caddis Emerger	12-16	May to September
Olive LaFontaine's Deep Sparkle Pupa	12-14	May to September
Tan, Olive Emergent Sparkle Pupa	12-14	May to September
Zug Bug	12-18	May to November
Yellow Caddis Larva	8	September to October
LaFontaine's Orange Sparkle Pupa	8	September to October
Streamers		
Brown, Olive, or Black Woolly Bugger	8-12	April to November
Muddler Minnow	8-12	April to November
Dry Flies		
Trico Spinner (Black Body/White Wing)	18-22	June to August
CDC Rusty Spinner	18-22	June to August
Light Cahill	16-18	June to August
Pale Morning Dun	16-18	June to August
Pale Olive Paradun	16	June to August
Little Yellow Stone	14	June to August
Burk's C.D.C. Stone	14-16	June to August
Golden Stone	8-10	April to June
Green Drake	12	April to May, October
Deer Hair Spider (Olive)	18	June to September
Elk Hair Caddis	14-16	May to September
Royal Wulff	14-16	May to September
Improved Sofa Pillow	8	September to October
Orange and Golden Stimulator	8	September to October
Orange Bucktail Caddis	8	September to October

* Timing of hatches and activity may vary each season.

Hidden World of Medicine Lake Highlands

One of the least visited areas in Northern California is the Medicine Lake Highlands area. Situated in portions of three national forests—Shasta Trinity, Modoc, and Klamath in Modoc and Siskiyou counties—the Highlands volcanic area surpasses 200 square miles. The basin lies east of the Cascade Range. Volcanic formations, lava flows, pumice deposits, cinder cones, craters, lava tubes, and faults are visible throughout this region. Jumbled, rugged plains of broken rock interspersed with timbered hills and buttes are some of the unique features surrounding several productive trout lakes.

Lying below Mt. Hoffman (7,913 feet) and the Glass Mountain Geologic Area in the western boundary of Modoc National Forest, 150-foot-deep Medicine Lake (6,676 feet) provides excellent trout fishing. The lake is equipped with a boat ramp, campground, and picnic area with breathtaking scenery. Nearby smaller lakes, Little Medicine Lake (6,700 feet) and Bullseye Lake (6,680 feet), are other waters to explore. At one time, Bullseye Lake was home to grayling. However, through the years, the fish have diminished. Now, Bullseye Lake has been stocked with brook, rainbow, and Eagle Lake trout. Little Medicine Lake also has these three species of trout. There are several U.S. Forest Service campgrounds at Medicine Lake. These three lakes are not accessible until late June or July because of heavy snow pack.

An access route to Medicine Lakes Highlands is from SR 89 east of McCloud to Bartle or west on SR 89 from the Four Corners of SR 299 and SR 89. Upon reaching Bartle, head north on Medicine Lake Road, which is also FSR 49. This route will take you directly to Medicine Lake, which is also a brook, rainbow, and Eagle Lake trout fishery.

The Splendid McCloud

The McCloud is one of the major tributaries of the Sacramento River, situated in Siskiyou and Shasta counties. Also known as the intermountain circuit, the McCloud Arm of Shasta Lake provides exhilarating experiences for adventurous fly-fishers seeking prime trout waters. Within this vast watershed two prominent Cascade Mountain peaks—Mt. Shasta and Lassen Peak—dominate the entire area and divide the Sierra Nevada Province from the Klamath Mountains Province.

In the early 1800s, Scotsman Alexander Roderick McLeod, leader of a Hudson Bay Company, was one of the first fur trappers and explorers to penetrate Northern California. In 1828-1829, his group located and crossed a river now bearing his name under a different spelling, the McCloud. The spelling of the river's name varies in early maps and reports. At one time, the name was associated with Ross McCloud who settled here in 1855. McCloud became prominent in the development of the region, and the river was associated with his name.

Upper McCloud River

With Mt. Shasta presiding over the McCloud, this moderate sized classic freestone river originates from Moosehead Creek, east of Mushroom Rock (6,224 feet). Moosehead Creek and its tributaries are closed to fishing all year. Much of the McCloud River comes from snowmelt out of Mt. Shasta, springs, and tributaries. Landscaped with lush forestland, strewn with volcanic lava rocks, dotted with grassland, willows, scrub oaks, and manzanita brush, the stream in this section of upper McCloud River is small, lined with brush, and water flows are slow for the most part.

The stream in this headwaters section meanders north through Colby Meadow paralleling SR 89 a short distance toward Bartle. It then turns west flowing through two Forest Service campsites at Algoma and Cattle camps with access roads from SR 89. Most of the upper river above the reservoir holds stocked rainbow trout from the Department of Fish and Game. There are also some resident rainbow and brown trout in this upper river. To increase your chances for success, hike up and down stream from these campsites. Much of the upper McCloud River lies in private ownership land. However, a small section of the stream above the reservoir is situated on U.S. Forest Service land.

The U.S. Forest Service acquired the Upper McCloud River during the spring of 1989 through a land exchange agreement with Champion International Corporation. Because of its scenic quality, the Forest Service had identified the river corridor as a top priority for acquisition. Through this exchange, the Forest Service gained 2,626 acres of land that included 13 miles of river, two spectacular waterfalls, and 50-acre Bigelow Meadow. With this acquisition, this section of the Upper McCloud River offers great potential for recreation activities.

Upper falls on the McCloud River.

Middle falls McCloud River.

Lower falls McCloud River.

The first access to the McCloud is near Colby Meadow. As the river heads west, it passes through three plummeting, magnificent waterfalls known as the Upper, Middle, and Lower falls that are visible to fly-fishers as well as visitors.

The Upper McCloud River is accessible by traveling on a scenic road that forms a loop. To reach the loop from Interstate 5 north of Redding, exit on SR 89. Continue east and pass the town of McCloud by 5 miles. The loop begins at the Fowlers Campground exit sign. From Fowlers Campground, the road winds along the river passing through various recreation sites for 6 miles until it reaches Cattle Camp and subsequently SR 89 forming a loop. The area provides excellent access for anglers to explore this stretch of stream for smaller trout. Be cautious in areas around waterfalls.

In this upper river, some good areas are Fourmile Flat, Skunk Hollow, Bigelow Meadow, Lower Falls, and Fowler Campground. Camping facilities, day-use, picnic units, undeveloped sites, and handicapped facilities are available in this upper river. Although the McCloud is a difficult river to access, once there, it is a fly-fisher's dream as you can hook on to native wild trout. However, please respect the rights of private landowners by not trespassing on their lands.

The major source of water in this freestone river is a large volcanic spring known as Big Springs (3,000 feet), located approximately two miles below the Lower Falls. Volcanic rocks in this part of the Cascade Range where the McCloud River lies give a greenish hue to the water. Below Big Springs, sedimentary and metamorphic rocks are common in the region. Also, limestone outcrops are characteristic landscapes of the area.

A large volume of water in the McCloud gushes out of lava rocks at Big Springs and down the canyon wall, which increases the size of the river. Large trout inhabit this area because of the consistent coldwater temperatures from springs and the rich food sources flowing down from the upper river. From Big Springs, the river continues its course and flows into Lake McCloud.

Exhilarating and Challenging Lower McCloud River

In the lower river canyon below McCloud Dam, the best lies are found in the miles of large terraced pools, rapids, classic pocket water, and deep runs. The secret of fishing the McCloud effectively is wading aggressively and nymphing in the smooth waters and tailouts of the deep pools.

Only experienced fly-fishers should attempt to manipulate these long boulder-strewn waters that vary in depth. This type of water characterizes the classic freestone river of the McCloud. Fish inhabit the areas behind boulders, rocks, deep pools and runs, cut-banks, downed trees, logs, and other debris. Within this fast section of the lower river, be aware of your footing as it is treacherous and slippery. Anglers should take precautionary measures when wading this torrential stream.

To avoid being dunked and swept downstream by strong currents, felt-soled boots, good balance, and a wading staff are mandatory to safely wade in the Lower McCloud. When possible, fish with a partner.

Special regulations of barbless hooks and a two-fish limit imposed in Lower McCloud River commence from below the dam downstream to the confluence of Lady Bug Creek. From the confluence of Lady Bug Creek downstream to the lower boundary of U.S.

The McCloud River.

Squaw Valley Creek on the McCloud River.

Forest Service loop which lies in the southern boundary of Section 36, Township 38 North, Range 3 West, has a zero-fish limit with the use of barbless hooks. However, the McCloud River is closed to fishing all year from the lower boundary of the U. S. Forest loop to the upper boundary of the McCloud River Club. It is important to check for any changes in these regulations before venturing out.

Pacific Crest National Scenic Trail Access: Castle Crags State Park to Squaw Valley Creek

Although a 154-mile section of the PCT passes in a west to east direction across the Shasta-Trinity National Forest, almost 60 miles of it covers the McCloud area. This portion of the PCT is the only maintained trail within the McCloud River District. There have not been any trailheads developed in this sector; however, the trail crosses several Forest Service roads, providing good access to hikers. Of particular interest, from the Soda Creek Trailhead at Castle Crags State Park (2,077 feet), the PCT heads east climbing approximately 10 miles to Girard Ridge (4,400 feet) and descends 6 miles to Cabin Creek (2,600 feet) at the confluence of Squaw Valley Creek.

Squaw Valley Creek and McCloud River PCT Fishing Access

The PCT crosses a footbridge at Squaw Valley Creek. After leaving Squaw Valley Creek, the PCT continues east 3.5 miles and gains 3,400 feet in elevation to Trough Creek. From Trough Creek, the PCT ascends another 2.5 miles to Bald Mountain Ridge (3,700 feet). The trail traverses high on the ridge with infrequent glimpses of the McCloud River. Subsequently, it

descends 4.5 miles to the McCloud River at Ah-Di-Na Campground. At Ah-Di-Na, the trail parallels the river above the steep, impressive canyon along the 2.5-mile stretch from Ah-Di-Na (2,160 feet) to Ash Camp (2,400 feet).

Pacific Crest National Scenic Trail: McCloud River to Lake Britton

As the PCT leaves Ash Camp, this portion of the trail passes through Butcherknife Creek and Deer Creek drainages before starting a steady 10-mile uphill climb toward Grizzly Peak (6,252 feet) and Mushroom Rock (6,224 feet). This sector of the trail passes through the headwaters area of Kosk Creek and Clark Creek, and then reaches its destination of the McCloud segment of the PCT to McArthur Burney Falls Memorial State Park at Lake Britton (2,733 feet). At Burney Falls State Park, the long journey continues with the beginning of the Lassen segment of the PCT.

Another access to reach the Squaw Valley Creek area is out of Squaw Valley Road. From McCloud, turn south on Squaw Valley Road toward Lake McCloud. Continue on this road for six miles. Then make a right turn on FSR 39N21 and proceed three miles beyond the concrete bridge. There is ample room to park at the trailhead. This tranquil, secluded, and scenic area is an ideal place to hike and fish. However, if you wish to reach the PCT and footbridge, you need to ford Cabin Creek, which is one-half mile downstream.

Ah-Di-Na River Access

Below Lake McCloud (2,680 feet), the first river access is at Ash Camp. At the mouth of Hawkins Creek is the rough campsite of Ash Camp. The campsite is approximately a mile downstream from the dam outlet. This section of the stream is extremely dangerous for wading above and a short distance below the camp because of unpredictable water releases from Lake McCloud. With the unreliable flows in the pocket waters and pools, fishing this area is tricky and requires some skill.

Approximately two and a half miles downstream from Ash Camp is Ah-Di-Na Campground which has 16 units and a water system fed by a spring. The stretch of stream above and below Ah-Di-Na Campground is best fished in the fall months because of minimum and more consistent flows for safer wading. This allows easier access for anglers to fish this section.

Average water flows in the Ah-Di-Na area are around 200 cubic feet per second (cfs). During the summer, the water is highly turbid. The turbidity is caused by glacial mud and volcanic ash from Mt. Shasta, which flows into the river from Mud Creek, a tributary to the McCloud River above the reservoir. The milky-green coloration of water is a common condition in glacially fed rivers.

Ah-Di-Na and its area has a rich and diversified background. At one time, many Native American tribes, such as the McCloud River Wintu, the Okwanuchu, and the Pit River Native Americans, claimed Ah-Di-Na as part of their tribal territory. However, further archaeological research is needed for in-depth clarification.

The Whittiers, a wealthy family from San Francisco, California, were the first owners of Ah-Di-Na. They purchased the property in 1896 from the Central Pacific Railroad. They had it in mind to develop the area as a sportsman's fishing and hunting paradise.

There are two original complexes still standing at Ah-Di-Na, one of which is the Stone Chimney, built in 1917. Other features include a guest cabin used as a "ladies cabin," an old pack rail lined with rock retaining walls, and an orchard which still bears cherries, pears, apples, chestnuts, and walnuts. There are also various unidentified foundations and some concrete-lined reservoirs. There is speculation that these reservoirs were used for irrigation and fishing pools.

In 1919, William M. Fitzhugh of San Francisco purchased Ah-Di-Na. Fitzhugh built a log cabin. Within the first few years, the cabin began to crack because the logs were not well cured. Ah-Di-Na deteriorated while Fitzhugh was the owner. It was mostly used for farming, fishing, and harvesting fruit. In 1926, the property was sold to a company in Nevada.

The wealthy San Francisco publisher William Randolph Hearst's family purchased Ah-Di-Na in 1936. Hearst remodeled the estate and furnished it lavishly. During these early years, many famous guests visited the estate and fished the area. However, in 1958, because of infrequent use, Ah-Di-Na was vandalized, and the caretaker burned all of the Hearst buildings. In 1965, the U.S. Forest Service acquired the property for public campground and river access. Although it is not clear how Ah-Di-Na received its name, it first appeared in the Shasta National Forest Map in 1936 when the Hearst family owned the property.

McCloud River Preserve

Six miles of the McCloud River lie within the McCloud River Preserve's jurisdiction. Its main purpose is to protect the wild-trout fishery, dense forest, and its limestone outcrops. The

Ladies house on the McCloud River.

McCloud River preserve sign.

California Nature Conservancy manages the preserve. Historically, with the completion of Shasta Dam in 1945, salmon and steelhead runs from the Sacramento River were blocked and approximately 15 miles of the lower canyon of the McCloud was inundated. As a result of the blockage, the waters were undisturbed until the construction of a hydroelectric diversion dam and logging roads upstream at Ah-Di-Na. With the availability of public access and campgrounds by the Forest Service in the early 1960s, fish activity increased with the fish stocking program by the Department of Fish and Game.

The impact of logging and fish poaching on the lands of the McCloud River Club located downstream from Ah-Di-Na caused some concern. As a result of this, in 1973 the River Club donated about one half of their holdings to the Nature Conservancy to protect the area from further damage.

The first objective of the Conservancy was to protect the native fishery in this 6-mile stretch. During the period of 1974 and 1975, funds acquired from the James Irvine Foundation and Trout Unlimited allowed the Conservancy to conduct an extensive biological inventory of the river. The outcome was that a portion of the Preserve could be opened for public use with careful management of catch-and-release fishing. In 1975, the California Fish and Game Commission recognized the value of the proposal and officially designated a section of the river, which includes the Preserve, as a Wild Trout Stream.

One special regulation by the Conservancy includes a limit of 10 anglers on the Preserve at any one time. Five anglers per day may be reserved through the Nature Conservancy's California Field Office at (415) 777-0487. The remainder slots are available on a first-come, first served basis. Fly-fishers who have reservations must be at the Preserve by 10:00 a.m., otherwise they could lose their reservations to other individuals waiting to get in. Non-fly-fishers who wish to hike do not need a reservation. The Preserve opens at sunrise and closes at sunset.

This 6-mile section of the river is catch-and-release only, with the use of barbless hooks. If you plan to fish the Preserve stretch of the stream, make your reservations way ahead of time. For example, reservations for the month of October are usually booked by the early season, so make reservations early once you decide when you plan to fish the Preserve.

During the early season, the cold 40-degree water temperatures and higher flows may hamper fly-fishing activity. So, the best time to fish this stretch of stream is late morning or early afternoon when the sun warms the water. When the water temperatures reach the low to mid-50s, Golden Stones, Nos. 8-10, Pheasant Tails, Hare's Ears, and Bird's Nests, Nos. 12-14 with indicators are the most productive patterns.

Mayflies, caddisflies, and stoneflies are abundant in the McCloud. However, most of the fish are tuned in to nymphs. June, July, October, and November are the best months to pursue the robust rainbows and browns. October is the prime month at the Preserve, especially when the large October caddis hatches. The hatch occurs at the same time that brown trout are more abundant in the river below the dam. If you time it right, the brown trout fishing can be fantastic on the Preserve and upstream at Ah-Di-Na because they usually move upstream from Shasta Lake during summer and fall months to spawn.

If you use one line, a floating line with strike indicator and weighted flies or bead heads works best. When fishing pocket waters, dap the fly on the surface similar to a caddis laying eggs on the surface of the water.

The Preserve and Ah-Di-Na area is approximately an hour's drive from SR 299 at the town of McCloud. Although the road is not steep, the approximate 10 miles of winding and rugged access road consists of some unpaved sections and is narrow with large or sharp rocks in some spots.

Parking is available at Ah-Di-Na Campground. If you plan to fish the Preserve, park at Ah-Di-Na and walk down the road to reach the trail to the Preserve cabin. There is no road to the Preserve area.

McCloud River Fly Patterns

Suggested Flies	Hook Sizes	Best Months*
Nymphs and Emergers		
Brassie	14-18	June to November
Bird's Nest	10-14	May to November
Golden Stone Nymph	8-10	May to June
Gold Ribbed Hare's Ear	8-14	May to November
A.P. Black Nymph	10-12	May to November
Bead Head Emerging Caddis	14-16	May to July
Prince Nymph	10-12	May to October
Kaufmann's Dark Stone Nymph	4	July to October
Pheasant Tail	14-16	May to November
BH Pheasant Tail (Bead Head)	14-16	May to November
Red Fox Squirrel Nymph	8-12	May to October
Black Rubberlegs (Heavily Weighted)	2-8	May to October
Ted Fay Black and Brown Bombers	8-10	May to October
Cream, Olive CDC Caddis Emerger	12-16	May to July
Tan Caddis Larva, Pupa	12-14	May to July
Olive LaFontaine's Deep Sparkle Pupa	12-14	May to July
Tan, Olive Emergent Sparkle Pupa	12-14	May to July
Yellow Caddis Larva	6-8	September to October
LaFontaine's Orange Sparkle Pupa	6-8	September to October
Streamers		
Brown, Olive, or Black Woolly Bugger	8-12	May to November
BH Olive, Crystal Bugger	8-12	May to November
Muddler Minnow	8-12	May to November
Olive or Cinnamon Marabou Leech	2-4	May to October
Dry Flies		
Adams	12-16	May to November
Yellow Humpy	10-16	June to September
Tan and Olive Elk Hair Caddis	12-16	May to July
Cream and Olive Paraduns	14-16	May to July
Improved Sofa Pillow	6-8	September to October
Orange Bucktail Caddis	6-8	September to October
Orange Elk Hair Caddis	6-8	September to October

* Timing of hatches and activity may vary each season.

McCloud conservancy water.

Expansive Sacramento River

Known in the early days as the Nile of the West, the nearly 400-mile-long Sacramento River is the state's longest river. It also has the largest flow of water in California. The river has an average annual runoff of nearly 17 million acre feet.

At the north end of the Sacramento Valley, four major forks flow out of the Klamath Mountains, Cascade Range, and Modoc Plateau provinces: Upper Sacramento River, McCloud River, Squaw Creek, and Pit River. Situated in a land of ancient lava flows and active volcanoes, these principal watersheds form California's largest four-fingered man-made body of water. Shasta Lake provide fantastic, multifaceted fly-fishing experiences. This segment of the Sacramento River covers the area from its headwaters in the Klamath Mountains downstream to the Central Valley. It also covers portions of the lower Sacramento River for those interested in fly-fishing for shad, often referred to as the poor man's steelhead or tarpon.

From ancient times up to a century ago, the river meandered through the expansive Sacramento Valley. The flood plains were approximately five miles in width. At more than 500 feet deep, Shasta Lake has a capacity of 4,552,000 acre feet of water and covers 46 square miles. Shasta Dam is the highest center spillway dam in the United States. It is also one of the largest concrete structures ever built. Besides recreational use, the lake serves as a site of vital importance for water storage and conservation, flood-control use, and hydroelectric power for the Central Valley.

Within this watershed, anglers can find large, healthy and robust trout hiding in roiling pocket waters of the Upper Sacramento River. Tributary waters provide clear streams, quiet creeks, and placid lakes. These waters offer swarms of mayfly, stonefly, and caddisfly hatches throughout the season.

The Upper Sacramento River is a nationally known trout water. However, all forms of life in the river were devastated with the catastrophic July 14, 1991 train derailment at Cantara Loop near Dunsmuir. Because of the pesticide spill from a punctured tank car, the Upper Sacramento River and its tributaries were closed to all fishing from Box Canyon Dam to Shasta Lake. After extensive research and restoration efforts the Upper Sacramento began to heal from wounds inflicted by the spill.

The stretch of river below Box Canyon Dam and Shasta Lake re-opened for the 1994 trout fishing season. Prior to the opening, aquatic plants and invertebrates such as stoneflies were making a comeback. Also, insects from unaffected tributary streams moved downstream into the main river system. The trout population also showed signs of return.

Special regulations have been imposed since the re-opening of the Upper Sacramento River. The river and tributaries from Box Canyon Dam downstream to the Scarlett Way Bridge in Dunsmuir is a catch-and-release water using artificial lures with barbless hooks.

The Sacramento River and its tributaries, excluding Soda Creek from Scarlett Way Bridge downstream to the mouth of Soda Creek, has no restrictions except for a 5-fish limit per day and 10 in possession.

The Sacramento River and tributaries, including Soda Creek from the mouth of Soda Creek downstream to Shasta Lake, are also catch-and-release and artificial lures with barbless hooks. Other special regulations also apply to the river below Keswick Dam.

Bewitching Upper Sacramento and Trinity Divide Country Waters

The Sacramento Arm, known as the Upper Sacramento River, is

Nymph flies.

one of the most developed and accessible arms of Shasta Lake. As the stream travels alongside most of the highway and railroad route, easy river access makes this premier stream a fly-fisher's paradise for trophy fish.

The Sacramento River drainage begins its course above Lake Siskiyou below Mount Eddy (9,025 feet) in the Klamath Mountains Province. The area is known as the Trinity Divide country. Lakes and streams on the east slope of the divide in Siskiyou and Shasta counties flow into the Sacramento River system. It is possible to explore a wide variety of roadside and back-country angling destinations in the high country. Major tributaries such as the North, Middle, and South forks of the Sacramento River support good fishing. Most trails or roads travel next to the stream. However, forested vegetation often limits access to some good holding waters.

North Fork Sacramento River

The North Fork Sacramento River originates from springs above 7,000 feet in elevation on the southern slope of The Eddys mountain range. Flowing east, the river's flow drops rapidly to 3,600 feet in 8 river miles before joining with the South Fork. The stream features a series of falls surrounded by heavily timbered land. These falls are breathtaking. When you find an opening to the stream that has deep pools below falls, the wild native rainbows will provide some unforgettable action. The Sisson-Callahan National Recreation Trail follows the stream from the trailhead west of Lake Siskiyou to Mt. Eddy. This is an alternative route to the Deadfall Lakes in the Trinity River system located west of Mt. Eddy.

Middle Fork Sacramento River

A couple of hidden headwater lakes in the Middle Fork Sacramento River and within the rugged terrain can be productive at times. Toad and Porcupine lakes are the principle drainage system for the Middle Fork Sacramento River. The most productive method to connect with larger fish in these two Middle Fork waters is from a raft or float tube.

Toad and Porcupine Lakes

Situated below The Eddys, Toad Lake (6,935 feet) and Porcupine Lake (7,236 feet) offer several species of trout. To reach 24-acre, 40-foot-deep Toad Lake and 9-acre, 50-foot-deep Porcupine Lake, be prepared to travel on a steep, bumpy, rocky, and narrow 12-mile winding gravel and dirt road. The main access route to Toad Lake is about two and a half miles past the concrete bridge on Forest Service Road 26 south of Lake Siskiyou. Turn right on Forest Service Route 41N53. After traveling one-half mile on this road, make a left turn on Route 40N64. Continue on this road until you reach a cabin site where the road changes to rugged and rocky, requiring a high-clearance vehicle in order to continue. From the parking area at the cabin site, you can cover two lakes with a short hike on a trail to Toad and another mile of well-marked trail to Porcupine. Both of these lakes are also accessible by hiking on the ridge from the PCT. Porcupine Lake sits in a crater-like depression. Because it sits in a depression, the surface level does not overflow. However, the shoreline is dotted with granitic rocks.

South Fork Sacramento River

A major portion of the eastern slope lakes in the Divide country drain into the South Fork. Lake Siskiyou is the principle holding reservoir for several tributaries of the Sacramento River system. Gumboot, Cliff, Terrace, and Cedar lakes are headwaters to the South Fork Sacramento River. Turnouts along the rock-strewn South Fork allow anglers to drift flies to waiting hungry trout during early season when water levels are conducive to fishing. Drainage waters from Gray Rock lakes also flow into the South Fork Sacramento River.

To reach the South Fork, Lake Siskiyou, and Wagon Creek, take the Central Mt. Shasta City Exit off Interstate 5. Follow the signs to the State Fish Hatchery. Where W. Jessie Street (also known as Hatchery Lane) ends, turn left on Old Stage Road. When you come to a fork, take a right on Wm. A. Barr Road. Access to Wagon Creek is found by making a right turn on North Shore Road off Wm. A. Barr Road. Continue on if you are headed toward Lake Siskiyou or South Fork Forest Service Road 26 to Gumboot Lake.

Gumboot Lake

Southwest of the city of Mt. Shasta is 7-acre, 15-foot-deep, Gumboot Lake. Gumboot is approximately 10 miles from Lake Siskiyou. This lake is one of the best waters and it is accessible by driving directly to the lake on Forest Service Road 26. You have the option to fly-fish from a float tube, boat, rubber raft, or from shore. No motor is allowed in this tree-lined meadow-type brook and rainbow trout lake.

On August 22, 1954, the Mt. Shasta Rod and Gun Club constructed a small dam at Gumboot Lake. The dam was erected to increase the water surface area of the lake. This allows Gumboot to be an ideal fly-fishing lake during the fall months. Nearby, shallow 8-foot-deep, 3.5-acres Upper Gumboot Lake requires a short hike from the outlet of the lower lake. However, during severe winters, the lake is subject to winter kill.

August and September are the best months to fish Gumboot with hatches occurring during this period. The best time to fish Gumboot is early in the morning before the bright sunlight hits the water. Another peak period is during the evening when the sun is going down. The most ideal nymph patterns are Pheasant Tails, Bird's Nest, gray, olive, and beige, Nos. 14 to 16 and a No. 12 Olive Woolly Worms. For dry-fly patterns, a Mosquito pattern, Adams and Light Cahill in Nos. 16 to 18 produce some rewarding rod-bending actions.

Cliff Lakes, Terrace Lake, and Gray Rock Lakes

Spur routes off Forest Service Road 26 lead to a couple of lakes in the South Fork Sacramento River drainage. For the most part, the road is extremely rocky and not suitable for low-clearance vehicles. The first lake you come across is 9-foot-deep Cedar Lake, a brook trout fishery. Choked with aquatic vegetation surrounding most of the shoreline and other parts of the lake, it is difficult to launch a craft into Cedar Lake. Therefore, the Cliff Lakes and Terrace Lake are the watersheds to venture into.

To reach the Cliff Lakes and Cedar Lake, after crossing the bridge on Road 26 by approximately seven and one-half miles, make a left turn onto a faint rocky road identified by a sign in vertical position reading 39N05Y. It is important to note whenever you encounter a sign showing numbers on a post in a vertical position on Forest Service Roads, it signifies high-clearance 4WD vehicle use only. Drive as far as you can, then park and walk. It is an easy hike to the lake.

Upon reaching Cedar Lake, the road crosses the outlet of Cedar Lake and passes Lower Cliff Lake and ends at Cliff Lake. Prior to reaching Cliff Lake, the road splits. The one to the right is a private road. Do not attempt to enter this road. The road to the left is also on private land. Be aware of private roads and lands in the area. Please respect the rights of the landowner. Drive and park carefully as you approach the lake. Depending on the amount of flow coming out of Cedar Lake, you may be able to drive the one and a half mile to Cliff Lake. However, if you are unable to cross the outlet creek, it is a short hike to the lake.

Sitting at 5,730 feet, 3-acre, 11-foot-deep Lower Cliff Lake has a continual flow from the outlet of Cliff Lake, thereby sustaining enough water during the summer months. However, the lake gets quite swampy and heavily surrounded with trees and brushes. Anglers often bypass Lower Cliff as they head for Cliff Lake.

Cliff Lake (5,770 feet) is one of the most visited. This beautiful lake has a landscape headwall of craggy rocks and jagged peaks towering above the lake. Cliff Lake receives flow from Terrace Lake during a major portion of the year. The majority of brushy Cliff Lake is on private property. This 90-foot-deep, 22-acre lake has dual ownership. The Forest Service holds 6 acres while 16 acres are in private possession. In order to effectively fish Cliff Lake, you need a floating device to get into the waters. This lake holds some nice fish to 12 inches, plus occasional larger ones.

Lying southwest of Cliff Lake, 11-foot-deep, 2.5-acre Upper Cliff Lake (6,330 feet) requires 560 feet of steep, strenuous climbing over high rock walls that rise abruptly in a short distance. This tiny body of pocket water is stocked with brook trout. Southeast of Cliff, larger 3.5-acre, 37-foot-deep Terrace Lake (6,214 feet), is reachable from a shorter, steep cross-country climb with over 400 feet elevation gain. Rainbow, brook, and Eagle Lake trout inhabit this glacial cirque lake.

Situated in the Castle Crags Wilderness, several off-the-beaten-track lakes, such as Gray Rock Lake (5,970 feet), Upper Gray Rock Lake (6,275 feet), Timber Lake (6,017 feet), and Scott Lake (6,190 feet), are reachable from a steep trail and cross-country route. Spring and fall are the best times to fish the Gray Rock Lakes group. The 20-foot-deep, 4.5-acre Upper Gray Rock Lake has the best fly-fishing because of its open space. Spring and fall are the best times to fish this watershed. On the other hand, the 2.5-acre, 10-foot-deep Scott Lake holds various species of trout, such as rainbow, brook, and Eagle Lake trout. This impoundment is surrounded by brush and heavy vegetation. It is over the ridge from the Gray Rock Lakes. The 11-acre, 20-foot-deep Gray Rock Lake and 2-acre, 15-foot-deep Timber Lake hold Eastern brook trout.

Off Forest Service Route 26 to Gumboot Lake, at the wooden bridge, turn left and take road 40N43. A spur road with a Forest Service road sign reading 39N45 in a vertical position leads to the Gray Rock Lakes Trailhead. These routes are extremely rocky for passenger cars. After traveling approximately 500 feet, make a right turn onto road 39N45 for one and one-half miles, then turn onto road 39N41. The road ends at the trailhead for the Gray Rock Lakes. To reach the Gray Rock Lakes, take Trail 5W07.

Seven Lakes Basin

Other possibile explorations include the waters of the Seven Lakes Basin. The 4-mile one-day or backpack trip to the basin provides some solitude. Situated in Siskiyou County, this small 2.5-acre, 46-foot-deep hike-in Helen Lake (6,700 feet) is one of the most attractive lakes in this basin. It has openings around the shorelines for fly-fishing.

Within this basin, 4.5-acre, 35-foot-deep Upper Seven Lake (6,300 feet) holds brook, rainbow, and Eagle Lake trout. The lake is surrounded by dense brush and timber. From FSR 26 where it ends at the PCT Gumboot Trailhead, a short descending hike on Trail 5W09 will get you into this Seven Lakes Basin watershed.

Castle Lake

Castle Lake is one of few lakes that is accessible by paved road. Early spring and again in the fall, rainbow and brook trout take flies readily. There's a Forest Service campground one-quarter mile below this popular lake. The largest, deepest, and one of the most attractive lakes in the Divide, 120-foot-deep, 47-acre Castle Lake (5,436 feet) flows into Castle Creek, a tributary to the Upper Sacramento River.

Many anglers frequent Castle Lake during the summer months. It's 11 miles from the town of Mt. Shasta. Upon reaching Lake Siskiyou, turn left on the first paved road after crossing Box Canyon Dam and continue uphill to Castle Lake. Most of the shoreline is brushy and forested. However, float tubes or other watercraft are ideal means for taking in some good fishing.

Lake Siskiyou and Wagon Creek

The North, Middle, South forks, and a host of tributary waters, such as Wagon, Cold, Castle, and Scott Camp, flow into Lake Siskiyou. The water gushes out of Box Canyon Dam near the town of Dunsmuir.

The headwaters of spring-fed Wagon Creek originate from the slope of 9,025-foot Mt. Eddy, the highest peak in the

Castle Lake.

Twelve-inch brook trout.

province. Wagon Creek inlet on the north arm of Lake Siskiyou, for example, is great fly-fishing water for brook, rainbow, and brown trout. These species of trout provide prolific action in the deep cool waters of the inlet cove. Be cautious when crossing rivulets along the creek because certain portions of the creekbed close to the lake are similar to quicksand.

Boating along the coves of tributaries also provides rewarding action. I have had my best luck in the cool fall months when lake levels are low and the fish move into inlet water areas. In addition, crowds have lessened and the trees are in colorful transition. Early spring is also a supreme time for fly-fishers to fish the Wagon Creek arm and along the eastern shores near the dam. Since water temperatures along the edge of the lake are warmer, baitfish tend to cruise the shorelines. Therefore, streamers such as Olive Matukas, Muddler Minnows, and Woolly Buggers in olive, brown, and black crystal hair in Nos. 4 to 8, are the most productive patterns.

Intimate Upper Sacramento River: Box Canyon Dam to Shasta Lake

Situated above Shasta Lake north of Redding, the Upper Sacramento River is one of Northern California's most productive and longest roadside streams. The stretch of river below Box Canyon Dam and Shasta Lake is known as the Upper Sacramento River. This segment runs along Interstate 5 from Dunsmuir to Shasta Lake. Easy stream access in many sections provide many opportunities for anglers to cover a host of waters. It is a unique stream often frequented by fly-fishers in this part of the state.

As the cool and crystal-clear Upper Sacramento River weaves through the charming and historic old railroad town of Dunsmuir, anglers can enjoy many magnificent scenic sights from Box Canyon Dam, Cantara Loop, Mossbrae Falls, to Castle Crags State Park in this upper section. A noticeable change takes place as the river expands into a larger river system below Dunsmuir to Shasta Lake.

In August 1886, the Southern Pacific arrived at an area now called the town of Dunsmuir. Historic Dunsmuir was named after Alexander Dunsmuir, a coal baron of British Columbia and San Francisco, who passed through Cedar Flat, which was a station consisting of a boxcar. He promised the settlers a fountain if the future town was named after him. In January 1887, the proposal for the name change from Pusher to Dunsmuir was accepted. Subsequently, the fountain was erected at the railroad station. Recently, the fountain was moved to a new home at Dunsmuir Park.

The Upper Sacramento River is dependent on releases out of Lake Siskiyou during the summer months when flows are low. This stream is best fished during early and late season. Before heavy snow pack melts in the spring, outstanding trout fishing is possible for a while. During summer, as water levels drop, the deeper, and shaded canyons above Dunsmuir to the Box Canyon area offer anglers better opportunities for cooperating trout. Despite its great accessibility to prime pocket waters, riffles, and runs, this stretch of the river does not seem to be crowded or over-fished. The river receives the majority of its water from snow runoff in the spring and the releases from Lake Siskiyou for most of its flow during the rest of the season.

After runoffs have subsided, one of my favorite waters for safe wading in the upper section from the Cantara Loop access upstream towards Box Canyon Dam. The mouths of Ney Springs and Stink Creek are also productive. There is also an option to hike downstream following the railroad tracks toward Big Canyon Creek. When walking the trails along the tracks of Cantara Loop, be sure to stay on the same side of the tracks. As the train approaches on this loop, stay on one side away from the tracks until the train passes the area.

One of the best fishing sections of the river that many anglers often overlook is in the center of town at Dunsmuir. Access is from the Prospect Avenue Foot Bridge, the access parking at Scarlett Way, the city park off of North Dunsmuir Avenue, Central and South exits to reach the center of town, River Avenue, and Soda Creek. The Soda Creek access to the Sacramento River is approximately 3 miles south of Dunsmuir.

As we head downstream to Castella, we come into more expansive waters. A series of deep pools hold larger trout in this section. There is much rock-climbing to maneuver in order to reach productive waters. Little runs, riffles, and pools dominate this section. Access to the pool waters is between Sweetbrier and Sweetbrier Creek. Eight miles south of Dunsmuir is the Sweetbrier access. This section has excellent waters for fly-fishing. However, reaching the waters gets complicated in some sections. You need to be surefooted and possess good balance to climb around large boulders. From Sweetbrier, head south to other river accesses and parking at Conant, Flume Creek, Upper Sims, and Sims to Shotgun Creek. Fly-fishers do not frequent the stretch of water from Shotgun Creek downstream to Shasta Lake as much as the upper river.

After runoff conditions have subsided, hatches occur throughout summer and fall, allowing anglers to fish their favorite stretches in this cold freestone stream. During hot weather days, the fish tend to hold up in deeper waters. However, once it cools down, they will surface to feed in shallower waters. Also, as the weather warms and water levels drop, the most productive sections are in the shaded and deeper canyons near the town of Dunsmuir.

Lake Siskiyou.

Dropper Fly Setup Combinations

An effective technique in the Upper Sacramento River and other streams is to set up two fly patterns in tandem. The method consists of tying the main fly at the end of the tippet and the dropper fly above it. For example, tie a weighted Black or Brown Bomber in Nos. 8-10 as the main fly. For the dropper fly, tie approximately an extra 12 to 18 inches of line to the tippet knot. Use either a triple surgeon's or blood knot for the connection. The Yellow Jackets, Caddis Larvaes, Burlaps, or Cro Flys in Nos. 8-10 are good candidates for the dropper fly.

This method gives you the opportunity to use two flies in succession. With this technique, you eliminate the ritual of changing flies when you have crucial periods. In many cases during a small window of time when trout are in a feeding frenzy, the dropper fly method is an ideal set up. Alternate fly patterns are a Caddis Pupa as the main fly and a small Elk Hair Caddis on the dropper, or a Woolly Bugger and Hare's Ear combination.

In many streams, my favorite combination includes a Pheasant Tail Nymph as the main fly with a Caddis Pupa or Elk Hair Caddis as the dropper. Other times, I use either a variation of two nymphs, or a combination of a nymph and a dry fly. In most instances, the Pheasant Tail Nymph is one of my all-around favorites.

Use the larger, heavier fly as the principal fly. Regardless of what fly pattern you plan to use for the dropper fly set up, you will need to vary the length of the tippet and dropper line as well as adjust the amount of weight of the fly in order to match the correct depth and speed of the current.

Upper Sacramento River Fly Patterns

Suggested Flies	*Hook Sizes*	*Best Months**
Nymphs and Emergers		
Bird's Nest	10-14	April to November
Golden, Black, Brown Stone Nymph	4-10	April to June
Gold Ribbed Hare's Ear	10-12	April to November
Hare's Ear Nymph	10-12	April to November
A.P. Black Nymph	10-12	April to November
BH Pheasant Tail	14-16	April to November
Black Bomber (Heavily Weighted)	8-10	May to August
Brown Bomber (Heavily Weighted)	8-10	August to November
Woolly Worm (Black with Grizzly Hackle)	8-10	June to November
Peacock Herl Nymph	8-12	June to November
(Grizzly or Brown Hackle)		
Red Fox Squirrel Nymph	8-12	May to October
Black Rubberlegs (Heavily Weighted)	2-6	April to October
Prince Nymph	10-12	May to October
Cream, Olive CDC Caddis Emerger	12-16	May to August
Tan Caddis Larva, Pupa	12-14	May to August
Olive LaFontaine's Deep Sparkle Pupa	12-14	May to August
Tan, Olive Emergent Sparkle Pupa	12-14	May to August
Yellow Caddis Larva	6-8	September to October
LaFontaine's Orange Sparkle Pupa	6-8	September to October
Streamers		
Brown, Olive, or Black Woolly Bugger	8-12	May to November
BH Olive, Crystal Bugger	8-12	May to November
Dry Flies		
Light Cahill	12-16	June to August
Yellow or Orange Humpy	10-14	June to September
Tan and Olive Elk Hair Caddis	14-16	May to July
Goddard Caddis	14-16	May to July
Yellow Jacket	8-10	August to October
Cro Fly	8-10	May to November
Improved Sofa Pillow	4-6	September to October
Orange Bucktail Caddis	6-8	September to October
Orange Elk Hair Caddis	6-8	September to October

* Timing of hatches and activity may vary each season.

Smaller Sacramento River Tributary Waters

A series of smaller trout waters lying east of the Sacramento River are blessed with sophisticated rainbows, brooks, and brown trout. These waters include the main stem Battle Creek, North and South Battle Creek, Lassen National Park waters, and other Sacramento River tributaries.

Battle Creek Drainage Waters

The Battle Creek drainage hosts phenomenal mountain lakes and miles of streams. North Fork Battle Creek originates from springs below Huckleberry Mountain (7,064 feet) and Latour Butte (6,740 feet). It then flows into North Battle Creek Reservoir. Other North Fork Battle Creek watersheds are: McCumber Reservoir, Nora and Grace lakes.

South Fork Battle Creek, on the other hand, begins its course from springs above 6,200 feet north of Mineral, McGowan Lake (6,072), a brook and brown trout fishery, Nanny Creek, and Martin Creek.

North Fork Battle Creek Reservoir

North Battle Creek Reservoir (5,571 feet)—a brown, rainbow, and Eagle Lake trout fishery—has 10 camp units and 5 walk-in camp units. This 28-foot-deep reservoir is accessible by taking SR 44, approximately 3.5 miles east of Viola. Turn north onto Road 32N17 and drive 5 miles; make a left turn onto Road 32N31 for 4 miles, turn right onto Road 32N18 and proceed for approximately one-half mile. Do not overlook North Fork Battle Creek where access is open.

McCumber Reservoir

Tucked away above SR 44 is another PG&E impoundment in the North Battle Creek drainage. McCumber Reservoir (4,086 feet) is home to some large rainbow and brown trout. The best time to fish this 35-foot-deep Shasta County reservoir is during the spring before it is choked with weeds near the shallow areas. The weed beds will generally bloom as soon as the water warms. However, if there is a considerable amount of snowmelt in some seasons, the weed growth can be delayed for several weeks or so.

McCumber is primarily a spring and early summer fishery because of its shallow water that heats up during the summer. However, during the fall months, brown trout will move in to shorelines to spawn making it an ideal time to fish again. The dam area, center of the lake, and the edges of weed beds are the most productive areas. You may be surprised with large trout hiding beneath or between the weed beds. At times, it is difficult to cast from shore. Marshy shorelines surround certain areas around the lake, so it is not conducive to foot traffic.

The reservoir is restricted to electric motors only since it is a water-supply impoundment. Prams, canoes, or similar watercraft are the best means to get to where the trout are. Effective fly patterns such as Woolly Buggers, Muddler Minnows, and other streamer patterns produce well in this lake.

To reach McCumber Reservoir, turn left on Lake McCumber Road from SR 44, which is located 4 miles west of Viola. Drive 2 miles from Lake McCumber Road to the parking lot near the dam.

The Idyllic Manzanita Lake

Set below the snowcapped mountain of Lassen Peak (10, 457 feet) in Lassen National Park is the serene beauty of Manzanita

Manzanita Lake.

Lake. Manzanita Creek begins its course between Lassen Peak (10,457 feet) and Loomis Peak (8,658 feet), and continues its flow to Manzanita Lake (5,847 feet). Originally, this was a natural lake. However, in 1912 Northern California Power Company built an outlet dam, raising the level of the lake. Several hundred feet below the outlet of the lake, the creek disappears into porous volcanic ashes. It then continues its flow to the confluence of North Fork Battle Creek below McCumber Reservoir.

A tributary to North Fork Battle Creek in the Sacramento River system, this prime trout stillwater fishery in Shasta County provides some spectacular fishing for large rainbow and brown trout. Mayflies, caddisflies, and damselflies provide the fish with an abundance of food. Look for mayfly hatches in the shallow areas. The fish are selective and at times it is difficult to arouse them to take artificial offerings. Use long leaders to 16 feet and 6X tippets with indicators on floating lines. Make delicate presentations with floating, sinking, or sink-tip lines. With a sink-tip or sinking line, change to a larger tippet and impart slower retrieves. Most fishing action occurs during late spring after snow melts, for most of the summer season, and

Float-tube rainbow trout.

fall. The best time to fish Manzanita is right after snow melt. If possible, avoid fishing this popular lake on weekends or holidays because large groups of anglers dot the waters. Early or late season and weekdays are the best bet to bypass the heavy angler traffic jam.

Callibaetis mayfly hatches occur early in the season, the trout are hungry and not as selective. Fishing is also successful at dusk in August with the large caddisfly (Dicosmoecus genus of Limnephilidae family) hatch, known as the motorboat caddis to many fly-fishers. The name is derived from this caddis skating across the water before taking off, creating a V-wake similar to one made by a ski boat. The commotion drives the trout into a frenzied state. Prepare to cast large Nos. 6-8 Rusty Oranges and Golden Stimulators or Orange Elk Hair Caddis when this action takes place.

Hike quietly along the banks wearing polarized glasses to spot cruising fish. Wading is possible in the shallows. However, float tubes, prams, and canoes, on the other hand, will cover more waters. This method is made more effective by casting to weed beds and working the coves, sand flats, and islands. Motorized boats are prohibited in this 32-foot-deep lake.

The northwest entry station to Lassen Volcanic National Park is 50 miles east of Redding on SR 44. Self-registering camping facilities next to the lake are available on a first-come, first-served basis.

A selection of Callibaetis nymphs, Pheasant Tails, Gold Ribbed Hare's Ears, and Bird's Nest nymphs—with and without bead heads—will work all season. The most effective patterns for Manzanita Lake are listed in the following table.

Mazanita Fly Patterns

Suggested Flies	Hook Sizes	Best Months*
Nymphs and Emergers		
Bird's Nest	12-14	May to November
Gold Ribbed Hare's Ear	12-14	May to November
Hare's Ear Nymph	12-16	May to November
A.P. Black Nymph	12-16	May to November
Pheasant Tail Nymph	14-18	May to November
Prince Nymph	10-12	May to October
Cream, Olive CDC Caddis Emerger	12-16	May to August
Tan Caddis Larva, Pupa	12-14	May to August
Olive LaFontaine's Deep Sparkle Pupa	12-14	May to August
Tan, Olive Emergent Sparkle Pupa	12-14	May to August
Damsel Fly	8-12	June to September
Dragonfly	6	June to September
Yellow Caddis Larva	8	Late July to August
LaFontaine's Orange Sparkle Pupa	8	Late July to August
Midge Pupa	18-22	June to September
Streamers		
Brown or Olive Woolly Bugger	6-10	May to November
BH Olive, Crystal Bugger	6-10	May to November
Zonker	6-10	May to November
Maribou Leech (Olive, Brown, and Black)	6-10	May to November
Dry Flies		
Light Cahill	16	June to August
Haystack Callibaetis	12-18	June to October
Tan and Olive Elk Hair Caddis	14-16	May to August
Damsel Fly	10	June to July
Caddis (Motorboat Rust/Orange)	8-10	Late July to August
Midge Adult	18-22	July to September
Parachute Adam	14-18	June to October
Black Ant	12-16	June to August
Beetle	12-16	June to August

* Timing of hatches and activity may vary each season.

Grace Lake.

Yellow Marabou Muddler.

Grace and Nora Lakes

Grace Lake (3,480 feet) is just a couple of hundred feet from Nora Lake (3,431 feet). Situated southeast of Shingletown, these two lakes are both well stocked with several species of trout and open to fishing all year. Do not overlook the inlet or outlet waters of these lakes. Nora Lake is an artificial lake located near the ruins of Noble's Castle. Nora and Grace were daughters of H. H. Noble of the Shasta Power Company.

Grace and Nora lakes have 10 picnic units each. Access to these two lakes is out of Shingletown on SR 44. Upon arrival at Shingletown, turn south onto Manton Road. Continue for a mile then turn left. Follow the dirt road for 0.8 mile to Grace Lake. From Grace, travel another one-half mile south to Nora Lake.

South Fork Battle Creek

A short distance northwest of Mineral off of SR 36, public access to the South Fork Battle Creek is in a portion of U.S. Forest Service land that offers some excellent rainbow, brook, brown, and Eagle Lake trout. The best stretch of water is the area above and below the bridge. There is a campground next to the stream.

An abundance of insect life, such as stoneflies and caddisflies, inhabit this cold and clear South Fork stream. I have had great success using short-line nymphing in this medium-sized stream. Effective patterns are Nos. 12-14 olive and brown nymphs such as Gold Ribbed Hare's Ears, Pheasant Tail Nymphs, Bird's Nests; Nos. 10-12 Cream and Olive Elk Hair Caddis, Tan Caddis Larva Pupas, and Nos. 6-10 Olive and Brown Woolly Bugger streamers. In the evenings just before dark, use a No. 12 Cream Elk Hair Caddis dry-fly pattern.

Main Stem Battle Creek

Great fly-fishing for rainbow and Eagle Lake trout is had on the main stem of Battle Creek. This stream meanders west toward the Sacramento River on the Shasta and Tehama County line near Balls Ferry. The stream is open to fishing 250 feet upstream from Coleman National Fish Hatchery to the Coleman Power House. The Coleman Hatchery Road is located east of Cottonwood and ends at the power house. Upstream from the power house, the stream enters into steep canyon waters.

Lassen Volcanic National Park Waters

Besides Manzanita Lake, there are other waters within the park you may wish to drive or hike to. However, always check at the Entrance Station for any closures or changes in fishing regulations from the California Department of Fish and Game is current Sport Fishing Regulations within the national park. The waters in the national park are home to native rainbow trout as well as introduced brook, and brown trout. Open season in the park conforms to the DFG regulation. The National Park lies within Lassen, Plumas, Shasta, and Tehama counties. Lassen National Park operates seven campgrounds. Campsites are available on a first-come, first-served basis and are self-registering.

Emerald Lake, Manzanita Creek above Manzanita Lake, and Manzanita Lake within 150 feet of the inlet of Manzanita Creek are closed to fishing at all times. Boating is permitted on all park lakes except Boiling Springs Lake, Emerald Lake, Lake Helen (8,164 feet), and Reflection Lake. Also, motorized boats are prohibited on all national park lakes and waterways. It is noted that all boaters must wear Coast Guard approved personal flotation devices. The trout fishing season in the park conforms with the DFG regulations, except that Grassy Creek connecting Horseshoe Lake and Snag Lake is closed to fishing between October 1 and June 15.

The following lakes and streams hold various species of trout in the national park. I organized the waters by Lakes and Streams, County, USGS 7.5' Topo Maps, Elevation, and Fish Species. Rainbow Trout (RT), Brown Trout (BN), Brook Trout (BK):

Lakes

Butte Lake	Lassen County	Prospect Peak	6,043 feet	RT
Crystal Lake	Lassen County	Mt. Harkness	7,299 feet	RT, BN
Dream Lake	Plumas County	Reading Peak	5,716 feet	BK
Hat Lake	Shasta County	West Prospect Peak	6,440 feet	BK
Horseshoe Lake	Shasta County	Mt. Harkness	7,299 feet	RT, BK
Ridge Lake	Shasta County	Lassen Peak	5,895 feet	RT
Snag Lake	Lassen County	Prospect Peak	6,076 feet	RT, PK
Summit Lake	Shasta County	Reading Peak	6,889 feet	RT
Terrace Lake	Shasta County	Reading Peak	7,680 feet	BK

Streams

Bailey Creek, NF	Shasta County	Lassen Peak	---	RT, BK
Grassy Creek	Lassen County	Prospect Peak	---	RT, BK
	Shasta County	Mt. Harkness		
Grassy Swale	Shasta County	Mt. Harkness	---	RT
		Reading Peak		
Hat Creek	Shasta County	Reading Peak	---	RT
Hot Springs Creek	Plumas County	Mt. Harkness	---	RT, BN
	Shasta County	Reading Peak		
Kings Creek	Plumas County	Mt. Harkness	---	RT
	Shasta County	Reading Peak		
Rice Creek, N. Arm	Plumas County	Childs Meadow	---	RT
	Shasta County			
Sulphur Creek (Below Falls)	Tehama County	Lassen Peak	---	RT, BN
Summit Creek	Shasta County	Reading Peak	---	RT

Cascading waterfall.

Mill Creek

Mill Creek, tributary to the Sacramento River, is an important spawning ground for spring and fall-run chinook salmon and steelhead. The upper creek provides miles of riffles, pocket waters, and small pools. Below the campgrounds, Mill Creek switches to miniature boulder-strewn pocket freestone water with cascading waterfalls through narrow canyon walls.

Spring-fed Mill Creek originates from the southwestern sector of Lassen Volcanic National Park below Diamond Peak (7,968 feet) from East and West Sulphur creeks. It then merges to form Mill Creek near the southern entrance of the national park. As the creek continues to flow south, additional springs increase the flow.

To reach Mill Creek from SR 36, turn south on SR 172 from Mineral until you reach Mill Creek. Mill Creek and Hole in the Ground campgrounds parallel the creek. The waters above Mill Creek Campground flow through a meadow setting. However, the Hole in the Ground stretch has a series of riffles, small pocket waters, small pools, and few runs in some spots. This section possesses a gradual elevation drop as it heads toward canyon waters. Hardy anglers can hike downstream for miles in the canyon waters to enjoy solitary fishing. In this long stretch, climbing over rocks and weaving in and out of trees and other vegetation is in order here. However, the beauty of the fantastic cascading waterfalls along its course heading to the confluence of the Sacramento River at Los Molinas is overwhelming.

Caddisflies and stoneflies make up the bulk of the hatches in this creek. So use caddisfly and stonefly patterns with bead heads in the faster waters. Short-line nymphing with strike indicators is the best method to work the pocket waters. In riffle waters, casting your line across the stream and letting it drift is another effective method. One of Mill Creek's special regulations is catch-and-release (0-limit) and the use of artificial lures with barbless hooks, from the Lassen Park boundary downstream to the U.S. Geological Survey gauging station cable crossing at the mouth of Mill Creek Canyon.

Majestic Lower Sacramento River

The lower Sacramento River below Keswick Dam in Redding downstream to Anderson is a trophy trout, salmon, and steelhead fishery. A 15-mile stretch of the lower Sacramento River below Keswick Dam downstream to Anderson supports an abundance of insect life, caddisflies, and eggs from spawning chinook salmon. This segment of the river, with riffles and pools, is a great all-year fly-fishing destination for some of the finest wild trophy native rainbow trout fishing. Floating or drifting with a boat is the best method for these waters. However, the ideal fishing conditions for wading are when the river's flow from Keswick Dam out of Shasta Lake is cut back to between 3,500 to 4,000 cubic feet per second (cfs) during fall, winter, and early spring.

The stretch of the lower Sacramento River is more expansive than the upper river. However, be cautious of slippery rocks in this

Sacramento River at Redding.

large river. For safety, wear wading shoes with cleat soles and use a strong wading staff at all times.

The flow fluctuates radically from 3,500 to above 14,500 cfs. The high flows generally start in May and during the summer months when the water is released down to the Central Valley for irrigation and flood control. By mid-summer, the water decreases for optimum fishing again. Therefore, the best time to fish the lower Sacramento River is when the stream drops during late winter, early spring, and mid-summer. It is important to check ahead for the cfs with the Bureau of Reclamation's hot line at (530) 246-7594. This same phone number also reports flows for the Trinity River.

When the caddis hatch is on, the river's silence is broken by large rainbows gorging themselves on the abundance of caddis. Other effective fly patterns are Bird's Nest and Hare's Ear nymphs. Most of these wild native trout are in the 14- to 18-inch range. However, larger fish from 20 to 24 inches can surprise you. This portion of the Sacramento River has a reputation of hosting many anglers from all over the state.

Some of the best fishing occurs in the city of Redding. When the flow is low, wading is possible in the Posse Grounds area in the city. For river access take the SR 299 West exit. Continue on SR 299 for approximately two miles to the Park Marina offramp. Make a right turn at the offramp. Continue north on the road to the Civic Auditorium and Posse Grounds. The Posse Grounds (Rodeo Grounds) is next to the Civic Auditorium and Trade Convention Center. River access with trails and a boat-launching site is near the parking lot.

Another river access in the city of Redding is below the SR 299 Bridge and is known as the East Turtle Bay Fishing Access. This site is accessible from Interstate 5 by taking the Cypress Avenue Exit and heading west. Make a right turn onto Bechelli Lane. Continue on Bechelli Lane until it dead ends near the SR 299 overpass Bridge.

Public River Trail Access

Local anglers mostly frequent a convenient public river access trail in the city of Redding. The trail encompasses the stretch between the Anderson-Cottonwood Irrigation District canal in the city limits of Redding and Keswick Dam. It runs from a parking area at the bottom of Dieselhorst Bridge five miles upstream where it crosses a newly constructed footbridge. It then drops down the river on the opposite bank, offering access to the entire stretch of approximately 10 miles of shorelines. In the gorge section, there are some excellent fly-fishing waters holding large trout in the deeper stretches. The entire segment of the river is open to the public, an ideal condition for anglers who do not own a boat.

Access to the river trail is from the Cypress Avenue exit from Interstate 5. Continue west until the highway signs direct you to SR 273. Make a left turn prior to crossing the bridge on Market Street and drop down to the parking area.

In the fall, chinook salmon arrive into the Sacramento River. This is an ideal time to fly-fish for salmon. Look for riffle waters below salmon pools. Single salmon-egg patterns such as Glo Bugs are ideal during this period when loose eggs drift from redds. Also, rainbows are vulnerable to the salmon patterns as they gorge on salmon eggs.

Four distinct races of chinook salmon are found in the Sacramento River: fall, late fall, winter, and spring runs. All species of salmon have declined substantially during the past years. Without immediate action, it is feared the fall and winter runs may soon become extinct. Steelhead populations have also declined in recent years. Therefore, special regulations have been imposed upon the salmon and steelhead fisheries.

Whiskeytown Lake and Tributary Waters

As part of the Whiskeytown-Shasta-Trinity National Recreation Area (NRA), the National Park Service administers the Whiskeytown Unit. Whiskeytown Lake (1,210 feet), within the Unit, is located 10 miles west of Redding on SR 299 West. This Shasta County lake has a constant water level because of water diverted from Lewiston Lake to the Trinity River. It then flows through Clear Creek Tunnel to Judge Francis Carr Powerhouse and into Whiskeytown Lake. Subsequently, water is released to the Sacramento River from Whiskeytown out of Clear Creek, a tributary of the Sacramento River.

You have several alternatives for fishing this Whiskeytown NRA water. When there is sufficient water above the lake in Clear Creek to maintain trout-stocking programs during the season, fishing is best from the inlet to about a mile above SR 299 within the NRA Unit jurisdiction. Also, you can fish in various sections of Clear Creek below the dam where there is access to the stream. Other tributaries, such as Brandy and Boulder creeks, flow into the lake, also provide some good fishing.

Float tubers or other small-craft users can relish fishing the coves at the western side of the lake near the inlet areas of Boulder, Dry, and Brandy creeks. There is a campground at Dry Creek and a campground and picnic area at Brandy Creek along the south shore.

If you are coming from Redding on SR 299, access routes to Clear Creek below the dam, Brandy, and Boulder creeks are from J.F. Kennedy Memorial Drive on the eastern side of the lake. To reach Brandy and Boulder creeks, and inlet coves of the lake, make a right turn on South Shore Drive.

An alternative route to the powerhouse and picnic areas is on the western side of the lake. From SR 299 turn south on Powerhouse Road, then to South Shore Drive Road to reach the Boulder Creek, Dry Creek, and Brandy Creek areas.

Small nymphs, such as Hare's Ear, Pheasant Tails, Bird's Nests, as well as caddis emergers and Bivisibles in Nos. 12-14 will produce phenomenal fly-fishing in mid-season. Use smaller sizes in the fall. At times, Nos. 8-12 olive and brown Woolly Buggers are effective.

Poor Man's Steelhead: American Shad

The lower Sacramento River from Red Bluff to Princeton hosts an excellent American shad fishery. Shad generally enter major river systems from late April to late June or early July when river flows are high.

The American shad (*Alosa sapidissima*) is an anadromous fish with great fighting ability. This fish is often referred to as the "poor man's steelhead or tarpon." Belonging to the herring family, the American shad does not have an adipose fin or a lateral line. A row of black spots appears on the forward and dorsal sides of the fish. Shades of metallic blue predominate on the top and sides while the bellies are bright silvery. Averaging 3 to 5 pounds, the female shad is considerably larger than the male. The American shad has a single dorsal fin on the middle of the back. The ventral fins are directly below the dorsal fin. Its sharp-edged and saw-toothed belly separates it from the herring and sardine. A row of spots high and to the front of the American shad separates it from the smaller threadfin shad.

The American shad was first introduced in the Sacramento River system in 1871. Several years later, additional stocking took place. A great number enter the Sacramento River and its major tributaries: Feather, Yuba, and American rivers. However, lower American River below Nimbus Dam has the best-designated access areas for shore fishing and wading throughout the river. In the lower Sacramento River, numerous shad filter into the river system when the run is in. A smaller run of shad also enters the Russian, Klamath, and Eel rivers. A lesser run of shad migrates to the San Joaquin River system.

If one is new to steelhead fly-fishing, shad fishing with a fly rod provides excellent practice. Traditionally, the ideal time to fish for shad is late May or early June. At this time, the run peaks when water temperatures range from 60 to 65 degrees. Shad take flies readily at this time. Patterns with chartreuse, orange, red, purple, white, yellow, and bright color combinations are the most productive. Nickel hooks in Nos. 4-8 with bead-chain eyes for added weight are often necessary to get flies down to the fish.

When shad are in the river system, the key is to locate the fish. In the early season, they congregate in schools. As the season progresses, shad hold in spawning grounds downstream from dams, the inner sides of bends in the river, or any depressions in stream bottoms. In Northern California, most spawning rituals occur over gravel or sand bottoms.

Several river accesses that accommodate excellent shad fly-fishing include north of Los Molinas, Woodson Bridge State Recreation Area at Corning, Road 29 south of Hamilton City, Ordbend, Road 44 north of Glenn, and the Princeton Gravel Bar in Princeton.

•**Los Molinas Area.** Good shore fishing 7 miles north of Los Molinas late in the season. Turn west off SR 99 on Le Claire Avenue and drive to the road's end.

•**Woodson Bridge State Recreation Area at Corning.** Campground facilities. No boating access. Good fly-fishing during the middle of the season. Woodson Bridge is accessible out of the Gardner Ferry Road from Interstate 5 at Corning or from SR 99 north of Chico.

•**Road 29 South of Hamilton City.** A good fly-fishing site throughout the season. Located approximately 10 miles south of Hamilton City off SR 45.

•**Ordbend.** Good fly-fishing here, south of the Ordbend Bridge on the east bank of the river. This site can be accessed from SR 45 by heading toward the river on the main intersection in Ordbend.

•**Road 44 North of Glenn.** This is an excellent long, open gravel bar for wading and accommodates many fly-fishers. Early season is best here. Road 44 is located off SR 45 just north of Glenn. Continue on this road toward the river.

•**Princeton Gravel Bar.** Good fly-fishing during the early season. This site is accessible by turning east off SR 45 in Princeton. Drive up over the levee and continue toward the river. However, do not drive over the gravel bar, there's a high risk of getting stuck.

Lesser-Known West Slope Waters

Two lesser-known waters in the western side of the Sacramento River system offer great fishing opportunities: Middle Fork Stony Creek and Putah Creek.

Middle Fork Stony Creek

Middle Fork Stony Creek is of significance to fly-fishers. This Mendocino National Forest creek is one of the streams Fish and Game Commission have designated as a Catch-and-Release Trout Water pursuant to the Trout and Steelhead Conservation and Management Planning Act of 1979.

Middle Fork Stony Creek begins its course from springs between Snow Mountain West (7,038 feet) and Snow Mountain East (7,056 feet) out of the Snow Mountain Wilderness in Colusa County. Immediately, it crosses into Lake County. The stream flows in a northwesterly direction, collecting spring waters before turning east below Crockett Peak (6,172 feet). After flowing a distance, it turns south into Glenn County and drops down to Red Bridge (1,680 feet) into the confluence of South Fork Stony Creek. Nearby North Stony Creek also joins the South Fork.

North Fork, South Fork, and Middle Fork Stony Creek at Red Bridge are accessible from Fouts Springs Road. Several campgrounds are in the area—North Fork Campground, Fouts and Mill Creek campgrounds located west of Stonyford. From Stonyford, this Sacramento River tributary flows north into Stony Gorge Reservoir.

The Department of Fish and Game has imposed special regulations on Stony Creek and the Middle Fork from Red Bridge upstream. Check the most current Sport Fishing Regulations before fishing this stream. Access to the Fouts Springs area is out of Interstate 5 to Maxwell and west to Stonyford. Then take the Fouts Springs Road to Red Bridge.

Situated in Letts Valley in Colusa County, nearby 15-foot-deep Upper Letts Lake (4482 feet) is a great stillwater fishery. The lake flows into Lett's Creek, then into South Fork Stony Creek. There are a few campgrounds around the lake.

Sacramento Valley's Putah Creek

Putah Creek brings back special memories for me. When I took up fishing many moons ago, I was overwhelmed with riffles, runs, pools, and the sound of rapids. I immediately fell deeply in love with this beautiful stream. It was a thrilling and challenging experience to catch and release native browns and rainbows in this splendid watershed. My obsession and the short drive to reach Putah Creek led me to continue my love affair with the fishery. The fall season brought tremendous fishing when trophy browns emerged for their spawning rituals.

Putah Creek Sacramento River drainage.

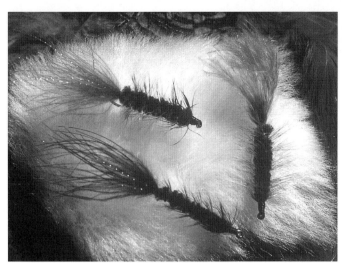

Woolly Buggers.

Fly-fishing in Putah Creek is an all-year event. An added attraction is its special winter fly-fishing season. The period from November 16 to the last Saturday in April is catch-and-release with the use of artificial flies and barbless hooks.

In early years, angler pressure was minimal, which allowed me to gain knowledge and experience. From then on, my passion for fly-fishing never ceased. I made countless trips to my rendezvous, fishing every accessible stretch of stream from below Monticello Dam to Lake Solano. Through the years, increased angler pressure, litter, and other abusive factors endangered the fishery in this once prolific, silent stream. Although fly-fishing in Putah Creek is great, it will never be the same as it once was.

Putah Creek is a medium-sized stream. It features resident rainbow trout, brown trout, and receives stocked fish on a regular basis. The stream is located west of Winters in Solano County. There are several county day-use access sites leading to magnificent riffles, runs, and pools.

The stream receives its water from releases out of Lake Berryessa. As it meanders through prime fishing waters down to Lake Solano, the stream's personality changes to slow smooth waters rather than riffles, runs, and pools. During irrigation periods, swift water releases and thick shoreline brush and trees make wading a dangerous way to reach holding fish.

Effective Fly Patterns and Tactics for Putah Creek

Successful fly patterns that brown trout will succumb to are olive Woolly Worms and Woolly Buggers in Nos. 6-8, with or without crystal hair and bead heads if the flow is high. Switch to Nos. 8-10 during fall and winter months. Other nymph patterns are Pheasant Tails, Bird's Nests, Hare's Ears in Nos. 12-14. However, when a hatch is on, use Adams' and Elk Hair Caddis in Nos. 12-14. As the season progresses toward fall, smaller fly patterns in Nos. 16-18 are your best bet. When winter approaches and flow is low, small Elk Hair Caddis, Midges, and Bivisibles are effective fly patterns.

The best fishing in Putah Creek is when the flow is low. I used to keep track of water releases from Monticello Dam. When the water is high, it is extremely difficult to fly-fish in the brushy vegetation that lines the stream. During low flow periods, fly-fishing is a wonderful experience.

From the San Francisco Bay area, take Interstate 80 east to Interstate 505 north to Winters. Take the SR 128 west exit, which will take you directly to Putah Creek. From the Sacramento Area,

take Interstate 80 west to SR 113 north. Exit on County Road E6 (West Covell Boulevard) to Winters. From Winters, take SR 128 and continue west on this route until you reach Putah Creek.

The California State DFG has designated Wild Trout (WT), Heritage Trout (HT), and Catch-and-Release (CR) waters under the Commission's Policy on Wild Trout. This program was implemented as a result of the Steelhead Conservation and Management Planning Act of 1979.

Wild Trout, Heritage Trout, and Catch-and-Release Waters

The California Wild Trout (WT) Program began in the early 1970s when selected streams were designated and managed with the goal of maximizing wild-trout angling opportunities. A priority was established to maintain an abundance of self-sustaining trout populations in which the number of larger and older fish was not significantly reduced by angler harvesting.

In order to qualify for the Wild Trout Program, a stream must be open to the public. It must be able to support, with appropriate angling regulations, wild-trout populations of sufficient magnitude and provide satisfactory catches in both number and size of fish. The program was managed with the stipulation that there would be no stocking of domestic strains of catchable-sized trout. However suitable strains of hatchery-produced wild or semi-wild trout may be planted, but only if natural trout reproduction is inadequate.

In 1998, the California Heritage Trout Program was established to emphasize restoration, education, and angling activities aimed at native trout. The California Fish and Game Commission amended its Wild Trout Policy in order to allow designation of specific lakes and streams as part of the California Heritage Trout waters. The selected waters feature one or more of the state's native trout.

A California Heritage Trout (HT) is a native trout, one that has existed in California since prehistoric times. The ancestors of trout that exist today arrived by natural means, such as migration through connecting waters when the climate and geology of the region were much different from today.

Through the years, these isolated populations have evolved into geographically distinct strains, races, subspecies, or species that are exceptionally adapted to their habitat. Many forms of redband trout found in the interior drainages of northeastern California in the Great Basin Province, Warner Valley, and the Cascade Range Province have been geographically isolated from coastal rainbow trout for thousands of years. Redband trout inhabit Goose Lake, and a few upper McCloud River and Warner Valley drainages. Since they have evolved in specific localities, native trout are an integral part of the natural history and ecosystem of their home waters.

Although the rainbow trout is still present in much of its original range, most of California's steelhead population and some inland native trout are now listed under the Federal Endangered Species Act. At present, several other native trout are being evaluated for possible listing. The bull trout, formerly known as the Dolly Varden, originally inhabited the waters of the McCloud River, but is no longer present in California. Through adverse land-use practices, dam construction, water diversion, pollution, and urban development, the native trout habitat has been substantially reduced. The special Eagle Lake rainbow trout, for example, has been threatened with extinction because its main source of available spawning habitat at Pine Creek has suffered extensive damage.

Through the years, the Department of Fish and Game, together with other resource management agencies, organizations, and individuals, has restored native trout species to their former historic habitats. Successful watersheds in the southern Sierra Nevada include the upper South Fork Kern River (Tulare County) for California golden trout and Slinkard Creek (Mono County) for Lahontan cutthroat trout. The California Heritage Trout Program is committed to continuing its efforts. However, with increased public support and involvement, the program can move ahead with greater speed.

A major goal of the California Heritage Trout Program is to restore depleted native trout populations. This includes implementing post-restoration management policies that would allow angling opportunities compatible with native trout conservation. Designated waters may have special angling regulations to insure that the fishery will provide angling without affecting the native trout populations or habitat. Waters that are of important refuge for native trout may be restricted to zero-limit, with catch-and-release angling only.

In order to be designated as a California Heritage Trout water, streams or lakes must meet specific criteria. The first criterion for inclusion in Heritage Trout waters is it must support populations of California native trout within their historic range. In addition, as a special subset of Wild Trout waters, Heritage Trout waters must be open to angling. Also, no domesticated strains of catchable-sized trout may be introduced. In Heritage Trout waters, angling must be consistent with native trout conservation. Therefore, some waters that are too small, lack suitable angling conditions, or have a critical sanctuary role will not be considered for designation.

In the future, as more populations are restored, other waters will be added to the list. However, the first six California Heritage Trout waters designated by the Commission on April 5, 1999 include one trout water in Northern California, and the other five waters in northern and southern Sierra Nevada:

Designated Water	Native Trout Present
Clavey River	Coastal rainbow trout
Eagle Lake	Eagle Lake rainbow trout
Golden Trout Creek	California golden trout
Heenan Lake	Lahontan cutthroat trout
Upper Kern River	Kern River rainbow trout
Upper Truckee River	Lahontan cutthroat trout

One of the objectives and benefits of the Heritage Trout Program is to increase public awareness concerning the beauty, diversity, historical significance, and special values of California's native trout and their habitat. It also allows diverse opportunities to fish for, observe, and experience native trout in their historic habitats. Another objective is to build public support and increase public involvement in native restoration efforts.

In 1979, the California State Legislature passed SB 192, defined as Catch-and-Release (CR) angling regulations as zero-, one-, or two-trout bag limits. It also has minimum and maximum size limits together with gear restrictions that may be used in combination with the bag limits. The regulations are grouped into four categories: zero-trout limits, two-trout limits, two-trout limits with minimum size restrictions, and two-trout limits with maximum

size restrictions. However, minimum and maximum size limits may be used in conjunction with one-and two-trout limits.

An inventory of streams and lakes that have been designated as Wild Trout (WT), Heritage Trout (HT), and Catch-and-Release (CR) waters in Northern California are noted below. Also, abbreviations for fish species and designated waters are as follows:

Fish Species	Designated Waters
RT: Rainbow Trout	WT: Wild Trout Water
BN: Brown Trout	HT: Heritage Trout Water
BK: Brook Trout	CR: Catch-and-Release Trout Water
CT: Cutthroat Trout	
SH: Steelhead Rainbow Trout	

Location/ Designated Water	Length (miles) or Area (acres)	Trout Species	Program Designated	Bag Limit	Size Limt Min/Max
Streams					
Upper Sacramento River	14*	RT	CR	0*	
Upper Klamath River	6.2	RT, BN	WT	5	
McCloud River	5	RT, BN	WT, CR	2	
McCloud River	2.3	RT, BN	WT, CR	0	
Pit River	5	RT	CR	2	18"/
Fall River	23	RT	WT, CR	2	/14"
Tule River	9	RT	CR	2	
Hat Creek	3.5	RT, BN	WT, CR	2	18"/
Burney Creek	1	RT, BN, BK	CR	2	/14"
Hayfork Creek	24	SH	CR	0	
Stony Creek MF	10	RT	CR	2,0**	
Lakes					
Big Lake	790	RT	CR	2	
Eastman Lake	60	RT	CR	2	
Grass Valley Creek Reservoir	40	RT	CR	2	
Manzanita Lake	53	RT, BN	CR	0	
Stone Lagoon	570	CT, SH	CR	2,0***	14"/
Eagle Lake	28,000	RT	HT	2	
Coastal Streams					
Eel River MF	28	SH	CR	0	
San Lorenzo River	15	SH	CR	1****	
Carmel River	12	SH	CR	0	
Big Sur River	6	SH	CR	0	

*Prior to the chemical spill in 1991, 14 miles of the upper Sacramento River were designated catch-and-release with a 2-trout limit. In 1994, following a two-year fishing closure to allow ecosystem recovery, 32 miles was opened with a 0-limit (including the original 14 miles).

**Two trout: Last Saturday in April through November 15; zero limit: November 16 through last Friday in April.

***Two trout limit, 14-inch minimum on cutthroat trout; steelhead must be released.

****One hatchery trout or steelhead; wild steelhead must be released.

Fly-Fishing Waters by County

Major and Secondary Drainages
Klamath Mountains, Great Basin, Modoc Plateau, and Cascade Provinces

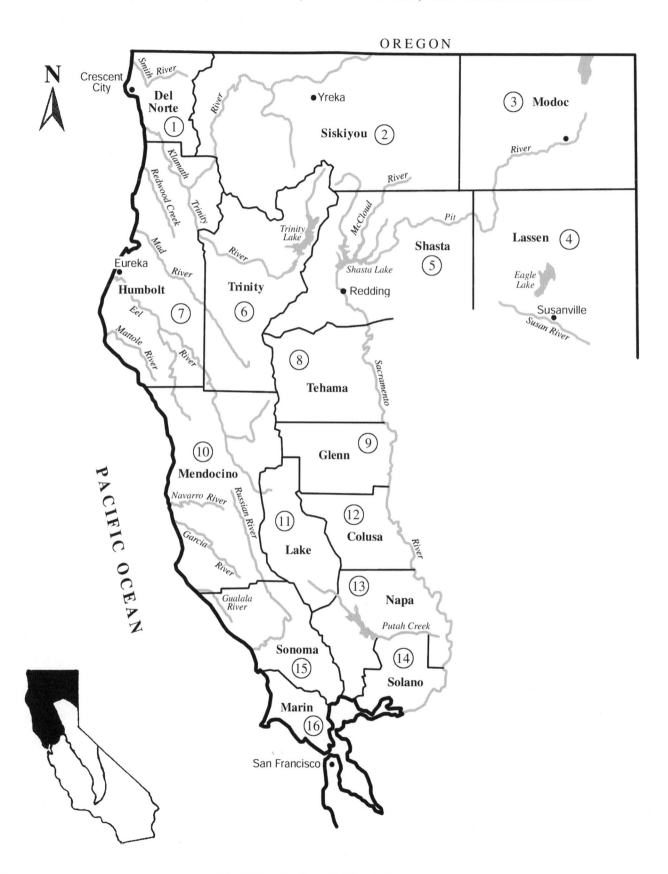

OREGON

N

Crescent City

Smith River

Del Norte ①

River

Yreka

Siskiyou ②

Modoc ③

River

Klamath

Redwood Creek

Trinity

Mad River

Eureka

Humbolt

Eel River

Mattole River

River

Trinity Lake

River

McCloud

Pit

River

Shasta Lake

Shasta ⑤

Lassen ④

Eagle Lake

Susanville

Susan River

Redding

Trinity ⑥

⑦

Tehama

⑧

Sacramento

PACIFIC OCEAN

Navarro River

⑩

Mendocino

Russian River

Garcia River

Glenn ⑨

Lake ⑪

⑫ Colusa

River

Gualala River

⑬

Napa

Putah Creek

Sonoma

⑮

⑭ Solano

Marin ⑯

San Francisco

Fly-Fishing Waters by County

1. Del Norte County
Six Rivers National Forest Map
Smith River
Klamath River
Illinois River
Pacific Ocean

2. Siskiyou County
Klamath National Forest Map
Shasta-Trinity National Forest Map
Modoc National Forest Map
Pacific Ocean
Applegate River
Klamath, Salmon, Scott, and Shasta Rivers
Sacramento and McCloud Rivers

3. Modoc County
Modoc National Forest Map
Goose Lake
Surprise Valley
Upper Alkali and Middle Alkali Lakes
Cowhead, Upper and Lower Lakes
Willow, Lassen, and Davis Creeks
Sacramento and Pit Rivers
Emerson Creek

4. Lassen County
Lassen National Forest Map
Modoc National Forest Map
Susan River
Honey Lake
Upper and Lower Lakes
Madeline Plains
Surprise Valley
Eagle Lake and Pine Creek
Sacramento and Pit Rivers

5. Shasta County
Shasta-Trinity National Forest Map
Lassen National Forest Map
Sacramento, Pit, and McCloud Rivers
Battle, Cottonwood, Kosk, and Mill Creeks
Feather River and Warner Creek (Shasta-Plumas County)
Klamath, Salmon, and Scott Rivers

6. Trinity County
Shasta Trinity National Forest Map
Six Rivers National Forest Map
Mendocino National Forest Map
Klamath, Trinity, Salmon, and Scott Rivers
Eel River
Mad River
Pacific Ocean

7. Humboldt County
Six Rivers National Forest Map
Eel, Mad, and Mattole Rivers
Klamath and Trinity Rivers

Humboldt County cont.
Redwood Creek
Pacific Ocean

8. Tehama County
Lassen National Forest Map
Mendocino National Forest Map
Shasta-Trinity National Forest Map
Sacramento River
Antelope, Battle, Cottonwood and Deer Creeks

9. Glenn County
Mendocino National Forest Map
Sacramento River
Stony Creek
Eel River
Black Butte River

10. Mendocino County
Mendocino National Forest Map
Albion River
Eel and Black Butte Rivers
Big River
Noyo River
Russian River
Tenmile River
Pacific Ocean

11. Lake County
Mendocino National Forest Map
Eel River
Sacramento River
Cache Creek

12. Colusa County
Mendocino National Forest Map
Sacramento River
Stony Creek

13. Napa County
Napa River
San Pablo Bay
Sacramento River
Putah Creek

14. Solano County
San Pablo Bay
Pacific Ocean
Sacramento River

15. Sonoma County
Pacific Ocean

16. Marin County
Pacific Ocean
Lagunitas Creek
San Francisco Bay

Part 3
Fish Distribution

The Fish Distribution depicts fish species inhabiting a wide range of waters in Northern California. Extensive research and raw data for each body of water were collected, analyzed, selected, tabulated, summarized, and incorporated into the inventory by counties to provide the user with a reference guide. I also included USGS 7.5 Minute Topo Map Series' for each lake and stream.

The current USGS 7.5 Minute Topo Map Series with greater detail has replaced the 15 Minute Map Series. The 15 Minute Topo Map Series was officially abandoned by the USGS as they have not been revised nor reprinted for many years. In the northwestern region of California, 10 USGS 7.5' X 15' Topo Maps cover some waters of the Trinity, Eel, and Mad rivers.

Generally more than one topo map covers an entire stream; however, I have selected the most appropriate map(s) depicting the water of an area. Do keep in mind that in any stream course fish will move from one section to another.

Depending upon many variables that may affect the waters mentioned, please note that the future status of fisheries is unknown or uncertain. Through the years, many lakes and streams have been vulnerable to environmental and other changes. Water diversion, bank erosion, logging, road construction, property resale, road or land closure, high-flow channeling, and pollution may alter any body of water. Deficient food production, mining, agriculture and grazing activities, excessive siltation, excessive angler use, deficient shelter-cover, and inadequate spawning areas are other problems interfering with fish habitat and their food sources in many watersheds.

Along with environmental factors, drought, and water conditions, some lakes in higher elevations face "winter kill" each season. "Winter kill" refers to complete or partial fish mortality in shallow lakes during the winter season. When heavy snow packs cover ice layers preventing light from penetrating into the water, vegetation dies and decomposes, causing a depletion of oxygen.

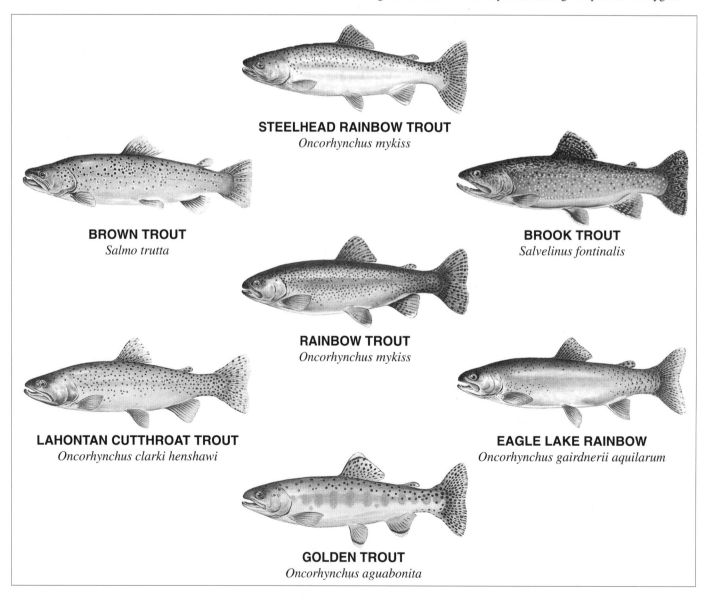

STEELHEAD RAINBOW TROUT
Oncorhynchus mykiss

BROWN TROUT
Salmo trutta

BROOK TROUT
Salvelinus fontinalis

RAINBOW TROUT
Oncorhynchus mykiss

LAHONTAN CUTTHROAT TROUT
Oncorhynchus clarki henshawi

EAGLE LAKE RAINBOW
Oncorhynchus gairdnerii aquilarum

GOLDEN TROUT
Oncorhynchus aguabonita

Fish Distribution Northern California Lakes and Streams

Various species of trout inhabit much of the roadside, back-country, and wilderness lakes and streams. However, the California Department of Fish and Game regularly stocks fingerling rainbow, brook, and golden trout in designated back-country and wilderness lakes by aerial methods. They also stock roadside waters with catchable and subcatchable trout.

Unforeseen closures or special regulations may occur and are subject to changes in some waters holding anadromous and freshwater fish. Many portions of major and tributary streams in Northern California have all-year closures imposed. Check the most current California Sport Fishing Regulations and its latest supplement for each body of water you intend to fish.

Research data on all lakes and streams was gathered from various sources and summarized with the following explanation:

County: Lake and stream in alphabetical order for each county.
Water: Name of lake or stream.
Drainage: Major stream and primary tributary.
USGS Topographic Map: 7.5 Minute Series Quadrangle delineating the water.
Elevation: Lake surface elevation in feet. Stream elevation not shown as they vary due to gradient.

Fish Species

RT: Rainbow Trout	RDT: Redband Rainbow Trout
BK: Brook Trout	KOK: Kokanee Salmon
CT: Cutthroat Trout	SH: Steelhead Rainbow Trout
CT-C: Cutthroat Trout, Coastal	KS: King Salmon (Chinook)
ELT: Eagle Lake Trout	SS: Silver Salmon (Coho)
BN: Brown Trout	AS: American Shad
GT: Golden Trout	

Water By County	Drainage	USGS Topographic Map 7.5 Minute Series	Elevation (Feet) Lakes Only	Fish Species
Colusa County				
FRENZEL CREEK	Sacramento River Stony Creek	Gilmore Peak	- - -	RT
HYPHUS CREEK	Sacramento River Stony Creek	Gilmore Peak	- - -	RT
LETTS LAKE, Upper	Sacramento River Stony Creek	Fouts Springs	4482	RT
MILL CREEK	Sacramento River Stony Creek	Fouts Springs	- - -	RT
PARADISE CREEK	Sacramento River Stony Creek	St. John Mountain	- - -	RT
STONY CREEK	Sacramento River	Stonyford St. John Mountain	- - -	RT
STONY CREEK, Little	Sacramento River Stony Creek	Gilmore Peak Fouts Springs	- - -	RT
STONY CREEK MF (Red Bridge upstream) (Also, see Glenn & Lake Co.)	Sacramento River Stony Creek	Crockett Peak St. John Mountain	- - -	RT
STONY CREEK NF	Sacramento River Stony Creek	St. John Mountain	- - -	RT
STONY CREEK SF	Sacramento River Stony Creek	St. John Mountain Potato Hill	- - -	RT
SULLIVAN CREEK	Sacramento River Stony Creek	Gilmore Peak Fouts Springs	- - -	RT
SULLIVAN CREEK, Little	Sacramento River Stony Creek	Gilmore Peak Fouts Springs	- - -	RT
TROUT CREEK	Sacramento River Stony Creek SF	Fouts Springs	- - -	RT
TROUT CREEK	Sacramento River Stony Creek, Little	Gilmore Peak Hough Springs	- - -	RT
Del Norte County				
BLUE CREEK	Klamath River	Ah Pah Ridge	- - -	RT, SH, KS SS, BK
CHICAGO CREEK	Illinois River	Broken Rib Mountain	- - -	RT, CT-C
DRY LAKE	Smith River Smith River SF	Cant Hook Mountain	1326	RT
DUNN CREEK	Illinois River	Polar Bear Mountain	- - -	SH, KS, RT, CT-C, SS

Water By County	Drainage	USGS Topographic Map 7.5 Minute Series	Elevation (Feet) Lakes Only	Fish Species
EARL, LAKE	Pacific Ocean Jordan Creek	Crescent City	07	RT, CT-C
FLAT IRON LAKE	Klamath River Blue Creek	Chimney Rock	4960	RT, ELT
HARRINGTON LAKE	Smith River Smith River SF	Presto Mountain	5150	RT
ILLINOIS RIVER E. FK	Illinois River	Polar Bear Mountain	- - -	SH, RT, KS CT-C, SS
ISLAND LAKE	Smith River Smith River SF	Devils Punchbowl	4980	RT, ELT
KLAMATH RIVER (Del Norte to Humboldt Co. line. Also, see Humboldt & Siskiyou Co.)	Pacific Ocean	Klamath Glen Requa	- - -	SH, KS, SS
MUSLATT LAKE	Smith River Smith River SF	Ship Mountain	2870	RT, ELT
RATTLESNAKE LAKE	Smith River Smith River SF	Cant Hook Mountain	1650	BK
SANGER LAKE	Smith River Smith River MF	Broken Rib Mountain	5150	BK
SMITH RIVER	Pacific Ocean North Coast	Smith River, Hiouchi Gasquet, Hurdygurdy Butte	- - -	SH, KS, SS CT-C, RT
SMITH RIVER MF	Pacific Ocean Smith River	Gasquet	- - -	KS, SS, SH RT, CT-C
SMITH RIVER NF	Pacific Ocean Smith River	Gasquet	- - -	SH, KS, SS RT, CT-C
SMITH RIVER SF	Pacific Ocean Smith River	Cant Hook Mountain	- - -	KS, SS, SH CT-C, RT
TALAWA LAKE	Pacific Ocean Lake Earl	Crescent City	0	RT, CT-C, SS

Glenn County

Water By County	Drainage	USGS Topographic Map 7.5 Minute Series	Elevation (Feet) Lakes Only	Fish Species
BRISCOE CREEK	Sacramento River Stony Creek	Saint John Mountain Stonyford	- - -	RT
BRISCOE CREEK NF	Sacramento River Stony Creek	Stonyford	- - -	RT
COLD CREEK	Eel River Black Butte River	Plaskett Ridge Plaskett Meadows	- - -	RT
CORBIN CREEK	Eel River	Kneecap Ridge Felkner Hill	- - -	RT
CORBIN CREEK NF	Eel River Corbin Creek	Felkner Hill	- - -	RT
GRINDSTONE CREEK	Sacramento River Stony Creek	Alder Springs Chrome	- - -	RT, BN
KELLER LAKE	Eel River Black Butte River	Plaskett Ridge	5570	BK
KILL DRY CREEK	Sacramento River Stony Creek	Plaskett Meadows Log Spring	- - -	RT
MILL CREEK	Sacramento River Stony Creek	Alder Springs Plaskett Meadows	- - -	RT
PANTHER CREEK	Sacramento River Stony Creek	Log Spring Mendocino Pass	- - -	RT
PLASKETT MEADOW PONDS	Eel River Black Butte River	Plaskett Meadows	5980	RT
SHEPHERD CREEK	Sacramento River Stony Creek	Alder Springs Plaskett Meadows	- - -	RT
STONY CREEK MF	Sacramento River Stony Creek	Saint John Mountain Crockett Peak	- - -	RT
STONY CREEK NF	Sacramento River Stony Creek	St. John Mountain	- - -	RT

Humboldt County

Water By County	Drainage	USGS Topographic Map 7.5 Minute Series	Elevation (Feet) Lakes Only	Fish Species
ALBEE CREEK	Eel River Eel River SF	Bull Creek	- - -	RT, SH, SS
AMMON CREEK	Klamath River Trinity River	Hennessy Peak	- - -	RT

Water By County	Drainage	USGS Topographic Map 7.5 Minute Series	Elevation (Feet) Lakes Only	Fish Species
BEAR CREEK NF	Mattole River Bear Creek	Honeydew	- - -	SH, RT
BEAR CREEK SF	Mattole River Bear Creek	Shelter Cove	- - -	SH
BEAR RIVER	Pacific Ocean	Cape Mendocino	- - -	SH, SS, KS RT
BEAR RIVER SF	Pacific Ocean Bear River	Capetown	- - -	SH, SS, RT
BEE LAKE	Klamath River Bluff Creek	Fish Lake	3580	RT
BENBOW, LAKE	Eel River Eel River SF	Garberville	374	KS, SH, SS, RT
BIG FINLEY CREEK	Mattole River Briceland	Shelter Cove	- - -	SH, SS, RT
BIG FLAT CREEK	Pacific Ocean	Shubrick Peak	- - -	SH, RT
BIG FLAT CREEK NF	Pacific Ocean Big Flat Creek	Shubrick Peak	- - -	SH
BIG LAGOON	Pacific Ocean	Rodgers Peak, Trinidad	6	SH, CT-C, RT
BLACKS LAKE (Packsaddle Ridge and Red Cap Prairie)	Klamath River Red Cap Creek	Salmon Mountain	5140	BK
BLANKET CREEK	Eel River Van Duzen River	Black Lassic	- - -	RT
BLUE LAKE	Klamath River Bluff Creek	Fish Lake	2750	BK, RT, ELT
BLUFF CREEK	Klamath River	Weitchpec, Fish Lake Lonesome Ridge	- - -	RT, SH, KS, SS
BOISE CREEK	Klamath River	Orleans	- - -	RT, SH, KS SS
BOISE CREEK, Little South Fork	Klamath River Boise Creek	Orleans Orleans Mountain	- - -	RT
BREMER CREEK	Klamath River Trinity River	Salyer	- - -	RT
BULL CREEK	Eel River Bull Creek	Weott	- - -	SH, SS, RT KS
CABIN CREEK	Eel River Eel River SF	Weott	- - -	RT, SH
CAMP CREEK	Klamath River Bark Shanty Gulch	Orleans	- - -	RT, SH, KS SS
CANOE CREEK	Eel River Eel River SF	Weott	- - -	SH, KS, RT
CEDAR CREEK	Klamath River Trinity River	Tish Tang Point Salyer	- - -	SH, RT
CHADD CREEK	Eel River	Redcrest	- - -	SS, SH, RT
CHEENITCH CREEK	Klamath River	Orleans	- - -	RT, SH
CHINA CREEK	Klamath River Camp Creek	Orleans, Fish Lake Lonesome Ridge	- - -	RT
COLEMAN CREEK	Eel River	Blocksburg	- - -	SH, RT
COON CREEK	Klamath River Trinity River	Willow Creek Salyer	- - -	SH, RT
COOSKIE CREEK	Pacific Ocean	Cooskie Creek	- - -	SH
CORRAL CREEK	Klamath River Trinity River	Tish Tang Point Trinity Mountain	- - -	BK
COW CREEK	Klamath River Trinity River	Board Camp Mountain Grouse Mountain	- - -	RT
COW CREEK	Eel River Eel River SF	Weott	- - -	SH
CUNEO CREEK	Eel River Eel River SF	Bull Creek Weott	- - -	SH, RT
DAVIS CREEK	Pacific Ocean	Capetown	- - -	SH, RT
DECKER CREEK	Eel River Eel River SF	Weott	- - -	RT, SH
DIVIDE LAKE	Klamath River Miners Creek	Fish Lake	3120	RT
DOBBYN CREEK, North	Eel River Dobbyn Creek	Alderpoint Black Lassic	- - -	RT

Water By County	Drainage	USGS Topographic Map 7.5 Minute Series	Elevation (Feet) Lakes Only	Fish Species
DONAHUE FLAT CREEK	Klamath River	Orleans Mountain Orleans	- - -	RT, SH
EAST CREEK	Mad River Pilot Creek	Blake Mountain	- - -	RT, SH
EEL RIVER (Alderpoint to Weott)	Pacific Ocean	Alderpoint, Fort Seward Blocksburg, Myers Flat Weott	- - -	SH, KS, SS RT
EEL RIVER (Weott to Fernbridge)	Pacific Ocean	Weott, Redcrest Scotia, Fortuna	- - -	SH, KS, SS AS
EEL RIVER SF	Pacific Ocean Eel River	Garberville, Miranda Myers Flat, Weott	- - -	KS, SH, SS, RT
FISH CREEK	Klamath River Bluff Creek	Fish Lake	- - -	RT
FISH LAKE	Klamath River Bluff Creek	Fish Lake	1773	RT, BK
FIVEMILE CREEK	Klamath River	Orleans	- - -	RT
FRESHWATER LAGOON	Pacific Ocean	Orick	0	RT
GROUSE CREEK	Klamath River Trinity River	Sims Mountain Board Camp Mountain	- - -	RT, SH, KS, SS
GROVES PRAIRIE CREEK	Klamath River Trinity River	Willow Creek Salyer, Denny	- - -	RT
HARPER CREEK	Eel River Eel River SF	Weott	- - -	SH, RT
HOME CREEK	Pacific Ocean	Fern Canyon	- - -	SH, CT-C
HONEYDEW CREEK	Pacific Ocean Mattole River	Honeydew Shubrick Peak	- - -	SH, SS, RT
HONEYDEW CREEK WF	Pacific Ocean Mattole River	Shubrick Peak	- - -	RT
HORSE LINTO CREEK	Klamath River Trinity River	Tish Tang Point	- - -	SH, KS, SS, RT
HORSE LINTO CREEK EF	Klamath River Trinity River	Denny	- - -	RT, BK
HORSE MOUNTAIN CREEK	Klamath River Trinity River	Grouse Mountain	- - -	RT
HORSE RANGE CREEK	Klamath River Trinity River	Salyer	- - -	RT
KERLIN CREEK	Klamath River Trinity River	Hyampom Mountain Hyampom	- - -	RT, SH
KLAMATH RIVER (Somes Bar to Weitchpec)	Pacific Ocean	Somes Bar, Orleans, Weitchpec	- - -	SH, KS, SS, RT
KLAMATH RIVER (Weitchpec to Humboldt Co. line. Also, see Del Norte & Siskiyou Co.)	Pacific Ocean	Weitchpec, French Camp Ridge, Johnsons, Holter Ridge, Ah Pah Ridge	- - -	SH, KS, SS, RT
LEARY CREEK	Klamath River Red Cap Creek	Hopkins Butte	- - -	RT
LITTLE LOST MAN CREEK	Redwood Creek Prairie Creek	Orick Holter Ridge	- - -	SH, SS, CT-C
LOST MAN CREEK	Redwood Creek Prairie Creek	Orick	- - -	SH, SS, KS CT-C
MAD RIVER (Mouth to Maple Creek)	Pacific Ocean	Arcata North, Blue Lake Tyee City, Korbel Maple Creek	- - -	SH, KS, SS RT, CT-C
MAD RIVER (Maple Creek to Trinity Co. line)	Pacific Ocean	Mad River Buttes Showers Mountain Dinsmore	- - -	SH, KS, SS, RT
MADDEN CREEK	Klamath River Trinity River	Salyer, Willow Creek Grouse Mountain	- - -	RT, SH
MATTOLE RIVER	Pacific Ocean	Petrolia, Buckeye Mountain Shubrick Peak	- - -	SH, KS, SS RT
MILL CREEK	Klamath River Trinity River	Hupa Mountain	- - -	SH, KS, SS RT
MILL CREEK	Eel River Eel River SF	Bull Creek Scotia	- - -	SH, SS, RT
MILL CREEK LAKE, Lower	Klamath River Trinity River	Trinity Mountain	5360	BK, RT, ELT

Water By County	Drainage	USGS Topographic Map 7.5 Minute Series	Elevation (Feet) Lakes Only	Fish Species
MOSQUITO CREEK	Klamath River Trinity River	Sims Mountain Board Camp Mountain	- - -	RT
NICKOWITZ CREEK	Klamath River Blue Creek	Blue Creek Mountain Lonesome Ridge	- - -	SH, RT, KS SS
ONION LAKE	Klamath River Pecwan Creek	Lonesome Ridge	4450	BK, RT
PEARCH CREEK	Klamath River Orleans Mountain	Orleans	- - -	RT, SH
PILOT CREEK	Mad River Sims Mountain	Blake Mountain	- - -	RT, SH
RED CAP CREEK	Klamath River Hopkins Butte	Orleans	- - - SS	RT, SH, KS
RED CAP LAKE	Klamath River Trinity River	Salmon Mountain	5650	BK, BN
RED MOUNTAIN LAKE	Klamath River Bluff Creek	Fish Lake	2450	BK
REDWOOD CREEK	Pacific Ocean Rodgers Peak	Orick	- - -	SH, RT, SS CT-C, KS
ROSALINA CREEK	Klamath River Orleans	Orleans Mountain	- - -	RT
RUBY CREEK	Klamath River Trinity River	Willow Creek	- - -	RT
SHIPMAN CREEK	Pacific Ocean	Shubrick Peak	- - -	SH
SIMS CREEK	Klamath River Trinity River	Sims Mountain	- - -	RT
SLATE CREEK	Klamath River	Fish Lake	- - -	RT, SH, KS SS
SLIDE CREEK	Klamath River Blue Creek	Blue Creek Mountain	- - -	RT, SH, KS
SQUASHAN CREEK	Pacific Ocean	Fern Canyon, Orick	- - -	SH, CT-C
SQUAW CREEK	Eel River Eel River SF	Bull Creek Weott	- - -	SH, SS, RT
SQUAW CREEK	Mattole River	Buckeye Mountain	- - -	SH, SS, RT
STONE LAGOON	Pacific Ocean	Rodgers Peak Orick	8	CT-C
THREE CREEK	Klamath River Trinity River	Willow Creek	- - -	RT
TISH TANG A TANG CREEK	Klamath River Trinity River	Hoopa Tish Tang Point	- - -	RT
TRINITY RIVER (Willow Creek to mouth at Weitchpec. Also, see Trinity Co.)	Klamath River	Willow Creek, Hoopa Weitchpec	- - -	KS, SH, SS RT, BN, AS
TRINITY RIVER SF	Klamath River Trinity River	Salyer, Hennessy Peak Hyampom Mountain	- - -	KS, SH, SS RT
TWIN LAKE, South Slate Creek	Klamath River	Fish Lake	3750	BK
VAN DUZEN RIVER	Pacific Ocean Eel River	Bridgeville, Redcrest Owl Creek, Hydesville	- - -	SH, KS, SS RT
VAN DUZEN RIVER SF	Eel River Van Duzen River	Larabee Valley Dinsmore, Black Lassic	- - -	SH, RT
WILDER CREEK	Klamath River Camp Creek	Orleans Bark Shanty Gulch	- - -	SH, RT
WILLOW CREEK	Klamath River Trinity River	Willow Creek Lord-Ellis Summit	- - -	SH, KS, SS RT
WILLOW CREEK EF	Trinity River Willow Creek	Willow Creek	- - -	RT

Lake County

Water By County	Drainage	USGS Topographic Map 7.5 Minute Series	Elevation (Feet) Lakes Only	Fish Species
ANDERSON CREEK	Eel River Crockett Peak	Kneecap Ridge	- - -	RT
BEAR CREEK Eel River Rice Fork	Eel River	Potato Hill	- - -	RT
BENMORE CREEK (Benmore Valley to SF Scotts Creek)	Tule Lake Scotts Creek	Lakeport Purdys Garden	- - -	RT

Water By County	Drainage	USGS Topographic Map 7.5 Minute Series	Elevation (Feet) Lakes Only	Fish Species
BENMORE CREEK (White Pebble Spring to Eel River)	Eel River	Lake Pillsbury Elk Mountain	- - -	RT, SH
BEVANS CREEK Lakes Pillsbury	Eel River	Elk Mountain	- - -	RT
Black Oak Springs (Black Oak Springs to Scotts Creek)	Eel River Tule Lake	Cow Mountain	- - -	RT
BLUE LAKE, Lower	Sacramento River Cache Creek (Clear Lake)	Cow Mountain	1605	RT
BLUE LAKE, Upper	Sacramento River Cache Creek (Clear Lake)	Cow Mountain	1700	RT
BOARDMAN CREEK	Eel River Lake Pillsbury	Lake Pillsbury Hull Mountain	- - -	RT
BUCKNELL CREEK	Eel River	Van Arsdale Reservoir	- - -	KS, SH, RT
CACHE CREEK (Lake, Colusa & Yolo Co.)	Sacramento River	Glasscock Mountain	- - -	RT
COLD CREEK	Eel River	Crockett Peak Saint John Mountain	- - -	RT
COPPER BUTTE CREEK	Eel River	Crockett Peak	- - -	RT. SH
CORBIN CREEK (Also, see Glenn Co.)	Eel River	Kneecap Ridge	- - -	RT
DEER CREEK	Eel River Eel River Rice Fk	Lake Pillsbury Elk Mountain	- - -	RT
DUTCH OVEN CREEK	Eel River Corbin Creek	Kneecap Ridge	- - -	RT
EEL RIVER RICE FK	Eel River Lake Pillsbury	Lake Pillsbury Elk Mountain	- - -	RT
FRENCH CREEK	Eel River Eel River Rice Fk	Potato Hill	- - -	RT
HORSE CREEK	Eel River Hull Mountain	Kneecap Ridge	- - -	RT, SH
INDIAN VALLEY RESERVOIR	Sacramento River Cache Creek	Benmore Canyon	1475	ELT
MILL CREEK	Eel River Salmon Creek	Lake Pillsbury Van Arsdale Reservoir	- - -	RT
PANTHER CREEK	Eel River Soda Creek	Lake Pillsbury Van Arsdale Reservoir	- - -	RT
PILLSBURY, LAKE	Eel River	Lake Pillsbury	1910	RT
RICE CREEK	Eel River Eel River, Rice Fk	Lake Pillsbury Elk Mountain	- - -	RT
ROCK CREEK	Eel River Eel River, Rice Fk	Potato Hill Elk Mountain	- - -	RT
SCOTTS CREEK	Sacramento River Cache Creek	Upper Lake Lakeport	- - -	RT
SKELETON CREEK	Eel River	Crockett Peak	- - -	RT
SMOKEHOUSE CREEK	Eel River	Lake Pillsbury Hull Mountain	- - -	RT
SODA CREEK	Eel River	Lake Pillsbury	- - -	RT
STONY CREEK MF (Snow Mtn. Wilderness, Mendocino NF)	Sacramento River	Crockett Peak	- - -	RT, BK
THISTLE GLADE CREEK	Eel River	Crockett Peak Lake Pillsbury	- - -	RT
TWIN VALLEY CREEK	Sacramento River Cache Creek	Bartlett Springs Bartlett Mountain	- - -	RT
WELCH CREEK	Eel River Soda Creek	Lake Pillsbury Van Arsdale Reservoir	- - -	RT
WILLOW CREEK	Sacramento River Scotts Creek	Purdys Gardens	- - -	RT

Lassen County

ASH CREEK	Sacramento River Pit River	Ambrose Valley	- - -	RT, BN, ELT
BALLS CANYON CREEK	Susan River	Litchfield	- - -	BN

Water By County	Drainage	USGS Topographic Map 7.5 Minute Series	Elevation (Feet) Lakes Only	Fish Species
BARE CREEK	Lower Lake	Snake Lake Little Hat Mountain	- - -	RT, BN
BATHTUB LAKE, North	Sacramento River Pit River	Prospect Peak	6160	BK
BATHTUB LAKE, South	Sacramento River Pit River	Prospect Peak	6160	BK
BEAVER CREEK	Sacramento River Pit River	Pittville	- - -	RT
BETTY LAKE	Honey Lake Susan River	Red Cinder	6457	BK
BLACK LAKE	Eagle Lake Pine Creek	Bogard Buttes	7100	ELT, RT
BLUE LAKE	Sacramento River Pit River	Jess Valley	6067	RT, ELT
BOOT LAKE	Madeline Plains	Boot Lake Little Hat Mountain	6800	ELT
BUTTE CREEK	Sacramento River Pit River	Prospect Peak	- - -	RT, BK
BUTTE LAKE	Sacramento River Pit River	Prospect Peak	6043	RT
CARIBOU LAKE	Honey Lake Susan River	Bogard Buttes	6620	RT, BN, BK ELT
CEDAR CREEK	Sacramento River Pit River	Tule Mountain Jess Valley	- - -	RT, BN
CRATER LAKE	Eagle Lake Pine Creek	Harvey Mountain	6852	BK
DODGE RESERVOIR	Madeline Plains	Dodge Reservoir	5739	RT, ELT
EAGLE LAKE	North Lahontan Susanville	Troxel Point, Pikes Point Gallatin Peak, Spalding Tract	5102	ELT
EAST CREEK (Lassen & Modoc Co.)	Sacramento River Pit River	Emerson Peak Jess Valley	- - -	BK, RT
EAST CREEK SF	Sacramento River Pit River	Emerson Peak	- - -	RT
FEATHER LAKE	Honey Lake Susan River	Pine Creek Valley	5701	RT
HOLBROOK RESERVOIR	Sacramento River Pit River	Ash Valley Holbrook Canyon	5372	ELT
LOST LAKE	Lower Lake	Emerson Peak	7250	RT
McCOY FLAT RESERVOIR	Honey Lake Susan River	Pegleg Mountain	5555	RT, ELT
MENDIBOURE LAKE	Madeline Plains	McDonald Peak Madeline	6000	RT
MOSQUITO CREEK	Sacramento River Pit River	Emerson Peak	- - -	RT, BN
NORTH CREEK	Lower Lake Bare Creek	Snake Lake	- - -	RT
NELSON CORRAL RESERVOIR	Sacramento River Pit River	Holbrook Canyon	5900	ELT
NEWLAND RESERVOIR	Lower Lake	Little Hat Mountain	5822	RT
PARSNIP CREEK	Sacramento River Pit River	Jess Valley	- - -	BN, RT
PINE LAKE	Eagle Lake Pine Creek	Bogard Buttes	6600	BK
PARSNIP CREEK	Sacramento River Pit River	Jess Valley	- - -	RT
PINE CREEK	Eagle Lake	Bogard Buttes Pine Creek Valley Champs Flat	- - -	BK, ELT
RED ROCK CREEK	Madeline Plains	Observation Peak Dodge Reservoir	- - -	RT
RIM LAKE	Honey Lake Susan River	Red Cinder	7000	BK
SECRET CREEK	Honey Lake Susan River	Karlo Shafter Mountain	- - -	BN
SILVER CREEK	Lower Lake Snake Lake	Emerson Peak	- - -	RT

Water By County	Drainage	USGS Topographic Map 7.5 Minute Series	Elevation (Feet) Lakes Only	Fish Species
SILVER LAKE	Honey Lake Susan River	Red Cinder	6480	RT, BK, ELT
SILVER CREEK	Lower Lake Bare Creek	Snake Lake Emerson Peak	- - -	RT, BK
SMOKE CREEK	State of Nevada Smoke Creek Reservoir	Mixie Flat Al Shinn Canyon	- - -	RT, BN
SMOKE CREEK RESERVOIR (Also in Nevada)	State of Nevada	Al Shinn Canyon	4400	BN
SNOWSTORM CREEK	Honey Lake Susan River	Karlo, Petes Valley Snowstorm Mountain	- - -	BN
SUSAN RIVER (Headwaters to McCoy Flat Reservoir)	Honey Lake Pegleg Mtn.	Red Cinder Swain Mountain	- - -	RT, BN BK ELT
SUSAN RIVER (Goumaz - Section 33, T30N, R10E to Devils Corral)	Honey Lake	Roop Mountain Susanville	- - -	RT, BN, BK ELT
SWORINGER RESERVOIR (Modoc & Lassen Co.)	Surprise Valley Bare Creek	Snake Lake	5860	RT, BN
TRIANGLE LAKE	Eagle Lake Pine Creek	Bogard Buttes	7100	BK, RT, ELT
TURNAROUND LAKE	Eagle Lake Pine Creek	Bogard Buttes	7000	BK, RT, ELT
TWIN LAKES	Eagle Lake Pine Creek	Bogard Buttes	7100	BK, RT, ELT
WILLARD CREEK	Honey Lake Susan River	Roop Mountain Fredonyer Pass	- - -	RT
WILLOW CREEK	Honey Lake Susan River	Tunnison Mountain Johnstonville	- - -	RT, BN
WILLOW CREEK	Sacramento River Pit River	Adin Lane Reservoir	- - -	RT, BN

Marin County

ALAMERE CREEK	Pacific Ocean	Double Point	- - -	SH
ALPINE LAKE	Lagunitas Creek San Rafael	Bolinas	645	RT
BON TEMPE LAKE	Lagunitas Creek	San Rafael	716	RT
CRYSTAL LAKE (Pt. Reyes National Seashore)	Pacific Ocean	Double Point	475	RT
COAST CREEK	Pacific Ocean	Double Point Inverness	- - -	SH, RT
KENT LAKE	Lagunitas Creek	Bolinas	335	RT
LAGUNITAS LAKE	Lagunitas Creek	San Rafael	783	RT
PELICAN LAKE (Pt. Reyes National Seashore)	Pacific Ocean	Double Point	200	RT
PHOENIX CREEK	Phoenix Lake Corte Madera Creek	San Rafael	- - -	RT
PHOENIX LAKE	San Francisco Bay Corte Madera Creek	San Rafael	183	RT
REDWOOD CREEK	Pacific Ocean	Point Bonita San Rafael	- - -	SH, SS
RODEO LAGOON, Upper	Pacific Ocean	Point Bonita	10	RT
STAFFORD LAKE	San Pablo Bay Novato Creek	San Geronimo	195	RT
WILDCAT LAKE (Pt. Reyes National Seashore)	Pacific Ocean	Double Point	200	RT

Mendocino County

ALBION RIVER	Pacific Ocean	Albion	- - -	SH, SS
ALBION RIVER NF	Pacific Ocean Albion River	Albion Elk	- - -	SS, SH
ALDER CREEK	Pacific Ocean	Malo Pass Creek Point Arena	- - -	SH, RT
BALDY CREEK	Eel River Eel River MF	Plaskett Ridge	- - -	SH, RT

Water By County	Drainage	USGS Topographic Map 7.5 Minute Series	Elevation (Feet) Lakes Only	Fish Species
BEAVER CREEK	Eel River Eel River MF	Leech Lake Mountain Buck Rock	- - -	RT
BIG RIVER	Pacific Ocean	Mendocino	- - -	SH, SS, KS
BLACK BUTTE RIVER (Glenn Co. line to Eel River MF)	Eel River Eel River MF	Newhouse Ridge Plaskett Ridge	- - -	SH, RT, KS
BUCKHORN CREEK	Eel River Eel River MF	Plaskett Ridge	- - -	RT, SH
BUTTE CREEK	Eel River Eel River MF	Plaskett Ridge	- - -	SH, RT
CASPER CREEK	Pacific Ocean	Mendocino Mathison Peak, Noyo Hill	- - -	SH
CHAMBERLAIN CREEK	Big River Big River NF	Comptche Northspur	- - -	SH, SS
CLEONE, Lake	Pacific Ocean North Coast	Fort Bragg	40	RT, SH
EEL RIVER (Confluence NF Eel to Humboldt Co. line)	Pacific Ocean	Van Arsdale Reservoir Dos Rios, Updegraff Ridge	- - -	SH, KS, SS
EEL RIVER MF (Dos Rios to Yolla Bolly- Middle Eel Wilderness)	Eel River	Leech Lake Mountain Newhouse Ridge, Dos Rios Covelo East, Jamison Ridge	- - -	SH, SS, KS
EEL RIVER SF (Leggett to Humboldt Co. line at Piercy)	Eel River	Leggett, Noble Butte Piercy	- - -	SH, RT, SS
FLY CREEK	Eel River Eel River MF	Leech Lake Mountain Buck Rock	- - -	SH, RT
GARCIA RIVER	Pacific Ocean	Point Arena Eureka Hill	- - -	SH, SS, RT
GUALALA RIVER (Mendocino-Sonoma Co. line)	Pacific Ocean	Gualala	- - -	SH, SS
HAMMERHORN CREEK	Eel River Eel River MF	Leech Lake Mountain Buck Rock	- - -	RT, SH?
HAMMERHORN LAKE	Eel River Eel River MF	Buck Rock	3520	RT
HARE CREEK	Pacific Ocean	Fort Bragg Noyo Hill	- - -	SH, SS
HAYSHED CREEK	Eel River Eel River MF	Thatcher Ridge	- - -	SH
HOWARD LAKE	Eel River Eel River MF	Buck Rock	1525	RT
JAMES CREEK	Big River Big River NF	Comptche Greenough Ridge	- - -	SH, SS
JUG HANDLE CREEK	Pacific Ocean	Fort Bragg Mendocino	- - -	SS, SH
JUMPOFF CREEK	Eel River Black Butte River	Newhouse Ridge Mendocino Pass	- - -	RT
McCLURE CREEK (Lake Co. line to Mill Creek)	Russian River Mill Creek	Ukiah Cow Mountain	- - -	SH, RT
MILL CREEK NF	Russian River Mill Creek	Ukiah Elledge Peak	- - -	SH, RT
MORRIS LAKE (Morris Dam)	Eel River	Laughlin Range Outlet Creek	1554	RT
NAVARRO RIVER	Pacific Ocean	Albion, Elk Navarro	- - -	SH, RT, SS
NOYO RIVER	Pacific Ocean	Fort Bragg Noyo, Northspur	- - -	SH, SS, ELT
NOYO RIVER NF of SF	Noyo River Noyo River SF	Noyo Hill	- - -	SH, SS
RUSSIAN RIVER	Pacific Ocean	Hopland Elledge Peak	- - -	SS, SH
RUSSIAN RIVER E. FK	Russian River Lake Mendocino	Ukiah Potter Valley	- - -	BN, RT
SMOKEHOUSE CREEK	Eel River Eel River MF	Buck Rock	- - -	RT
STICK LAKE CANYON CREEK	Eel River Eel River MF	Leech Lake Mountain	- - -	SH

Water By County	Drainage	USGS Topographic Map 7.5 Minute Series	Elevation (Feet) Lakes Only	Fish Species
TEN MILE RIVER	Pacific Ocean	Inglenook Dutchmans Knoll	- - -	SS, SH
TEN MILE RIVER MF	Pacific Ocean Ten Mile River	Dutchmans Knoll	- - -	SH, SS
THATCHER CREEK	Eel River Eel River MF	Thatcher Ridge Sanhedrin Mountain	- - -	RT
TOM LONG CREEK	Eel River Eel River SF	Harris, Noble Butte Bell Springs	- - -	SH, KS
UMBRELLA CREEK	Eel River Eel River MF	Hull Mountain	- - -	SH
WHITE HAWK CREEK	Eel River Eel River MF	Mendocino Pass	- - -	SH
WILLIAMS CREEK	Eel River Eel River MF	Potter Valley Redwood Valley	- - -	RT, SH, KS

Modoc County

Water By County	Drainage	USGS Topographic Map 7.5 Minute Series	Elevation (Feet) Lakes Only	Fish Species
ANNIE LAKE	Surprise Valley	Lake Annie	5000	RT, BK, BN ELT, CT-L
ASH CREEK	Sacramento River Pit River	Ambrose Valley	- - -	BN, RT
BALLARD RESERVOIR	Sacramento River Pit River	Canby	4600	BK, ELT
BASEBALL RESERVOIR	Sacramento River Pit River	Weed Valley	5300	RT
BAYLEY RESERVOIR	Sacramento River Pit River	Graven Ridge	4960	RT, BK, ELT
BIDWELL CREEK	Upper Alkali Lake	Mount Bidwell Fort Bidwell	- - -	RT, BN
BRILES RESERVOIR	Goose Lake	Sugar Hill	5237	RT, ELT, BK
BUCK CREEK	Goose Lake Willow Creek	Sugar Hill Willow Ranch	- - -	RT, RDT
CAVE LAKE	Goose Lake Pine Creek	Mount Bidwell	6450	RT, BK
CEDAR CREEK	Middle Alkali Lake	Cedarville Payne Peak	- - -	RT
CLEAR LAKE	Sacramento River Pit River	Soup Creek	5805	RT, BN, BK
COLD CREEK	Goose Lake Lassen Creek	Sugar Hill	- - -	RT, RDT
COTTONWOOD CREEK	Middle Alkali Lake	Warren Peak	- - -	RT
COTTONWOOD CREEK	Goose Lake	Willow Ranch	- - -	RDT
COUCH CREEK	Sacramento River Pit River	Payne Creek Davis Creek	- - -	RT
DAVIS CREEK MF	Goose Lake Davis Creek	Davis Creek	- - -	RT, RDT
DAVIS CREEK NF	Goose Lake Davis Creek	Davis Creek	- - -	RT, BN
DAVIS CREEK SF	Goose Lake Davis Creek	Davis Creek	- - -	BN, RT
DEEP CREEK, North	Middle Alkali Lake	Cedarville	- - -	RT
DEEP CREEK, South	Middle Alkali Lake	Cedarville	- - -	RT
DELTA LAKE	Sacramento River Pit River	Likely Infernal Cavern	5165	ELT
DISMAL CREEK	Cow Head Lake	Mount Bidwell	- - -	RT
DORRIS RESERVOIR	Sacramento River Pit River	Dorris Reservoir	4400	RT
DRY CREEK	Sacramento River Pit River	Shields Creek	- - -	RT
DUNCAN RESERVOIR	Sacramento River Pit River	Ambrose	4950	RT, ELT
EAGLE CREEK	Lower Lake	Eagle Peak	- - -	RT
EAST CREEK	Sacramento River Pit River	Jess Valley Emerson Peak	- - -	RT, BN, RDT
EAST CREEK NF	Sacramento River Pit River	Emerson Peak	- - -	RT, BN

Water By County	Drainage	USGS Topographic Map 7.5 Minute Series	Elevation (Feet) Lakes Only	Fish Species
EMERSON CREEK	Lower Lake	Eagle Peak	- - -	RT, BN
EMERSON LAKE NORTH	Lower Lake Emerson Creek	Eagle Peak	7740	BK
EMERSON LAKE SOUTH	Lower Lake Emerson Creek	Eagle Peak	7950	BK, RT, ELT
FEE RESERVOIR	Upper Lake	Larkspur Hills	5239	RT, ELT, CT-L
FITZHUGH CREEK	Sacramento River Pit River	Dorris Reservoir Little Juniper Reservoir	- - -	RT, BN
FITZHUGH CREEK NF	Sacramento River Pit River	Soup Creek Little Juniper Reservoir	- - -	RT, BN, BK
FITZHUGH CREEK SF	Sacramento River Pit River	Soup Creek Little Juniper Reservoir	- - -	RT, BK
FRANKLIN CREEK	Sacramento River Pit River	Davis Creek	- - -	RT
GOOSE LAKE	Lakeview	West of Willow Ranch McGinty Point Willow Ranch	4715	RT, RDT
HOUSEHOLDER RESERVOIR	Sacramento River Pit River	Pease Flat	5298	RT
HULBERT CREEK	Sacramento River Pit River	Happy Camp Mountain	- - -	RT
INDIAN SPRINGS RESERVOIR	Sacramento River Pit River	Mahogany Ridge	4960	ELT, RT
JANES RESERVOIR	Sacramento River Pit River	Weed Valley	4104	RT, BN
JIM CREEK	Sacramento River Pit River	Dorris Reservoir	- - -	RT
JOSEPH CREEK	Sacramento River Pit River	Payne Peak	- - -	RT
LASSEN CREEK	Goose Lake	Sugar Hill	- - -	RDT, RT
LILY LAKE	Goose Lake Pine Creek	Mount Bidwell	6000	RT, BK, ELT
McGINTY RESERVOIR	Goose Lake	McGinty Reservoir	5000	RT, ELT
MILL CREEK	Sacramento River Pit River	Jess Valley Soup Creek	- - -	RT, BN, RDT
MILL CREEK	Upper Lake	Mount Bidwell	- - -	RT, BN
MILL CREEK (Lake City Canyon)	Upper Lake	Davis Creek Lake City	- - -	RT
OWL CREEK	Middle Alkali Lake	Eagle Peak Warren Peak	- - -	RT
PARKER CREEK	Sacramento River Pit River	Dorris Reservoir Shields Creek	- - -	RT
PARKER CREEK MF	Sacramento River Pit River	Shields Creek	- - -	RT
PARKER CREEK NF	Sacramento River Pit River	Shields Creek	- - -	RT
PARKER CREEK SF	Sacramento River Pit River	Shields Creek	- - -	RT
PATTERSON LAKE	Sacramento River Pit River	Warren Peak	9040	RT, ELT
PAYNE RESERVOIR	Sacramento River Pit River	Dorris Reservoir	4646	BN
PINE CREEK	Sacramento River Pit River	Dorris Reservoir Shields Creek	- - -	RT, BN
PINE CREEK MF	Sacramento River Pit River	Shields Creek	- - -	RT, BK
PINE CREEK NF	Sacramento River Pit River	Shields Creek	- - -	RT
PINE CREEK SF	Sacramento River Pit River	Soup Creek	- - -	RT, BK
PINE CREEK BASIN	Sacramento River Pit River	Eagle Peak	7400	BK, RT, RDT
PINE CREEK RESERVOIR	Sacramento River Pit River	Dorris Reservoir	4953	BK, RT, ELT
PIT RIVER SF	Sacramento River Pit River	Jess Valley Tule Mountain	- - -	BN, RT

Water By County	Drainage	USGS Topographic Map 7.5 Minute Series	Elevation (Feet) Lakes Only	Fish Species
RAIDER CREEK	Middle Alkali Lake	Eagle Peak, Eagleville	- - -	RT
RENNER SIBLEY (CAL-OR)	Goose Lake	Pease Flat	4984	CT-L
RESERVOIR "C"	Sacramento River Pit River	Boles Meadows East	4943	RT, BN, ELT
RESERVOIR "F"	Sacramento River Pit River	Ambrose Jacks Butte	4960	RT, ELT
RUSH CREEK, Upper	Sacramento River Pit River	Hermit Butte	- - -	RT, BN
RUSH CREEK, Lower	Sacramento River Pit River	Hermit Butte Adin Pass	- - -	RT, BN
SHIELDS CREEK	Sacramento River Pit River	Shields Creek Dorris Reservoir	- - -	RT
SHIELDS CREEK NF	Sacramento River Pit River	Shields Creek	- - -	RT
SHIELDS CREEK SF	Sacramento River Pit River	Shields Creek	- - -	RT
SNAKE LAKE	Lower Lake	Snake Lake	5249	RT, BK
SOLDIER CREEK	Upper Lake	Cedarville	- - -	RT
SOUP CREEK	Sacramento River	Soup Creek	- - -	RT
SWORINGER RESERVOIR (Modoc & Lassen Co.)	Lower Lake Bare Creek	Snake Lake	5860	RT, BN
THOMS CREEK	Sacramento River Pit River	Payne Peak	- - -	BN, RT
TWELVE MILE CREEK	Cow Head Lake	Lake Annie	- - -	RT
WEST VALLEY RESERVOIR	Sacramento River Pit River	Tule Mountain	4760	RT, ELT
WASHINGTON CREEK	Sacramento River Pit River	Washington Mountain Happy Camp Mountain	- - -	RT
WILLOW CREEK	Goose Lake	Willow Ranch Sugar Hill	- - -	RT, RDT
WILLOW CREEK NF	Klamath River Lost River	Sagebrush Butte Swamp	- - -	RT

Napa County

Water By County	Drainage	USGS Topographic Map 7.5 Minute Series	Elevation (Feet) Lakes Only	Fish Species
BELL CANYON CREEK	Napa River Bell Canyon Reservoir	Saint Helena	- - -	RT, SH
BELL CANYON RESERVOIR	San Pablo Bay Napa River	Saint Helena	415	RT
BERRYESSA, LAKE	Sacramento River Putah Creek	Monticello Dam Lake Berryessa Waller Springs	440	ELT, RT
HINMAN, LAKE	Napa River	Rutherford	364	RT
RITCHIE CREEK	Napa River	Calistoga	- - -	SH

Shasta County

Water By County	Drainage	USGS Topographic Map 7.5 Minute Series	Elevation (Feet) Lakes Only	Fish Species
BACKBONE CREEK	Sacramento River	Bohemotash Mountain	- - -	RT, BN
BAILEY CREEK	Sacramento River Battle Creek	Manton Viola	- - -	ELT, RT
BAILEY CREEK NF	Sacramento River Battle Creek	Lassen Peak	- - -	RT, BN
BAILEY CREEK SF	Sacramento River Battle Creek	Lassen Peak	- - -	RT, ELT
BAKER CREEK	Pit River Kosk Creek	Big Bend	- - -	RT
BAKER FLAT CREEK	Sacramento River Cottonwood Creek	Beegum (7.5' X 15') Chanchelulla Peak (7.5' X 15')	- - -	RT
BARRETT LAKE	Sacramento River Pit River	Thousand Lakes Valley	6470	BK
BATTLE CREEK (Also see Tehama Co.)	Sacramento River	Tuscan Buttes NE Balls Ferry	- - -	RT, ELT
BATTLE CREEK NF	Sacramento River Battle Creek	Manton Viola	- - -	RT, BN, ELT
BATTLE CREEK RESERVOIR, NORTH	Sacramento River Battle Creek	Viola	5571	BN, RT, ELT

Water By County	Drainage	USGS Topographic Map 7.5 Minute Series	Elevation (Feet) Lakes Only	Fish Species
BAUM LAKE	Sacramento River Pit River	Cassel	2978	RT, BN, BK ELT
BEEGUM CREEK (Shasta-Tehama Co. line)	Sacramento River Cottonwood Creek	Beegum (7.5' X 15')	- - -	RT, KS, SH
BEEGUM CREEK MF (Lower 5 miles of stream Shasta-Tehama Co. line)	Sacramento River Cottonwood Creek	Beegum (7.5' X 15') Pony Buck Peak (7.5' X 15')	- - -	RT
BEEGUN CREEK NF	Sacramento River Cottonwood Creek	Beegum (7.5' X 15')	- - -	RT
BIG LAKE	Sacramento River Pit River	Jacks Backbone Hatchet Mountain Pass	5862	RT
BLUE LAKE	Sacramento River Cow Creek	Miller Mountain	5680	RT
BOULDER CREEK	Sacramento River	Whiskey Town French Gulch	- - -	RT
BOX LAKE	Sacramento River Pit River	Thousand Lakes Valley	6430	BK
BRANDY CREEK	Sacramento River	Igo	- - -	RT, KOK, ELT
BRITTON, Lake	Sacramento River Pit River	Burney Falls	2733	ELT
BUCKHORN LAKE	Sacramento River Cow Creek	Miller Mountain	7100	RT
BURNEY CREEK (Lower, Middle, Upper)	Pit River	Burney Falls, Burney Burney Mountain West	- - -	RT, BN, BK ELT
CASTLE CREEK	Sacramento River	Dunsmuir Seven Lakes Basin	- - -	RT, BN
CASTLE CREEK NF	Sacramento River Castle Creek	Dunsmuir	- - -	RT
CEDAR SALT LOG CREEK	Pit River Iron Canyon Creek	Big Bend	- - -	RDT
CHATTERDOWN CREEK	Sacramento River McCloud River	Bollibokka Mountain	- - -	RT
CLARK CREEK (Lower, Upper)	Pit River	Burney Falls	- - -	RT
CLEAR CREEK (Below Whiskeytown Lake)	Sacramento River	Igo	- - -	RT, KS, SH ELT
CLEAR CREEK (Above Whiskeytown Lake)	Sacramento River	Schell Mountain Damnation Peak	- - -	RT, ELT
CLEAR CREEK E. FK	Sacramento River Clear Creek	Schell Mountain	- - -	RT
CLOVER CREEK	Sacramento River Cow Creek	Palo Cedro Clough Gulch	- - -	RT, ELT
COLEMAN RESERVOIR	Sacramento River Battle Creek	Tuscan Buttes NE	870	RT
COTTONWOOD CREEK MF	Sacramento River Cottonwood Creek	Chanchelulla Peak (7.5' X 15') Chickabally Mountain (7.5' X 15')	- - -	RT, KS, SH
COTTONWOOD CREEK NF	Sacramento River Cottonwood Creek	Ono (7.5' X 15')	- - -	RT, KS, SH
COW CREEK, Old and POWER HOUSE	Sacramento River Cow Creek	Palo Cedro Clough Gulch	- - -	ELT, RT
COW CREEK SF	Sacramento River Cow Creek	Palo Cedro	- - -	RT, BN, KS, SH, ELT
CRYSTAL CREEK	Sacramento River Clear Creek	French Gulch	- - -	RT, KOK
CRYSTAL LAKE	Sacramento River Pit River	Cassel	3000	RT, BN
DEADLUN CREEK	Pit River Iron Canyon Creek	Big Bend	- - -	RT
DEEP CREEK	Pit River	Chalk Mountain	- - -	RT
DEVILS CANYON CREEK	Pit River Kosk Creek	Big Bend Grizzly Peak	- - -	RT
DIGGER CREEK (Also see Tehama Co.)	Sacramento River Battle Creek	Manton	- - -	RT, BN, SH ELT
DURBIN LAKE	Sacramento River Pit River	Thousand Lakes Valley	6460	RT, ELT
EASTMAN LAKE	Sacramento River Pit River	Fall River Mills	3311	RT

Water By County	Drainage	USGS Topographic Map 7.5 Minute Series	Elevation (Feet) Lakes Only	Fish Species
EILER, LAKE	Sacramento River Pit River	Thousand Lakes Valley	6403	RT, ELT, BK
EVERETT LAKE	Sacramento River Pit River	Thousand Lakes Valley	7181	RT, ELT, BK
FLAT CREEK	Pit River	Devils Rock	- - -	RT
GAP CREEK	Pit River Iron Canyon Creek	Shoeinhorse Mountain	- - -	RDT
GRACE LAKE	Sacramento River Battle Creek	Manton	3480	RT, BK, ELT
GREY ROCK LAKE	Sacramento River Castle Creek	Chicken Hawk Hill	5500	BK, RT, ELT
HAT CREEK, Upper (Below Lassen NP to Cassel)	Sacramento River Pit River	West Prospect Peak	- - -	RT, BN, BK
HAT CREEK, Lower (Hat P.H. 1, Hat P.H. 2 to Lake Britton)	Sacramento River Pit River	Cassel	- - -	RT, BN, BK
HAT CREEK E. FK (Lassen NP)	Sacramento River Pit River	West Prospect Peak	- - -	RT, BK
HAT CREEK W. FK (Lassen NP)	Sacramento River Pit River	West Prospect Peak	- - -	RT, BK
HAT LAKE	Sacramento River Pit River	West Prospect Peak	6440	BK
HATCHET CREEK	Sacramento River Pit River	Hatchet Mountain Pass	- - -	RT, BN, BK ELT
HAWKINS CREEK	Sacramento River McCloud River	Shoeinhorse Mountain	- - -	RT, BN
HAZEL CREEK	Sacramento River	Tombstone Mountain	- - -	RT, BN
HAZEL CREEK SF	Sacramento River Hazel Creek	Tombstone Mountain	- - -	RT, BN
HEART LAKE	Sacramento River Pit River	Lassen Peak	6560	RT, BK
HELEN, LAKE	Sacramento River Castle Creek	Seven Lakes Basin	6700	BK
HORSESHOE LAKE	Sacramento River Pit River	Mount Harkness	6550	BK, RT
HUFFORD LAKE	Sacramento River Pit River	Thousand Lakes Valley	6749	RT, BK
IRON CANYON CREEK	Sacramento River Pit River	Big Bend	- - -	RT, RDT
IRON CANYON RESERVOIR	Sacramento River Pit River	Big Bend Shoeinhorse Mountain	2664	RT, ELT, BK
JERUSALEM CREEK	Sacramento River Cottonwood Creek	Ono (7.5' X 15')	- - -	RT
KESWICK DITCH (Canal to Nora Lake)	Sacramento River Battle Creek	Manton	- - -	ELT, BK
KESWICK RESERVOIR	Sacramento River	Redding	585	RT
KILARC RESERVOIR	Sacramento River Cow Creek	Miller Mountain	3789	RT, BN, ELT
KINGS CREEK, Upper (Shasta-Plumas Co.)	Feather River Warner Creek	Mount Harkness (Plumas Co.) Reading Peak (Shasta Co.)	- - -	RT, BK
KNOWNOTHING CREEK	Klamath River Salmon River	Youngs Peak	- - -	SH, KS, RT, SS
KNOWNOTHING CREEK, E. FK	Klamath River Salmon River	Youngs Peak	- - -	RT
KNOWNOTHING CREEK, W. FK	Klamath River Salmon River	Youngs Peak	- - -	RT
KUNTZ CREEK	Klamath River	Hamburg	- - -	RT
KOSK CREEK	Sacramento River Pit River	Big Bend Dead Horse Summit	- - -	RT, BN
LEWIS CREEK	Klamath River Salmon River	Hamburg	- - -	RT
LICK CREEK	Klamath River Dillon Creek	Bear Peak	- - -	RT
LICK CREEK	Klamath River Elk Creek	Huckleberry Mountain	- - -	RT
LITTLE BEAR VALLEY CREEK	Klamath River Clear Creek	Bear Peak	- - -	RT

Water By County	Drainage	USGS Topographic Map 7.5 Minute Series	Elevation (Feet) Lakes Only	Fish Species
LITTLE CASTLE CREEK	Sacramento River	Dunsmuir	- - -	RT
LITTLE ELK LAKE CREEK	Klamath River Scott River	Marble Mountain	- - -	RT
LITTLE GRIDER CREEK	Klamath River	Happy Camp	- - -	RT
LITTLE GRIZZLY CREEK	Klamath River Salmon River	Thompson Peak	- - -	RT
LITTLE MILL CREEK	Klamath River Scott River	Callahan, Billys Peak	- - -	RT
LUMGREY CREEK	Klamath River Cottonwood Peak	Badger Mountain	- - -	SH, RT
LOST CREEK	Sacramento River Pit River	Murken Bench	- - -	RT
LOST CREEK	Sacramento River Pit River	West Prospect Peak	- - -	RT
MAGEE LAKE	Sacramento River Pit River	Thousand Lakes Valley	7198	RT, ELT, BK
MANZANITA LAKE	Sacramento River Battle Creek	Manzanita Lake	5847	RT, BN
MATTHEWS CREEK	Klamath River Salmon River	Cecilville	- - -	SH, RT
McADAM CREEK	Klamath River Scott River	Indian Creek Baldy	- - -	SH, RT
McCASH FORK CREEK	Klamath River Ukonom Creek	Ukonom Mountain	- - -	RT
McCLOUD, LAKE	Sacramento River McCloud River	Lake McCloud	2680	RT, BN, ELT
McCLOUD RIVER, Lower (Below Lake McCloud, Ash Camp to Nature Conservancy) (Upper McCloud, see Siskiyou Co.)	Sacramento River	Shoeinhorse Mountain Yellowjacket Mountain	- - -	RT, BN, BK
McCUMBER RESERVOIR	Sacramento River Battle Creek	Viola	4086	RT, BN
McGILL CREEK	Pit River Iron Canyon Creek	Big Bend	- - -	RDT
McKINNEY CREEK	Klamath River	Horse Creek McKinley Mountain	- - -	SH, RT
McNEIL CREEK	Klamath River Salmon River	Thompson Peak Caribou Lake	- - -	RT, SH
MEARS CREEK	Sacramento River	Tombstone Mountain Chicken Hawk Hill	- - -	RT
MEDICINE CREEK	Klamath River Dillon Creek	Chimney Rock	- - -	RT
MERRILL CREEK	Klamath River Salmon River	Somes Bar	- - -	RT
METHODIST CREEK	Klamath River Salmon River	Cecilville, Youngs Peak	- - -	SH, SS, RT
MIDDLE CREEK	Klamath River Horse Creek	Hamburg, Dutch Creek	- - -	SH, RT, KS, SS
MIDDLE CREEK	Klamath River Scott River	Scott Bar, Grider Valley	- - -	SH, RT
MILL CREEK	Sacramento River Clear Creek	French Gulch	- - -	RT
MONTGOMERY CREEK	Sacramento River Pit River	Montgomery Creek	- - -	RT
NELSON CREEK	Sacramento River Pit River	Big Bend Skunk Ridge	- - -	RT
NELSON CREEK E. FK	Pit River Nelson Creek	Skunk Ridge	- - -	RT
NORA LAKE	Sacramento River Battle Creek	Manton	3431	RT, BN, ELT, BK
PAIGE BOULDER CREEK	Sacramento River Clear Creek	Igo	- - -	RT
PIT RIVER (Shasta Co.) (Pit 1 P.H. to Lake Britton)	Sacramento River	Hogback Ridge Cassel	- - -	RT, BN
PIT RIVER (Shasta Co.) (Lake Britton to Pit 3 P.H.)	Sacramento River	Dana, Burney Falls Burney	- - -	RT, BN

Water By County	Drainage	USGS Topographic Map 7.5 Minute Series	Elevation (Feet) Lakes Only	Fish Species
PIT RIVER (Shasta Co.) (Pit 3 P.H. to Big Bend	Sacramento River	Chalk Mountain Big Bend	- - -	RT, BN
PIT 5 RESERVOIR	Sacramento River Pit River	Chalk Mountain	2056	RT
PIT 6 RESERVOIR	Sacramento River Pit River	Roaring Creek	1430	RT
RAINBOW LAKE	Sacramento River Cottonwood Creek	Shasta Bally	2012	RT
REFLECTION LAKE	Sacramento River Battle Creek	Manzanita Lake	5895	RT, BN
RIDGE LAKES	Sacramento River Mill Creek	Lassen Peak	7920	BK
RIPGUT CREEK	Pit River Goose Gap	Devils Rock	- - -	RT, BN
ROCK CREEK	Pit River Skunk Ridge	Burney Falls	- - -	RT, BN
SACRAMENTO RIVER, Upper (Castle Crag to Shasta Lake. Above Dunsmuir, see Siskiyou Co.)	Sacramento River	Dunsmuir Tombstone Mountain Chicken Hawk Hill, Lamoine	- - -	RT, BN
SACRAMENTO RIVER, Lower (Keswick Dam to Anderson)	Sacramento River	Redding, Enterprise Cottonwood	- - -	RT, KS, SH
SCREWDRIVER CREEK	Sacramento River	Burney Falls Skunk Ridge	- - -	RT
SEVEN LAKE NO. 3	Sacramento River Pit River	Miller Mountain	5960	RT
SEVEN LAKE, Lower	Sacramento River Pit River	Miller Mountain	6200	BK
SHADOW LAKE	Sacramento River Pit River	Reading Peak	7640	BK, RT
SHASTA LAKE	Sacramento River	Shasta Dam, O'Brien	6665	RT, ELT, BN
SHOTGUN CREEK NF	Sacramento River	Chicken Hawk Hill	- - -	RT
SILVER LAKE	Sacramento River Cow Creek	Miller Mountain	4730	BN, RT
SLATE CREEK	Sacramento River	Lamoine	- - -	RT, BN
SLATE CREEK SF	Sacramento River Slate Creek	Lamoine Damnation Peak	- - -	RT
SQUAW CREEK	Sacramento River	Minnesota Mountain Devils Rock	- - -	RT
SQUAW VALLEY CREEK	Sacramento River McCloud River	Girard Ridge	- - -	RT, BN
SUGARLOAF CREEK	Sacramento River	Bohemotash Mountain	- - -	RT
SUMMIT LAKE	Sacramento River Pit River	Reading Peak	6889	BK, RT
TOM DOW CREEK	Sacramento River McCloud River	Yellowjacket Mtn	- - -	RT
TOM NEAL CREEK	Sacramento River McCloud River	Yellowjacket Mtn	- - -	RT
TULE LAKE	Sacramento River Pit River	Fall River Mills	3300	RT, BN
TWIN LAKE, Lower	Sacramento River Pit River	Prospect Peak	6880	RT, BK
TWIN LAKE, Upper	Sacramento River Pit River	Prospect Peak	6530	RT
WHISKEYTOWN LAKE	Sacramento River	Whiskeytown French Gulch, Igo	1220	RT, KOK, BK ELT, BN

Siskiyou County

Water By County	Drainage	USGS Topographic Map 7.5 Minute Series	Elevation (Feet) Lakes Only	Fish Species
ABBOTT LAKE	Klamath River Salmon River	English Peak	5663	BK
ABRAMS LAKE	Sacramento River Wagon Creek	City of Mount Shasta	3700	RT
ALBERT LAKE, Lower	Klamath River Scott River	Eaton Peak	6900	BK, ELT
ALBERT LAKE, Upper	Klamath River Scott River	Eaton Peak	7150	RT, BK

Water By County	Drainage	USGS Topographic Map 7.5 Minute Series	Elevation (Feet) Lakes Only	Fish Species
ANGEL LAKE	Klamath River Scott River	Boulder Peak	6500	BK
ANTELOPE CREEK	Klamath River Butte Valley	Bray, Tennant Rainbow Mountain	- - -	BN, RT, BK
ANTELOPE CREEK LAKE	Klamath River	Rainbow Mountain	6800	BK
APPLEGATE RIVER	Applegate River, OR	Kangaroo Mountain	- - -	RT
APPLEGATE RIVER BUTTE FK	Applegate River	Kangaroo Mountain Figurehead Mountain	- - -	RT
APPLEGATE RIVER MF	Applegate River	Kangaroo Mountain Figurehead Mountain	- - -	RT
ASH CREEK	Klamath River	Hawkinsville	- - -	SH, RT
ASPEN LAKE	Klamath River Scott River	Boulder Peak	7100	BK
ATKINS CREEK	Klamath River Salmon River	Yellow Dog Peak English Peak	- - -	RT
AUBREY CREEK	Klamath River	Dillon Mountain	- - -	RT
AZALEA LAKE	Rogue River, OR Applegate River	Figurehead Mountain	5380	BK
BABS FORK	Klamath River Scott River	Boulder Peak Yellow Dog Peak	- - -	RT
BABS LAKE	Klamath River Scott River	Yellow Dog Peak	5500	BK, RT
BARKHOUSE CREEK	Klamath River	McKinley Mountain	- - -	SH, RT, SS
BASS LAKE	Klamath River Shasta River Little Shasta River	Little Shasta	- - -	RT, BK
BEAR CREEK	Klamath River Elk Creek	Huckleberry Mountain Grider Valley	- - -	RT, BK
BEAR CREEK	Klamath River Beaver Creek	Buckhorn Bally	- - -	RT
BEAR LAKE	Klamath River Elk Creek	Grider Valley	5950	BK
BEAR LAKE, Lower	Klamath River Clear Creek	Bear Peak	4350	RT, ELT
BEAR LAKE, Upper	Klamath River Clear Creek	Bear Peak	4380	BK
BEAVER CREEK	Klamath River	McKinley Mountain Buckhorn Bally	- - -	SH, KS, SS, RT
BIG BLUE LAKE	Klamath River Salmon River	Eaton Peak	6836	RT, ELT, BN
BIG BEND CREEK	Klamath River Salmon River	Thompson Peak Caribou Lake	- - -	RT
BIG CREEK	Klamath River Salmon River	Sawyers Bar Forks of Salmon	- - -	RT
BIG ELK LAKE	Klamath River Salmon River	Marble Mountain	6050	RT
BIG MEADOWS CREEK	Klamath River Salmon River	English Peak	- - -	RT
BIG MILL CREEK	Klamath River Scott River	Callahan, Scott Mountain Tangle Blue Lake	- - -	SH, RT, SS
BINGHAM LAKE	Klamath River Salmon River	Eaton Peak	7080	RT, BK, ELT
BISHOP CREEK	Klamath River Elk Creek	Huckleberry Mountain	- - -	RT
BLACK BEAR CREEK	Klamath River Salmon River	Cecilville Sawyers Bar	- - -	RT
BLUE GRANITE LAKE	Klamath River Elk Creek	Ukonom Lake	5255	RT, ELT
BLUEBERRY LAKE	Klamath River Salmon River	English Peak	6050	RT, BK
BOLES CREEK	Klamath River Shasta River	Weed, Hotlum	- - -	RT
BOULDER CREEK	Klamath River Scott River	Scott Bar Boulder Peak	- - -	RT, SH
BOULDER CREEK	Klamath River Scott River SF	Callahan	- - -	SH, RT

Water By County	Drainage	USGS Topographic Map 7.5 Minute Series	Elevation (Feet) Lakes Only	Fish Species
BOULDER LAKE, East	Klamath River Scott River	Billys Peak	6676	RT, BK, ELT
BOULDER LAKE, Lower	Klamath River Scott River	Billys Peak	6223	RT, BK, ELT
BOULDER LAKE, Middle	Klamath River Scott River	Billys Peak	6512	RT, BK, ELT
BOULDER LAKE, Upper	Klamath River Scott River	Billys Peak	6777	RT, BK, ELT
BOULDER LAKE, West	Klamath River Scott River	Billys Peak	6963	RT
BRIDGE CREEK	Klamath River Salmon River	Medicine Mountain Ukonom Lake	- - -	RT, SH
BROWNS CREEK	Klamath River	Clear Creek	- - -	RT
BUCK LAKE	Klamath River Clear Creek	Devils Punchbowl	4300	BK, RT
BUCKHORN CREEK	Klamath River	Hamburg, Horse Creek Comfrey Mountain	- - -	RT, SH, KS, SS
BUCKHORN LAKE	Klamath River Scott River	Boulder Peak	6800	RT, BK, ELT
BUG CREEK	Klamath River Thompson Creek	Figurehead Mountain	- - -	RT
BULL CREEK	Sacramento River McCloud River	Kinyon, Bartle, Dead Horse Summit	- - -	BK
BULLSEYE LAKE	Sacramento River Pit River	Medicine Lake	6680	BK, RT, ELT
BURNEY LAKE	Klamath River Elk Creek	Ukonom Lake	5650	BK
BURNEY VALLEY CREEK	Klamath River Elk Creek	Ukonom Lake	- - -	RT, BK
BUTLER CREEK	Klamath River Salmon River	Orleans Mountain	- - -	SH, RT
BUTTE CREEK	Butte Valley Meiss Lake	MacDoel, Bray, Penoyar West Haight Mountain	- - -	RT
BUZZARD LAKE	Klamath River Scott River	Boulder Peak	6700	BK, RT
CABIN MEADOW LAKE	Klamath River Scott River	South China Mountain	6893	RT, ELT
CADE CREEK	Klamath River	Slater Butte	- - -	RT, SH
CALDWELL LAKE, Lower	Klamath River Shasta River	South China Mountain	6835	BK
CALDWELL LAKE, Middle	Klamath River Shasta River	South China Mountain	7100	BK
CALDWELL LAKE, Upper	Klamath River Shasta River	South China Mountain	7100	BK
CALF LAKE	Klamath River Scott River	Boulder Peak	7000	BK
CAMP CREEK	Klamath River	Iron Gate Reservoir	- - -	RT
CAMPBELL LAKE	Klamath River Scott River	Boulder Peak	5758	RT, BK, ELT
CANYON CREEK	Klamath River Seiad Creek	Seiad Valley Kangaroo Mountain	- - -	RT, SH
CANYON CREEK	Klamath River Scott River	Scott Bar, Boulder Peak, Marble Mountain	- - -	SH, SS, RT
CARIBOU LAKE	Klamath River Salmon River	Caribou Lake	6822	BK, RT, ELT
CARIBOU LAKE, Little	Klamath River Salmon River	Caribou Lake	7165	BK
CARIBOU LAKE, Lower	Klamath River Salmon River	Caribou Lake	6520	RT, BK, ELT
CARTER CREEK	Klamath River Ukonom Mountain	Dillon Mountain	- - -	RT
CASTLE LAKE	Sacramento River Castle Lake Creek	Seven Lakes Basin	5436	RT, BK, ELT
CASTLE LAKE, Little	Sacramento River Ney Springs Creek	Dunsmuir	5590	RT, BK, ELT
CASTLE LAKE CREEK	Sacramento River	City of Mount Shasta Mount Eddy	- - -	RT

Water By County	Drainage	USGS Topographic Map 7.5 Minute Series	Elevation (Feet) Lakes Only	Fish Species
CECIL CREEK	Klamath River Salmon River	Cecilville Cecil Lake	- - -	SH, RT
CEDAR CREEK	Klamath River Thompson Creek	Preston Peak	- - -	RT
CEDAR LAKE	Sacramento River Sacramento River SF	Seven Lakes Basin	5700	BK
CHINA CREEK	Klamath River	Thompson Peak	- - -	RT, SH
CHARMAINE LAKE	Klamath River Salmon River	English Peak	6300	RT, BK, ELT
CHIMNEY ROCK LAKE	Klamath River Salmon River	Forks of Salmon	6100	BK, RT, ELT
CHINQUAPIN LAKE	Klamath River Scott River	Boulder Peak	7150	BK, RT, ELT
CHIPMUNK LAKE	Sacramento River Sacramento MF	Mount Eddy	6363	BK
CLEAR CREEK	Klamath River	Clear Creek	- - -	SH, KS, SS, RT
CLEAR CREEK SF	Klamath River Clear Creek	Clear Creek Bear Peak	- - -	RT, SH
CLEAR CREEK WF	Klamath River Clear Creek	Devils Punchbowl Presto Mountain	- - -	RT, SH
CLEAR LAKE	Klamath River Salmon River	Medicine Mountain	5790	RT, ELT
CLIFF LAKE	Klamath River Scott River	Boulder Peak	6109	ELT, BK
CLIFF LAKE	Sacramento River Sacramento River SF	Seven Lakes Basin	5770	BK, RT
CLIFF LAKE, Lower	Sacramento River Sacramento River SF	Seven Lakes Basin	5730	BK
CLIFF LAKE, Upper	Sacramento River Sacramento River SF	Seven Lakes Basin	6330	BK
COLD CREEK	Sacramento River	City of Mount Shasta	- - -	RT
COLE CREEK	Klamath River Indian Creek	Happy Camp Deadman Point	- - -	RT
COOK AND GREEN CREEK	Applegate River Dutch Creek	Kangaroo Mountain	- - -	RT
COON CREEK	Klamath River	Ukonom Mountain Dillon Mountain	- - -	SH, RT
COPCO RESERVOIR	Klamath River	Copco	2590	RT
COPPER CREEK	Klamath River Dillon Creek	Chimney Rock	- - -	RT
CRAPO CREEK	Klamath River Salmon River	Forks of Salmon	- - -	RT, SH
CRATER LAKE, Little	Klamath River Shasta River	Mount Eddy	7581	BK
CRATER LAKE, Lower	Klamath River Scott River	China Mountain	7505	RT, BK
CRATER LAKE, Upper	Klamath River Scott River	China Mountain	7508	BK, ELT, RT
CRAWFORD CREEK	Klamath River Salmon River	Cecilville Grasshopper Ridge	- - -	SH, RT
CUB CREEK	Klamath River Ukonom Creek	Ukonom Mountain	- - -	RT
CUDDIHY LAKE, No. 1	Klamath River Salmon River	Ukonom Lake	5650	BK
CUDDIHY LAKE, No. 2	Klamath River Salmon River	Ukonom Lake	5650	BK, ELT
CUDDIHY LAKE, No. 3	Klamath River Salmon River	Ukonom Lake	5700	BK
CUDDIHY LAKE, No. 4	Klamath River Salmon River	Ukonom Lake	5700	RT
DALE CREEK	Klamath River Shasta River	Weed Mount Eddy	- - -	BN
DEADMAN LAKE	Klamath River Salmon River	Ukonom Lake	5680	BK
DEADWOOD CREEK	Klamath River Scott River	Indian Creek Baldy McKinley Mountain	- - -	RT

Water By County	Drainage	USGS Topographic Map 7.5 Minute Series	Elevation (Feet) Lakes Only	Fish Species
DEEP LAKE	Klamath River Scott River	Boulder Peak	6350	RT, BK, ELT
DEEP LAKE CREEK	Klamath River Scott River	Boulder Peak	- - -	RT
DEER CREEK	Sacramento River	Buckhorn Bally	- - -	RT
DEER LICK CREEK	Klamath River Salmon River	Somes Bar	- - -	RT
DEVILS PUNCHBOWL LAKE	Klamath River Clear Creek	Devils Punchbowl	4800	BK, RT, ELT
DILLON CREEK	Klamath River	Dillon Mountain Chimney Rock	- - -	RT, SH, KS, SS
DILLON CREEK NF	Klamath River Dillon Creek	Dillon Mountain Bear Peak	- - -	RT
DOBKINS LAKE	Klamath River Shasta River	Mount Eddy	6788	RT, BN
DOE CREEK	Klamath River Clear Creek	Devils Punchbowl	- - -	RT, BK
DOGGETT CREEK	Klamath River	Horse Creek Condrey Mountain	- - -	SH, RT
DOGWOOD LAKE	Klamath River Scott River	Boulder Peak	7250	RT, BK
DONA CREEK	Klamath River	Horse Creek	- - -	RT
DOOLITTLE CREEK	Klamath River Elk Creek	Huckleberry Mountain	- - -	RT
DOOLITTLE CREEK	Klamath River Indian Creek	Happy Camp	- - -	RT
DUCK LAKE	Klamath River Butte Valley	Tennant	8540	BK, RT
DUCK LAKE, Big	Klamath River Scott River	Eaton Peak	6459	RT, ELT
DUCK LAKE, Little	Klamath River Scott River	Eaton Peak	6710	RT, BK
DUNCAN CREEK	Klamath River Salmon River	Orleans Mountain	- - -	RT, SH
DURNEY LAKE	Klamath River Shasta River	Mount Eddy	7045	BK
DUTCH CREEK	Applegate River Elliott Creek	Dutch Creek	- - -	RT
EATON LAKE, Lower	Klamath River Scott River	Eaton Peak	6560	RT
EATON LAKE, Middle	Klamath River Scott River	Eaton Peak	6610	RT, ELT
EATON LAKE, Upper	Klamath River Scott River	Eaton Peak	6620	RT, ELT
ECHO LAKE	Applegate River	Kangaroo Mountain	5510	BK
EDDY CREEK	Klamath River Shasta River	Weed, China Mountain, South China Mountain	- - -	RT
EDSON CREEK	Sacramento River McCloud River	Kinyon, Rainbow Mountain, Bartle	- - -	RDT
ELK CREEK	Klamath River Happy Camp	Huckleberry Mountain	- - -	SH, KS, SS, RT
ELK CREEK EF	Klamath River Elk Creek	Huckleberry Mountain	- - -	RT, SH
ELK CREEK, Upper	Klamath River Elk Creek	Huckleberry Mountain	- - -	RT
ELK LAKE, Big	Klamath River Salmon River	Marble Mountain	5900	RT, ELT
ELK LAKE, Little	Klamath River Scott River	Marble Mountain	5400	RT, ELT
ELLIOTT CREEK	Applegate River	Dillon Mountain	- - -	RT, CT
ENGLISH LAKE, Lower	Klamath River Salmon River	English Peak	5828	RT, BK, ELT
ENGLISH LAKE, Upper	Klamath River Salmon River	English Peak	5847	BK
ETHEL, Lake	Klamath River Salmon River	English Peak	5697	BK

Water By County	Drainage	USGS Topographic Map 7.5 Minute Series	Elevation (Feet) Lakes Only	Fish Species
ETNA CREEK	Klamath River Scott River	Etna	- - -	SH, SS, RT
FAWN CREEK	Sacramento River Sacramento River SF	Seven Lakes Basin Mumbo Basin	- - -	RT
FISH CREEK	Klamath River Grider Creek	Grider Valley	- - -	RT
FISH LAKE	Klamath River Salmon River	Deadman Peak	6050	RT
FIVEMILE CREEK	Klamath River Clear Creek	Bear Peak	- - -	RT
FLEMS FORK	Klamath River Ukonom Creek	Ukonom Mountain Ukonom Lake	- - -	RT
FORT GOFF CREEK	Klamath River	Slater Butte Figurehead Mountain	- - -	SH, RT
FORT GOFF CREEK MF	Klamath River Fort Goff Creek	Figurehead Mountain	- - -	RT
FORT GOFF CREEK WF	Klamath River Fort Goff Creek	Figurehead Mountain	- - -	RT
FOUR MILE CREEK	Klamath River	Clear Creek	- - -	RT
FOX CREEK	Klamath River Scott River	Billys Peak	- - -	RT, SH
FOX CREEK LAKE	Klamath River Scott River	Billys Peak	6571	RT, BN, ELT
FRYING PAN LAKE	Klamath River Scott River	Marble Mountain	5760	BK
GATE LAKE	Klamath River Scott River	Marble Mountain	5550	RT, BK, ELT
GOLD GRANITE LAKE	Klamath River Elk Creek	Ukonom Lake	5600	BK
GOLDEN RUSSIAN LAKE (Russian Wilderness)	Klamath River Salmon River NF	Eaton Peak	6080	BK, GT
GRANITE CREEK	Klamath River Elk Creek	Ukonom Lake	- - -	RT, BK
GRAY ROCK LAKE	Sacramento River Sacramento River SF	Seven Lakes Basin	5970	BK
GRAY ROCK LAKE, Upper	Sacramento River Sacramento River SF	Seven Lakes Basin	6275	BK
GREEN GRANITE LAKE	Klamath River Elk Creek	Ukonom Lake	5350	BK
GREENHORN CREEK	Klamath River Shasta River	Yreka	- - -	RT
GREENHORN RESERVOIR	Klamath River Shasta River	Yreka	2754	RT
GRIDER CREEK	Klamath River	Seiad Valley Grider Valley	- - -	SH, RT, KS, SS
GRIDER CREEK, West	Klamath River Grider Creek	Seiad Valley	- - -	SH, RT, KS, SS
GROUSE CREEK	Klamath River Beaver Creek	McKinley Mountain	- - -	SH, RT
GROUSE CREEK	Klamath River Scott River	Scott Mountain	- - -	SH, RT
GROUSE CREEK LAKE	Klamath River Scott River	Scott Mountain	6182	BK
GUMBOOT LAKE, Lower	Sacramento River Sacramento River SF	Mumbo Basin	6050	RT, BK
GUMBOOT LAKE, Upper	Sacramento River Sacramento River SF	Mumbo Basin	6350	BK
HALVERSON CREEK	Klamath River	Bark Shanty Gulch	- - -	SH, RT
HAMMEL CREEK	Klamath River Salmon River	Orleans Mountain	- - -	RT
HANCOCK CREEK	Klamath River Salmon River	Medicine Mountain	- - -	SH, RT
HANCOCK LAKE, Big	Klamath River Salmon River	English Peak	6345	RT, BK, BN, ELT
HANCOCK LAKE, Little	Klamath River Salmon River	English Peak	6700	BK

Water By County	Drainage	USGS Topographic Map 7.5 Minute Series	Elevation (Feet) Lakes Only	Fish Species
HAYPRESS CREEK	Klamath River Salmon River	Somes Bar	- - -	RT
HEART LAKE	Sacramento River Sacramento River SF	Seven Lakes Basin	6035	BK
HEATHER LAKE	Klamath River Salmon River	English Peak	7400	BK
HELLO LAKE	Applegate River Applegate River Butte Fk	Kangaroo Mountain	5420	BK
HEMLOCK LAKE	Klamath River Antelope Creek	Rainbow Mountain	6200	B
HIDDEN LAKE	Klamath River Salmon River	Deadman Peak	6658	BK
HIGH LAKE	Klamath River Scott River	Eaton Peak	7300	RT, BK
HINES CREEK	Klamath River Camp Creek	Bark Shanty Gulch	- - -	RT
HOGAN LAKE	Klamath River Salmon River	Eaton Peak	5950	RT, BK, ELT
HOOLIGAN LAKE	Klamath River Salmon River	Ukonom Lake	5160	RT, ELT
HORN CREEK	Klamath River Salmon River	Forks of Salmon	- - -	RT
HORSE CREEK	Klamath River Dutch Creek	Hamburg	- - -	SH, KS, SS, RT
HORSE CREEK EF	Klamath River Horse Creek	Dutch Creek	- - -	RT
HORSE CREEK WF	Klamath River Horse Creek	Dutch Creek	- - -	RT
HORSE RANGE CREEK	Klamath River Scott River	Eaton Peak	- - -	RT
HORSE RANGE LAKE (Marble Mtn Wilderness)	Klamath River Salmon River	English Peak	5984	BK
HORSE RANGE LAKE (Russian Wilderness)	Klamath River Scott River	Eaton Peak	6600	BK
HORSESHOE LAKE	Klamath River Scott River	Eaton Peak	6400	RT, ELT
HOUSTON CREEK	Klamath River Scott River	China Mountain Gazelle Mountain	- - -	RT, SH
HUMBUG CREEK	Klamath River	Badger Mountain McKinley Mountain	- - -	SH, RT, SS
HUMBUG CREEK, Little	Klamath River Humbug Creek	McKinley Mountain	- - -	SH, RT
HUMBUG CREEK MF	Klamath River Humbug Creek	Badger Mountain	- - -	SH, RT
HUMBUG CREEK SF	Klamath River Humbug Creek	Badger Mountain	- - -	SH, RT
HUNGRY CREEK	Klamath River Beaver Creek	Buckhorn Bally Cottonwood Peak	- - -	SH, RT
HUNGRY CREEK NF	Klamath River Beaver Creek	Cottonwood Peak	- - -	RT
INDEPENDENCE CREEK	Klamath River	Ukonom Lake	- - -	RT, SH, BK
INDEPENDENCE LAKE	Klamath River Independence Creek	Ukonom Lake	5950	BK, ELT
INDIAN CREEK	Klamath River Deadman Point	Happy Camp	- - -	SH, KS, SS, RT
INDIAN CREEK	Klamath River Salmon River	Cecilville Sawyers Bar	- - -	SH, RT
INDIAN CREEK	Klamath River Scott River	Greenville Russell Peak	- - -	SH, RT
INDIAN CREEK EF	Klamath River Indian Creek	Deadman Point	- - -	SH, RT
INDIAN CREEK, Little SF	Klamath River Indian Creek	Happy Camp Preston Peak	- - -	SH, RT
INDIAN CREEK SF	Klamath River Indian Creek	Deadman Point Preston Peak	- - -	SH, RT, SS, KS
INDIAN CREEK, West Branch	Klamath River Indian Creek	Deadman Point	- - -	SH, RT

Water By County	Drainage	USGS Topographic Map 7.5 Minute Series	Elevation (Feet) Lakes Only	Fish Species
INDIAN CREEK WF of Little SF of SF	Klamath River	Preston Peak	- - -	RT
INDIAN TOM LAKE	Lower Klamath River, OR	Dorris, Sheepy Lake	4060	CT-L
IRON GATE RESERVOIR	Klamath River	Iron Gate Reservoir Copco	2330	RT
IRVING CREEK	Klamath River	Somes Bar	- - -	RT, SH
JACKSON CREEK	Klamath River Scott River	Eaton Peak	- - -	RT, SH
JACKSON LAKE	Klamath River Scott River	Eaton Peak	6200	RT
JACKSON LAKE, Little	Klamath River Scott River	Deadman Peak	5997	BK
JOHNSON CREEK	Klamath River Elk Creek	Huckleberry Mountain	- - -	RT
JOSEPHINE LAKE (Trinity Alps)	Klamath River Salmon River	Caribou Lake	5818	RT, BK
JOSEPHINE LAKE (Russian Wilderness)	Klamath River Scott River	Eaton Peak	7350	BK
JUANITA LAKE	Klamath River	MacDoel, Panther Rock	5160	RT, BN
KANGAROO CREEK	Klamath River Scott River	Scott Mountain	- - -	SH, RT
KANGAROO LAKE	Klamath River Scott River	Scott Mountain	6020	RT, ELT
KATHERINE, LAKE	Klamath River Salmon River	English Peak	5741	RT, BK, ELT
KELLY LAKE	Klamath River Indian Creek	Polar Bear Mountain	4310	RT
KELSEY CREEK	Klamath River Scott River	Scott Bar	- - -	SH, RT, SS
KIDDER CREEK	Klamath River Scott River	Boulder Peak	- - -	SH, SS, RT
KIDDER LAKE	Klamath River Scott River	Boulder Peak	5900	RT, ELT
KING CREEK	Klamath River	Ukonom Mountain	- - -	RT, SH
KLAMATH RIVER (Oregon Border to Iron Gate Reservoir)	Pacific Ocean	Secret Spring Mountain, Copco, Iron Gate Reservoir	- - -	RT
KLAMATH RIVER (Iron Gate Reservoir to Horse Creek)	Pacific Ocean	Iron Gate Reservoir, Hornbrook Hawkinsville, Badger Mountain, McKinley Mountain, Horse Creek	- - -	SH, KS, SS, RT
KLAMATH RIVER (Hamburg to Happy Camp)	Pacific Ocean	Hamburg, Seiad Valley, Slater Butte, Happy Camp,	- - -	SH, KS, SS, RT
KLAMATH RIVER (Clear Creek to Somes Bar)	Pacific Ocean	Clear Creek, Dillon Mountain, Ukonom Mountain, Bark Shanty Gulch, Somes Bar	- - -	SH, KS, SS, RT
KLEAVER LAKE	Klamath River Salmon River	Marble Mountain	6450	RT, BN, BK
LAKE OF THE ISLAND	Klamath River Salmon River	English Peak	5682	BK, RT, ELT
LILY LAKE	Klamath River Salmon River	Medicine Mountain	5980	BK
LILY PAD LAKE	Klamath River Scott River	Scott Mountain	5940	BK, RT
LIPSTICK LAKE	Klamath River Scott River	Eaton Peak	6350	BK
LOG LAKE (Marble Mountain Wilderness)	Klamath River Scott River	Boulder Peak	5400	RT, ELT
LONESOME LAKE Butte Fk Applegate River	Applegate River	Figurehead Mountain	5510	BK
LONG GULCH LAKE	Klamath River Salmon River	Deadman Peak	6406	RT, ELT
LONG HIGH LAKE	Klamath River Scott River	Boulder Peak	7150	BK
LOST LAKE	Klamath River Salmon River	Medicine Mountain	5650	RT, ELT
MACKS CREEK	Klamath River	Hamburg	- - -	RT
MAN EATEN LAKE	Klamath River Salmon River	Marble Mountain	6200	RT, ELT

Water By County	Drainage	USGS Topographic Map 7.5 Minute Series	Elevation (Feet) Lakes Only	Fish Species
MAVIS LAKE Scott River	Klamath River	Billys Peak	6686	BK
McCLOUD RIVER, Upper (Above Lake McCloud. Below Lake, see Shasta Co.)	Sacramento River	Bartle, Kinyon Lake McCloud	- - -	RT, BN, BK ELT
MEDICINE LAKE	Sacramento River Pit River	Medicine Lake	6676	BK, RT, ELT
MEDICINE LAKE, Little	Sacramento River Pit River	Medicine Lake	6700	RT, BK, ELT
MEEKS MEADOW LAKE	Klamath River Scott River	Etna	6150	RT, ELT
METEOR LAKE	Klamath Salmon River	Ukonom Lake	5750	RT, ELT
MILL CREEK	Klamath River Indian Creek	Deadman Point	- - -	RT
MILL CREEK	Klamath River	Hamburg	- - -	RT
MILL CREEK	Klamath River Scott River	Etna	- - -	RT
MILL CREEK SF	Klamath River Scott River	Russell Peak	- - -	RT
MILL CREEK LAKE	Klamath River Trinity River	Billys Peak	6590	RT, BK, ELT
MILNE LAKE	Klamath River Salmon River	English Peak	6750	BK
MINERS CREEK	Klamath River Scott River	McConaughy Gulch Callahan, Eaton Peak	- - -	SH, SS, RT
MONTE CREEK	Klamath River Salmon River	Orleans Mountain	- - -	RT
MONUMENT LAKE	Klamath River Salmon River	Ukonom Lake	5780	BK, RT, ELT
MOREHOUSE CREEK	Klamath River Salmon River	Orleans Mountain Forks of Salmon	- - -	RT, SH
MOUNTAIN HOUSE CREEK	Klamath River Scott River	China Mountain	- - -	RT
MUSIC CREEK	Klamath River Salmon River	Tanners Peak	- - -	RT
MUSKGRAVE CREEK	Klamath River Meiss Lake	Panther Rock	- - -	BK
NATUCKET CREEK	Klamath River	Bark Shanty Gulch	- - -	RT
NEGRO CREEK	Klamath River Salmon River	Youngs Peak Forks of Salmon	- - -	RT, SH
NEYS SPRINGS CREEK	Sacramento River	City of Mount Shasta Dunsmuir	- - -	RT
NORDHEIMER CREEK	Klamath River Salmon River	Forks of Salmon Orleans Mountain	- - -	SH, RT, KS, SS
NORTH RUSSIAN CREEK	Klamath River Salmon River	Tanners Peak Yellow Dog Peak	- - -	SH, RT, KS, SS
OAK FLAT CREEK	Klamath River	Clear Creek Happy Camp	- - -	RT, SH
OGAROMTOC LAKE	Klamath River	Bark Shanty Gulch	2000	ELT, BK
O'NEIL CREEK	Klamath River Seiad Valley	Hamburg	- - -	RT, SH
ONEMILE CREEK	Klamath River Ukonom Creek	Ukonom Mountain Ukonom Lake	- - -	RT, ELT
ONEMILE LAKE	Klamath River Ukonom Creek	Ukonom Lake	5700	RT, ELT
ORR LAKE	Klamath River	Bray	4643	RT, BN
PANTHER CREEK	Klamath River Ukonom Creek	Ukonom Mountain	- - -	RT
PARKS CREEK	Klamath River Shasta River	China Mountain	- - -	SH, RT, BK
PARKS CREEK WF	Klamath River Shasta River	China Mountain	- - -	RT, CT
PARADISE LAKE	Klamath River Scott River	Marble Mountain	5430	BK
PAYNES LAKE	Klamath River Scott River	Eaton Peak	6520	RT, ELT

Water By County	Drainage	USGS Topographic Map 7.5 Minute Series	Elevation (Feet) Lakes Only	Fish Species
PINE LAKE	Klamath River Salmon River	English Peak	6240	BK
PLEASANT LAKE	Klamath River Salmon River	Ukonom Lake	5520	BK
PLUMMER CREEK	Klamath River Salmon River	Cecilville Cecil Lake	- - -	RT, SH
POISON LAKE	Klamath River Salmon River	Deadman Peak	7920	RT, BK
PORCUPINE LAKE	Sacramento River Sacramento River SF	South China Mountain	7236	BK, RT, ELT
PORTUGUESE CREEK	Klamath River	Seiad Valley Kangaroo Mountain	- - -	SH, RT
PORTUGUESE CREEK EF	Klamath River Portuguese Creek	Seiad Valley Kangaroo Mountain	- - -	RT
PRESTON CREEK	Klamath River Clear Creek	Devils Punchbowl	- - -	RT
RACCOON CREEK	Sacramento River McCloud River	Kinyon, Grizzly Peak Dead Horse Summit	- - -	RT
RAIL CREEK	Klamath River Scott River	Scott Mountain	- - -	RT, SH
RAINY LAKE	Klamath River Elk Creek	Marble Mountain	5510	RT, BK, ELT
RANCHERIA CREEK	Klamath River Grider Creek	Grider Valley	- - -	RT
RASPBERRY LAKE	Klamath River Clear Creek	Preston Peak	5380	RT, ELT
RED ROCK CREEK	Klamath River Scott River	Marble Mountain	- - -	RT
REYNOLDS CREEK	Klamath River	Bark Shanty Gulch	- - -	RT, SH
ROCK CREEK	Klamath River	Dillon Mountain Bark Shanty Gulch	- - -	RT, SH
ROCK CREEK	Klamath River Salmon River	Medicine Mountain	- - -	RT
ROCK LAKE	Klamath River Salmon River	Youngs Peak Salmon Mountain	6150	BK
ROCK FENCE LAKE	Klamath River Scott River	South China Mountain	6700	BK
RODGERS CREEK	Klamath River	Somes Bar	- - -	SH, RT
RUFFEY LAKE, Lower	Klamath River Scott River	Etna	6050	BK
RUFFEY LAKE, Upper	Klamath River	Etna	6400	BK
RUSH CREEK	Klamath River Salmon River	Thompson Peak Caribou Lake Deadman Peak	- - -	RT
RUSH CREEK LAKE	Klamath River Salmon River	Deadman Peak	6600	BK, RT, ELT
RUSSIAN LAKE, Lower	Klamath River Salmon River	Eaton Peak	6500	BK
RUSSIAN LAKE	Klamath River Salmon River	Eaton Peak	7100	RT, ELT
SACRAMENTO RIVER, Upper (Headwaters to Dunsmuir Below Dunsmuir See Shasta Co.)	Sacramento River	City of Mount Shasta Dunsmuir	- - -	RT, BN
SACRAMENTO RIVER, Upper (Railroad Park)	Sacramento River	Dunsmuir	- - -	BK, RT
SACRAMENTO RIVER MF	Sacramento River	Mount Eddy	- - -	RT
SACRAMENTO RIVER NF	Sacramento River	Mount Eddy	- - -	RT
SACRAMENTO RIVER SF	Sacramento River	Mount Eddy Seven Lakes Basin	- - -	RT, BK
SAINTE CLAIRE CREEK	Klamath River Salmon River	Cecilville Cecil Lake	- - -	RT, SH
SALMON LAKE	Klamath River Salmon River	Siligo Peak	7087	BK
SALMON RIVER (Mouth to Forks of Salmon)	Klamath River	Somes Bar Orleans Mountain Forks of Salmon	- - -	SH, KS, SS, RT

Water By County	Drainage	USGS Topographic Map 7.5 Minute Series	Elevation (Feet) Lakes Only	Fish Species
SALMON RIVER EF of SF	Klamath River Salmon River	Deadman Peak Grasshopper Ridge	- - -	SH, RT, KS, SS
SALMON RIVER, Little NF	Klamath River Salmon River	English Peak Sawyers Bar	- - -	SH, RT
SALMON RIVER, Little SF	Klamath River Salmon River	Thompson Peak	- - -	RT
SALMON RIVER NF	Klamath River Salmon River	Forks of Salmon Sawyers Bar	- - -	SH, KS, SS, RT
SALMON RIVER SF	Klamath River Salmon River	Forks of Salmon Youngs Peak	- - -	SH, KS, SS, RT
SANDY BAR CREEK	Klamath River	Bark Shanty Gulch Ukonom Mountain	- - -	RT, SH
SCOTT CAMP CREEK	Sacramento River Lake Siskiyou	City of Mount Shasta Mount Eddy	- - -	RT, BK, BN
SCOTT LAKE	Sacramento River Scott Camp Creek	Seven Lakes Basin	6190	RT, BK, ELT
SCOTT RIVER	Klamath River	Hamburg, Scott Bar Russell Peak	- - -	SH, KS, SS, RT
SCOTT RIVER EF	Klamath River Scott River	Scott Mountain Callahan, Gazelle Mtn.	- - -	RT, SH
SCOTT RIVER SF	Klamath River Scott River	Eaton Peak Deadman Peak	- - -	SH, RT, SS, KS
SECRET LAKE	Klamath River Ukonom Creek	Ukonom Lake	5300	RT, ELT
SECTION LINE LAKE	Klamath River Scott River	Billys Peak	7050	RT, ELT
SEIAD CREEK	Klamath River	Seiad Valley Kangaroo Mountain	- - -	SH, RT, SS
SEIAD CREEK EF	Klamath River Seiad Creek	Kangaroo Mountain	- - -	RT
SEIAD CREEK WF	Klamath River Seiad Creek	Kangaroo Mountain	- - -	RT
SEVEN LAKE, Upper	Sacramento River Castle Creek	Seven Lakes Basin	6300	BK, RT, ELT
SHACKLEFORD CREEK	Klamath River Scott River	Boulder Peak	- - -	SH, SS, RT
SHADOW CREEK	Klamath River Salmon River	Grasshopper Ridge	- - -	RT, SH
SHADOW LAKE	Klamath River Scott River	Marble Mountain	6500	BK
SHASTA RIVER	Klamath River Shasta River	Hawkinsville Montague, Little Shasta	- - -	SH, KS, SS, RT
SHASTA RIVER, Little	Klamath River Shasta River	Little Shasta	- - -	SH, RT, BN
SHASTINA, Lake	Klamath River Shasta River	Lake Shastina Juniper Flat	2805	RT, BN, BK
SHELLY LAKE	Klamath River Salmon River	Yellow Dog Peak	6710	BK
SHOVEL CREEK	Klamath River Panther Rock	Secret Spring Mountain	- - -	RT, BN
SINGLETON CREEK	Klamath River Scott River	Russell Peak	- - -	RT
SISKIYOU, Lake	Sacramento River	City of Mount Shasta	1000	RT, BK, BN
SIXMILE CREEK	Klamath River Salmon River	Grasshopper Ridge Deadman Peak	- - -	RT
SKY HIGH LAKE, Lower	Klamath River Scott River	Marble Mountain	5765	RT, ELT
SKY HIGH LAKE, Upper	Klamath River Scott River	Marble Mountain	5780	RT, ELT
SLIDE CREEK	Klamath River Thompson Creek	Figurehead Mountain Slater Butte	- - -	RT
SLIPPERY CREEK	Klamath River Clear Creek	Bear Peak	- - -	RT
SMITH LAKE	Klamath River Scott River	Eaton Peak	7100	RT, ELT
SNOWSLIDE LAKE	Klamath River Salmon River	Caribou Lake	6600	RT, BK, ELT

Water By County	Drainage	USGS Topographic Map 7.5 Minute Series	Elevation (Feet) Lakes Only	Fish Species
SNYDER LAKE	Klamath River Elk Creek	Ukonom Lake	5820	RT, ELT
SOAPSTONE CREEK	Sacramento River Sacramento River SF	Seven Lakes Basin	- - -	RT
SODA CREEK	Klamath River Beaver Creek	Buckhorn Bally	- - -	RT
SOMES CREEK	Klamath River Salmon River	Orleans Mountain	- - -	RT, SH
SOUTH FORK LAKE, Little	Klamath River Salmon River	Thompson Peak	5959	RT
SOUTH FORK LAKE, Lower	Klamath River Scott River	Deadman Peak	6689	RT, ELT
SOUTH FORK LAKE, Upper	Klamath River Scott River	Deadman Peak	6748	RT, ELT
SOUTH RUSSIAN CREEK	Klamath River Salmon River	Tanners Peak Eaton Peak	- - -	SH, KS, SS, RT
SPECIMEN CREEK	Klamath River Salmon River	Sawyers Bar Tanners Peak	- - -	SH, RT
SPIRIT LAKE	Klamath River Salmon River	Ukonom Lake	5920	BK
STANSHAW CREEK	Klamath River	Bark Shanty Gulch	- - -	RT, SH
STANZA CREEK	Klamath River Elk Creek	Huckleberry Mountain	- - -	RT
STATUE LAKE	Klamath River Salmon River	Eaton Peak	7200	BK
STEINACHER CREEK	Klamath River Salmon River	Somes Bar Medicine Mountain	- - -	RT
STEINACHER LAKE	Klamath River Salmon River	Forks of Salmon	5900	RT, ELT
SUCKER CREEK	Klamath River Humbug Creek	Badger Mountain	- - -	RT
SUGAR CREEK	Klamath River Scott River	Eaton Peak	- - -	SH, RT, SS
SUGAR LAKE, South	Klamath River Scott River	Eaton Peak	6000	RT, ELT
SUMMIT LAKE	Klamath River Scott River	Marble Mountain	6300	RT, BK, ELT
SUMMIT MEADOW LAKE	Klamath River Scott River	Marble Mountain	6100	BK
SUTCLIFF CREEK	Klamath River Indian Creek	Deadman Point Polar Bear	- - -	RT
SWAMP CREEK	Sacramento River McCloud River	Rainbow Mountain	- - -	RDT
SWILLUP CREEK	Klamath River	Ukonom Mountain Dillon Mountain	- - -	RT, SH
TATE CREEK	Sacramento River McCloud River	Kinyon Grizzly Peak	- - -	RT, BK, BN
TAYLOR CREEK (Russian Creek)	Klamath River Salmon River	Tanners Peak Eaton Peak	- - -	RT
TAYLOR CREEK	Klamath River Salmon River	Grasshopper Ridge Deadman Peak	- - -	RT, SH, SS
TAYLOR CREEK SF	Klamath River Salmon River	Grasshopper Ridge	- - -	RT
TAYLOR LAKE	Klamath River Salmon River	Eaton Peak	6492	RT, ELT
TELEPHONE LAKE	Klamath River Scott River	Billys Peak	6886	RT, ELT
TENEYCK CREEK	Klamath River	Bark Shanty Gulch	- - -	RT
TENMILE CREEK	Klamath River Clear Creek	Bear Peak Preston Peak	- - -	RT, SH
TERRACE LAKE	Sacramento River Sacramento River SF	Seven Lakes Basin	6214	RT, BK, ELT
THOMPSON CREEK	Klamath River	Slater Butte Figurehead Mountain	- - -	SH, RT, KS, SS
TI CREEK	Klamath River	Dillon Mountain Ukonom Mountain	- - -	RT,SH

Water By County	Drainage	USGS Topographic Map 7.5 Minute Series	Elevation (Feet) Lakes Only	Fish Species
TITUS CREEK	Klamath River	Clear Creek	- - -	RT, SH
TICKNER LAKE	Klamath River Elk Creek	Ukonom Lake	6300	BK
TIMBER LAKE	Sacramento River Sacramento River SF	Seven Lakes Basin	6017	BK
TOAD LAKE	Sacramento River Sacramento River SF	South China Mtn. Mount Eddy	6935	RT, BK, BN ELT
TOBACCO LAKE	Klamath River Salmon River	English Peak	6500	RT, ELT
TOM MARTIN CREEK	Klamath River	Hamburg Scott Bar	- - -	RT
TOMPKINS CREEK	Klamath River Scott River	Scott Bar	- - -	SH, RT, SS
TOMS LAKE (Elk Peak)Elk Creek	Klamath River	Ukonom Lake	5160	RT, BK, ELT
TOMS LAKE (English Peak)	Klamath River Salmon River	English Peak	6720	RT, ELT
TOWHEAD LAKE	Applegate River	Kangaroo Mountain	5900	BK
TRAIL CREEK	Klamath River Salmon River	Deadman Peak Eaton Peak	- - -	RT
TRAIL GULCH LAKE	Klamath River Salmon River	Deadman Peak	6436	RT, ELT
TROUT CREEK	Sacramento River McCloud River	Kinyon Rainbow Mountain	- - -	RDT
TWIN LAKE, Lower	Klamath River Salmon River	Eaton Peak	6700	BK
TWIN LAKE, Upper	Klamath River Salmon River	Eaton Peak	6720	BK
TWIN VALLEY CREEK	Klamath River Indian Creek	Preston Peak Polar Bear Mountain	- - -	SH, RT, CT-C
UKONOM CREEK	Klamath River Ukonom Lake	Ukonom Mountain	- - -	RT, SH, SS
UKONOM LAKE	Klamath River Ukonom Creek	Ukonom Lake	6080	RT, ELT
VANN CREEK	Klamath River Dillon Creek	Bear Peak	- - -	RT
VIRGINIA LAKE	Klamath River Scott River	Billys Peak	6893	RT, ELT
WAGON CREEK	Sacramento River Lake Siskiyou	City of Mount Shasta	- - -	RT, BK, BN
WALKER CREEK	Klamath River	Seiad Valley	- - -	RT, SH
WASHBASIN LAKE	Klamath River Scott River	Billys Peak	7022	BK
WATERDOG LAKE	Klamath River Salmon River	Eaton Peak	6700	BK, RT, ELT
WEST PARK LAKE, Middle	Klamath River Shasta River	China Mountain	7435	BK
WEST PARK LAKE, Lower	Klamath River Shasta River	China Mountain	7232	BK
WHISKEY CREEK	Applegate River	Kangaroo Mountain	- - -	RT
WICKS LAKE	Klamath River Salmon River	Etna	5700	RT, ELT
WILD LAKE	Klamath River Salmon River	English Peak	5888	RT, ELT
WILLOW CREEK SF	Klamath River Shasta River	China Mountain	- - -	RT
WINGATE CREEK	Klamath River	Clear Creek	- - -	RT
WOLVERINE LAKE	Klamath River Scott River	Boulder Peak	6800	BK
WOOLEY CREEK Salmon River	Klamath River Medicine Mountain	Somes Bar	- - -	SH, KS, SS
WOOLEY CREEK, Cuddihy FK	Klamath River Salmon River	Ukonom Lake	- - -	RT
WOOLEY CREEK NF	Klamath River Salmon River	Medicine Mountain Ukonom Lake	- - -	SH, RT
WOOLEY CREEK SF	Klamath River Salmon River	English Peak Marble Mountain	- - -	RT

Water By County	Drainage	USGS Topographic Map 7.5 Minute Series	Elevation (Feet) Lakes Only	Fish Species
WOOLEY LAKE	Klamath River Salmon River	English Peak	6676	RT, ELT
WRIGHT LAKE, Lower	Klamath River Scott River	Boulder Peak	6930	RT, ELT
WRIGHT LAKE, Upper	Klamath River Scott River	Boulder Peak	7300	RT, BK

Solano County

CHABOT, Lake	San Pablo Bay	Cordelia	81	RT
MADIGAN, Lake	San Pablo Bay	Mount George	367	RT
PUTAH CREEK (Also in Yolo County)	Sacramento River	Merritt, Winters	- - -	RT, BN

Sonoma County

GUALALA RIVER	Pacific Ocean North Coast	Gualala	- - -	SH, SS
RUSSIAN RIVER, Lower	Pacific Ocean North Coast	Duncan Mills Guerneville, Healdsburg	- - -	SS, KS SH, AS
SALMON CREEK	Pacific Ocean North Coast	Bodega Head	- - -	SH, SS

Tehama County

ANTELOPE CREEK MF	Sacramento River Antelope Creek	Finley Butte	- - -	RT
ANTELOPE CREEK NF	Sacramento River Antelope Creek	Finley Butte Panther Spring	- - -	RT, BN, ELT
ANTELOPE CREEK SF	Sacramento River Antelope Creek	Panther Spring	- - -	RT, BK, ELT
BATTLE CREEK	Sacramento River Balls Ferry	Tuscan Buttes NE	- - -	RT, ELT
BATTLE CREEK SF	Sacramento River Battle Creek	Mineral Lyonsville	- - -	RT, BK, BN ELT
BEEGUM CREEK (Tehama & Shasta Counties)	Sacramento River Cottonwood Creek	Beegum (7.5' X 15')	- - -	RT, KS, SH
BEEGUM CREEK MF (Tehama & Shasta Counties)	Sacramento River Cottonwood Creek	Beegum (7.5' X 15')	- - -	RT
BEEGUM CREEK SF	Sacramento River Cottonwood Creek	Beegum (7.5' X 15')	- - -	RT, BN
CEDAR CREEK	Sacramento River Cottonwood Creek	Tomhead Mountain	- - -	RT
COTTONWOOD CREEK, Cold ForkCottonwood Creek	Sacramento River Cold Fork	Oxbow Bridge	- - -	RT
COTTONWOOD CREEK SF	Sacramento River Cottonwood Creek	South Yolla Bolly Cold Fork, Oxbow Bridge	- - -	KS, SH, RT
DEER CREEK	Sacramento River	Onion Butte Devils Parade Ground	- - -	RT, BN, SH, KS, BK, ELT
DIGGER CREEK (Also, see Shasta Co.)	Sacramento River Battle Creek	Manton	- - -	RT, BN, SH ELT
DIAMOND LAKE (Turner Mountain)	Sacramento River Antelope Creek	Lyonsville	6240	ELT
DRY CREEK, Big	Sacramento River Toomes Creek	Acorn Hollow Ishi Caves	- - -	KS, SH
ELDER CREEK NF	Sacramento River Elder Creek	Raglin Ridge Lowrey	- - -	RT
ELDER CREEK SF	Sacramento River Elder Creek	Riley Ridge	- - -	RT
GURNSEY CREEK	Sacramento River Deer Creek	Childs Meadow	- - -	RT, ELT
JUDD CREEK	Sacramento River Antelope Creek	Finley Butte Lyonsville	- - -	RT
LONG LAKE	Sacramento River Cottonwood Creek	South Yolla Bolly (7.5' X 15')	7087	BK, ELT
LOST CREEK	Sacramento River Deer Creek	Stover Mountain Childs Meadow	- - -	RT

Water By County	Drainage	USGS Topographic Map 7.5 Minute Series	Elevation (Feet) Lakes Only	Fish Species
MARTIN CREEK	Sacramento River Battle Creek	Mineral Lassen Peak	- - -	RT
McGOWAN LAKE	Sacramento River Battle Creek	Lassen Peak	- - -	BK, BN
MILL CREEK	Sacramento River	Mineral Onion Butte	- - -	KS, SH, RT, BN, BK, ELT
NORTH YOLLA BOLLY LAKE	Sacramento River Cottonwood Creek	North Yolla Bolly (7.5' X15')	6522	BK, RT
POLE CORRAL CREEK	Sacramento River Cottonwood Creek	Pony Buck Peak (7.5' X 15') Beegum (7.5' X 15')	- - -	RT
SACRAMENTO RIVER, Lower (Cottonwood to Woodson Bridge State Park Recreation)	Sacramento River	Ball Ferry, Bend, Red Bluff East, Los Molinos, Vina	- - -	KS, SH, AS
SQUARE LAKE	Sacramento River Cottonwood Creek	South Yolla Bolly (7.5' X 15')	7021	BK, RT
SUMMIT CREEK	Sacramento River Battle Creek	Mineral Lassen Peak	- - -	RT
THOMES CREEK	Sacramento River	Flournoy Henleyville	- - -	SH, KS, RT
WILLOW CREEK	Sacramento River Thomes Creek	Log Spring Mendocino Pass	- - -	RT

Trinity County

Water By County	Drainage	USGS Topographic Map 7.5 Minute Series	Elevation (Feet) Lakes Only	Fish Species
ADAMS CREEK	Klamath River Trinity River	Caribou Lake	- - -	RT
ADAMS LAKE	Klamath River Salmon River	Caribou Lake	6243	BK
ALDER BASIN CREEK	Eel River Eel River MF	Four Corners Rock (7.5' X 15')	- - -	RT
ALLEN CREEK	Klamath River Trinity River	Hyampom Mountain	- - -	RT
ALPINE LAKE	Klamath River Upper Trinity River	Siligo Peak	6112	BK, RT
ANNA LAKE	Klamath River Upper Trinity River	Siligo Peak Covington Mill	7550	BK
BACKBONE CREEK	Klamath River Trinity River	Thurston Peaks Mount Hilton	- - -	RT
BALM OF GILEAD CREEK	Eel River Eel River MF	Four Corners Rock (7.5' X 15') South Yolla Bolly (7.5' X 15')	- - -	RT, SH
BARRY CREEK	Mad River	Shannon Butte	- - -	RT
BATTLE CREEK	Klamath River Upper Trinity River	Ycatapom Peak	- - -	RT
BEAR CREEK	Klamath River Upper Trinity River	Ycatapom Peak Covington Mill	- - -	ELT, RT
BEAR CREEK	Klamath River Upper Trinity River	Tangle Blue Lake	- - -	RT
BEAR CREEK (Hayfork Creek)	Klamath River Trinity River	Hyampom Mountain	- - -	RT, SH
BEAR LAKE, Big	Klamath River Upper Trinity River	Tangle Blue Lake	5844	BK, RT
BEAR LAKE, Little	Klamath River Upper Trinity River	Tangle Blue Lake	6220	BK, RT
BEAR LAKE, Wee	Klamath River Upper Trinity River	Tangle Blue Lake	6184	BK
BIG EAST FORK LAKE	Klamath River Upper Trinity River	Rush Creek Lakes	5850	BK, RT
BIG FRENCH CREEK	Klamath River Trinity River	Del Loma	- - -	RT
BLACK LASSIC CREEK	Eel River Van Duzen River	Ruth Lake Black Lassic	- - -	RT
BLACK ROCK LAKE	Klamath River Trinity River	Black Rock Mountain (7.5' X 15')	6250	RT, BK, ELT
BLUFF LAKE	Klamath River Upper Trinity River	South China Mountain	6300	BK, RT, ELT
BOULDER CREEK (Coffee Creek)	Klamath River Upper Trinity River	Ycatapom Peak	- - -	RT

Water By County	Drainage	USGS Topographic Map 7.5 Minute Series	Elevation (Feet) Lakes Only	Fish Species
BOULDER CREEK (Stuart Fork)	Klamath River Upper Trinity River	Siligo Peak	- - -	RT
BOULDER LAKE (Coffee Creek)	Klamath River Upper Trinity River	Ycatapom Peak	6070	BK, RT, ELT
BOULDER LAKE, Little (Coffee Creek)	Klamath River Upper Trinity River	Ycatapom Peak	6318	BK, RT, ELT
BOULDER CREEK LAKE (Canyon Creek)	Klamath River Upper Trinity River	Mount Hilton	5709	BK, RT
BROWNS CREEK Trinity River	Klamath River Weaverville	Hossimbim Mountain	- - -	SH, KS, RT
BUCK LAKE	Klamath River Upper Trinity River	Deadman Peak	6800	BK
BUCKEYE CREEK	Klamath River Trinity River	Trinity Dam	- - -	RT, KOK
BUCKHORN CREEK	Klamath River Trinity River	Hyampom Mountain	- - -	RT
BULL LAKE	Klamath River Upper Trinity River	South China Mountain	6350	BK, RT
CABIN CREEK	Klamath River Trinity River	Cecil Lake	- - -	SH, RT
CANADIAN CREEK	Klamath River Trinity River	Del Loma Ironside Mountain	- - -	RT
CANYON CREEK	Klamath River Trinity River	Junction City Dedrick, Mount Hilton	- - -	SH, RT, KS GT, BN
CANYON CREEK, Big East Fork	Klamath River Trinity River	Dedrick	- - -	RT, SH
CANYON CREEK LAKE, Lower	Klamath River Upper Trinity River	Mount Hilton	5606	BK, RT, ELT
CANYON CREEK LAKE, Upper	Klamath River Upper Trinity River	Mount Hilton	5688	BK, RT, GT
CEDAR CREEK	Klamath River Trinity River	Whisky Bill Peak Carrville	- - -	RT, KOK
CEDAR FLAT CREEK	Klamath River Trinity River	Ironside Mountain Hyampom Mountain	- - -	RT
CHANCHELULLA CREEK	Klamath River Trinity River	Chanchelulla Peak (7.5' X 15')	- - -	RT
CHINA CREEK (New River)	Klamath River Trinity River	Denny Jim Jam Ridge	- - -	RT
CHINA CREEK (Trinity River NF)	Klamath River Trinity River	Thurston Peaks Mount Hilton	- - -	SH, RT
CLAIR ENGLE LAKE	Klamath River Trinity River	Carrville, Trinity Center Covington Mill, Trinity Dam Papoose Creek	2370	RT, KOK, BN
CLARK CREEK	Klamath River Trinity River	Hyampom Mountain	- - -	RT
COFFEE CREEK	Klamath River Upper Trinity River	Ycatapom Peak Caribou Lake, Carrville	- - -	RT, BN, KOK
COFFEE CREEK E FK	Klamath River Upper Trinity River	Ycatapom Peak Billys Peak	- - -	RT, KOK
COFFEE CREEK N FK	Klamath River Upper Trinity River	Deadman Peak Billys Peak	- - -	RT, KOK
COFFEE CREEK S FK	Klamath River Upper Trinity River	Deadman Peak	- - -	RT
CONWAY LAKE	Klamath River Upper Trinity River	Ycatapom Peak	6838	BK
COPPER CREEK	Klamath River Upper Trinity River	Carrville	- - -	RT
CORRAL CREEK (Hayfork Creek)	Klamath River Trinity River	Hyampom Mountain Big Bar	- - -	RT, SH
CROOKS CREEK	Eel River Van Duzen River	Dinsmore	- - -	RT
DEADFALL CREEK	Klamath River Upper Trinity River	South China Mountain	- - -	RT, BK
DEADFALL LAKE, Lower	Klamath River Upper Trinity River	South China Mountain	7139	BK
DEADFALL LAKE, Middle	Klamath River Upper Trinity River	South China Mountain	7259	BK, RT, ELT

Water By County	Drainage	USGS Topographic Map 7.5 Minute Series	Elevation (Feet) Lakes Only	Fish Species
DEADFALL LAKE, Upper	Klamath River Upper Trinity River	Mount Eddy	7790	BK
DEADWOOD CREEK	Klamath River Trinity River	Lewiston French Gulch	- - -	SH, RT
DEEP CREEK (Stuart Fork)	Klamath River Upper Trinity River	Siligo Peak	- - -	RT
DEER CREEK	Klamath River Upper Trinity River	Siligo Peak	- - -	RT, BK, ELT
DEER CREEK	Klamath River Trinity River	Big Bar	- - -	RT, BK
DEER LAKE	Klamath River Upper Trinity River	Siligo Peak	7150	BK
DEVILS CANYON CREEK	Klamath River Trinity River	Jim Jam Ridge	- - -	RT
DEVILS LAKE	Klamath River Upper Trinity River	Whisky Bill Peak	6112	BK, BN
DIAMOND LAKE	Klamath River Upper Trinity River	Siligo Peak	7250	BK
DOE LAKE	Klamath River Upper Trinity River	Billys Peak	6992	BK
DON JUAN CREEK	Klamath River Trinity River	Ironside Mountain	- - -	RT
DUTCH CREEK	Klamath River Trinity River	Junction City	- - -	RT, SH
EAGLE CREEK	Klamath River Trinity River	Helena Hayfork Bally	- - -	RT, SH
EAGLE CREEK	Klamath River Upper Trinity River	Tangle Blue Lake Billys Peak	- - -	RT, KOK
EAST WEAVER LAKE	Klamath River Upper Trinity River	Rush Creek Lakes	6350	RT, BK
ECHO LAKE	Klamath River Upper Trinity River	Siligo Peak	7250	BK
EEL RIVER MF	Pacific Ocean Eel River	Four Corners Rock (7.5' X 15')	- - -	SH, RT
EEL RIVER NF of MF	Pacific Ocean Eel River	Four Corners Rock (7.5' X 15')	- - -	SH, RT
ELEANOR, Lake	Klamath River Upper Trinity River	Covington Mill	4950	BK, BN
ELTAPOM CREEK	Klamath River Trinity River	Hyampom Mountain	- - -	RT, SH, SS
EMERALD LAKE	Klamath River Upper Trinity River	Caribou Lake	5500	BK, RT, ELT
FISHER GULCH	Klamath River Trinity River	Dedrick	- - -	RT
FORBIDDEN LAKE, Upper	Klamath River Trinity River	Mount Hilton	6168	BK
FOSTER LAKE	Klamath River Upper Trinity River	Ycatapom Peak	7245	BK, ELT
FOUND LAKE	Klamath River Upper Trinity River	Ycatapom Peak	6866	BK
GRANITE CREEK (Swift Creek)	Klamath River Upper Trinity River	Covington Mill Siligo Peak	- - -	RT, BK
GRANITE CREEK (Coffee Creek)	Klamath River Upper Trinity River	Billys Peak	- - -	RT
GRANITE LAKE (Coffee Creek)	Klamath River Upper Trinity River	Billys Peak	6446	BK, CT-L, ELT
GRANITE LAKE (Swift Creek)	Klamath River Upper Trinity River	Covington Mill	6000	BK, RT, CT-L ELT, BN
GRASS VALLEY CREEK	Klamath River Trinity River	Lewiston Bully Chop Mountain	- - -	SH, RT, KS
GRASS VALLEY CREEK RESERVOIR (Reservoir not in GNIS or on Topo Map. See Trinity River text)	Klamath River Trinity River	Lewiston	2526	RT SH (landlocked)
GRASSY FLAT CREEK (Hayfork Creek)	Klamath River Trinity River	Hyampom Mountain Big Bar	- - -	RT

Water By County	Drainage	USGS Topographic Map 7.5 Minute Series	Elevation (Feet) Lakes Only	Fish Species
GRIZZLY CREEK	Klamath River Trinity River	Cecil Lake Thompson Peak	- - -	RT, BK, SH
GRIZZLY LAKE	Klamath River Upper Trinity River	Thompson Peak	7105	RT, BK
GROUSE LAKE	Klamath River Upper Trinity River	Whisky Bill Peak	5888	BK, BN
GWIN GULCH	Klamath River Trinity River	Dedrick	- - -	RT, SH
HARDSCRABBLE CREEK	Klamath River Trinity River	Caribou Lake Deadman Peak	- - -	RT
HAYFORK CREEK	Klamath River Trinity River Big Bar	Hyampom Hyampom Mountain	- - -	SH, KS, SS RT
HAYSHED CREEK (Hayfork Creek)	Klamath River Trinity River	Big Bar	- - -	RT
HAYSHED CREEK EF (Hayfork Creek)	Klamath River Trinity River	Big Bar	- - -	RT
HAYSHED CREEK WF (Hayfork Creek)	Klamath River Trinity River	Big Bar Hyampom Mountain	- - -	RT
HENNESSY CREEK	Klamath River	Hennessy Peak	- - -	RT
HETTEN CREEK	Mad River	Ruth Lake	- - -	RT
HICKORY CREEK	Klamath River Upper Trinity River	Caribou Lake Deadman Peak	- - -	RT
HIGH CAMP CREEK	Klamath River Upper Trinity River	South China Mountain	- - -	RT
HIGHLAND LAKE	Klamath River Upper Trinity River	Whisky Bill Peak	5726	BK, RT, ELT
HORSE CREEK	Klamath River Upper Trinity River	Tangle Blue Lake	- - -	RT
HORSESHOE LAKE	Klamath River Upper Trinity River	Siligo Peak	6850	BK, ELT
INDIAN CREEK	Klamath River Trinity River	Weaverville Hossimbim Mountain	- - -	SH, RT, KS, SS
ITALIAN CREEK	Klamath River Trinity River	Del Loma	- - -	RT
JUD CREEK (Hayfork Creek)	Klamath River Trinity River	Halfway Ridge	- - -	RT
KALMIA LAKE	Klamath River Upper Trinity River	Mount Hilton	7480	BK
"L" LAKE	Klamath River Upper Trinity	Mt. Hilton	6562	BK
LANDERS LAKE	Klamath River Upper Trinity River	Caribou Lake	7042	RT, BK, ELT
LANDERS CREEK	Klamath River Upper Trinity River	Caribou Lake Ycatapom Peak	- - -	ELT
LEWISTON LAKE	Klamath River Trinity River	Trinity Dam	1910	RT, BN, KOK ELT
LILY PAD LAKE	Klamath River Upper Trinity River	Ycatapom Peak	6300	BK
LION LAKE	Klamath River Upper Trinity River	Ycatapom Peak	6996	BK
LITTLE BROWNS CREEK	Klamath River Trinity River	Weaverville Rush Creek	- - -	SH, RT, KS
LITTLE FRENCH CREEK	Klamath River Trinity River	Del Loma Helena	- - -	RT
LOG LAKE (Trinity Alps Wilderness)	Klamath River Upper Trinity River	Tangle Blue Lake	6076	BK
LOIS LAKE	Klamath River Upper Trinity River	Thompson Peak	7600	BK
LOST LAKE	Klamath River Scott River	Scott Mountain	5600	BK, BN
LUELLA LAKE	Klamath River Upper Trinity River	Siligo Peak	6950	BK
MAD RIVER (Ruth Lake to Humboldt Co. line) (Also see Humboldt Co.)	Pacific Ocean	Ruth Lake Sportshaven	- - -	RT, SH

Water By County	Drainage	USGS Topographic Map 7.5 Minute Series	Elevation (Feet) Lakes Only	Fish Species
MAD RIVER NF	Pacific Ocean Mad River	Blue Lake Korbel	- - -	RT
MAD RIVER SF	Pacific Ocean Mad River	Black Rock Mountain (7.5' X 15')	- - -	RT
MANZANITA CREEK	Klamath River Trinity River	Hayfork Bally Helena	- - -	RT, SH, SS
MARSHY LAKE, Big	Klamath River Upper Trinity River	Billys Peak	6297	BK
MARSHY LAKE, Little	Klamath River Upper Trinity River	Billys Peak	6196	BK
MASTERSON MEADOW CREEK	Klamath River Upper Trinity River	Scott Mountain	- - -	RT
MASTERSON MEADOW LAKE	Klamath River Upper Trinity River	Scott Mountain	6200	BK, BN
McDONALD LAKE	Klamath River Upper Trinity River	Billys Peak	5896	BK, RT
MILL CREEK	Klamath River Trinity River	Ironside Mountain Hyampom Mountain	- - -	RT
MINERS CREEK (Hayfork Creek)	Klamath River Trinity River	Big Bar	- - -	SH, RT
MINNIE CREEK	Eel River Eel River MF	Four Corners Rock (7.5' X 15') South Yolla Bolly (7.5' X 15')	- - -	RT
MIRROR LAKE	Klamath River Upper Trinity River	Mount Hilton	6600	RT, BK
MOONEY GULCH (Lewiston Dam)	Klamath River Trinity River	Trinity Dam	- - -	RT, BN
MORRIS LAKE	Klamath River Upper Trinity River	Siligo Peak Mount Hilton	7350	GT, BK
MOSQUITO LAKE	Klamath River Upper Trinity River	Billys Peak	6613	BK, RT, BN
MULE CREEK	Klamath River Upper Trinity River	Trinity Dam Covington Mill	- - -	RT, KOK
MUMBO CREEK	Klamath River Upper Trinity River	Whiskey Bill Peak Mumbo Basin	- - -	RT, BK
MUMBO LAKE	Klamath River Upper Trinity River	Mumbo Basin	6100	RT, BK, ELT
MUMBO LAKE, Upper	Klamath River Upper Trinity River	Mumbo Basin	6150	BK
OWENS CREEK	Klamath River Upper Trinity River	Siligo Peak	- - -	RT
PANTHER CREEK	Klamath River Trinity River	Denny	- - -	RT
PAPOOSE LAKE	Klamath River Upper Trinity River	Mount Hilton	6653	RT, BK, ELT
PARKER CREEK	Klamath River Upper Trinity River	Ycatapom Peak	- - -	ELT
PICAYUNE CREEK	Klamath River Upper Trinity River	South China Mountain Mumbo Basin	- - -	RT, BK
PICAYUNE LAKE	Klamath River Upper Trinity River	Mumbo Basin	6080	BK, RT, ELT
POND LILY LAKE	Klamath River Upper Trinity River	Whisky Bill Peak	5817	BK, RT
PONY CREEK	Klamath River Trinity River	Hennessy Peak	- - -	RT, SH
QUINBY CREEK	Klamath River Trinity River	Salyer	- - -	RT
QUINBY CREEK	Klamath River Trinity River	Denny	- - -	RT
RAMSHORN CREEK	Klamath River Upper Trinity River	Tangle Blue Lake Mumbo Basin	- - -	RT
RAMSHORN CREEK NF	Klamath River Upper Trinity River	Tangle Blue Lake Mumbo Basin	- - -	RT
RANCHERIA CREEK	Klamath River Trinity River	Trinity Center Carrville	- - -	KOK
READING CREEK	Klamath River Trinity River	Weaverville Hossimbim Mountain	- - -	SH, KS, RT

Water By County	Drainage	USGS Topographic Map 7.5 Minute Series	Elevation (Feet) Lakes Only	Fish Species
ROBINSON CREEK	Eel River Eel River MF	South Yolla Bolly (7.5' X 15') North Yolla Bolly (7.5' X 15')	- - -	RT
ROCK CREEK	Eel River Eel River MF	Four Corners (7.5' X 15')	- - -	SH, RT
RUSCH CREEK (Hayfork Creek)	Klamath River Trinity River	Halfway Ridge	- - -	SH, RT
RUSH CREEK	Klamath River Trinity River	Lewiston, Trinity Dam Rush Creek	- - -	RT, SH, KS BN
RUSH CREEK LAKE, Lower	Klamath River Trinity River	Rush Creek Lakes	6250	BK, RT
RUSH CREEK LAKE, Middle	Klamath River Trinity River	Rush Creek Lakes	6479	BK, RT
RUSH CREEK LAKE, Upper	Klamath River Trinity River	Rush Creek Lakes	6900	RT, BK
RUTH LAKE	Mad River Forest Glen	Ruth Lake	2655	RT
SALOON CREEK	Klamath River Upper Trinity River	Billys Peak Deadman Peak	- - -	RT
SALT CREEK	Klamath River Upper Trinity River	Siligo Peak	- - -	RT
SALT CREEK (Hayfork Creek)	Klamath River Trinity River	Hayfork	- - -	SH, RT
SAPPHIRE LAKE	Klamath River Upper Trinity River	Thompson Peak Mount Hilton	5700	BK, RT, ELT
SCORPION CREEK	Klamath River Upper Trinity River	Carrville	- - -	RT
SEVEN UP LAKE	Klamath River Upper Trinity River	Covington Mill	7000	BK
SHANTY CREEK	Eel River Van Duzen River	Ruth Lake Black Lassic	- - -	RT
SHARBER CREEK	Klamath River Trinity River	Salyer	- - -	RT, SH
SHERER CREEK	Klamath River Upper Trinity River	South China Mountain Mumbo Basin	- - -	RT
SHIMMY LAKE	Klamath River Upper Trinity River	Ycatapom Peak	6300	BK, BN
SLATE CREEK	Klamath River Trinity River	Trinity Dam Rush Creek Lakes	- - -	SH, RT
SLIDE CREEK	Klamath River Trinity River	Dees Peak	- - -	SH, RT
SLIDE LAKE	Klamath River Upper Trinity River	South China Mountain	5440	BK
SMITH LAKE	Klamath River Upper Trinity River	Siligo Peak	6500	BK, RT
STODDARD LAKE	Klamath River Upper Trinity River	Billys Peak	5832	BK, RT, ELT
STONEY CREEK	Klamath River Upper Trinity River	Trinity Dam Covington Mill	- - -	KOK
STROPE CREEK	Klamath River Upper Trinity River	Covington Mill	- - -	RT, KOK
STUART FORK	Klamath River Upper Trinity River	Trinity Dam Rush Creek Lakes Siligo Peak	- - -	RT, KOK, BN, BK
STUART FORK E FK	Klamath River	Covington Mill	- - -	RT, KOK
SUGAR PINE LAKE	Klamath River Upper Trinity River	Ycatapom Peak	6579	BK
SUMMIT LAKE	Klamath River Upper Trinity River	Siligo Peak	7700	BK
SWEDE CREEK	Klamath River Trinity River	Del Loma	- - -	RT
SWIFT CREEK	Klamath River Upper Trinity River	Trinity Center Covington Mill	- - -	RT, KOK, BN
SWIFT CREEK NF	Klamath River Upper Trinity River	Covington Mill	- - -	RT, KOK
TAMARACK LAKE, Big	Klamath River Upper Trinity River	Chicken Hawk Hill	5862	BK, RT

Water By County	Drainage	USGS Topographic Map 7.5 Minute Series	Elevation (Feet) Lakes Only	Fish Species
TAMARACK LAKE, Little	Klamath River Upper Trinity River	Chicken Hawk Hill	5862	BK, RT
TANGLE BLUE CREEK	Klamath River Upper Trinity River	Tangle Blue Lake	- - -	RT
TANGLE BLUE LAKE	Klamath River Upper Trinity River	Tangle Blue Lake	5746	BK, RT, ELT
TAPIE LAKE	Klamath River Upper Trinity River	Ycatapom Peak	6501	BK
TRELOAR CREEK	Klamath River Trinity River	Big Bar	- - -	RT
TRINITY RIVER, Upper	Klamath River Trinity River	South China Mountain Tango Blue Lake, Carrville	- - -	BN, RT
TRINITY RIVER (Lewiston Dam to Junction City)	Klamath River	Lewiston, Weaverville Junction City	- - -	KS, SH, SS, BN, RT
TRINITY RIVER (Junction City to Del Loma)	Klamath River	Junction City, Dedrick Helena, Hayfork Bally Big Bar, Del Loma	- - -	KS, SH, SS, BN, RT
TRINITY RIVER (Del Loma to Willow Creek) (See Humboldt Co. for Willow Creek to Mouth)	Klamath River	Del Loma, Ironside Mountain Hennessy Peak, Salyer Willow Creek	- - -	KS, SH, SS, BN, RT
TRINITY RIVER E FK	Klamath River Trinity River	Whisky Bill Peak Mumbo Basin Seven Lakes Basin	- - -	RT, KOK, BN, BK
TRINITY RIVER, Little	Klamath River Upper Trinity River	Scott Mountain	- - -	RT
TRINITY RIVER NF (Helena to Hobo Gulch Campground)	Klamath River Trinity River	Helena Thurston Peaks	- - -	SH, KS, RT
TRINITY RIVER SF (Mouth of South Fork to Hyampom Bridge)	Klamath River Trinity River	Hyampom Mountain Hyampom	- - -	KS, SH, SS, RT
TRINITY RIVER, Upper (Headwaters to Clair Engle Lake)	Klamath River Trinity River	South China Mountain Tangle Blue Lake, Carrville	- - -	KOK, RT, BN, BK
TULE CREEK (Hayfork Creek)	Klamath River Trinity River	Hayfork	- - -	SH, RT
TULE CREEK EAST (Hayfork Creek)	Klamath River Trinity River	Hayfork	- - -	RT
TULE CREEK WEST (Hayfork Creek)	Klamath River Trinity River	Hayfork	- - -	RT
TWIN LAKE, Lower	Klamath River Upper Trinity River	Chicken Hawk Hill	5773	RT, BK
TWIN LAKE, Upper	Klamath River Upper Trinity River	Chicken Hawk Hill	5776	BK, RT, ELT
TWIN LAKE, Upper (Swift Creek)	Klamath River Upper Trinity River	Covington Mill	5090	BK
UNION CREEK	Klamath River Upper Trinity River	Caribou Lake	- - -	RT, ELT
UNION LAKE	Klamath River Upper Trinity River	Caribou Lake	6023	RT, BK
VAN DUZEN RIVER (Headwaters to Humboldt- Trinity Co. line. Also, see Humboldt Co.)	Eel River	Sportshaven Ruth Lake	- - -	SH, RT, KS SS
VAN DUZEN RIVER, W FK	Eel River Van Duzen River	Ruth Lake Black Lassic	- - -	RT
VAN HORN CREEK	Mad River	Shannon Butte	- - -	RT
VAN MATRE CREEK	Klamath River Trinity River	Rush Creek Lakes	- - -	RT
VAN NESS CREEK	Klamath River Trinity River	Papoose Creek	- - -	KOK
WARD LAKE	Klamath River Upper Trinity River	Caribou Lake	7118	RT, BK, BN, ELT
WATTS LAKE	Eel River	Ruth Lake	4950	RT
WEAVER CREEK	Klamath River Trinity River	Weaverville	- - -	SH, KS, RT,

Water By County	Drainage	USGS Topographic Map 7.5 Minute Series	Elevation (Feet) Lakes Only	Fish Species
WEAVER CREEK, East	Klamath River Trinity River	Weaverville Rush Creek Lakes	- - -	SH, RT, KS, BN
WEAVER CREEK, East Branch	Klamath River Trinity River	Rush Creek Lakes	- - -	RT
WEAVER CREEK, West	Klamath River Trinity River	Weaverville	- - -	SH, RT, KS
WILLOW CREEK	Eel River	Four Corners Rock (7.5' X 15')	- - -	SH, RT
WHITES CREEK LAKE	Klamath River Trinity River	Thurston Peaks	6150	BK
YELLOWJACKET CREEK	Klamath River Trinity River	Thurston Peaks Mount Hilton	- - -	SH, RT
YELLOWJACKET CREEK	Eel River Eel River MF	Four Corners Rock (7.5' X 15')	- - -	RT

Conclusion

In this publication, *Fly-Fishing Northern California Waters*, I presented and shared with you written and visual memories on the complex mysteries of trout, anadromous fish, and the many wild and splendid fly-fishing waters of Northern California.

During the course of creating this book, I tried to provide as much information as possible to capture the beauty of the wide range of territories, its placid lakes, the majesty of its rivers, and the thrill of fly-fishing for trout, steelhead, or salmon.

I described in great detail the beauty of Northern California's magnificent mountain ranges with its watersheds, geological and geographical features, and the origin of historical names that played a significant role in this book. I also focused on species of fish from rainbow, brook, brown, redband to golden trout, insect habitats, food sources, effective fly patterns, scenic views, and landscape changes when traveling from one expanse to another. Each area contains priceless fly-fishing waters, from the most prominent to lesser-known lakes and streams, to the unknown sleepers. My intention was to provide as much information as possible to create a reference and guidebook that communicates the exciting fly-fishing found in Northern California.

My passion for fly-fishing is an analogy in many ways to the same feelings I have for listening to both dramatic and serene operas and classical music. During the creative writing of this book, my devoted companions were Bizet's The Pearl Fishers, Puccini's Madama Butterfly and Turandot, and other opera arias.

Listening to these powerful collections mesmerized me, helping me return spiritually to the outdoors I so dearly love. My thoughts would wander to the many fly-fishing empires that are extremely meaningful to me. Towering granitic cliffs, spectacular cascading waterfalls, lush meadows, wildflowers and vegetations, fertile valleys, stillwaters, raging and tranquil streams possess a tremendous amount of spiritual forces. These forces have been sacred to me.

I presented much information for experiencing the beauty, tranquility, and pleasures associated with the adventurous roadside, backcountry, and wilderness waters of Northern California. They will be cherished forever. Fly-fishing in these waters has greatly increased in popularity. However, there are plenty of watershed destinations to discover throughout Northern California. They have survived through the years and will continue to do so if they are left as we found them.

A key point in evaluating which stillwater or stream to explore is to keep in mind you have unlimited resources available to you. Angling opportunities are yours to savor, from roadside adventures to remote wilderness expeditions.

May your fly-fishing experiences be pleasurable and memorable. In the meantime, through other creative projects, we shall meet some day in the future . . .

Appendix A: California Fly-Fishing and Environmental Organizations

Fly fishing and environmental organizations provide anglers with rewarding benefits and social pleasure. New acquaintances, conservation, and educational programs are a few amenities for members. Regardless of age, gender, or experience, new adventures are available to all anglers.

Through my experiences in the fly-fishing community, as past officer in several capacities in a fly-fishing organization, and working with peers and newcomers, I recognized the need of individuals seeking organizations. I contacted fly-fishing clubs in Northern California, as well as environmental and educational organizations, to ascertain if they wish to share their knowledge, programs, and projects with others. The organizations listed in the Directory below responded to my requests.

As this publication pertains to Northern California waters, I will furnish names and addresses of organizations concerning this region. However, while some organizations are located in Northern California, their programs also cover the High Sierra region. Calendar events offered to members range from fly-casting instruction, seminars, conservation projects, education, fly-tying clinics and fish-outs. Other benefits include valuable tips from national and local speakers at the monthly meetings.

Environmental and educational organizations offer conservation and educational projects to protect, restore, and enhance our state's fisheries. Please note that each club and organization furnishes a variety of fisheries and conservation programs. I urge anglers to support these organizations.

Fly-Fishing Organizations

Amador Fly-Fishers
P.O. Box 935, Sutter Creek, CA 95685

Calaveras Fly-Fishers
P.O. Box 451, Arnold, CA 95223

California Fly-Fishers Unlimited
P.O. Box 162997, Sacramento, CA 95816

Delta Fly-Fishers
P.O. Box 7270, Stockton, CA 95207

E.C. Powell Flyfishers
P.O. Box 1135, Yuba City, CA 95992

Flycasters, Inc. of San Jose
P.O. Box 821, Campbell, CA 95009

Fly-Fishers of Davis
P.O. Box 525, Davis, CA 95617

Gold Country Fly-Fishers
P.O. Box 2988, Grass Valley, CA 95945

Golden West Women Flyfishers
790 N. 27th Avenue, San Francisco, CA 94121

Granite Bay Flycasters
P.O. Box 1107, Roseville, CA 95678

Livermore Fly-fishermen
P.O. Box 231, Livermore, CA 94551

Merced Flyfishing Club
c/o Hal Thompson, 9111 W. Bell Drive, Atwater, CA 95301

Mission Peak Fly Anglers
P.O. Box 7263, Fremont, CA 94537

Monterey Peninsula Flycasters
P.O. Box 222673, Carmel, CA 93922

Napa Valley Fly-Fishermen
P.O. Box 2373, Napa, 94558

Pacific Coast Flyrodders
286 Wendall, Crescent City, CA 95531 (Conservation, DFG Political)

Peninsula Fly-Fishers, Inc.
P.O. Box 207, Belmont, CA 94002

Russian River Fly-Fishers
P.O. Box 2673, Santa Rosa, CA 95405

Salinas Valley Fly-Fishermen
P.O. Box 1793, Salinas, CA 93902

Santa Cruz Fly-Fishermen
P.O. Box 2008, Santa Cruz, CA 95063

Santa Lucia Flyfishers
P.O. Box 166, San Luis Obispo, CA 93406

Shasta Fly-Fishers
P.O. Box 2, Redding, CA 96099

Solano Fly-Fishers
P.O. Box 3082, Fairfield, CA 94533

Tahoe-Truckee Flyfishers
P.O. Box 5704, Tahoe City, CA 96145

Tehama Fly-Fishers and Red Bluff Fisheries Forum
P.O. Box 224, Red Bluff, CA 96080

Truckee River Fly-Fishers
2875 Northtownee Lane, #323-F, Reno, NV 89512

Environmental Organizations

California Trout, Inc.,
870 Market Street, #859, San Francisco, CA 94102. (415) 392-8887
Mission: To protect and restore wild trout,
native steelhead, and their habitat.

Federation of Fly-Fishers
P.O. Box 1595, Bozeman, MT 59771. (406) 585-7592
Conserving, restoring, and educating through fly-fishing.

The Nature Conservancy
785 Market Street, San Francisco, CA 94103. (415) 777-0487
California Field Office. Manages McCloud River Preserve
For reservations to fish the McCloud River Preserve.

Sierra Club
730 Polk Street, San Francisco, CA 94109. (415) 776-2211
Environmental organization promoting
conservation programs of natural environment.

Friends of the River
915 - 20th Street, Sacramento, CA 95814, (916) 442-3155
Watershed, stream, and river conservation in California.

Appendix B: Fly Shops, Lodging, and Other Services

American Fly-Fishing Co.
3523 Fair Oaks Blvd., Sacramento, CA 95864
(916) 483-1222, 1-800-410-1222

Clearwater Trout Tours
Lodging and Fly Fishing. 274 Star Route, Muir Beach, CA 94965
Winter (415) 381-1173, Summer (530) 335-5500

Creative Sports Enterprises
1924C Oak Park Blvd., Pleasant Hill, CA 94523
(925) 938-2255. Outside Bay Area: 1-800-407-FISH (3474)

Eagle Lake General Store, Spalding Resort
503-150 Mahogany Way, Susanville, CA 96130
(530) 825-2191

Ernie's Casting Pond
4845 Soquel Drive, Soquel, CA 95073
(831) 462-4665

Eureka Fly Shop
1632 Broadway, Eureka, CA 95501
(707) 444-2085

Hiouchi Hamlet R.V. Resort
2000 Highway 199 Crescent City, CA 95531
(707) 458-3321

Jay Fairs
687-900 Linden Way, Eagle Lake, Susanville, CA 96130
(530) 825-3401

Flies Unlimited
27 St. Francis Way, Salinas, CA 93906
(831) 758-1539

The Fly Shop
4140 Churn Creek Road, Redding, CA 96002
1-800-669-3474

Kiene's Fly Shop
2654 Marconi Avenue, Sacramento, CA 95821
(916) 486-9958, 1-800-4000-FLY

Lakeview Terrace Resort
HC01, Box 250, Lewiston, CA 96052
(530) 778-3803

Lava Creek Lodge
Glenburn Star Route, Fall River Mills, CA 96028
(530) 336-6288

Mel Kreiger Club Pacific
Fly Fishing School and Trips
790 - 27th Avenue, San Francisco, CA 94121
(415) 752-0192

The Midge Fly Shop, Inc.
271 State Street, Los Altos, CA 94022
(650) 941-8871

Mike Monroe's Flyrodder Guide Service
5313 Ridgefield Ave., Carmichael, CA 95608
(916) 481-9133

Oasis Springs Lodge, Fly Fishing Ranch.
32400 Highway 36 East, Paynes Creek, CA 96075
(510) 653-7630, 1-800-239-5454

Otter Bar Lodge, Lodging and fly-fishing school
Box 210, Forks of Salmon, CA 96031
(530) 462-4772

Pit River Lodge
Pit One Power House Road, Fall River Mills, CA 96028-0920
(530) 336-5005

Pit Stop Store
P.O. Box 87, Big Bend, CA 96011
(530) 337-6254

Rick's Lodge, Fly Fishing Fall River
Glenburn Star Route, Fall River Mills, CA 96028
(530) 336-5300

Shasta Angler
SR 299 East, Box 430, Fall River Mills, CA 96028
(530) 336-6600

Stewarts Point Store
P.O. Box 40, 32000 South Highway 1, Stewarts Point, CA 95480
(707) 785-2406

Ted Fay Fly Shop
P.O. Box 47, Dunsmuir, CA 96025
(530) 235-2969

Trinity Fly Shop
P.O. Box 176, Lewiston, CA 96052
(530) 623-6757

Trinity Outfitters, Inc.
Packing Service, P.O. Box 1973, Weaverville, CA 96093
(530) 623-2476

Vaughn's Sporting Goods
37307 Main Street, Burney, CA 96013
(530) 335-2381

Bibliography

Amesbury, R. 1971. *Eagle Lake*. Sparks, NV: Western Printing.

Arbona, F.L., Jr. 1980. *Mayflies, The Angler, and the Trout*. Piscataway, NJ: Winchester Press.

Bailey, E.H. (Ed), 1966. *Geology of Northern California*. Bulletin 190. San Francisco, CA: California Division of Mines and Geology.

California Department of Fish and Game, Resources Agency. 1969. *Anglers' Guide to Lakes and Streams*. Sacramento, CA: State of California.

California Department of Fish and Game, Wildlife and Inland Fisheries Division. Statewide and Regional Wild Trout Staff. 1999. *California Heritage Trout*. Sacramento, CA: State of California.

California Department of Water Resources, Resources Agency. July, 1964. *Klamath River Basin Investigation*. Bulletin No. 83. Sacramento, CA: State of California.

Cavender, T.M. 1978. Taxonomy and Distribution of the Bull Trout, *Salvelinus Confluentus* (Suckley), American Northwest. California Fish and Game, 64 (3), 139-174. Sacramento, CA: State of California.

Combs, T. 1991. *Steelhead fly-fishing*. NY: Lyons & Burford.

Combs, T. 1976. *Steelhead fly-fishing and Flies*. Portland, OR: Frank Amato.

Deinstadt, J.M. 1987. Catch-and-Release Fishing, A Decade of Experience. A National Sport Fishing Symposium. *California's Use of Catch-and-Release Angling Regulations on Trout Waters*. Proceedings from Humboldt State University, Fisheries Department & AFS Chapter, California Cooperative Fishery Research Unit & California Trout, Inc., Arcata, CA. California Department of Fish and Game. Rancho Cordova, CA: State of California.

Deinstadt, J. M., Lentz, D. C., Sibbald, G. F., Murphy, K. D. 1993. Fishing Success on California Wild Trout Waters in 1990-91: Reports from Angler Box Surveys. *Inland Fisheries Administrative Report No. 93-1*. California Department of Fish and Game. Sacramento, CA: State of California.

Evermann, B. W. 1906. *The Golden Trout of the Southern High Sierras*. Bulletin of the U. S. Bureau of Fisheries. Vol. XXV, 1905 (1906): 1-51. WA: Government Printing Office.

Ferguson, B., Johnson, L., & Trotter, P. 1985. *Fly-Fishing for Pacific Salmon*. Portland, OR: Frank Amato.

Fisk, L. 1983. *Golden Trout of the High Sierra*. California Department of Fish and Game. Sacramento, CA: State of California.

Gudde, E. G. 1960. *California Place Names*. Berkeley, CA: University of California Press.

Hafele, R. & Hughes, D. 1981. *The Complete Book of Western Hatches*. Portland, OR: Frank Amato.

Hart, J. D. 1978. *A Companion to California*. New York, NY: Oxford University Press.

Hoopaugh, D. A. October, 1974. Status of the Redband Trout (*Salmo SP.)* in California. *Inland Fisheries Administrative Report , No. l74-7*. Sacramento, CA: California Department of Fish and Game.

Kroeber, A.L. 1976. *Handbook of the Indians of California*. NY: Dover Publications.

LaFontaine, G. 1981. *Caddisflies*. NY: Nick Lyons. A Winchester Press.

Loomis, B. F. 1926. *Pictorial History of the Lassen Volcano*. San Francisco, CA: California Press.

McClane, A. J. 1965. *McClane's Standard Fishing Encyclopedia*. NY: Holt,Rinehart & Winston.

McMillan, B. 1987. *Dry Line Steelhead and Other Subjects*. Portland, OR. Frank Amato.

Meyer, D. 1992. *Advanced fly-fishing for Steelhead*. Portland, OR: Frank Amato.

Moyle, P.B., Williams, J.E., & Wikramanayake, E.D. October, 1989. *Fish Species of Special Concern of California*. Sacramento, CA: California Department of Fish and Game.

Moyle, P.B. 1976. Inland Fishes of California. Berkeley, CA: University of California Press.

Muir, J. 1988 . *The Mountains of California*. Edited by R. C. Baron. Golden, CO: Fulcrum.

Pister, P. 1991. Golden Trout (Oncorhynchus Aguabonita). In J. Stolz & J. Schnell (Eds.), *The Wildlife Series Trout* (pp. 280-285). Harrisburg, PA: Stackpole Books.

Purdy, T. I. 1988. *Purdy's Eagle Lake*. Susanville, CA: Lahontan Images.

Resources Agency. SB 1086. Nielsen, J., Advisory Council. January, 1989. *Upper Sacramento River*. Fisheries and Riparian Habitat Management Plan. Sacramento, CA: State of California.

Richards, C., Swisher, D., & Arbona, Jr., F. 1980. *Stoneflies*. New York: Nick Lyons.

Rode, M. 1990. Bull Trout, Salvelinus Confluentus Suckley, In the McCloud River: Status and Recovery Recovery Recommendations. *Inland Fisheries Administrative Report*, No. 90-15. Sacramento, CA: California Department of Fish and Game.

Schaffer, J. P., Schifrin, B., Winnett, T., & Jenkins, R. 1989. *The Pacific Crest Trail*, Volumne 1: California. Berkeley, CA: Wilderness Press.

Scott, J. 1982. *Greased Line Fishing for Salmon [and Steelhead]*. Portland, OR: Frank Amato.

Sigler, W. F. & J. W. 1987. *Fishes of the Great Basin*. Reno, NV: University of Nevada Press.

Steger, G. A. & Jones, H. H. *Place Names of Shasta County*. Glendale, CA: La Siesta Press.

Swisher, D. & Richards, C. 1971. *Selective Trout*. NY: Crown Publishers.

Usinger, R.L. (Ed.). 1956. *Aquatic Insects of California*. Berkley CA: University of California Press.

Other Helpful Titles

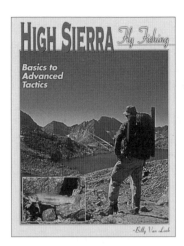
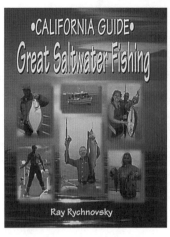
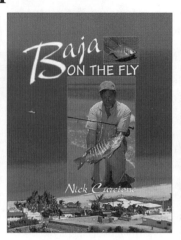
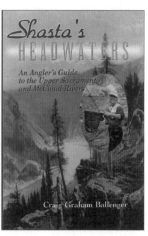

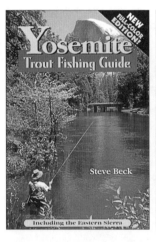
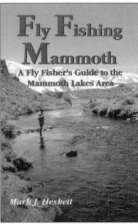
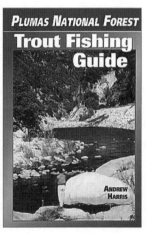
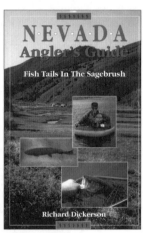
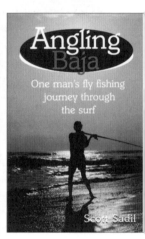

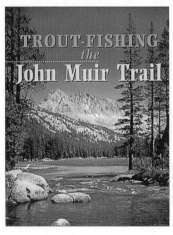
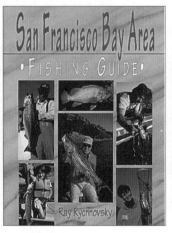
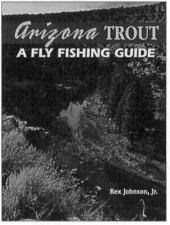